Feminist Philosophy and the Problem of Evil

A *Hypatia* Book

HYPATIA

EDITED BY ROBIN MAY SCHOTT

Feminist Philosophy and the Problem of Evil

INDIANA UNIVERSITY PRESS

Bloomington and Indianapolis

This book is a publication of

Indiana University Press
601 North Morton Street
Bloomington, IN 47404-3797 USA

http://iupress.indiana.edu

Telephone orders 800-842-6796
Fax orders   812-855-7931
Orders by e-mail iuporder@indiana.edu

The paper used in this publication meets the minimum requirements of American National Standard for Information Sciences—Permanence of Paper for Printed Library Materials, ANSI Z39.48-1984.

Manufactured in the United States of America

Library of Congress Cataloging-in-Publication Data

Feminist philosophy and the problem of evil / edited by Robin May Schott.
      p. cm. — (Hypatia books)
   Includes bibliographical references and index.
   ISBN 978-0-253-34858-6 (cloth : alk. paper) — ISBN 978-0-253-21901-5 (pbk. : alk. paper) 1. Good and evil. 2. Feminist theory. I. Schott, Robin May.
   BJ1401.F39 2007
   170—dc22
                                                                                    2006029516

          1 2 3 4 5   12 11 10 09 08 07

To my parents

In memory of Iris Marion Young
(January 2, 1949–August 1, 2006)

Iris Marion Young, a contributor to this volume, died at the height of her philosophical powers on 1 August 2006. Young received her Ph.D. from Pennsylvania State University in 1974. She was trained in continental European philosophy, and much of her early work on theorizing female body experience used a phenomenological method. Young wrote boldly about topics hitherto ignored in academic philosophy: women's motility and sexual objectification in the society of the 1970s, the experience of pregnancy, breasted experience, and women's relation to clothes. "Throwing Like a Girl" became a much-loved classic in this genre.

Young finally gained the attention of mainstream political philosophers in 1990 with the publication of her landmark book *Justice and the Politics of Difference.* This book criticized most philosophical theories of justice for being overly preoccupied with distributive justice and insufficiently concerned with domination and oppression. Young defined these concepts to reveal aspects of justice that are excluded by the distributive model. They included: exploitation, marginalization, powerlessness, cultural imperialism, and violence.

Young's second major book, *Inclusion and Democracy,* explores how the ideals of deliberative democracy can be approached not in some ideal world but in our actually existing world of systematic differences, inequality, and segregation. She calls her work "democratic theory for unjust conditions." In her work on democracy, Young is still concerned ultimately with justice. For her, the value of democracy is not intrinsic but rather instrumental to remedy injustice. At the time of her death, Young was working on a book exploring the responsibility of citizens in affluent countries for abuses such as sweatshops.

Young's work bridged divides between analytic and European philosophy and between high-level theory and grassroots activism. In addition to her philosophical contributions, Iris was a committed political activist, an inspiring teacher, a loving partner and mother, and a loyal friend.

Alison M. Jaggar and Robin May Schott

Contents

Acknowledgments

It takes a very long time to make a book, and what happens during that time can be decisive for the character of that book. This is particularly the case for this book, which was planned as a *Hypatia* Special Issue on Feminism and the Problem of Evil well before the terrorist attacks of September 11, 2001. Those of us working on the issue quite naturally expanded its scope and character following these events.

I would like to thank Nancy Tuana and Laurie Shrage, who were co-editors of *Hypatia* when I worked on the Special Issue. From its inception both of them were enthusiastic about having an issue devoted to feminist philosophical analyses of the problem of evil. Laurie Shrage in particular urged me to expand the Special Issue to include a forum on terrorism after the attacks on 9/11. The articles in part two of this book develop this forum and have been (with one exception) substantially revised and expanded for this edition. I would like to thank Hilde Lindemann, current editor of *Hypatia,* for her unfailingly positive spirit of cooperation, which has smoothed the transformation of the Special Issue into a Hypatia book.

Claudia Card, whom I met originally in 1995 at an IAPh meeting in Vienna on the theme of war, is largely responsible for calling my attention to the problem of evil in relation to war rape. I would also like to thank Sara Ruddick for her longstanding work on gender and war and for her ongoing support of my own work in this area. And I thank Debra Bergoffen both for her work with the theme of vulnerability and for her personal courage in facing it. I am grateful to all of the contributors of this volume, leading figures in the field, many of whom have worked for years with the issues they discuss here. Their work does indeed illustrate why feminist interventions are crucial for addressing some of the central ethical and political problems of our time.

Dee Mortensen, editor at Indiana University Press, has been an outstanding editor in every sense. Not only has she provided constant encouragement and support in dealing with the publication process, but she gave me invaluable feedback for my own contribution to this book. I would like to thank Elizabeth Yoder, copy editor of the manuscript. Though many authors cringe at the thought of a copy editor changing their words, Elizabeth's work has elicited only praise and enthusiasm from the contributors.

I would like to thank Alison Jaggar for her contribution to the memorial reflections for Iris Marion Young. The recent death of Iris Young is a brutal reminder that we must thank not only the living, but those who have died after having worked so hard to create the conditions under which philosophy, and feminist philosophy, can flourish.

Feminist Philosophy and the Problem of Evil

1 Evil, Terrorism, and Gender

Robin May Schott

Why Discuss Evil Now?

If anyone should think that evil is a problem of the past and not of the present, a glance at the history of the twentieth century proves otherwise. In that century, the atrocities of war escalated dramatically; between 1900 and 1990, there were over four times as many war deaths as in the preceding four hundred years. In 1990 battlefields included Afghanistan, Angola, Colombia, El Salvador, Ethiopia, Guatemala, India, Kuwait, Lebanon, Liberia, Mozambique, Peru, Somalia, South Africa, Sri Lanka, Sudan, and Tibet (Vickers 1993, 2). To these one must add the battles of the Gulf War and the genocides in Bosnia and Rwanda. And if Americans thought that events that give rise to reflections on evil matter to other peoples but not to them, then they came to a rude awakening on the morning of September 11, 2001.

The Special Issue of *Hypatia* on Feminist Philosophy and the Problem of Evil, which appeared in the winter and spring of 2003, was conceived well before the terrorist attacks on 9/11. By that time, I had already collected a substantial body of feminist reflections on evil. These essays covered a range of historical and theoretical issues, from the sixteenth-century witch hunts to the genocides and war rapes of the twentieth century, from an analysis of American popular ideology with its belief that every cloud has a silver lining to an analysis of the texts of leading women philosophers.

Five days after the attacks, Laurie Shrage, co-editor of *Hypatia*, made the suggestion that I expand the special issue on evil to include a forum on terrorism, with short commentaries by feminist philosophers invited to write on the recent tragedies. Given the willingness of conservative intellectuals and politicians to point to the existence of "the radical evil emanating from the Muslim world" (Peretz 2001), the pressing question was whether the term *evil* could be used in reference to these terrorist attacks. And given the fact that all the suicide attackers were male; that according to reports in the *New York Times* on September 15, three of the terrorists had spent a few hundred dollars on lap dances and drinks at a Daytona Beach strip club the night before the attack; and that young male Muslim suicide bombers are reportedly promised that they will be greeted by seventy black-eyed virgins in heaven, the question of gender seemed troublingly relevant.[1] On September 11, women and men alike were victims of this terrible tragedy. Can feminist perspectives provide insights for understanding and responding to terrorism?

The urgency of these questions has increased rather than decreased in importance over the last four years. We find ourselves now in what some writers have called the "9/11 syndrome," in which the events of 9/11 are viewed as a turning point in global politics. The 9/11 syndrome refers to the responses to the terrorist attacks on the United States, including the renewed faith in violence, the resurgence of narrow definitions of nationalism, and the intensification of an us/them mentality with regard to racial, ethnic, and religious differences. Here one can refer to the enlargement of the "zone of mistrust" that extends beyond the usual black/white divide in the United States (Joseph and Sharma 2003, xi–xv).[2]

The conviction that animates my work on this book is that evil is indeed one of the central issues of our time. Such a conviction is hardly new. The problem of evil is older than the story of Job, a just and faithful man who experienced evil events through the loss of family, health, and property. His story poses the question: Why should any individual or community, especially those who seek to live justly, suffer inexplicably? Job ultimately accepted the voice of God from the whirlwind, recognized that humans are not competent to judge whether God is just, and was redeemed. Many of Job's successors have followed his example by demanding an explanation of unjust suffering, but have refused to accept Job's solution. For modern authors, it is not God but human beings who become judges of the significance of evil in human affairs (Cicovacki 2001, 83–94).

The problem of evil has haunted modern thought. Susan Neiman writes in *Evil in Modern Thought: An Alternative History of Philosophy* that one can read modern philosophy as a story about how to make sense of a world that is ineradicably a place of suffering (2002, 2). The specifically modern conception of evil refers to moral evils, to evils that human beings are responsible for, as opposed to the catastrophes of natural disasters or the suffering implicit in the finitude of the world, which were earlier classified as forms of evil. Joan Copjec observes that Immanuel Kant's *Religion within the Boundaries of Mere Reason* (1793) enacted a conceptual revolution by which evil "ceases to be a religious or metaphysical problem and becomes, for the first time, a political, moral and pedagogical problem" (Copjec 1996, xi). By situating evil as an effect of freedom rather than of human finitude, Kant opened the way to what María Pía Lara calls a postmetaphysical understanding of evil (2001, 1).

The proposal that the story of evil is the central story of modernity is bound to meet resistance. Typically, we are presented with the story of the Enlightenment as marking the triumph of human reason and the irrepressible march of progress in history in technological, scientific, rational, and ethical domains. Yet a closer look at the work of Kant, who is taken to be the paragon of this position, shows a different story. In his late work on *Religion*, Kant set out to analyze the "*radical* innate *evil* in human nature" ([1793] 1996, 80).[3] He explains evil ultimately through the human capacity for freedom: "The human being is *evil* cannot mean anything else than that he is conscious of the moral law and yet has incorporated into his maxim the (occasional) deviation from it" (79). Kant's story of radical evil tells us that evil is intrinsic to human existence because we are not transparent to ourselves and because there is always a dimension of self-alienation in human freedom. Kant's story tells us that evil is fundamentally a *collective* condition. He wrote, for example, that when he speaks of the human being as good or evil, he means not individuals but the whole species (74). And since evil is a collective condition, the overcoming of evil is a collective historical task. Kant's essay "To Perpetual Peace: A Philosophical Sketch" (1795), published just two years after his book on religion, took the collective problem of war as the central problem of evil and the overcoming of all wars as the central historical task of humankind. His view of the collective dimension of evil is eerily prescient of the dilemmas of the present. So is his demand that the world order be reorganized in order to eliminate the conditions that tend to war.

Twentieth-century thinkers had good reason to take Kant's views about the link between evil and war to heart. But when Hannah Arendt declared in 1945, "The problem of evil will be the fundamental question of postwar intellectual life in Europe," she was wrong (Bernstein 1996, 137). As Richard Bernstein notes, most postwar intellectuals avoided addressing the problem of evil directly. But evil did become a fundamental problem for Arendt's work, and the last decade has seen a renewed interest in reflecting on the problems of evil.

The current resurgence of intellectual interest in the question of evil in the United States and Western Europe can be explained by at least three factors. The first is the *psychological* effect of the proximity of the evils that have marked the 1990s. While atrocities in Africa—represented as a racialized other, as Sherene Razack notes in this volume—may not seem threateningly close, the atrocities in the former Yugoslavia do hold that threat. Yugoslavia was, after all, the place for numerous conferences and vacations for Western Europeans and Americans alike, and hence the atrocities in the former Yugoslavia hit close to home. The second factor is connected to changes in *historical* consciousness that have taken place through the burgeoning of literature and scholarship on the Holocaust, especially the publishing of people's memoirs after decades of silence. This literature has led to a greater awareness about genocides in general, although philosophers after Arendt have been slower than other researchers in turning their attention to this theme. The third factor is linked to changes in the *philosophical* discourse of the last decades. Ewa Ziarek notes in the *Hypatia* "Special Cluster on Feminist Philosophy and the Problem of Evil" that evil is an inherent inspiration of postmodern reflection, which focuses on the irreducible dimension of antagonism and power in discourse, embodiment, and politics (Ziarek 2001, 1).

It hardly needs to be said that developments since 9/11 have intensified public intellectuals' interest in the problem of evil. Here it is important to distinguish between philosophical concepts of evil and the rhetoric of evil. The political rhetoric of evil has deservedly received a bad name. Recall former president Ronald Reagan's Star Wars rhetoric denouncing the Soviet Union as the "Evil Empire." Now that the United States and Russia have entered into a new NATO brotherhood, President George W. Bush has found other countries to target as part of the "axis of evil": Iran, Iraq, and North Korea (State of the Union Address 2002). But does this rhetoric mean that the term *evil* can have no meaning in moral, social, or political domains? Many thinkers have worked to develop definitions of evil that are both conceptually sound and can be guides for assessing the behavior of individual and collective subjects. One example is Claudia Card's definition of evil as "foreseeable intolerable harms produced by culpable wrongdoings" (2002, 3).

We would do well to bear this definition in mind when evaluating the decision of U.S. officials to ignore the Geneva Convention. Recent instances of abuse are reported by Human Rights Watch, which described soldiers' accounts of abusing Persons Under Control (PUCs) in Iraq by "smoking" detainees—exhausting them with physical exercise to the point of unconsciousness or forcing them to hold painful positions for extended amounts of time—and by "fucking" detainees—beating or torturing them severely. One sergeant reported, "Everyone in camp knew [that] if you wanted to work out your frustration, you show up at the PUC tent. In a way it was sport. . . ." The officer quoted in the Human Rights Watch report believes the abuses he witnessed in both Afghanistan and Iraq were caused by President Bush's 2002 decision not to apply the Geneva Conventions to detainees captured in Afghanistan: "We knew where the Geneva Conventions drew the line, but then you get that confusion when the Sec Def [Secretary of Defense] and the President make that statement [that Geneva did not apply to detainees]. . . . Had I thought we were following the Geneva Conventions, as an officer I would have investigated what was clearly a very suspicious situation" (Human Rights Watch 2005). The International Committee of the Red Cross (ICRC) reported on the pattern of abuses at Abu Ghraib—the prison formerly used by Saddam Hussein's forces under his regime and now run by the American military. Abuses occurred at every stage, from arrest to final internment, and included handcuffing with tight (plastic) flexi-cuffs; threats of imminent executions and reprisals against family members; being held naked in solitary confinement with insufficient sleep, food, or water; being paraded naked before other prisoners; exposure to loud music; and prolonged sun exposure. Coalition Forces intelligence officers told the ICRC that between 70 and 90 percent of detainees were arrested by mistake (Randall 2004).

These actions by the American military violate international human rights conventions regarding the treatment of prisoners in wartime, as does the CIA's secret use of prisons outside of the United States to interrogate suspected terrorists (Carr 2005). Hence, these actions are unjust. Are they also evil? The answer to this question, I think, is yes. These physical and psychic abuses are instances of foreseeable intolerable harm. And the convictions of seven soldiers at Abu Ghraib point to their culpability.[4] But why is the language of injustice inadequate to characterize these abuses? Why should we turn to a moral language that goes beyond the language of social and juridical relations? The post-metaphysical approach to evil focuses on the human origin of evil, but so does a juridical approach. What does the language of evil do that the language of injustice does not? Does the term *evil* provide an emotional intensification of discourse linked to a sense of revulsion? And does this emotional shock help us develop the ability to make judgments? I agree with María Pía Lara that the language of evil can shock us with new meanings and stimulate a reorientation in our thinking. Narratives of negative examplaries, such as the story of Adolf Eichmann or the stories of the American inquisitors in Abu Ghraib or Guantánamo Bay, can be linked to what Jürgen Habermas calls learning by catastrophes (Lara 2007). Some individuals, such as the American interrogator in Iraq who later admitted to the helplessness, rage, and sadism that was unleashed in him when he was instructed to get harsher with the prisoners, do learn from their wrongs. When you feel that you are entirely in control of other human beings and they refuse to do what you want, he explained, you will do anything do get your way—even unleashing dogs on them while they are blindfolded or breaking their bones. Other perpetrators of evil actions, such as the Nazi head of the *Einsatzgruppe* responsible for the mass murder of civilians, who never admitted that he committed atrocities, never learn from their wrongs. But we who read their stories learn by holding ourselves and our leaders to account.

Hannah Arendt caught sight of another important function of the concept of evil in her book *The Origins of Totalitarianism* (1951). Radical evil, she argued, "has emerged in connection with a system in which all men have become equally superfluous." For Arendt, what was at stake in the Nazi death factories was not the well-known evil motives of "greed, covetousness, resentment, lust for power and cowardice." She wrote, "human nature as such is at stake" (1951/1973, 459). What is at stake in totalitarianism, and when democratic governments employ abuses known under totalitarian regimes, is the annihilation of the concept of the human being, the annihilation of the individual as a cohabitant and cobuilder of a shared world. Arendt's use of the word *evil* points to the destruction of the possibility of a plurality of human beings living together in the world. And in undermining plurality, one also violates the conditions for democracy.

In one of Jacques Derrida's last publications before his death, he wrote of the self-destruction of democracy, the "autoimmune pervertibility of democracy" (2005, 34). He saw this autoimmunity, sometimes called the death drive, at work in American politics. He wrote:

> Is there, after the Algerian example, a more visibly autoimmune process than the one seen in the aftermath of what is called "September 11"? We see an American administration, potentially followed by others in Europe and the rest of the world, claiming that in the war it is waging against the "axis of evil," against the enemies of freedom and the assassins of democracy throughout the world, it must restrict within its own country certain so-called democratic freedoms and the exercise of certain rights by, for example, increasing the powers of police investigations and interrogations, without anyone, any democrat, being really able to oppose such measures. One can thus do little more than regret some particular abuse in the a

priori abusive use of force by which a democracy defends itself against its enemies, justifies or defends itself, of or from itself, against its potential enemies. It must thus come to resemble these enemies, to corrupt itself and threaten itself in order to protect itself against their threats. (2005, 39–40)

When Iraqi police who are trained by the United States imprison and torture civilians much as they did in the times of Saddam Hussein, then Derrida's claim that a democracy that restricts democratic freedom and rights comes to resemble its enemies is a diagnosis of the present. Using the term *evil* in the context of torture, and of torture carried out in the name of democracy, draws our attention to central features of human existence and of democratic political life that are transgressed by these abuses and therefore to what is at stake: not just the misdemeanors of particular individuals, but the threat to the social and political conditions for democracy.

There is yet another effect of the concept of evil: it reminds us that the worst threats to human existence come from human beings themselves. This is an aspect of evil that it is particularly important for Americans to remember today. Americans all too readily adopt a Manichean worldview, distinguishing between good and evil as distinct and opposing categories, where "we" are identified with the good, and "they" are identified with evil. This worldview was prevalent in 1947, when Simone de Beauvoir took her first journey to America. In *America Day by Day* she reflected on how Americans viewed the Japanese as the devil incarnate, and hence how they could justify the internment of Japanese living in the United States during World War II (Beauvoir 1998, 75).[5] And it is surely present today, when Americans view the sanctity of some lives (Americans) as worth more than others (e.g., Arabs and Muslims) (Butler 2004). It is this attitude that lies behind the rush to impute evil to the terrorists who attacked the United States on 9/11 and those who applauded this event. I too would characterize these events as evil. The terrorists killed more than three thousand persons—leaving many more thousands of lives in ruins—and disregarding the fragile distinction between combatants and civilians that just war theorists seek to maintain. But as Derrida noted, it was also a public and political event constituted "by a powerful media-theatricalization calculated on both sides" (2005, 103). Both sides are also responsible for the attack on the conditions of human plurality and democracy that we are now witnessing. Hence, no discussion of the question of evil in relation to the hijackers on 9/11 should be detached from a discussion of the evils committed by the United States in its response.

It would be well for us to recall the evils that undermine human plurality not only in the battles we fight but also in the battles we refuse to fight. Genocide is one clear example of evil in this sense. It is defined in the Genocide Convention as "deliberately inflicting on the group conditions of life calculated to bring about its physical destruction in whole or in part."[6] Yet on the tenth anniversary in 2004 of the genocide in Rwanda, the United Nations failed to recognize that genocide was taking place in Darfur. Instead, the UN resolution on Darfur re-

ferred to the "ongoing humanitarian crisis and widespread human rights violations."[7] Observers note that by summer of 2005, 250,000 people had died, 2
million people had been displaced, and hundreds of women and girls had been
gang-raped and branded, often in front of their families (Stanton 2005; Reeves
2004). At this writing, now in late fall 2005, the violence is escalating rather than
diminishing, with an increase in rapes of women and girls and in the killing of
children, who are recruited as soldiers by all sides of the conflict.[8] One might
well argue that the "benumbing indifference" that characterizes the international response has "exposed the quiet savagery of the rest of the world" (Nally
2004). Funds previously promised by the U.S. House of Representatives to support African Union peacekeepers have now been cut, leaving the peacekeepers
vulnerable and ill-equipped to respond. A British police liaison to the African
Union reported, "You would not see any other forces like the U. N. or NATO left
alone like this" (Wax 2005). With this failure to provide adequate intervention,
the international community once again commits the evil of omission that allows the continued escalation of genocidal violence.[9]

So far I have addressed three aspects of the problem of evil: the evils for
which individuals or groups have moral responsibility; the evils that threaten
the plurality that is essential to human existence; and the evils that threaten the
political conditions for democracy. Why should the existence of these moral,
ontological, or political evils be a problem that *feminist* philosophers might want
to confront?

One reason for feminist philosophers to address the problem of evil is that
many evils are gender-specific. Think, for example, of the practice of female
genital mutilation (FGM), which has been performed on some 100 to 130 million women and girls worldwide—a practice that also takes place in the United
States (Burstyn 1995, 2). Think of the random attacks against women in Bangladesh by men who throw acid over them, causing permanent pain and grotesque disfiguration, thus ruining the futures of these young women (Jantzen
2002). Think of the mass war rapes in recent years in Yugoslavia, Rwanda, and
Darfur. As Joseph and Sharma note, "In times of peace, as well as war, their
[women's] right to physical security is routinely violated through a range of violent acts, including rape, sexual harassment and sexual exploitation. During periods of social upheaval or political discord they experience heightened levels
of violence and trauma, both physical and psychological, both within the home
and outside it. . . . In times of conflict, they bear the additional social and economic burdens as they often find themselves solely responsible for their families" (2003, xii). Hence, attention to women's situation often brings with it a
heightened awareness of the evils that are linked to the uses of violence.

But many evils are not gender-specific, as Card notes in her contribution to
this volume. Both men and women lost their lives during the attacks of 9/11,
and both men and women were left bereaved on that day. Both men and women
suffer when innocent male members of a family are arrested, and it is the male
detainees who have been the target of abuses in Guantánamo Bay and Abu
Ghraib. Both men and women suffer during genocide. Hence, issues of terror-

ism, genocide, and prisoner abuse risk being overlooked by feminist scholars. But it is crucial for feminist philosophers to analyze both gendered and non-gendered forms of evil as part of a general commitment to incorporate feminist values and methodologies in analyses of ethical and political relations. Women philosophers such as Arendt have been particularly important in bringing the issue of evil to debate in a nonmetaphysical way. Hence, for feminist philosophers, it is often an analysis of the *particularity* of harms that enables reflection on evil. Given the historical representation of women as Other in philosophy, feminist philosophers are also attentive to problems of *otherness*. And given the way the figure of woman has been used to represent symbolically the points of vulnerability of the human life cycle—birth and death—feminist philosophers are attuned to the problem of human *vulnerability* in general.[10]

A Few Reflections on Structure

This book is divided into two sections: part one deals with feminist philosophical reflections on the problem of evil; part two deals with feminist reflections on the problem of terrorism as it came to American's reality on September 11, 2001. The continuing threat of terrorism became evident in Europe when ten bombs exploded on four packed commuter trains in Madrid on the morning of March 11, 2004, leaving 191 people dead and more than 1,800 injured. And terrorists struck London on July 7, 2005, when 52 people died during attacks on trains and buses. A mere two weeks later, on July 21, there were again attempted bombings in London, but none of the explosives were detonated.

Perhaps the simplest way to think about the relationship between the two parts of this book is to view them chronologically. In part one, the essays were written before the attacks in the United States, Spain, and Great Britain. The essays in part two were written after the 9/11 terrorist attacks and are revised for this book. One of the new contributions of this section is an essay by Spanish philosopher María Isabel Peña Aguado reflecting on the terrorist attacks in Spain. Thinking of the sections of the book chronologically helps to avoid certain misunderstandings about their relation. It would be a mistake to think of the essays in the first part as being primarily concerned with historical problems of evil, while those in part two deal with its contemporary manifestations. Although part one does indeed include essays of particular historical interest, for example on the witch hunts, a number of the essays in this section deal with issues that are highly contemporary: the problem of genocide, the trials of Bosnian war criminals, the situation of women in Afghanistan, and the issue of the violence of homegrown American terrorists. Similarly, it would be a mistake to think of the structure of the volume as making a statement about historical time: that history is to be divided into the events *before* and *after* 9/11. As I will discuss below, it is important to emphasize the continuity of the issues of militarization and terrorism before and after this symbolic date.

But there are two aspects that are related to the chronological divide in the book. One aspect is the thematic difference. Part two is focused specifically on the problem of terrorism, which only one contributor in part one addresses (Lynne Arnault in her essay on the Oklahoma City bombing). The second aspect is the relationship to the present. One is now forced to relate to what has been called the 9/11 syndrome, with the renewal of mistrust and hostility in the United States against racial, ethnic, and religious groups that are defined as "other." The contributors in this section (whether U.S., Canadian, Mexican, or Spanish) are explicitly critical of the resurgence of national and ethnic prejudices.[11] In the remainder of this introduction, I will discuss four themes that are pronounced in contemporary discourse in the wake of the 9/11 syndrome: the relation between terrorism and militarization; the role of pain in political discourse; the question of whether 9/11 should be understood as historical rupture or continuity; and the relation between moral and political discourse.

Contemporary Themes

Terrorism and Militarization

One of the strands of debate that emerged immediately after the 9/11 attacks was the call by critical intellectuals to analyze the relationship between terrorism and militarization, focusing on their overlaps and similarities. This task is not made easier by the reluctance of U.S. government officials to define terrorism. Eqbal Ahmad, after going through twenty U.S. documents on terrorism, came to the conclusion that that lack of definition was deliberate: "If you're not going to be consistent, you're not going to define."[12] However, if one roughly defines terrorism as the threat or use of violence against unarmed civilians in the pursuit of political goals, then parallels emerge between terrorism and the militarization that provided some of the preconditions for terrorist acts and that have shaped the U.S. response to it. Both terrorism and U.S. militarization share certain attitudes in common about the use of violence: (1) Force rather than political negotiation or dialogue is considered to be the appropriate response to political conflict. As Rohini Hensman notes about the U.S. strategies after 9/11, dialogue is invoked *after* the enemy has been vanquished. (2) Violence against unarmed civilians is considered to be an acceptable political cost. (3) Some lives are considered to be worth more than others. These last two points were illustrated by Madeleine Albright's response to an interviewer, who in 1996 questioned her about the half-million Iraqi children who had died because of sanctions. Albright replied, "We think the price is worth it."

There are other similarities between a discourse of terrorism and a discourse of militarization, which leads Rosalind Petchesky to refer to them as the "phantom Twin Towers."[13] Both discourses are characterized by an extreme form of *nationalism* with imperialistic tendencies. One can hear nationalism in bin Laden's invocation of "the Arab nation" or "brotherhood" that seeks to drive out "the infidels" from about a third of the globe. And one can hear this nationalism in President Bush's claim, "Either you are with us or you are with the terrorists." Bush thereby claims that the United States is the leader of the civilized world, while terrorists remain outside of civilization.

Both discourses are characterized by an invocation of *religious symbolism* to justify political purposes. Bin Laden declares a jihad, or holy war, against the United States, and Bush declares a crusade against the terrorists.[14] Lt. General William "Jerry" Boykin, promoted in 2003 to Deputy Undersecretary of Defense for Intelligence, told an audience about his battle against a Muslim warlord in Somalia: "I knew that my God was bigger than his. I knew that my God was a real God and his was an idol." And Boykin, an evangelical Christian, told an audience in Oklahoma that bin Laden and Saddam Hussein were not the enemy: "Our enemy is a spiritual enemy because we are a nation of believers. . . . His name is Satan." In light of this political invocation of a Manichean religious worldview, it is well to recall Eduardo Galeano's comment that "in the struggle of Good against Evil, it's always the people who get killed."

Both discourses operate with *racist* undertones. Bin Laden's anti-Semitism is explicit. In a 1998 interview he asserted that "the Americans and the Jews . . . represent the spearhead with which the members of our religion have been slaughtered. Any effort directed against America and the Jews yields positive and direct results." And in the United States the ongoing racism becomes even more virulent in times of national crisis, making vulnerable women who wear headscarves and Arab and Indian men.

Furthermore, *masculinism* characterizes the discourses of both terrorism and militarization. Bin Laden's Taliban protectors expressed extreme misogyny and violence against women. The Revolutionary Association of the Women of Afghanistan has documented how women were punished for sexual offenses and dress code offenses. Some Taliban followers threw vials of acid in the faces of women students who refused to wear veils, disfiguring them for life. The masculinism of the American military is also evident when it sends single mothers, who signed up for the National Guard when their welfare was cut, to die in its holy war, and when it refuses accountability before the International Criminal Court for acts of rape and sexual assault committed by American soldiers stationed around the globe.

The Role of Pain in Political Discourse

Another dimension of the contemporary political discourse is the invocation of pain as a justification for political response. Here one should underline with Lauren Berlant that nonrational factors become pivotal in political discourse.[15] Hence, one can ask how pain becomes a way of constituting political subjectivity.

Pain has entered the ethical discourse since Auschwitz, in particular with the publication of the substantial literature by survivors of the death camps. In this context, the role of pain has been important in rethinking the central ethical categories for understanding human extremes, and the role of the witness as an ethical category has had a major impact on ethics over the last decades. The work of Primo Levi has been pivotal, a focal point of Giorgio Agamben's analysis in *Remnants of Auschwitz*. Instead of theorizing ethics primarily in terms of guilt or punishment or responsibility, Agamben argues that the role of the witness shows the irreducible residue of the unspeakable and unrepresentable in extreme pain and dehumanization.

Pain has also played a significant role in religious discourse. The history of Christianity is closely connected with the idea of religious exaltation in sacrificing oneself for one's beliefs. Grace M. Jantzen writes of the public spectacles of pain in the Colosseum in ancient Rome, where mass killings were staged for the enjoyment of the Roman population. The spectacles of pain became one means of attaining martyrdom for early Christians. One second-century writer complained, "The poor wretches have convinced themselves, first and foremost, that they are going to be immortal and live for all time, in consequence of which they despise death and even willingly give themselves into custody most of the time" (in Jantzen 2004, 330–35).

Religious sacrifice and exaltation has found its way into political discourse, not only in relation to the militaristic interventions of the medieval church, but also in the theory of just war to which St. Augustine made such a substantial contribution. I would argue that the hidden premise of much contemporary discussions of just war is the view that *sacrifice* is necessary to maintain the meaningfulness of our values. Only by believing that some values (i.e., our values) are worth dying for, can a society maintain its own self-understanding. In his monumental *Just and Unjust War*, Michael Walzer argues that what is fundamentally at stake in just war is defending "rights that are worthy dying for" (1977/1992, 53). And even such a compelling and moderate spokeswoman for just war theory as Jean Bethke Elshtain has significantly changed the tenor of her reflections since September 11 with its challenge to "American values" (2003, 183–84).[16] Since the terrorist attacks on the United States, she has put her emphasis on showing that "we must and will fight . . . to defend who we are and what we, at our best, represent" (2003, 6). For Elshtain and others, Bush's war against terror functions as a means to rearticulate the perception that one must be willing to sacrifice oneself to defend the Americanness of democratic values.[17]

Pain has entered the contemporary political discourse not just in terms of what Americans willingly sacrifice, but in terms of what it means for Americans to see themselves as victims. The attacks on September 11, 2001, were the first foreign attacks on U.S. soil since the Japanese attack on Pearl Harbor on December 7, 1941, which precipitated U.S. entry into World War II. Even though people from over one hundred different nationalities died on September 11th, the attacks specifically targeted symbols of American economic and military power. Suddenly, the United States was put in the position of being the victim in a violent conflict. In this context, it is *our* pain that is put in the eyes of a public that is accustomed to viewing the pain of *others* at a distance. As Susan

Sontag noted in *Regarding the Pain of Others,* while focusing on the *pain* of others, we institute a criteria for who matters—whose pain and suffering and dying are made visible to the public and whose remain unnoticed and hence the subject of unconcern.[18] Moreover, regarding the pain of *others* helps us disregard the evils that are committed on American soil. In this context Susan Sontag notes that the Holocaust Memorial Museum and the future Armenian Genocide Museum and Memorial are about what *didn't* happen in America: "To have a museum chronicling the great crime that was American slavery in the United States of America would be to acknowledge that the evil was *here.* Americans prefer to picture the evil that was *there*" (2003, 79).

When Americans do acknowledge that evils are committed by their country, then it is when they are the victims of evils. But in assuming the role of victim in the wake of 9/11, the United States justifies its own role as military aggressor. Since it is the victim of attack, it can be justified in fighting for and maintaining its worldwide supremacy without losing its special status as victim. Thus the binary opposition between victim and aggressor can sometimes cover over much more complex relations.[19] In this case, *our* pain becomes a mirror for the preexisting political and economic hierarchies in international relations that we seek to sustain.

Rupture or Continuity

There may well be a tendency for each age to view itself as of special importance, dividing history into the before-and-after of a particular conflict. Hence, for some, 1939 was the decisive point in history, dividing the world into a prewar past and the horrors of World War II. After this momentous date, even nature was drawn into war—as manifest in the image of hundreds of cavalry horses frozen into a Finnish lake in their attempted flight from enemy fire, with only their heads visible as if chopped off cleanly by an axe (Parks 2005, 28–31). So too, the language after 9/11 takes on the character of a crisis of epochal importance, dividing history into that which preceded it, for which one could have a certain nostalgia, and that which follows it, in which terrorism is a constant threat for humankind.

As the German intellectual historian Reinhart Koselleck points out, there are three historical models of crisis. One model is the view of history as an ongoing crisis, marking every situation by an urgent sense of decision. A second model treats crisis as the crossing of a threshold which brings about a new situation that can repeat itself in an unending process (2002, 236–84). A third model treats crisis as the final crisis in history, after which history would look entirely different. It is this latter sense of crisis that one can invoke in relation to the Nazi death camps during World War II, where what was at stake was the very concept of humanity itself. Arendt argued that the death camps gave evidence of a massive experiment that sought to transform human nature by making all human beings equally superfluous (1951/1973, 458–59).

Which of these notions of crisis might be applicable to the discourse after September 11? The rhetoric found in the union of a religious and political right-wing movement in the United States invokes fighting Satan as the enemy in the battle of Good against Evil and as such seems to locate this discourse in this third sense of final crisis. But this would be a misguided analysis of the 9/11 attacks. The terrorists did treat their victims as objects and not as persons, but as objects who were strictly superfluous to their mission of attacking the so-called infidels.[20] Nonetheless, these attacks do not have the character of total destruction of humanity. It is the violation of democracy from within its own ranks and the possession of technologies of mass destruction that more radically undermine the concept of humanity.

One could plausibly argue that the events of September 11 qualify as a crisis in the second sense of the term, as bringing about a new situation. This sense of crisis addresses one of the effects of terrorism, that of destroying the trust in the everyday rhythms of ordinary existence. This trust has been dramatically undermined in Europe by the subsequent terrorist attacks in Madrid and London, and it has been undermined for ordinary Iraqis, whose daily security cannot be guaranteed. Yet this use of crisis has the danger of covering over the marked continuities before and after the September 11 attacks that are evident in the similarities between terrorism and militarism discussed above.

Hence, it may well be the first sense of crisis that is most useful in this situation. For the view that history is marked by an urgent sense of decision reminds us of the temporality and fragility of historical constellations. It is this notion of the fragility of certain institutions that may be most pressing for us to bear in mind, and that Derrida stressed when he analyzed the autoimmunity of democracy. And it is this notion that Adorno earlier warned against when he stated, "I consider the survival of National Socialism *within* democracy to be potentially more menacing than the survival of fascistic tendencies *against* democracy" (1998, 90). This notion of crisis reminds us that what is at stake in the current climate is a crisis of democracy, with the reminder that the historical life of democracy is relatively brief and that there is no absolute guarantee of its continued existence.

Moral and Political Discourses

In the present climate, the relationship between moral and political discourses has become a charged issue. Many philosophers argue against the use of moral language such as the term *evil* in relation to the problem of terrorism. This use of moral language risks trespassing the borders that distinguish issues proper to the political sphere—such as issues of rights and coercion in relations between citizens and their governments—and issues that are proper to the moral sphere—such as the rightness and wrongness of acts or social conditions.[21] From this point of view, using moral language reduces politics to morality and undermines the possibility of criticizing institutionalized injustices.

However, one can maintain a distinction between moral and political categories and still consider where these spheres overlap. In "To Perpetual Peace," Kant wrote, "I can actually think of a *moral politician*, i.e., one who so interprets the principles of political prudence that they can be coherent with morality, but I cannot think of a *political moralist*, i.e., one who forges a morality to suit the statesman's advantage" (1795/1983, 128).

As a citizen, one should be concerned not only with whether one's politicians are moral but also with whether one can judge one's role as a citizen to be moral. Here an existentialist approach sheds light on areas where the political and the moral overlap. Simone de Beauvoir's book *America Day by Day* maps out the ways in which the political institutions of racism—including segregation in the South in the 1940s—become the architecture for moral relations between persons. When a white woman does not dare offer a seat in the front of the bus to a black woman who had fainted, then she too is responsible for the privileges of her skin (Beauvoir 1998, 231). Similarly, when citizens are the beneficiaries of the violent colonialist policies of their government—as the French were during the war in Algeria—then they too are responsible for evil even as they act to oppose it. For Beauvoir, since political institutions are a framework for relations between individuals, then ethics also includes an analysis of this dimension of the political within its domain. Because ethics is much more than questions of individual will or intention in an existentialist approach, it is easier to catch sight of the complexity and contradictions in moral relations from this perspective. Beauvoir introduces the notion of ambiguity to highlight this complexity and to disavow a Manichean worldview that reduces the world to clear-cut oppositions of right and wrong.

As citizens in the post-9/11 world, we too live with ambiguity. We need to acknowledge the irremediable harms to the thousands of individuals and families who have suffered tragic losses through the terrorist attacks. And we need to acknowledge the evils for which our own governments are responsible. We need to recognize moral complexity rather than moral binaries in order to respond to the crises of the present. Moral complexity is central for an understanding of evil, which is central for an understanding of the present. As evidenced in this collection, feminist philosophers provide invaluable resources for understanding both the complexity and the vulnerability of human existence that is at stake in the problem of evil.

Notes

1. On September 15, 2002, Susan Brison included this information in a note on the FEAST listserv.
2. For a discussion of the 9/11 syndrome, see Ammu Joseph and Kalpana Sharma's fine introduction to *Terror, Counter-Terror: Women Speak Out*. For the phrase "zone of mistrust," see Rosalind P. Petchesky's article "Phan-

tom Towers: Feminist Reflections on the Battle between Global Capitalism and Fundamentalist Terrorism," in Joseph and Sharma 2003, 61.

3. My comments on Kant are based on my paper, "From Radical Evil to Perpetual Peace," forthcoming in Danish in *Introduktion til Kant* (Århus: Århus Universitetsforlag, 2007).

4. Convicted soldiers are Lynndie England, Sabrina Harman, Charles Graner Jr., Ivan Frederick, Jeremy Sivits, Roman Crol, Armin Cruz, and Javal Davis. http://msnbc.msn.com/id/7709487/, accessed November 22, 2005.

5. See my "Beauvoir and the Ambiguity of Evil" in Card 2003, 235.

6. See Article 2, clause c, of the Convention on the Prevention and Punishment of the Crime of Genocide, ratified by the General Assembly, December 9, 1948. http://www.unhchr.ch/html/menu3/b/p_genoci.htm, accessed November 22, 2005.

7. UN resolution on Darfur, July 30, 2004, http://news.bbc.co.uk/go/or/fr/-/hi/world/africa/3940527.stm, accessed November 18, 2005.

8. See Reuters, "Darfur descending into total lawlessness: Annan," November 22, 2005, http://www.alternet.org/thenews/newsdesk/N21325396.htm, accessed November 23, 2005.

9. For a discussion of the importance of the role of the bystander, see Staub 1989, 151–58. Staub discusses not only the passivity of German bystanders during the Nazi regime but the passivity of foreign governments that failed to deter Germany or act to save the Jews.

10. See Debra Bergoffen's article in this collection, "February 22, 2001: Toward a Politics of the Vulnerable Body."

11. Unfortunately, the French philosopher Michèle le Doeuff had to withdraw from this volume for reasons of health.

12. Cited in Rohini Hensman, "The Only Alternative to Global Terror," in Joseph and Sharma 2003, 23. The references in this paragraph are to pages 25, 33–34 of her article.

13. Petchesky, "Phantom Towers," in Joseph and Sharma 2003, 53. My comments on terrorism and militarization are based on her discussion on pages 55–61.

14. Although when informed that this phrase recalled the medieval Christian crusaders' invasion of Islamic nations, Bush retracted the word "crusade" (Cooper 2003). The following remarks by Boykin are cited here and in Schrift 2005, 3.

15. See Sherene H. Razack's essay in this volume, "Those Who 'Witness the Evil': Peacekeeping as Trauma." See also Lauren Berlant, "The Subject of True Feeling: Pain, Privacy, and Politics" in Bronfen and Kavka 2001, 126–60.

16. Elshtain was one of the primary authors of this public letter, signed by sixty prominent U.S. intellectuals. The letter is a defense of American values (though Europeans may wonder why the belief in dignity, moral truths, civic behavior, and freedom of conscience and religion are specifically *American*). And it is a defense of Bush's war against terror under the aegis of just war theory.

17. See my discussion in "Just War and the Problem of Evil" in Bat-Ami Bar On, ed., *Hypatia: Special Issue on Just War,* forthcoming 2008.

18. Judith Butler (2004, 35) also discusses the way in which the grief and vulnerability of some people are excluded from the public domain. She cites the story of a Palestinian citizen of the United States who submitted statements "in

memoriam" to the *San Francisco Chronicle* for two Palestinian families who had been killed by Israeli troops. The memorials were rejected on the grounds that the newspaper did not wish to offend anyone.

19. One sees the same kind of logic at work with regard to Serbian ideology in the 1990s. By virtue of its identity as victim, the Serbian nation could become the aggressor without losing its status as threatened victim. See Schott 2003, 113.

20. See Sara Ruddick's "The Evils of the September Attacks" in this volume.

21. In this volume see, for example, Bat-Ami Bar On's article, "Terrorism, Evil, and Everyday Depravity" and Alison M. Jaggar's "Naming Terrorism as Evil." Bar On argues that it is not desirable to assume a seamless connection between ethics and politics. Jaggar argues that the appropriate language for responding to terrorism is the language of international law. The language of evil should instead be used in reference to injustice, poverty, and political exclusion.

References

Adorno, Theodor W. 1998. *Critical Models: Interventions and Catchwords*. Ed. and trans. Henry W. Pickford. New York: Columbia University Press.

Agamben, Giorgio. 1999. *Remnants of Auschwitz: The Witness and the Archive*. Trans. Daniel Heller-Roazen. New York: Zone Books.

Arendt, Hannah. [1951] 1973. *The Origins of Totalitarianism*. New York: Harcourt Brace Jovanovich.

Beauvoir, Simone de. 1998. *America Day by Day*. Trans. Carol Cosman. London: Phoenix.

Berlant, Lauren. 2001. The Subject of true feeling: Pain, privacy, and politics. In *Feminist Consequences: Theory for the New Century*, ed. Elisabeth Bronfen and Misha Kavka, 126–60. New York: Columbia University Press.

Bernstein, Richard J. 1996. *Hannah Arendt and the Jewish Question*. Cambridge: Polity Press.

Bronfen, Elisabeth, and Misha Kavka, eds. 2001. *Feminist Consequences: Theory for the New Century*. New York: Columbia University Press.

Burstyn, Linda. 1995. Female circumcision comes to America. *Atlantic Monthly* (October): 1–13.

Bush, George W. 2002. State of the Union Address, 29 January. Retrieved 13 September from http://www.whitehouse.gov/news/releases/2002/01/20020129–11.html.

Butler, Judith. 2004. *Precarious Life: The Powers of Mourning and Violence*. London: Verso.

Card, Claudia, ed. 2003. *The Cambridge Companion to the Philosophy of Simone de Beauvoir*. Cambridge: Cambridge University Press.

———. 2002. *The Atrocity Paradigm: A Theory of Evil*. Oxford: Oxford University Press.

Carr, Rebecca. 2005. Who told of CIA's hidden prisons? *Austin American Statesman*. 9 November. Retrieved 17 November from http://statesman.com/news/content/auto/epaper/editions/wednesday/news_3417fa20b1db001400df.html.

Cicovacki, Predrag. 2001. The trial of man and the trial of God: Reflections on Job and the grand inquisitor. *Diotima: A Philosophical Review* 2 (2): 83–94.

Cooper, Richard T. 2003. General casts war in religious terms. *Los Angeles Times.* 16 October. Retrieved 1 December 2005 from http:/www.commondreams .org/cgi-bin/print.cgi?file=headlines03/1016-01.html.

Copjec, Joan, ed. 1996. *Radical Evil.* London: Verso.

Derrida, Jacques. 2005. *Rogues.* Trans. Pascale-Anne Brailt and Michael Naas. Stanford, Calif.: Stanford University Press.

Elshtain, Jean Bethke. 2003. *Just War Against Terror.* New York: Basic Books.

Hensman, Rohini. 2003. The only alternative to global terror. In *Terror, Counter-Terror: Women Speak Out,* ed. Ammu Joseph and Kalpana Sharma, 23. London: Zed Books.

Human Rights Watch. 2005. New accounts of torture by U.S. troops. 24 September. Retrieved 17 November 2005 from http://hrw.org/english/docs/2005/09/ 25/usint11776_txt.htm.

Jantzen, Grace M. 2004. *Foundations of Violence.* London: Routledge.

Jantzen, Ulrik. 2002. Aetsede for altid (Corroded forever). *Berlingske Tidende.* 12 May.

Joseph, Ammu, and Kalpana Sharma. 2003. *Terror, Counter-Terror: Women Speak Out.* London: Zed Books.

Kant, Immanuel. 1795/1983. To Perpetual Peace: A Philosophical Sketch. Trans. Ted Humphrey. In *Perpetual Peace and Other Essays.* Indianapolis/Cambridge: Hackett.

Kant, Immanuel. [1793] 1996. Religion within the boundaries of mere reason. In *Religion and Rational Theology,* ed. Allen W. Wood and George Di Giovanni. Cambridge: Cambridge University Press.

Koselleck, Reinhart. 2002. *The Practice of Conceptual History: Timing History, Spacing Concepts.* Trans. Samuel Presner and others. Stanford, Calif.: Stanford University Press.

Lara, María Pía. 2007. *Narrating Evil: A Postmetaphysical Theory of Reflective Judgment.* New York: Columbia University Press.

———, ed. 2001. *Rethinking Evil.* Berkeley: University of California Press.

Nally, David. 2004. Genocide in Darfur? In *Counterpunch,* ed. Alexander Cockburn and Jeffrey St. Clair, 31 July. Retrieved 17 November 2005 from http://counterpunch.org/nally07312004.html.

Neiman, Susan. 2002. *Evil in Modern Thought: An Alternative History of Philosophy.* Princeton, N.J.: Princeton University Press.

Parks, Tim. 2005. The Horrors of War. Review of *Kaputt* by Curzio Malaparted. *New York Review of Books,* 1 December, 28–31.

Peretz, Martin. 2001. Israel, the United States, and evil. *New Republic.* 24 September, 1–3.

Petchesky, Rosalind P. Phantom towers: Feminist reflections on the battle between global capitalism and fundamentalist terrorism. In *Terror, Counter-Terror: Women Speak Out,* ed. Ammu Joseph and Kalpana Sharma, 61. London: Zed Books.

Randall, Kate. 2004. Red Cross report documents U.S. torture of Iraqi prisoners. World Socialist Web site, 14 May. Retrieved 17 November 2005 from http://www.wsws.org/articles/2004/icrc-m14_prn.shtml.

Reeves, Eric. 2004. Genocide in Sudan. *In These Times.* 6 May. Retrieved 18 November 2005 from http://www.inthesetimes.com/site/main/print/genocide_i_sudan/.

Schott, Robin May. 2003. *Discovering Feminist Philosophy*. Lanham, Md.: Rowman and Littlefield.

———. Forthcoming 2008. Just war and the problem of evil. In *Hypatia: Special Issue on Just War Theory*, ed. Bat-Ami Bar On. Bloomington: Indiana University Press.

Schrift, Alan D., ed. 2005. *Modernity and the Problem of Evil*. Bloomington: Indiana University Press.

Sontag, Susan. 2003. *Regarding the Pain of Others*. London: Hamish Hamilton.

Stanton, Gregory H. 2005. Genocide emergency: Darfur, Sudan; twelve ways to deny a genocide. Retrieved 18 November 2005 from http://www.genocidewatch.org/ SudanTwelveWaysToDenyAGenocidebyGregStanton.

Staub, Ervin. 1989. *The Roots of Evil*. Cambridge: Cambridge University Press.

Vickers, Jeanne. 1993. *Women and War*. London: Zed Books.

Walzer, Michael. [1977] 1992. *Just and Unjust Wars*. New York: Basic Books.

Wax, Emily. 2005. Peace force in Darfur faces major challenges. *Washington Post*, 21 November. Retrieved 23 November 2005 from http://www.washingtonpost .com/wp-dyn/content/article/11/20/AR20051120010.

Ziarek, Ewa. 2001. *An Ethics of Dissensus*. Stanford, Calif.: Stanford University Press.

Part One   *Feminist Perspectives on Evil: Historical and Contemporary Perspectives*

2 The Devil's Insatiable Sex: A Genealogy of Evil Incarnate

Margaret Denike

For my part, who have been so long and continuously exercised and confirmed in the examination of witches, I shall not fear to proclaim freely and openly my opinion of them, and to do all in my power to bring the very truth to light: namely, that their lives are so notoriously befouled and polluted by so many blasphemies, sorceries, prodigious lusts and flagrant crimes, that I have no hesitation in saying that they are justly to be subjected to every torture and put to death in flames; both that they may expiate their crimes with a fitting punishment, and that its very awfulness may serve as an example and a warning to others.

Judge Nicholas Remy, *Demonalatry* (1602)

Preliminary Remarks on Genealogical Method

In part, this chapter takes up a challenge that Michel Foucault (1989) posed in an interview and that he himself had entertained throughout his genealogical histories of madness and sexuality. The challenge, specifically, is "to write a political history of truth," a history—or histories—that ascertain the kinds of power relations that are implicated in the production and circulation of knowledge, and particularly, in the "official discourses" that are accepted as "true." Such a genealogical approach, as Foucault defined it in the context of this interview (1989, 137–39), concerns the truth games played with "sex" and "sexuality," though there is nothing restricting such an approach to these discursive domains. His method purports to assess the collective, political, and institutional investments in the economies of knowledge that produce or invent certain subjects, like the "homosexual" or the "hysteric." For his own part, Foucault claims to look to the "misery" of those criminally sexualized and pathologized figures and characters who have "paid the price" for truth to be produced about them (1989, 139)—to the "perverts" and "deviants" who are literally subjected by institutions like the church, the judiciary, psychiatric hospitals, prisons, and schools—all of which have a political stake in constituting them and producing official discourses about them.

The possible variations to such genealogical analyses, whatever their scope or

historical trajectory, could furnish countless fragments and "fleeting appearances" of sexualized and criminalized monsters and marvels that speak volumes about those—and the world of those—who speak incessantly about them.
My interest rests with a subject about whom Foucault had almost nothing to
say: the "witch," and particularly, the heretic-witch who haunted the fifteenth
through to the late seventeenth centuries of most European countries. The price
she has paid—and the cost incurred by the "weaker sex" that she was made to
represent—is arguably well documented throughout the volumes of official and
unofficial discourses produced about her. Demonological treatises issued by
church and crown or state officials typically sexualize, demonize, and criminal-
ize her as the incarnation of evil, the "infidel," "servant of Satan," or the "enemy
of God" who wreaked havoc on his greatest glory: man. They speak of the torture and other "exceptional" punishments that their crimes justify, and they
often tell the tales themselves of the tragic fate of countless women who have
suffered them, as Nicholas Remy, Chief Justice of Lorraine, essentially does in
the epigraph quoted above from his 1602 treatise on the demon-idolatry of
witches. Indeed, inquisitors, jurists, and judges have spoken incessantly about
her, preaching, testifying, lecturing about the nature and scope of her demonic
allegiances and insipid weakness; about the reason she was such an ominous
threat; the reason she was to be "put to the question"; the reason she must die.
In the subsequent sections of this chapter, I attempt to sketch the history of the
specific concept "evil" that underlies this scapegoating of women.

One look at the bulk of official discourses issued from the church or crown
during the period that is otherwise dubbed the "Golden Age of Man" makes
apparent that one of the primary preoccupations of the officials of this age was
the wickedness of the "weaker sex" and why she was "given to the craft" so much
more than men, as King James VI of Scotland (James I of England) put it in
1604 (1924, 44). That is to say, why she was culpable of the one crime that war-
ranted what would otherwise, by any existing legal standard, be illegal, cruel,
and unusual punishment, especially for women. For James, "the reason is easie:
for as that sexe is frailer then men is, so is it easier to be intrapped in the gross
snares of the Devill, as was over well proved to be true, by the Serpents deceiving
of Eve at the beginning, which makes him the homelier with that sexe ever
since" (1924, 44).

Such tautological truth claims about women's propensity toward "so odious
a treason" as this "capital crime" were disseminated by a new Latin edition of his
Daemonologie (1604), within a year of James's ascension to England's throne,
just before he repealed existing witchcraft laws for much harsher ones.[1] Of
course, his reasoning echoes that of the notorious inquisitor's manual, the *Malleus Maleficarum* [1486], proffered more than a century earlier when, similarly,
the church was struggling for exclusive jurisdiction over the "heresy" and "treason" of witchcraft. Inquisitors Heinrich Kramer and James Sprenger went to
great lengths to make female sexuality synonymous with heresy and to explain
"why it is that women are chiefly addicted to Evil Superstitions" (1971: 41): "All
witchcraft comes from carnal lust, which in women is insatiable" (47). These

claims capture the spirit of the deeply misogynist campaigns launched by the church and the state during man's "renaissance," which relied on Christianity's historical demonization of female sexuality and which specifically and ruthlessly aimed to bring a brutal, punitive, and regulative machinery to bear directly on women. They speak of a self-legitimizing war on women, of a myriad of jurisdictional battles to colonize her, if not to outright kill her. They give us pause to consider what it is, other than historical happenstance, that finds such femicidal outbreaks to coincide with the "rebirth" of man, with inaugural conquests for autonomy such as those buttressing the rise of the modern state.

Considering that, on various occasions, Foucault took pains to elucidate the relations between the confessional production of truth and operations of ecclesiastical, juridical, and medical regimes of power (e.g., 1978, 1980, 1989), and considering how much he had to say about torture, confinement, internment, and the spectacles of cruelty that occurred at the interstices of judicial and medical knowledge (e.g., 1965, 1989, 1995), one might think that the regimes of knowledge and power invested in the witch would be an obvious point of return in his genealogical inquiries. The "witch"—or rather the colonizing forces and truth games that invented her "heretical depravity"—seems so immediately pertinent, and even exemplary, of the specific scenes of subjection and the construction of deviant subjectivities that engaged Foucault's genealogies of madness, sexuality, and criminality.[2] My interest, however, points less to questioning why such things as the construction of the "witch" and the proliferation of debates about her are so often eclipsed in sociopolitical and philosophically minded histories than what it means to come to terms with a phenomenon as formidable and as consequential as a church- and state-backed campaign, conducted in the name of eradicating evil, of unmitigated violence against women and particularly against those who are elderly, feeble, ailing, poverty-stricken, and socially ostracized.

This question would perhaps carry less significance if the regimes of knowledge and power produced around the witch had not had so profound and irreversible an effect on the institutionalization of the politics of sexual difference for the centuries to come. To date, we have yet to embrace the relevance of the historically unprecedented criminalization and sexualization of women *as witches* to questions as particular as the fate of debates like the *querelles de femmes* and to events as general as the shaping of early modern scientific and humanistic regimes of knowledge and the differential relations of the sexes to the truth games that are proper to them.[3] After all, we have only begun to scratch the surface of women's relation to, and subjection under, the Law of the Father and to understand what it has imposed on women and *others,* what places and roles it has assigned, and what many forms of resistance have been pitted against it.

The appearance on the historical stage of the criminal witch—the malignant and powerful woman plagued with carnal desire—is a remarkable example of how politically motivated truth games, and the official discourse derived from them, effectively invent certain subjectivities or identities by infusing with meaning and power the body and being of the female sex. She is a remarkable example of how the concept of "evil" has been deployed in Western cultures, how it sustains the systemic degradation and devaluation of women, and how it facilitates the will-to-power of patriarchal hegemonies. Throughout the extensive discourses written about her, investing and vested in her, we are witness to the complex power struggles between various authorities and institutions that appear to have *needed* her to be "evil" in order to make themselves and their persecutorial practices so holy. Religious, judicial, and medical treatises of the late sixteenth century, in particular, provide archival testimony of vast machineries of power/knowledge derived from witchcraft accusations and investigations and developed through the confessional hermeneutics of witch trials (see, e.g., Bodin 1580/1995; Boguet 1605/1971; James I, 1604/1924; and Remy 1602/1974).

Perhaps such literature is not unlike what Michel Foucault and contemporary feminists have found proliferating in the nineteenth century when the *scientia sexualis* "spoke incessantly" about the hysteric's confessions, the spectacle of her sexed body, and the performance of her diagnosis and treatment (see, e.g., Veith 1965; Foucault 1978; Showalter 1985; Evans 1991; Beizer 1994). The dissemination of discourses on witches and melancholics in the sixteenth and seventeenth centuries, like those on the hysteric in the nineteenth century, bear witness to certain economies of truth and power about women that are patriarchal struggles for autonomy that take the form aggressive campaigns both to repudiate and extirpate the feminine, and/or to implement systems of her regulation and control. To speak of the institutional interest in women's sexual subordination, historically minded feminist scholars have written extensively about the sexual politics of late modernity's truth games on hysteria, but far less has been said about those of the Renaissance, although one could argue that this is an age that witnessed the most sudden and most adverse changes to women's social and legal status. The criminalization of women during the witch craze is a testament to this.

One of the more revealing features of the discourses that give form to the heretical or criminal witch (and to affiliated constitutive subjects, such as the witch-melancholic or witch-hysteric) is their extensive negotiation between the incongruous and conflicting traits ascribed to women. Her place within and under the law is circumscribed by paradox: women are at once cast with children and the insane, deemed too "weak" or "feeble" to be taken seriously or to be included in the early institutions of the church, judiciary, and universities; and yet at the same time, they are said to be powerful and dangerous enough to "defy the laws of nature," to form covenants with the devil, to devastate crops, to introduce plagues, and to cause the death and impotence of men—as witches were typically accused of doing.

How is it that, despite their alleged incompetence and incapacity, which justified women's exclusion from inquisitorial and legal processes in most European countries, women could be brought before ecclesiastical and secular courts in unprecedented numbers and convicted of crimes of witchcraft that bore the harshest penalties as yet known in Western legal history? What trace have these truth games left in the institutions of modernity, and what impact have they had on the social and legal status of women? What can they tell us about the holy wars of today's forms of hegemony and modes of colonization? The answers to such questions have much to add to feminist analyses of evil, or at least to understanding "evil" as a discursive construct—a construct that has been ascribed to women in precise and strategic ways, deployed in the service of the masculinist struggles for individual and institutional autonomy, of the contests for power that define Western patriarchy. Understanding the institutional obsession with her reputed insatiability (and all the imputed strengths and weaknesses this entails) is critical to grasping the modes of "evil" that this obsession unleashed and its reliance on, and reinforcement of, ambivalent myths and conflicting representations of women as *other*. As set out below, this may be approached by elucidating the relation between the repudiation of femininity and the construct of "evil."

It is clear that a significant departure from Foucault would be required to conduct certain feminist genealogies of the "sexuality"—or the "evil"—historically constituted, deployed, and forced on women. That is to say, to document within a "history of sexuality" the political economy of the fear and cruelty directed at woman *because* of the evil that has been made of her sex, and the political purpose such evil has served; to trace the changing faces of productive power (such as those reflected in the historically contingent, invented subjectivities of the heretic-witch, witch-melancholic, or witch-hysteric) in a way that does not lose sight of the background of such figures, that is, the pervasiveness of male supremacy and female subordination; to document within the "history of truth" the political utility and effect of telling lies about women's "evil" and about her carnality and insatiability, while repeatedly proclaiming how "true" they are.

When it comes to thinking historically and critically about women's experience of men's (inventions of, and practices of) "sexuality," one of the real challenges, as Catharine MacKinnon (1992) has taught us, is to devise creative methodologies to expose and document the part of sexuality's history that is entombed in silence, the part that "its victims likely took to their graves" (120): that "sex, as practised, includes abuse, of women and children principally" (121). What would such genealogical histories look like if, as MacKinnon suggests, we were to "take as the primary historical impulse . . . *not* forgetting" this part of sexuality's history; "not forgetting about the meaning of what is not there, not known, maybe not even knowable" (125)? To take this seriously, we need ways get beneath the "ebbs and flows" of "sexuality's" history, beneath the many faces we find etched in the sand at the edge of the sea—"witches," "melancholics," or "hysterics" for example, that seem to appear and disappear in the politics of time and space.

So how might our genealogical tools and methods get at what MacKinnon calls the "bedrock" of male supremacy, which is to say, to that part of sexuality's history that "has not changed much" (123): the historically pervasive feature of patriarchy's will-to-power, or of the Law of the Father that informs the countless struggles for autonomy and for jurisdiction over women's sexual and sexualized bodies? In the course of this chapter, in order to broach this foundational feature of sexuality's history—which, admittedly, is rather unintelligible to the genealogical method Foucault had in mind—I turn to, and draw on, the structural and psycho-symbolic methodological analyses of Mary Douglas (1966) and Julia Kristeva (1982). Their blend of historically minded—yet transhistorical—analyses of the relation between pollution, abjection, and feminine repudiation helps to elucidate how "evil" has been made to operate in "sexuality's" history.

Introducing and Deploying "Evil" Incarnate

The fact that we continue to live with the fatal consequences of how "evil" has been deployed by the church and the state over the past two millennia makes it difficult to speak of evil as something that exists as a discernible presence or form in the world, singularly or diversely manifest to us and available for our analysis. To the extent that "evil" has been given a tangible and material existence in Western theological and political discourse, it has long been in the service of cruelty and brutality against the *other* to whom it is ascribed.

Christianity has given a unique form to the concept of "evil," introduced with the New Testament and entrenched through centuries of colonization. From its inaugurating discourses, Christianity was quick to find evil everywhere in the fallen world, to sketch its demonic and human faces and forms, to locate it in certain behaviors, rituals, or practices, and to rail against it at every opportunity. We're all too familiar with the ascription of "evil" to identifiably "befouled" groups—Jews, Muslims, heretics, witches, blacks, homosexuals—to manifestations of difference or deviation, such as madness, disability, sexuality, criminality, or even to gestures of resistance to, and defiance of, the One God, the Father(s) of the One Church, the One Sovereign State. And even still, and certainly since September 11, 2001, it is a common feature of the public discourses of U.S. and other state officials—from presidential addresses to military press conferences—to find "evil" materially envisaged and repeatedly ascribed to the odious "infidels" (typically rendered fundamentalist Muslim terrorists). Such evil is to be "rooted out" from every corner of the Middle East (beginning with Afghanistan but not stopping there), "hunted down" and "brought to justice." About this, as President George W. Bush's refrain goes, "Make no mistake!"[4]

"Evil" incarnated and embodied as "the infidel," the demonic "enemy of God," is central to the historical and contemporary rhetorical campaigns and propaganda machinery of self-righteous warfare against chosen scapegoats. "Evil" is a tool of war that allows systemic attack and colonization to be conducted under the auspices of "the greater good" or of the greater glory of God. Evil has long been in the service of church- and state-sanctioned practices of surveillance, interrogation, persecution, torture, and genocide through a sacrificial mechanism that targets demonized groups, and especially women. Even when evil is ascribed to a gender-neutral "people"—such as Jews or Muslims—it is typically rendered though themes of infidelity and tropes of sexual insatiability, fecundity, pollution, and corporeal defilement, all of which, in patriarchy's mythic universe, are constituted as feminine.

Cast invariably as the "adversary of God" and the essence of man's sinful affliction, and rendered through tropes of women's weakness and impurity, the predominant conception of "evil" that was launched in the New Testament takes a form that radically departs from its Greco-Roman and Judaic predecessors. It is neither a mere abstraction or principle nor a device like that used by the Hebrew God to test and tempt his loyal subjects, as we find, for example, in the trials of Job. From the Christian writings of the first century C.E. onward, no longer do we find the many serpents and satans of the Judaic tradition; there is but one: Satan, fully personified in his singularity as the "enemy of God," one who has in his service a minion of devils plaguing and befouling the fallen world. This new "evil" is made manifest in Satan's conspiratorial and treasonous trickery, which is performed, first and foremost, through woman, the "devil's gateway," as Tertullian calls her (1999: 133). Represented through images of seduction, temptation, sacrifice, and conspiratorial pacts with the devil himself, "evil" is inscribed with themes of sexual abjection, and it is cathected to, and incarnated as, the "weaker sex."

In the discourses of the inquisitors, judges, and doctors who preoccupy themselves with witches, evil is articulated in a way that paradoxically renders woman the passive fool and conduit of demonic trickery, yet at the same time, an odious threat that denigrates the greater glory of man and impedes his rightful access to the divine. She is the scene of "prodigious lust," powerful and dangerous, demonic, and defiant enough to bring about the fall of man. Yet she is also the embodiment of the sex that is feeble, decrepit, melancholic, and mad enough to be delusional about the dark demon intruders that she falsely imagines to be molesting and tormenting her. Deeply imbricated in the will-to-power of Western patriarchal law, such mythic projections onto female sexuality have ensured that *woman* will be the one to pay a price in "evil's" political economy.

The truth games played with these tales of evil sustain centuries of debates about the moral and intellectual superiority/inferiority of the sexes; they circumscribe her roles and status in institutions such as the church, the state, and the family; they demarcate where and how she stands in and under the Law of the Father. So, too, are they implicated in the political contests over who, exactly—inquisitors, judges, or doctors—should be the ones to take up the investigation, intervention, punishment, treatment or cure. In other words, in more ways than one, the demonization of femininity—and the correlative feminization of evil—is a function of masculinist *jurisdiction*. Patriarchal hegemonies are built on the backs of the *other's* evil. This is a discursive economy of evil incarnate, and it has as its currency the myth of voracious female sexuality.

In the writings of the church fathers, the papal decrees and canons of the

Middle Ages, the inquisitorial manuals of the fifteenth century, and the judicial treatises and trial records of the sixteenth and seventeenth centuries, evil is found to "befoul and pollute" the world, lurking and seething everywhere in the malice begotten of conspiracies or "pacts" with the devil. Persecution discourses provide a documentary history of a way of thinking and speaking about "evil" and of taking courageous action against it that weaves themes of abjection into incredulous tales of demonic seduction, aerial transvection, nocturnal gatherings, devil-worship, child sacrifice, and secret plots of malefice against "man." The world, for Christianity, was tormented by the immanence and presence of Satan and haunted by his minions of fallen angels and "familiars" who, through women, wreaked perpetual havoc on the proper social and symbolic order of the Father. The proliferation of such claims granted license to the church, and subsequently to the state, to sanction mass executions and command conformity on the basis that the sorcerers, heretics, and pagan idolaters were "servants of Satan" (Klaits 1985) and "enemies of God" (Larner 1981).

In what follows I look first to the internal motivations and/or psycho-symbolic relations of the specific construction and deployment of "evil" within patriarchal Christianity, and second to the concrete effects and discursive contests that such constructions gave rise to. I trace the repudiation of femininity and female sexuality at the inauguration of Christianity and Christian demonology, while mapping the mythical foundations of the sexualization of "evil" and the demonization of desire. I link these to the stereotypes of "heretical depravity" that the inquisitorial mechanisms saw as their business to eradicate and that are implicated in the early church's will-to-power, its inquisitorial aggression against "pagan error," its mobilization against nonconforming groups, and the forms of surveillance and punishment that darkened the late Middle Ages and the Renaissance. Themes of abjection abound within Christian conceptions of evil and the demonological discourses that dwell on it, and they sustain a logos of persecution, colonization, and institutionally sanctioned mass murder, as exemplified by the witch craze that swept throughout Europe from the late fifteenth through to the mid-seventeenth centuries.

Defilement and the Law of the Father

Mary Douglas (1966) and Julia Kristeva (1982) do well to assist in developing an analysis of the internal logic of repudiation and abjection that appears to inform the function of "evil" in patriarchal monotheistic cultures. Their respective theories of pollution and abjection help to sketch processes by which the fear and hatred are projected onto the abject *other*, as a matter of the subject's ceaseless struggle for purification, order, and autonomy. The mechanics of purity explored by Douglas and later by Kristeva lends itself to understanding the dynamic at work in the economy of evil, seen in relation to the Law of the Father and the symbolic order of patriarchy.

In her anthropological study of the concepts of purity and danger, Mary

Douglas has shown that ideas of pollution and contagion, whether or not they are associated with evil or sin, as they are in Christianity, have functioned in various cultures and historical contexts in relation to the imposition and maintenance of social order. "Defilement," she notes, "is never an isolated event," since it "only occurs in view of, and in relation to, a systematic ordering of ideas, . . . a total structure . . . whose boundaries, margins and internal lines are held in relation by rituals of separation" (1966, 41). In Hebrew scripture, for example, the abominations of Leviticus, including the strict dietary taboos, may be understood as gestures of separation aimed at the perfection and purity of the moral and social structure, the body worthy of presentation at the temple. They speak of the struggle for the unity and order of the body politic, mimetically reproduced in preoccupations about the purity/impurity of the physical body. Pollution fears, rules, and rituals operate through the symbolic medium of the physical body to work upon the body politic (128). A certain corporeality is constructed through taboos of incest and adultery, and through purification rituals relating to menstrual blood, food, and hygiene that alert us to the insecurity and permeability of the boundaries and margins that define the social body. For Douglas, the logic of defilement that belongs to these codes and practices is inherent to a systemic ordering of bodies of ideas, practices, and sociopolitical relations through which the religiosity of various groups define themselves (124–28). As Friedrich Nietzsche curiously puts it, "Wherever on earth the religious neurosis has appeared we find it tied to three dangerous dietary demands: solitude, fasting and sexual abstinence. . . . We also find the most sudden, the most extravagant voluptuousness which then, just as suddenly, changes into a penitential spasm and denial of the world and will" (1966, 61). The context of the repudiation/order, I suggest, helps to throw into relief the political economy of "evil" within Western Christianity and its inseparability from the defilement of the material/feminine.

Julia Kristeva (1982) looks to Douglas's cultural analyses to elucidate the "deep psycho-symbolic economy" that underlies all the anthropological variants of the social structures and religious rules to which Douglas applies her analysis. For Kristeva, corporal defilement signals "the imposition of a strategy of identity" that is as definitive of monotheism as it is of "the struggle each subject must wage during the entire length of his personal life in order to become separate, that is to say, to become a speaking subject and/or subject to Law" (95). Defilement rites, prohibitions, taboo, and sin are the mere "particulars" in the cultural/historical and individual struggle for separation and individuation. And to the extent that this struggle is pitted against the "virulent power of the other sex, . . . the feminine becomes synonymous with a radical evil that is suppressed" (70). The rites and rhetoric of defilement, expressed in themes of corporal abjection, mark the separation that "concatenates" the order of law and language (72), and for Kristeva, it amounts to the desire to "throttle matrilineality, an attempt at separating the speaking being from his body in order that the latter accede to the status of clean and proper" (78).

Leviticus's abominations tell of Judaism's struggle against the fecund mother, the "archaic Mother Goddess who actually haunted a nation at war with the surrounding polytheism" (100). The pure/impure mechanism, Kristeva says, "testifies to the harsh combat Judaism, in order to constitute itself, must wage against paganism and its maternal cults" (95). Psychically and socially, the process of self-identification marks violent separation as the inaugural foundations of monotheism (5). The place and law of the One, the One God, do not exist without the violence of negation, the repudiation of the fertility cults and especially the feminine deities of the ancient world, whose fecund bodies threaten to engulf the ascetically purified, rational soul of man. When Leviticus outlines "all the ways" whereby man's souls are "made abominable and unclean," it prescribes the rituals required to sanctify and purify the children of Israel (Leviticus 20:2, King James Version). In the will-to-purity, a body worthy of the temple must avoid all "Whoredom," adultery, female nakedness, and the abhorrent "fountain of her blood" (Leviticus 20:9–21). To cleanse the community, the "law" (15:32) imposes a sentence of death on those who engage in incest, homosexuality, or bestiality, as well as on those who are witches, wizards, or who have "a familiar spirit" (20:12–13, 16). It demands eradication of the "blemish therein" (22:21), while it dictates the precise details of the sacrifice and atonement that need to be made to restore the order threatened by the trace of the maternal/pagan powers.

In contrast to Hebrew scriptures, Kristeva finds within the New Testament "a new arrangement of differences . . . whose economy will regulate a wholly different system of meaning, hence a wholly different speaking subject" (1982, 113). In the gospels of Matthew and Mark, in particular, we witness the definitive "interiorization of impurity" (115), a displacement of abjection, and a transposition of Levitican abominations from the "exteriority" that they occupy in Hebrew scripture. The site of the impure is construed less in terms of what needs to be avoided than in terms of what needs to be expelled, for "the threat comes no longer from the outside but from within" (114). What threatens to defile the Christian man is the "ineradicable repulse of his henceforth divided and contradictory being" (116). This reversal may be read in tandem with what cultural historians have described as a feature that is new to Christianity and that gives form to its emerging demonology: the world is suddenly and irrevocably constituted as the domain of Satan, one now plagued by what Norman Cohn (1975) calls "Europe's inner demons." As Luke has it, the Lord himself says he "beheld Satan as lightning fall from heaven" (Luke 10:18, KJV). Once transposed as internal to the world, tangible evil and depravity will need to be eradicated and extirpated, at least by the committed and protected followers of the Word: "Behold I give unto you power to tread on serpents and scorpions, and over all the power of the enemy: and nothing by any means shall hurt you" (Luke 10:19).

At the risk of overly literalizing Kristeva's theory of abjection, and particularly the "psycho-symbolic" economy she examines, consider how her terms of reference could highlight the politicized campaigns of the early church fathers against pagan maternal cults—most notably, that of Diana. Indeed, one could trace throughout several centuries of official treatises (from canon law of the tenth century to inquisitor's treatises of the sixteenth century) a preoccupation with Diana and her followers, including debates about the truth/fantasy of her alleged powers to draw thousands of followers to fly through the night to secret, conspiratorial nocturnal gatherings (see Lea 1957). At once associated with fertility, growth, and harvest, and celebrated by women, Diana winds up in inquisitorial rhetoric widely detested, shouldering the blame for impotency, infertility, drought, famine, and disease. The theme is frequently revisited in discourses such as the *Malleus* (1486) that are typically recognized by most historians of the witch craze to be instrumental in the mass scapegoating and punitive brutality launched against women. Whether or not this amounts to a desire to "throttle matrilineality," as Kristeva might call it, the demonization of Diana and her followers drew a link between "heresy" or "infidelity" and the belief that life, death, fertility, and fecundity were in the hands of anyone other than the One True God, much less in the hands of a widely worshipped, and consequently hated, maternal goddess.

Though we've heard little if anything about it in contemporary scholarship, Diana was clearly and unequivocally demonized as God's enemy, particularly to the extent that she was directly affiliated with the devil and devil-worship, as will be shown below. Indeed, it is striking how frequently and brutally this maternal goddess and her followers did get "throttled" by church fathers and inquisitors when they were trying to impose and justify their law in her place. Where we find them speak of Diana, we tend to find reference to the devil himself, to the evil incarnate, whose carnal relation to *woman* forms the basis of a campaign to treat women as treasonous "vermin" and to sanction the use of torture and execution against her. Whatever Diana's deluded worshippers might "think" they are doing, they are mistaken; *in fact*, Kramer and Sprenger held, they are really but "servants of Satan" secretly consorting not to furnish life but to destroy it: as these inquisitors put it, they are "more bitter than death, . . . destroying the generative force in women, . . . procuring abortions, . . . offering children to devils, besides other animals and fruits of the earth with which they work much harm" (1486/1971, 47). For Kramer and Sprenger, while "these women imagine they are riding (as they think and say) with Diana or with Herodias, in truth they are riding with the devil, who calls himself by some such heathen name and throws a glamour before their eyes" (5).

Because it conveniently symbolizes the misogynistic dynamic at work in patriarchy's mythic universe, I pick up on this Dianic theme below in the ensuing analysis of the witchcraft debates. For the moment, I want to turn to other significant aspects of the ancient struggle that marked the inauguration of Christian monotheism and to the truth claims about women's evil that preoccupied the church fathers. I want to consider, in particular, the arguments of those who incidentally served as the leading authorities for the inquisitors, those whose logic and language was recreated and reiterated centuries later in the colonizing, femicidal treatises of the official demonological discourses of the fifteenth and sixteenth centuries.

The Church Fathers and the Repudiation of Woman

Various studies on early Christian demonology and theology conducted by historians of witchcraft beliefs have effectively traced the semiotics of abjection within the ideological contests between paganism, ancient Judaism, and early Christianity, although they would not necessarily describe the dynamics they identify in such terms. H. C. Lea (1957), Jeffrey Burton Russell (1972), and Norman Cohn (1975) have all noted that the kinds of allegations and testimonies made in witch trials (such as secret nocturnal gatherings and conspiracies; ritual murder and sacrifice; incest, cannibalism, and child-murder) are old and familiar ones. There is plenty of evidence to show that they were typically circulated among, and launched against, rival cultures and religions in the Greco-Roman pagan world, including accusations made by and against pagans, Jews, and Christians alike. These historians document an abundance of such bloody tales of repudiation and defilement of the *other* at the inauguration of Christianity and the articulation of its patriarchal law.[5]

At least one notable difference in how such allegations take shape in early Christian discourse—as is clear in the writings of Paul and the church fathers— is that they are explicitly linked to a tangible, personified, and embodied form of evil: the devil (see Lea 1957, 36–38; Cohn 1975, 17–18). Under the authority of the New Testament's doctrine of the fall (that is, a doctrine unique to Christianity), the sacrificial and purification rituals of paganism and Judaism were made to signify the "false idolatry" and worship of the devil; any idolatry of one other than the Father came to be specifically reconstrued as taking place under the direct supervision of Satan and his devils, who were seen to preside in material form (Cohn 1975, 18). For Paul, the Greeks and Jews were "fools" whose sacrificial offerings signaled a false idolatry born of a "fellowship with devils": "The things which the Gentiles sacrifice they sacrifice to the devils and not to God" (1 Corinthians 10:20, KJV). To put an end to pagan and Jewish "idolatry," and to affirm the One Law of the Father, as Paul calls upon his new Christians to do, would entail exposing the *others'* conspiratorial pact with the enemy of God, which would allow for the heroic mobilization of the sign of the cross against them. Such visions of Satan and his devils conspiring together with those who worship him construe "evil" not as an abstract "enemy of man," but as the substantial "enemy of God" (Cohn 1975, 17). Only Christians, the true believers of the one true religion, were to be free of the taint of impurity that this new figure of the Prince of Darkness was said to bring to the world through women, that is, through the sex that Tertullian describes as "the first deserter of divine law," the one upon whom "the sentence of God . . . lives in this age" (1999: 133). The new Law of the Father kept as its central tactic the repudiation of female sexuality: the filth of fornication, the flesh of the harlot's body, defiled the purity of man's "glorified" body, the "temple of the Holy Ghost" (1 Corinthians 6:15–20, KJV).

In his 1971 book on the rise and decline of witchcraft, and later in his 1998 study of early Catholic theology, Julio Caro Baroja directly links the "diabolization" of ancient deities and the attribution of demonic powers to the pagan rituals and practices of sorcery and magic with the New Testament's doctrine of the fall (1998, 22). With the "triumph of Christianity," Baroja says, pagan deities became nothing more than devilish figures (1971, 42). Circe's antics and spells, Calypso's seductive wiles, Medea's magic (1998, 23) thus live on in the laws, decrees, and theology of medieval Catholicism. Such "archetypes of witches," adopted from Greek antiquity, Baroja notes, are often represented as protected by, and associated with, feminine nocturnal divinities such as Diana, by which association they possessed the powers of coercion and conjuration (1971, 65; 1998, 23).

As the worship of pagan deities and the rites of fertility cults were perceived by the church as forms of devil worship, so too did pagan imagery become constitutive of the archetypes of Satan and his demons. Christian demonology relied heavily on the icons it repudiated to proliferate the ideology of heretical idolatry. The horned goat and the cloven-foot Pan, for example, were readily appropriated tropes to animate the tales of demonic temptation in the writings of the Desert Fathers (see the Waddell 1998 compilation of the "Sayings of the Fathers," especially those of or relating to St. Jerome and St. Anthony). Satan and his fallen angels roamed the world in grotesque animal forms to test the limits of these Fathers' faith. The same figures are surreptitiously concealed in human or "familiar" forms of the sexually voracious *incubus* or *succubus,* as Augustine and Aquinas described them, and they thrive in imagery of the fearsome icon that heads up the "devil's sabbath" of the fifteenth and sixteenth centuries. This composite stereotype of evil incarnate was also thoroughly interwoven with themes of fecundity and orgiastic transgression that emphasized its feminine associations.

The sexualized demonology born of the doctrine of the fall and elaborated through Christian asceticism speaks of a deep ambivalence toward femininity and female sexuality. It ensures that, on the one hand, *woman* was to remain the weaker, feeble, *other* sex—an embodied passivity, prone to deception and seduction—and that, on the other hand, she represented a destructive force and malevolent power; in consorting with the devil, woman became dangerous enough to pose a perpetual threat to the world, and especially to man. In law, she is constituted as the former; and before the symbolic Law of the Father, the latter. Witness, for example, the curtailment of her legal capacity in every facet of Roman-canonical law, wherein, like children, women are increasingly relegated to the non-status of chattel during the Christianization of the Roman Empire under Constantine (Brundage 1987, 71–88). At the same time, however, as is articulated through the demonological themes of asceticism and monasticism in the first five centuries C.E., woman's affinity with evil cast her demonic sexuality on par with the most heinous abuses of power. Justin Martyr speaks of fallen angels having intercourse with women to beget demon children and "spread among men the seeds of all vices, lust, murder, war and adultery" (quoted in Lea 1957, 42). Tertullian (ca. 160–225 C.E.) takes this one step further: "all spiritual and material evils which afflict man" can be ascribed to the multiplication of demons through the intercourse of angels with women. Known for his rigorous asceticism, he rebukes women as sexual temptresses: the carnal sex that *is* woman is the "odium," the "cause . . . of human perdition" (1999: 133). Thus, for Tertullian, every woman was "an Eve" (132), vain temptresses and "harlots" who bear all the guilt for perpetuating a race of demons, and for any man who falls to the allure of the trickery of their sex.

As the source and perpetual threat to man's godly purity, the taint of woman's sex was enough for the church fathers, on the authority of Paul, to condemn her to silence and obedience, to forbid her to preach or to administer the holy sacraments. For Origen, woman's embodiment was the essence of moral imperfection: all sin, he says, begins with the "incitement of the body," the medium of the devil's work. And this was so as to make it "impossible for the holiest to maintain the struggle against the flesh and the devil without the aid of God" (in Lea 1957, 46). Chrysostom (ca. 347–407), in turn, reasoned that woman had "misused her power . . . and ruined everything"; he appealed to men to see through the beautiful female body to the "white sepulchre" it truly is: while a rage covered in phlegm and spittle is repulsive to all, Chrysostom complained how men are nevertheless continually attracted to the "store houses and depositories of these things" (Easlea 1980, 43).

Fuelled by asceticism, this new Christian economy of demonic evil paradoxically relies on the abjected feminine that is "guilty of everything" (Cixous 1986, 97) in order to wrest from the world of chaos a holy, unified, and pure Christian masculinity, empowered to harness and conquer her. In Kristeva's terms, evil is projected out from the flesh of man onto the loathsome other: the heretic, the witch. It is woman who will come to bear the brunt of ascetic guilt and shame as, by contrast, they render truly heroic those men who "extirpate" in flames that pollution of desire that once plagued their own being. Such is what we find reverberating more than ten centuries later with the visions of women's wanton weakness and murderous infidelity by inquisitors and judges of witches, who rely extensively on these particular misogynist patriarchs.

For the purpose of understanding the scapegoating of women that we find with the later witch hunts, the significance of this rendering of "evil" in a personified form as the devil incarnate cannot be overstated. It forms the very basis of the reasoning and the institutional self-justification for unchecked cruelty in investigative, inquisitorial procedures and the extreme forms of punishment used, for example, by the *Inquisition Against Heretical Depravity* (as it was once called). It posits the dark, secretive, conspiratorial threat—the worst kind of enemy, the one that lurks *within* the Christian body politic, the one that must be eradicated to preserve its autonomy.

The fact that non-Christian (that is, heretical) beliefs and practices could be associated with a form of treason enabled the "exceptional" punitive proceedings, including the use of torture, that had, with Roman-canonical law, always been reserved for this "highest" of crimes—conspiracy against the king himself, the arbiter of the law.[6] So, for example, as various witchcraft historians have noted, the references we find to witches and sorcerers as "servants of Satan" (Klaits 1985) and "enemies of God" (Larner 1981) in the early Renaissance demonological writings of inquisitors and witch-hunters bear little relation to those found in Greco-Roman law and literature, where they were of little legal interest or consequence. It was only once witchcraft became directly associated with "heresy" and/or conspiracy with the devil himself that it was taken up within a persecutorial machinery that treated "witches" with the brutality reserved for treason. The notion that Satan was the "enemy of God" and that women were vessels of Satan's evil sustained the rationale we find, for example, in the introductory arguments of *Malleus maleficarum*: "For witchcraft is high Treason against God's Majesty. And so they are to be put to the torture and made to confess" (1486/1971, 6). Such is the sentence imposed on those deluded followers of Diana, whose carnal allegiance to the devil is reason enough to proclaim the need for witchcraft suspects to be treated as swiftly and harshly as those accused of treason, and that "extraordinary" measures be taken against them. Such is the legal rationale, at least, as to why they must be tortured and why they must die—despite their legal "incapacity" and infirmity.

Demonizing Diana: Inventing the Witch

It is important to note *how* the pagan legend was incorporated into early modern demonological theory, to fully appreciate the local struggles and political contests that imbued official discourses about witches and debates about how they should be dealt with. While the association between pagan ceremonies and devil worship tended toward the former being constituted as forms of treason against God, it also entailed what Baroja, like Lea before him, describes as a contradictory tendency of "belittling the reality of the supposedly diabolic acts" (1998, 23) of magic, conjuration, aerial transvection, and goddess worship. As Lea describes it, "No one did more than St. Augustine" to translate into theological demonology "the superstitions of antiquity." Lea notes that Augustine's late-fifth-century book, *The City of God*, in particular, provided inquisitors such as Johann Nider in his 1435 *Formicarius*, Jean Vineti in his 1450 *Tractatus contra demonum invocators*, and Kramer and Sprenger in their 1486 *Malleus maleficarum* with "an unfailing source to justify all their assertions" (1957, 122) about the prevalence of the devil and his allies, pagan sorceries, idolators, all of which Augustine held "are to be classed with those which result from pacts and contracts with demons" (*Confessions* XXII 58).

It's worth noting that *The City of God* was particularly popular at the time that the Inquisition's aggression against "heretical depravity" turned specifically against so-called witches. As the translator Marcus Dods remarks, between 1467 and the end of the fifteenth century, the press issued a new edition roughly every eighteen months (in Schaff 1997, 12). At this time, Augustine was typically ushered in by the witch-hunters to substantiate what was clearly shrouded in doubt and met with skepticism: that witches "truly exist" and "truly make a compact with devils in order to bring about real and true hurts and harms" (Kramer and Sprenger 1486/1971, 3). Augustine's strange tales that blend pagan myth, magic, illusion, spells, and bestial transformations, Lea notes, inevitably forced scholastics to admit and explain them, and to employ them against those skeptical of the demonic feats and themes that were paradoxically constituted in Catholic theology, largely under Augustine's authority (1957, 121). Though on the one hand, Augustine treated various tales of pagan lore as "truth," we see a parallel tendency to treat them as diabolical trickery and illusion. For Augustine, demons were in the business of producing illusions and deceptions (such as the strange effects of magic and sorcery) that many mistakenly take for truth. Those "who desire such evil things," he claimed, are subjected to the illusion and deception, mocked and deceived by those lying angels (*Confessions* XXIII 58). Devils haunt the world and consort with man, but there may be little reality to the actual powers and magical effects that such a union can and may provide. The essential paradox of the Augustinian thesis, which Baroja (1998, 24–27) shows to be later codified in the tenth century *Canon Episcopi,* captures the spirit of the demonological beliefs that imbued medieval theology. One could argue that it came to be the central conflict of the debates on the true/illusory powers of women/witches that proliferated during the witch trials from the mid-fifteenth through the mid-seventeenth centuries. These debates translated directly into the question of the power and the jurisdiction of the church and the state to eradicate witchcraft/woman.

The position developed by the early church, as captured in Augustine's ambivalent treatment of the strange tales encountered on his travels and later in the *Canon Episcopi* of the tenth century, is that powers and persuasions of pagan figures such as Diana and her followers, like the acts attributed to sorcerers and magicians, were mere dreams, illusions, or "false persuasions" created by the devil: "Let it be loudly proclaimed," the *Canon* declared, "that those who believe such things have lost the faith and no longer belong to God, but only to him in whom they believe, that is the devil" (in Baroja 1998, 26). Though the powers of pagan sorcerers and goddesses were stripped of their reality, this did not stop them from being seen as evil. While the *Canon* affiliates Diana's followers to worshippers of Satan, it sees the former to be lacking in reality, to be a delusion of mere "pagan error." Treating the *idea* as more criminally problematic than the *act,* it calls upon bishops to denounce as false the notably popular belief in the nocturnal flights and gatherings of Diana and her followers. "No credence," it says, should be given to the ideas "that certain women, perverted and dedicated to Satan, seduced by diabolical fantasies and deceits, believe and profess that they ride at night-time with Diana, goddess of the pagans, and with Herodias, astride certain beasts, in a company of innumerable other women, traversing spaces and obeying Diana's orders like those of a mistress who convokes them on certain nights" (in Baroja 1998, 26).

The *Canon* goes on to implicitly acknowledge the existence and popularity of the allegedly nonexistent and illusory Dianic cults, which "attract many others" who believe in and "follow" them: "Great throngs, deceived by this false persuasion, believe in all these lies and thus fall back into pagan error. Therefore priests should preach wherever it may be necessary to point out the falsity of these errors and make it known that such tricks are produced by the Evil One who seduces the mind by vain imaginations. . . . The soul that has abandoned itself to him imagines that it is accomplishing in the body things that take place only in the mind" (in Baroja 1998, 26). The *Canon* finds the devil embroiled in the pagan practice, but the real evil lies in the delusional trickery that has fooled "many followers" to believe in the "lie" of Diana. The double gesture of this law was to acknowledge yet repudiate the power and presence of a mother goddess and to mock her very existence as the trickery of the Evil One. The "first word" of the bishops finds the feminine principle suspended between her power and persuasion on the one hand, and her weak-minded tendency to be fooled by devil's seductive illusions on the other. The movement and exchange between the competing representations of power and powerlessness, between the truth and falsehood, or true danger and mere delusion, especially around this particular icon of fertility, is a basic feature of patriarchy's jurisdictional struggles. It is typical of most ecclesiastical and judicial demonological discourses that proliferated during the witch hunts.

Bishop Prum's decree on Diana and her many followers (see Baroja 1998, 26) is one of the most frequently cited passages from the canon law to appear in demonological treatises on the heresy and crime of witchcraft. As Lea's (1957) compilation and summary of numerous treatises demonstrates, there are dozens of these treatises that invoke this passage to espouse conflicting positions on the existence of demonic pacts. These treatises include those of persecutors vying for the authority to treat as "true" what the law clearly describes as "false persuasion" and dreams, as well as those "defenders of witches"—the skeptics and critics of the hunts who drew on this very law to refute the claims of persecutors. The *Canon* clearly created a legal obstacle for the persecutorial logic that required, as the *Malleus* had insisted, that "amongst Pagans" such forms of heretical worship suggested by the *Canon* "actually [do] happen" (Kramer and Sprenger 1486/1971, 5). It is noteworthy that Kramer and Sprenger, for example, launch their text and begin its first Question with an attempt to explain how their position is not inconsistent with that set out by the *Canon* (6–7). As noted above, attempting to justify why inquisitors should be empowered to torture and execute those who confess to the very things that the *Canon* says are mere illusions produced by the devil, they reason that those who think they follow a pagan goddess like Diana are quite mistaken, for "in truth" they follow the devil (7). Although canon law might seem to say that such women are merely deluded, they argue it is *also* "a most certain and most Catholic opinion that there are sorcerers and witches who by the help of the devil, on account of a compact which they have entered into with him, . . . produce real and actual evils and harm" (6). For such acts of treason, they must die.

A final consideration offered about those who confess to such things is that these women are not mere pagans but an "entirely different" creature: witches, and about the latter, the *Canon* has nothing to say. In any case, what marks their guilt is their treasonous allegiance to the enemy of God. By reconfiguring Diana's followers, and reconstituting them as devil-worshipping *witches*, the foundation was laid for other inquisitors to justify a *new* law, far more severe and callous than the restrictive one in place. In other words, if they were to follow existing canon law, which diminished the reality and seriousness of Dianic cults and treated them as deluded followers of false beliefs, church leaders would have no legal justification for launching an inquisition against them. Church courts could hardly get away with the use of torture and execution of those who are merely "falsely persuaded." Thus, if anything, the provision impeded persecution.

Defying the *Canon*'s position and imposing their own interpretation and their own new law, inquisitors Kramer and Sprenger were essentially aiming to reconstitute these women as devil-worshipping heretics deserving of the punishment reserved for treason. One of the immediate effects was to remove the legal obstacles preventing them and other inquisitors from unleashing their regimes of brutality against those (women) who otherwise lacked legal capacity within the law. Treason, after all, had a very low threshold for justifying the use of torture and expediting prosecution. The expansion of such regimes of power/knowledge, and the refinement of tactics for targeting and annihilating women, was not without immediate resistance, for it entailed jurisdictional contests with secular officials, who also had a vested interest defining and controlling women.

The Politics of Skepticism and Resistance

At every turn in the misogynist rationale of the *Malleus*, one detects the voices of skepticism and resistance to Kramer and Sprenger's view of women's and witches' powers, and to their authority to punish women in accordance with their ideas of them as Satan's cohorts. The resistance is clear in the Papal Bull of Innocent VIII (1484), included as a preface to most editions of the *Malleus*. After cataloguing the incredible crimes and heresies committed by women powerful enough to cause famine, hailstorms, and male impotence, the pope rails against "all rebels of whatsoever rank" who "hinder or harass inquisitors," those who have argued that these men "have no legal right to exercise their powers of inquisition in the provinces" (Kramer and Sprenger 1486/1971: xliv). Such a struggle for jurisdiction over the evil sought out by the church, and such correlative resistance from the secular body, is apparent as early as 1298 with the *Decretal* of Boniface VIII (*Ut inquisitionis*), which aims to ensure "that the business of the Inquisition against heretical depravity should prosper." It expressly bans interference by secular officials or appeals on the basis that it is "as much by the ordination of our predecessors as by imperial law, the right of appeal or further legal process is expressly forbidden to heretics, believers in heresy and their hosts, supporters and defenders." Making explicit the conflict over jurisdictional control, the *Decretal* declares that lords, rectors, officials, and any other "secular powers" are restricted "from judging or having any cognizance of this crime, for it is purely an ecclesiastical concern" (in Davidson and Ward 1993, 72).

The church's struggle to expand jurisdiction was intricately linked with attempts to justify "exceptional" procedures that would otherwise be held in check by secular processes. As noted above, the key strategy of the church was to employ a specific notion of witchcraft's "evil" as treasonous heresy, which, thus defined, located it within the jurisdiction of the Inquisition. We find this initiative in one of the earliest recorded trials to associate witchcraft with heresy, the 1324 trial of Alice Kyteler in Ireland (initiated by a bishop from France who had recently moved there). On the basis of allegations of making sacrifices to demons, holding nocturnal meetings, engaging in ceremonial sacrifices and cannibalism, and having "carnal relations" with an *incubus* of the devil, the French bishop had insisted that perpetrators of such heresy "be handled differently from other excommunicates" than the secular process would allow (Davidson and Ward 1993, 31). The chancellor, however, refused to grant a warrant on this basis, which in turn led to a series of initiatives to circumvent secular restrictions. The evidentiary and procedural rules of the secular courts posed an obstacle to what the church deemed appropriate for casting out the evil that plagued its world. Its peculiar construction of evil, embodied as a pact with the devil, and its self-endowed power to identify, punish, and extirpate it, were essential to the church's expansion and to the extension of its power to communities that did not embrace its beliefs. More immediately, it was synonymous with the institutional control over the bodies and minds of the accused.

Through the course of the institutionally sanctioned persecution of heretics and witches, first by the church and later by the secular courts, the skeptics turned to the competing conception of evil set out in the *Canon Episcopi's* reference to the "false persuasion" of Diana's followers. In dozens of treatises, such as those identified and summarized in Lea's *Materials* (1957), we encounter the proposition that the many things attributed to witches were mere illusion and deception, though evil nonetheless. This was precisely the position adopted by the most famous of the skeptics, the Dutch physician Johann Weyer, whose monumental 1563 treatise, *On the Tricks of Demons* committed some 500 pages to his proposition that the confessions of women accused of witchcraft revealed little more than the power of the devil to "trick" the feeble imagination of the women to believe in things that were otherwise impossible and even heretical to entertain. Elderly, feeble, and ailing women, tricked by the devil and caught in the machinery of the witch-hunts were *mad* enough and frightened enough to confess to powers and practices that they *did not have*. In this way, they are no different from the "madman or fools, and infants, to whom no crime whatsoever is imputed, even if they should do what is done by persons who are guilty of high treason" (Weyer 1563/1991, 567).

Weyer develops this point throughout his lengthy and highly controversial treatise on the kinds of tricks, deceptions, delusions, hallucinations, and madness that devils were prone to produce. Like the legends and tales that informed them, the many feats attributed to witches were "pure falsehoods, . . . more mythical than the myths themselves" (170); they were the substance of dreams, hallucinations, or delusions, the product of a "natural" humoral affliction of the melancholics' fragile, feeble minds (571–73). The central tenet of many of Weyer's arguments was his suggestion that the disproportion in the distribution of sexual difference among "suspects" of witchcraft was not a sign of a disproportionate propensity to the heresy of "carnal lust" or criminal insatiability between men and women, but of a disproportionate propensity to precise forms of madness (melancholy and delirium) that happened to bear identical symptoms to those of confessed witches, and to be suffered primarily by women. Women possessed, not extraordinary power, but exceptional weakness.

Weyer's contentious "medical" interpretation makes evident the institutional and ideological stakes involved in negotiating the truth of sex and the truth of evil in the domain of criminal jurisprudence. The possibility that the thousands of women who confessed to such powers were just "like madmen and fools," and were merely possessed by a kind of weakness of the mind prone to delirium, hallucinations, and false memories directly undermined the ecclesiastical and judicial presumption of women's guilt (her willful intent to commit heinous crimes), and in effect undermined the authority of persecuting officials such as Kramer and Sprenger and Jean Bodin to know the truth of what afflicted these women. No less did it undermine these officials' authority to examine, interrogate, investigate, torture, and convict them. How the "poetic fictions" confessed by elderly women were to be interpreted—as evidence of formidable evil or as a symptom of a "deluded imagination" (Weyer 1563/1991, 571)—was a question with profound implications and consequences for women (not to mention for the concept of madness), whose answers raised sometimes controversial issues of what form of professional expertise should properly be called upon to take up "the burden of the cure" (447).

The disputed questions of the existence, nature, power, and pleasures of witches produced an array of "best-selling" treatises by demonologists, and though apparently fewer, their critics. They furnished an elaborate demonological mythology on the evil powers and pleasures of this otherwise "feeble sex." The discursive economy of evil maintained paradoxical conceptions of the nature of woman, and they carved out her various subjected spaces within the patriarchal institutions of the church, the state, and the medical profession.

The disputed questions situated at the heart of these debates find various parallels within the *querelles des femmes* of the late Middle Ages—the popular debates about woman's capacity to be educated; her worth or depravity, inferiority or superiority; or the merits of her chastity, beauty, and limited intellect that were widely circulated among the exclusive Latin readership. However much theorists may be inclined to treat the *querelles* as paradigmatic of intellectual "banter" about the truth games of the feminine sex, its themes are interwoven with the debates about witches and devils, and its more famous participants, such as Martin Le Franc in his 1442 *Champion des Dames* and Cornelius

Agrippa—to whom Johann Weyer had apprenticed for four years as a young adult—in his 1529 *Declamation,* make frequent appearance in the persecution discourses vying for power and control over the evil of the weaker sex. As Simone de Beauvoir has reminded us, there is nothing trifling about the *querelles* or its consequences: "If the 'woman question' seems trivial, it is because masculine arrogance has made it a 'quarrel'" (1974, xxxi). Debates about the power of women and the nature of the evil within her exacted an inordinate price on women, both by sanctioning the excessive violence of the law against her alleged power, and by excluding her from the law on account of her fragility and idiocy.

The witchcraft debates concerned themselves with such questions as: Did women actually have the supernatural power, the *maleficia,* the carnal knowledge, or the insatiable sex that they voluntarily and involuntarily confessed to having, or were they somehow deluded, victimized not by the *crime* of having been seduced by incubus, but by the *natural malady* of "believing falsely" that such events take place? Could women actually be capable of the crimes that were increasingly being heard before the courts at the time? Or was the wicked, "insatiable sex" merely "feeble-minded" enough, if not mad enough, to confess to them? These debates were not unlike the *querelles*—to use Joan Scott's terms—in that they were primarily discourses by men, between men, and about women: men who had to offer, with or without a measure of satire, the *truth* of this sex (1997: 70), the truth of her evil. They were also not unlike the *querelles* in that they deployed and reproduced competing representations of the power and powerlessness of woman, both of which could lend themselves to authorizing different forms of institutional control or expulsion. Significantly, they corresponded with aggressive campaigns to reconfigure the status of women in the public discourses and domains of law.

Resisting the Skeptics: Secular Campaigns for the Extraordinary Punishment of Witches

Christina Larner and Margaret King have both made the point that in Renaissance Europe, for almost all criminal offenses, "women did not exist," and that with only the two exceptions of infanticide and witchcraft, women in most localities were neither responsible nor admissible as witnesses in criminal trials (Larner 1981, 51; King 1993, 10). That upward of 100,000 witches could be executed by the secular courts for a "crime"—witchcraft—reflects the extraordinary price paid by women as scapegoats and sacrificial victims in the discursive and political contests for autonomy and jurisdiction over the evil they represented. As Brian Levack describes it, "the great European witch-hunt was essentially a judicial operation," a phenomenon of "rough country justice" (1995, 68) in rural areas of continental Europe, particularly in the late 1500s and early 1600s. He and other historians (e.g., Midelfort 1972; Soman 1989; Larner 1981) have described the secular craze as a legal anomaly: the persecutorial activities of lower courts with respect to witch hunting are seen as "fundamentally inconsistent" with the traditional standards of justice, particularly in criminal procedure (Levack 1995, 93).

As a judicial operation across continental Europe, the witch hunts were facilitated by the introduction of the "inquisitorial" procedural system; the rise of secular jurisdiction over witchcraft (Levack 1995, 89); the revival of Roman-canonical law, including its practice of judicial torture; and perhaps most importantly, the ability of local courts to function autonomously, "independent of central political and judicial control" (Levack 1995, 93). As Alfred Soman's legal research demonstrates in the case of France, Christina Larner in the case of Scotland, and Brian Levack in the case of Germany, in those regions where local, parvenue judges held "virtual autonomy over judicial life," and where there was little regulation and almost no accountability to higher courts or officials, the accounts of torture were most barbarous and the execution rates were highest (Levack 1995, 94–95). Archival records tell what Soman describes as an "eloquent story of a struggle to combat the centrifugal tendencies of the lower courts—particularly in villages and small towns—and of the institutional innovation to achieve this goal" (1989, 3).

The struggle for officers of the court to obtain the right to both initiate legal proceedings and determine their outcome also tells the story of a specific and aggressive campaign on the part of lower court judges to construct witchcraft as a *crimen exceptum,* an "exceptional crime," the prosecution for which "certain procedural rules, such as those regarding the disqualification of witnesses, did not apply" (Levack 1995, 79–80). Following the analogy established by the Inquisition, which constituted the "heresy" of witchcraft as an exceptional and heinous offense against God, the secular courts found cause to expand the previously limited category of treason.

Until the late sixteenth century, when witchcraft became a capital crime within the secular domain in most European countries, standard practice was to treat it like almost all other crimes (except treason)—as a *crimen ordinaire* involving ordinary procedural rules (Ewen 1929, 13–20).[7] To the extent that witchcraft could be recognized as exceptional, judges were granted a number of ancillary shortcuts for convictions and expedient executions. For "exceptional" crimes, unlike ordinary ones, there was no restriction on the use of torture to extort confessions and no right for suspects to appeal their convictions. Nor was there any process of appeal, and hence no scrutiny of the evidence and no procedure for recourse to a centralized higher court. There were also relaxed rules for the use of witnesses, which entailed, for example, that women and children could testify in trials for the first time (Levack 1995; Soman 1989).

Through this judicial contest that saw an opposition develop between the more autonomous rural courts and the centralized urban courts, women were endowed with a power as yet unknown in criminal jurisprudence. Promoted by prolific judges and magistrates, it entailed nothing short of a radical reconfiguration of women as subjects of law. As the secular courts assumed jurisdiction over witchcraft, they embraced the same rationale employed by the *Malleus* in linking demonic pacts to a form of treason. The analogy is central to various popular treatises by French magistrates, the most noted of which include Bodin's 1580 *Demon-Mania* (1995); Nicholas Remy's 1602 *Demonolatry* (1974); Henri Boguet's 1605 *Examen des Sorcieres* (1971); and Pierre de Lancre's 1613 *Tableau*. Like the inquisitors before them, judicial officials argued against a palpable resistance and skepticism about the evil epidemic of witchcraft; why women, much more than men, were so susceptible to this crime; and why this crime should be treated so "exceptionally," such that it would be unparalleled by that of any crime other than the treason it became.

In his 1580 *Demon-Mania*, the French jurist Bodin did everything he could to render women subjects of exceptional criminal law. His objective was to expand and sharpen existing procedures for witchcraft/treason, and to implement new ones as yet unrecognized in French jurisprudence. Central to Bodin's treatise is a refutation of skeptics and defenders of witches, and particularly Weyer, who, Bodin claimed, had no business discussing witchcraft because this subject properly required the expertise of lawyers and criminal legal scholars.[8] Against Weyer's argument that women who confessed to demonic pacts were feeble-minded and deluded melancholics, Bodin claimed that there was no theoretical foundation for establishing the effects melancholy had on postmenopausal women. If for every male witch there were fifty female witches, as Bodin held, it was not because of women's propensity to illness but because far more women than men suffer from "bestial cupidity," and so are much more likely to lust after demons, as Kramer and Sprenger (1486/1971) had argued. What was true for Kramer and Sprenger, that "all witchcraft comes from carnal lust which in women is insatiable" (47), is true for Bodin one century later. Presupposing that a profound demonic and malign power inheres in the essential spiritual weakness and sexual prowess of women, Bodin reads the confessions of accused witches in a way that empowers not doctors but judges, to harness, to control, to annihilate her.

Bodin's 1580 treatise, and especially his instructions and evidentiary rules for judges (1995, 181–218), works toward developing a system of jurisprudential rationality for defining witchcraft as the one crime that women were always at high risk of committing, the one that justified the discretionary use of torture, expedient execution, and the automatic denial of an appeal to a higher court. His recommendations and instructions for admitting any and every suggestion, suspicion, or allegation carefully situated witchcraft among the order of those crimes for which, as for treason, it is incumbent upon "competent" judges to act more expeditiously, definitively, and harshly, "to adopt an entirely different exceptional approach" (188), effectively removing the limits on judicial cruelty. What holds for the highest crime of treason should also hold for what Bodin defines as "the crime of Treason against God, and in a wickedness that outweighs all others" (187). Bodin sounds a veritable call-to-arms for judges not to let this "crime of divine and human treason" escape prosecution (200). For insofar as it is *like* treason, it is exceptional; ergo, "it is permitted to apply the *question* [torture] on a simple presumption *as has always been the practice*" (201); and the same should stand for those who hold a pact with the devil.

In direct opposition to the analogy between witches and "madmen or fools" promoted by Weyer, Bodin's analogy between witchcraft and treason served to justify the judiciary's exceptional jurisdiction over the "suspects," and further, to eliminate any restrictions that might impede the autonomous, free exercise of the harshest investigative and punitive measures conceivably available to them. Even the "least" of the fifteen "detestable" crimes of witches that he describes in detail "merits a painful death" (207). Targeting Weyer and any other potential "defenders" of witches, Bodin insists that a failure to prosecute and execute witches is itself an offense against God and a betrayal of the faith. Leniency against witches was a crime itself, and the role of the judiciary was to act in God's interest by administering punishments of "gradually roasting and burning them over a fire," that is to say, punishments akin to the eternal fires awaiting them in hell.

As Soman (1989) shows, the anti-pagan/anti-feminine rhetoric and imagery that linked witchcraft to impious treason, such as we find in Bodin, was not advanced within French jurisprudence until the late 1500s and was never fully accepted by the High Court, the *Parlement* of Paris. This was not for lack of trying. It is quite remarkable that despite the official and unofficial skepticism toward the beliefs of demon-fearing judges such as Remy, Boguet, and de Lancre, these prolific magistrates would come to be known as experts on the witches' sabbat, providing for the Latin readership the minutest detail of its rituals—in a secular reconstruction of the pagan idolatry: nocturnal flights, secret ceremonies, banquets, gatherings, sacrifices, and demonic orgies.

To set the record straight for any skeptics, including magistrates of the Paris *Parlement,* Remy's *Demonolatry* of 1602 professed that more than mere acts and practices of harmful magic, the conspiratorial ceremonies of witches were nothing less than "the crowning evil of all misery and calamities into which our times have fallen" (1974, v): "the monstrous assemblies of the witches, who were very frequently among those who came before me for trials" (ix). Indeed, Remy admits to being compelled to write this work not only against what might be thought "too strange a matter for truth" but also to clear his own mind of haunting "thoughts of their banquetings, dancings, charms, and spells, their journeyings through the air, the horrid practices of their carnal relations with the Demon, their frequent transmutation into other shapes and forms (for so it seemed), and all the crimes and blasphemies with which it is well known that their lives are polluted and utterly befouled" (ix). To distinguish what "these women" *really do* from the "metamorphoses, spells, strange leechcraft, glamours, raising storms, and other such portents" (that the traditional legal concept of witchcraft assumes they do), he says he chose the term *Demonolatry* as the title of his treatise to lay greater emphasis on the evil idolatry of the sabbat, "the abominable blasphemy of their impious cult," the origin of "all other manifestations of witchcraft" (xi). In other words, he made explicit his effort to incorporate into criminal jurisprudence on heresy and treason the "single feature" that made mass trials possible and "made accusations and trials more likely and more perilous" (Midelfort 1972, 19).

The sabbat made its way into criminal trials not simply because of its popularity in local folklore. As Soman says, "What it attests to is the suitability, convenience, and admissibility of the concept for the purpose of litigation" (1989, 14). Conjuring visions of the secrecy of pagan idolatry, conspiratorial plotting, and carnal transgression, the mythology of the sabbat operated as strategy that, when sharpened through juridical confession, enabled persecutors to rationalize witchcraft as a treasonous conspiracy involving many participants—a crime against the Father so secretive and severe that it required the circumvention of all the evidentiary rules and procedures that otherwise set limits on the judicial autonomy to freely resort to torture and to execute suspects. Tales of demonic temptation were used in this way to mobilize systemic mass murder against the evil of women that such restrictions might otherwise have prevented. If then, Remy explained, "an eminently noble man could be convicted of treason" (as had recently been done by the *Parlement* of Paris) for simply conspiring to commit treason or "plotting" to assassinate the king without actually carrying out the act, then so too should witches be exceptionally tried and judged on the basis of their evil intentions alone and similarly subjected to "all the provisions of law . . . which decree the most terrible punishment for blasphemous opinions concerning God and religion" (1602/1974, 183). If subjects are to be tortured and executed without appeal for intending to commit treason, should not the same hold true for insatiable witches, that is, for those who "resolve in the mind and plot and desire that which all other men regard with horror and apprehension . . . in a word to use their every effort and endeavour to please [devils] alone as much as they possibly can" (183)? Women/witches don't even need to be culpable *of something* to be guilty. It is enough for them to be accused of desiring to defy the Law of the Father for these men to justify their extirpation.

As for the voices of resistance, Remy finds recourse to his "first hand" knowledge of some eight hundred capital trials. His long judicial practice in hearing confessions and sentencing witches, he says, could substantiate the "error of the skeptics," for he *knows* that there are witches; he *knows* of women's evil, of their propensity to commit the exceptional crime of carnal treason: "For when a man has himself seen and heard these things, it gives him the greater confidence to speak of them, and the greater resolve in defending his opinion against those who dissent from it" (1602/1974, xiii).

If indeed there was good reason to doubt whether women/witches could and did perform the deeds for which they were brought to trial, if indeed there was cause to question whether women enjoyed true seductions by demons, sabbat gatherings, and conspiracies detailed as evidence of their exceptional malefice, then there was good reason to question the legality, much less the sanity, of the work of these magistrates. In the telling words of the famous jurist Bodin, "if the whole body of the state [does] not diligently . . . search out and severely punish witches, . . . there is a danger that the people will stone both magistrates and witches" (1580/1995, 174). The pathetic rationale and the apparent credulity about their authority, right, and jurisdiction to eradicate the evil they projected onto women betray the deep insecurity of the tenuous autonomy and integrity of their authority.

Conclusion

The demonological literature of the witchcraft debates provides us with a particularly cogent demonstration of the mechanisms through which the personification of evil and the correlative demonization of femininity are deployed in the service of the will-to-power and the jurisdictional contests that define Western patriarchy's institutions. In this economy, the repudiated feminine is caught within the productive and performative hermeneutics of the opposition between an all-powerful pagan goddess and conspiratorial "enemy of God," and a deluded, feebleminded fool prone to demonic trickery. To the extent that women were made to simultaneously symbolize an unchecked evil power, on the one hand, and a pathetic and decrepit weakness on the other, they were paradoxically constituted so as to justify the ruthless persecutorial practices used by inquisitors and judges such as Kramer and Sprenger, Bodin, Remy, Boguet, and de Lancre. So too did they facilitate for the medical "defenders" of these weak-minded witch/melancholics and hysterics the development of new etiologies of the disease that the feeble sex *is*. The "quarrel" between these men about the nature of *woman*—women's evil, women's strength or weakness, women's passivity or aggression—is of no trivial matter. The debates are constitutive of the jurisdictional power struggles they are engaged in. It is to the dissenting voices of secular skeptics like medical doctors, for example, who profess to have original theories, diagnoses, and cures—that these religious and judicial persecutors speak in vituperatively announcing the voracious criminal insatiability of woman as a treasonous enemy of God, thereby laying claim to their authority, autonomy, and jurisdiction over her.

The struggle to impose their law relies on a particular discursive economy of "evil" operating through centuries of strategies of abjection, repudiation, and expulsion. "Evil" is one way that patriarchal violence, warfare, and genocide—and the myriad battles for autonomy, jurisdiction, and control related to them—can sanction and sanctify themselves, while all along ensuring that the *other* is to pay the price. The terror that "evil" incites belongs not to *man,* whose anatomical proximity to the "body of Christ"—as Kramer and Sprenger argued—"has so far preserved the male sex from such a great crime" as witchcraft and found him free of sin and full of glory (1486/1971, 47). It belongs, rather, to the sex that is made to wear the sin of his desire, to the insatiable one, whose incarnate evil sufficed to betray the likelihood that she was not just hallucinating, not just dreaming when she voluntarily or involuntarily confessed to succumbing to the seductions of dark demon intruders and, by implication, to committing the one treasonous crime for which her torture and execution became legal: having heretical, carnal relations with the devil himself. The *logos*—or the logic of the law's sanctimonious brutality—is aimed at eradicating *woman*, and it is constitutive of the "sexuality" that has been invented and imposed on us. It is the part of "sexuality" that patriarchy likes to conceal; the part that must be written into its history.

Even though the figures of the heretic-witch and the witch-melancholic make fleeting appearances on the historical stage, and even though the specific jurisdictional battles through which she is produced may come and go, there remain constant underlying relations of power that appear to be fundamental to the "body politic" of Western Christian male supremacy. I speak specifically to the processes of *othering*, the dynamic of sexual abjection, corporeal defilement, and the repudiation of femininity. As Mary Douglas (1966) asks consideration of the relation between the operation of the pure/impure mechanism of the body and the body politic, Julia Kristeva (1982) reveals the paradoxical place of the abject in the identity formation of the subject—that is, the abject is that which must be expelled as a guarantor of autonomous identity; yet, paradoxically, it is needed in order to provide this guarantee. Such analyses of the psycho-symbolic processes of subjection and abjection can perhaps reveal some of the darker foundations of Christian patriarchy, historically and otherwise, and the function that "evil" is made to play within it. In distinguishing themselves and their law from the Jewish and pagan *others*, we find with the inaugural discourses of the Fathers of the church a marriage of asceticism and feminine abjection that infuses the sexualization of evil and the demonization of female sexuality. The latter signifies and embodies the abject threat to their One Law and One God; at the same time its expulsion guarantees this very same law.

In such a political economy, where there are prices to be exacted and blood to be shed, Diana and her followers, as archetypes of the fecund power of woman's sexuality, are central tropes underlying the anxieties expressed in demonological theology and subsequent inquisitorial and judicial campaigns aimed at "extirpating" her. For it is in trading on the misogynist metamorphosis of Diana and her followers into Satan's conspiratorial accomplices that the justification is based for the "extraordinary" inquisitorial and juridical practices that find woman guilty of the treason her sex embodies. That is to say, we find in this metamorphosis all that is needed to bring the law to bear on *woman*, to sanction and sanctify her torture and murder, if not her regulation and control. It is with the aim of *not forgetting* the instrumentality of "evil" in the history of "sexuality" that this genealogy is written.

Notes

This chapter draws on some of the archives and observations taken from an ongoing genealogical research project, initiated with my doctoral dissertation, on the religious, judicial, and medical debates about women's moral and criminal culpability that were implicated in the criminalization and persecution of women for "witchcraft" between the fifteenth and the late seventeenth centuries in most European countries. I am indebted to Karlene Faith, Linda Nicholson, and Sal Renshaw for their inspiration and generosity in reviewing earlier drafts of this paper and in helping to sketch impossibly broad questions such as, What is it that makes *woman* the scapegoat of man's "golden age?" I am grateful to have had available the resources of the Rare and Manuscript Collections of the Carl A. Kroch Library at Cornell University, and the Woodward Memorial Library at the University of British Columbia, Canada.

1. The statute of 1604 changes the focus of the criminality of witchcraft from *maleficia* to a "pact with the devil," rendering this crime a form of "treason" deserving of capital punishment.

2. While Foucault makes the odd passing reference to the witches' sabbat in *Madness and Civilization* (1965), he briefly broaches this subject in a short interview, "Sorcery and Madness," where he discusses the work of Thomas Szasz (Foucault 1989, 107–11). Here he acknowledges Szasz's *Manufacture of Madness* (1970) to be "an important book in the history of the related techniques of power and knowledge," in part because it shows that the forms of power exercised through the Inquisition, including the interrogations and surveillances, are "still recognizable" in the psychiatric setup of today: "It interrogates us still, questions our desires and our dreams, disturbs our nights, hunts down secrets and traces boundaries, undertakes purifications and assures the functioning of order" (1989, 108).

3. Consider, for instance, the implications of the witch craze for writing women's legal history. To date, the latter tends to be treated as if it were inaugurated with white woman's suffrage—as if the most notable struggles for autonomy began as recently as the nineteenth century. Resistance also has a history, though it tends to be marked by silences, and it requires creative strategies to give them voice.

4. In *Thinking about Gender,* Janet McCracken presents the following translation of 1 Corinthians 6: "Make no mistake: no fornicator or idolator, none who are guilty either of adultery or of homosexual perversion, no thieves or grabbers or drunkards or slanderers or swindlers, will possess the kingdom of God" (1977, 199). It is in the same letter, of course, that Paul shuns all fornication and suggests in the next verse: "It is a good thing for a man to have nothing to do with women."

5. Cohn and Russell identify multiple variations of corporeal abjection, cannibalistic consumption, and voracious sexuality in the vitriolic rhetoric launched between rival groups of ancient cultures. In the Greco-Roman world, Christians were widely characterized as incestuous, cannibalistic, ritual murderers who sacrificed and ate children (Cohn 1975, 8–9; Russell 1972, 89). The very same allegations appear again in the writings of Christian apologists and church fathers, launched, in turn, against pagans, and especially Jews. In their apologetic writings, Justin Martyr, Origen, Tertullian, and Clement of Alexandria all make reference to the wild accusations against Christians. Martyr and Origen both accused the Jews of spreading the calumnies of incest and cannibalism. As Russell (1972, 92) summarizes, Origen ridiculed the pagan Celsus for believing that Christians sacrificed and ate children, invoked demons, and held revels at night where they engaged in carnal lust. Tertullian, in his *Apologia,* argued that the "pagans practised vicious acts and then blamed the Christians for incest and the sacrifice of babies" (in

Russell 1972, 91–92; Schaff 1997). With Clement of Alexandria (ca. 150–215), Russell notes, accusations of such "bloodthirsty rituals" became "standard procedure," systematically launched against other religious sects and practices: "The Carpocratians, he argued, were licentious, practising incestuous orgies. . . . The Montanists used the blood of children in their unholy sacrifices. The gnostics cooked and ate embryos for their Passover meal, and they partook of a horrible Eucharist confected of semen and menses" (Russell 1972, 92–93; see Schaff 1997). But also standard to Clement's prescriptions for purity and his depictions of orgiastic heretics is an ethic of sexual abstinence that renders any pagan system of beliefs akin to licentiousness. As he explains in his treatise "On Marriage," while the Greeks had counseled that we "should fight desire and not be subservient to it, so as to bring it to practical effect . . . our ideal is not to experience desire at all" (in Heyward 1982, xx).

Roberts and Donaldson (1997) and Schaff (1997) collectively comprise an excellent resource for any research on these and other ante-Nicene, Nicene, and post-Nicene writings: the full collection of the works of such "Church Fathers" is compiled digitally on CD-rom.

6.　Trying to defend the "true heroism" of aggressive witch-hunters like Judge Nicholas Remy, his twentieth-century translator and commentator Montague Summers paints him as a warrior for the kingdom of God and reasons that "a certain suspicion or vein of treason" was clearly "commingled with witchcraft, since the person had transformed his allegiance from the lawful sovereign, the Prince of the land, to an alien, the devil. The idea was afterwards elaborated in fuller detail by the jurists, and an even darker shade was given to it when the witch was held to be guilty of lese-majesty, a false traitor to Almighty God" (in Remy 1971, xx).

7.　The Criminal Code, *Carolina* (1532) promulgated for the Holy Roman Empire by Charles V was similar to the early witchcraft statute passed by Henry VIII in 1542 and repealed by Edward VI in 1547 in that it associated witchcraft, not with sabbat rituals or covenants with the devil but with the use of charms, "conjugations," and "enchantments . . . to the destruction of the neighbours persones and goodes" (see Ewen 1929, 18). The crime was originally defined in terms of acts and practices, and was processed with relatively small penalties in the secular courts. Not until the end of the century is this crime linked in law, for example, to what the statute of James I referred to as an individual who "shall consult, covenant with, entertaine, employ, feed or reward any evill and wicked Spirit to or for any intent or purpose" (see Ewen 1929, 14). These statutes are reprinted, along with the new statutes of promulgated by Elizabeth I in 1563 and 1580, and James I in 1604, in Ewen 1929, 13–20.

8.　In the postscript to the 1583 edition of *Tricks*, Weyer, in turn, addresses Bodin's arguments and acknowledges the hostility of the "legal experts" who themselves seem to contrive "monstrous mockeries" in labyrinths of demonic illusions. "If the legal experts are vexed that I disagree with popular belief . . . , then I am receiving ill will in return for my kindness, because I wished to give them every opportunity to seek out the truth from others in this sort of argument and to bring forth and duly pronounce criminal sentence not according to the dictates of an age that is blind with respect to the Christian religion but on the basis of the very mysteries of truth" (1995, 582–83).

References

Agrippa, Cornelius. [1529] 1996. *Declamation on the Nobility and Preeminence of the Female Sex*. Trans. Albert Rabil Jr. Chicago: University of Chicago Press.

Aquinas, St. Thomas. [1274] 1997. *Summa Theologica*. Albany, N.Y.: Ages Software.

Augustine, St. [c. 426] 1958. *On Christian Doctrine*. Trans. D. W. Robertson. New York: Macmillan.

——. 1961. *Confessions*. Trans. R. S. Pine-Coffin. Harmondsworth: Penguin.

——. 1997. *City of God*. In *Nicene and Post-Nicene Fathers*, vol. 3. Ed. Philip Schaff, trans. Marcus Dods. Albany, N.Y.: Ages Software.

Baroja, Julio Caro. 1971. *The World of Witches*. Trans. O. N. V. Glendinning. Chicago: University of Chicago Press.

——. 1998. Witchcraft and Catholic theology. In *Early Modern European Witchcraft: Centres and Peripheries*, ed. Bengt Ankarloo and Gustav Henningsen. Oxford: Clarendon Press.

Beizer, Janet. 1994. *Ventriloquized Bodies: Narratives of Hysteria in Nineteenth-century France*. Ithaca, N.Y.: Cornell University Press.

Bodin, Jean. [1580] 1995. *On the Demon-mania of Witches*. Trans. Randy A. Scott. Toronto: Centre for Reformation and Renaissance Studies.

Boguet, Henri. [1605] 1971. *An Examen of Witches* [*Examen des Sorcieres*]. Trans. E. A. Ashwin. New York: Barnes and Noble.

Brundage, James A. 1987. *Law, Sex, and Christian Society in Medieval Europe*. Chicago: University of Chicago Press.

Chrysostom. [c. 380-83] 1997. *On the Priesthood*. In *The Nicene and Post-Nicene Fathers*, vol. 9. Ed. Philip Schaff. Albany, N.Y.: Ages Software.

Cixous, Hélène. 1986. Sorties. In Hélène Cixous and Catherine Clement, *The Newly Born Woman*. Trans. Betsy Wing. Manchester: Manchester University Press.

Clement of Alexandria. [c. 180-193] 1997. *Exhortation to the Heathen*. In *The Ante-Nicene Fathers*, vol. 2. Ed. Alexander Roberts and James Donaldson. Albany, N.Y.: Ages Software.

Cohn, Norman. 1975. *Europe's Inner Demons: An Inquiry Inspired by the Great Witch-hunt*. New York: Meridian.

Davidson, L. S., and John O. Ward, eds. 1993. *The Sorcery Trial of Alice Kyteler: A Contemporary Account*. Binghamton: Medieval and Renaissance Texts and Studies.

de Beauvoir, Simone. 1974. *The Second Sex*. Trans. H. M. Parshley. New York: Vintage.

Douglas, Mary. 1966. *Purity and Danger: An Analysis of the Concepts of Pollution and Taboo*. New York: Routledge.

Easlea, Brian. 1980. *Witch Hunting, Magic and the New Philosophy: An Introduction of the Debates of the Scientific Revolution*. Atlantic Highlands, N.J.: Humanities Press.

Evans, Martha Noel. 1991. *Fits and Starts: A Genealogy of Hysteria in Modern France*. Ithaca, N.Y.: Cornell University Press.

Ewen, C. L'Estrange, ed. 1929. *Witch Hunting and Witch Trials: The Indictments*

for Witchcraft from the Records of 1373 Assizes Held for the Home Circuit
A.D. 1559–1763. London: Kegan Paul.

Foucault, Michel. 1965. *Madness and Civilization: A History of Insanity in the Age of Reason.* Trans. Richard Howard. New York: Mentor.

———. 1978. *History of Sexuality.* Trans. Robert Hurley. New York: Pantheon.

———. 1980. *Herculine Barbin: Being the Recently Discovered Memoirs of a Nineteenth-century French Hermaphrodite,* trans. Richard McDougall. New York: Pantheon.

———. 1989. *Foucault Live: Interviews, 1966–1984.* Trans. John Johnston. Ed. Sylvère Lotringer. New York: Semiotext(e).

———. 1995. *Discipline and Punish: The Birth of the Prison.* Trans. Alan Sheridan. New York: Vintage.

Heyward, Isabel Carter. 1982. *The Redemption of God.* New York: University Press of America.

Innocent VIII, Pope. [1486] 1971. The Bull of Innocent VIII. In Heinrich Kramer and James Sprenger, *Malleus maleficarum,* trans. Montague Summers. New York: Dover.

James I, King of Scotland. [1604] 1924. *Daemonologie.* New York: E. P. Dutton.

King, Margaret. 1993. *Women of the Renaissance.* Chicago: University of Chicago Press.

Klaits, Joseph. 1985. *Servants of Satan: The Age of the Witch Hunts.* Bloomington: Indiana University Press.

Kramer, Heinrich, and James Sprenger. [1486] 1971. *Malleus maleficarum.* Trans. Montague Summers. New York: Dover.

Kristeva, Julia. 1982. *The Powers of Horror: An Essay on Abjection.* Trans. Leon S. Roudiez. New York: Colombia University Press.

———. 1984. *Histoires d'Amour—Love Histories.* London: Institute of the Contemporary Arts.

Lancre, Pierre de. 1613. *Tableau de L'inconstance des mauvais anges et demons.* Paris: Nicolas Bvon.

Larner, Christina. 1981. *Enemies of God: The Witch-hunt in Scotland.* London: Chatto and Windus.

Lea, H. C. 1957. *Materials Toward a History of Witchcraft.* New York: Thomas Yoseloff.

Le Franc, Martin. [1442] 1968. *Le Champion des dames.* Lausanne: Librairie Payot.

Levack, Brian. 1995. *The Witch-hunt in Early Modern Europe.* 2nd ed. New York: Longman.

MacKinnon, Catharine. 1992. Does sexuality have a history? In *Discourses of Sexuality,* ed. Domna Stanton. Ann Arbor: University of Michigan Press.

Martyr, Justin. 1997. *First Apology.* In *The Ante-Nicene Fathers,* vol. 1. Ed. Alexander Roberts and James Donaldson. Albany, N.Y.: Ages Software.

McCracken, Janet, ed. 1977. *Thinking about Gender.* Orlando, Fla.: Harcourt Brace College Publishers.

Midelfort, H. C. Erik. 1972. *Witch Hunting in Southwestern Germany 1526–1684: The Social and Intellectual Foundations.* Stanford, Calif.: Stanford University Press.

Nietzsche, Friedrich. 1966. *Beyond Good and Evil.* Trans. Walter Kaufmann. New York: Vintage.

Origen. 1997. *Origen against Celsus.* In *The Ante-Nicene Fathers,* vol. 3. Ed. Alexander Roberts and James Donaldson. Albany, N.Y.: Ages Software.

Remy, Nicholas. [1602] 1974. *Demonalatry.* Trans. E. A. Ashwin. Secaucus, N.J.: University Books.

Roberts, Alexander, and James Donaldson, eds. 1997. *The Ante-Nicene Fathers.* Albany, N.Y.: Ages Software.

Russell, Jeffrey Burton. 1972. *Witchcraft in the Middle Ages.* Ithaca, N.Y.: Cornell University Press.

Schaff, Philip, ed. 1997. *The Nicene and Post-Nicene Fathers.* Albany, N.Y.: Ages Software.

Scott, Joan. 1997. "La querelle des femmes" in the late twentieth century. *Differences* (Summer) 9:2.

Showalter, Elaine. 1985. *The Female Malady: Women, Madness, and English Culture.* New York: Pantheon.

Soman, Alfred. 1989. Decriminalizing witchcraft: Does the French experience furnish a European model? *Criminal Justice History* 10:1–22.

Szasz, Thomas. 1970. *The Manufacture of Madness: A Comparative Study of the Inquisition and the Mental Health Movement.* New York: Harper and Row.

Tertullian. [c. 200] 1997. *Prescriptions Against the Heretics.* In *The Ante-Nicene Fathers,* vol. 3. Ed. Alexander Roberts and James Donaldson. Albany, N.Y.: Ages Software.

———. 1999. *On the Apparel of Women.* Trans. S. Thelwell. In *Eve and Adam: Jewish, Christian, and Muslim Readings on Genesis and Gender,* ed. Kristen E. Kvam, Linda S. Schearing, and Valarie H. Ziegler. Bloomington: Indiana University Press.

Veith, Ilza. 1965. *Hysteria: The History of the Disease.* Chicago: University of Chicago Press.

Waddell, Helen. 1998. *The Desert Fathers: Translations from the Latin with an Introduction by Helen Waddell.* London: Constable.

Weyer, Johann. [1563] 1991. *On the Tricks of Demons.* Trans. John Shea. Binghamton: Medieval and Renaissance Texts and Studies.

3 Irigaray's *To Be Two:* The Problem of Evil and the Plasticity of Incarnation

Ada S. Jaarsma

> Any universal corresponding to a single gender or claiming to be neuter sins against spirit. And to sin against spirit is absolute. Everything else can be forgiven. Apart from that other infamy: destroying nature itself as the source of life for each and every man and woman.
>
> Luce Irigaray, *I Love to You*

As this epigraph signals, an awareness of "sin" emerges out of Luce Irigaray's central assertion of sexual difference as the essential ethical and philosophical problem. Irigaray asserts that a rejection or refutation of sexual difference risks committing an ultimate sin. Through this claim, we can glimpse a problematic of evil emerging out of Irigaray's project that cannot be easily or quickly delimited. Irigaray herself traverses this problematic in her texts, elaborating sources of brokenness and violence as well as concomitant possibilities for regeneration (see, e.g., 1993b, 1993d, and 1996). Rather than mobilizing traditional concepts like "moral evil" or "natural evil," Irigaray's project cuts across such categories, putting into play an analysis that elaborates structural as well as individual blindness toward sexual difference as the central problem of evil.

At various points in her texts, Irigaray mobilizes Christian stories in order to carry out her analysis. "Sin," in this context, works as a specific narrative, diagnosing sites of violence and possibilities for redemption. The very telling of traditional stories of sin and salvation must be excavated and reenacted in order for Irigaray to actualize her interpretation of the problem of evil. As Irigaray's readers, then, we must attend to this double traversal that makes up her analysis, reading "sin" as one particular site at which judgment against the tradition is leveled and healing is invoked. We are called to travel through her excavation and retelling of religious stories in order to discern both the scope of her project and the actual implications for us as her readers.

Irigaray states that the "same breath circulates" between her texts, from *The Forgetting of Air in Martin Heidegger* (1999) to *I Love to You* (1996) and *To Be*

Two (2001b; 2001a, 309). By attending to this breath that moves continuously throughout her texts, we may discern the consistent parameters of the problematic of evil that emerges throughout her project. The lack of love, as well as the concomitant urgent need for rethinking the possibilities of love, acts as a continually rearticulated preoccupation of Irigarayan texts. Irigaray invokes love as necessary in the prologue to *To Be Two:* "Is it not because I do not know you that I know that you are? Only love consents to a night in which I will never know you. Between those who love each other, there is a veil. In solitude, perhaps setting out with a lamp is necessary, but in love? Does such a night correspond to blind faith or to respect for the one I will never know? Is it not this unknown which allows us to remain two?" (2001b, 9). The relationality of this invocation of love, continuous throughout Irigaray's project, operates horizontally as well as vertically, calling for transformed relations between individuals and themselves, between men and women, and between humanity and divinity. Her project is itself alive, invigorating itself and also invoking relations with the reader, both man and woman, and their communities.

By acknowledging the horizontal and vertical dimensions of love invoked by Irigaray, we can begin to identify her traversal of a problem that concerns not only human relations but also relations between humanity and the divine. While her project is not in itself a theology, Irigaray mobilizes religious narratives in order to restore the possibility of healing through sacred stories. The stories themselves are in need of healing so that they can then be deployed as sources of spiritual renewal. Irigaray's retelling of the incarnation and annunciation stories, for example, elaborates means of mediating between speech and touch—providing answers to the question that she poses in her early text, *This Sex Which Is Not One* (1993d), a question that continues to resonate on critical levels in her more recent writing. In *This Sex,* Irigaray asks, "How can I put 'I love you' differently?" (207) She poses the question again in *I Love to You* (1996, 129). As a parallel question, in both *This Sex* and *To Be Two,* she asks, "How can I touch you if you are not there?" (1993d, 205; 2001b, 94). These questions operate implicitly as well as explicitly throughout Irigaray's theoretical project, elaborating both a motivation behind the Irigarayan problematic—the need to reenvision discourse as we know and use it in order to transform our immediate relationships—and a performative enactment of this analysis in and through the discursive movements of her own texts.

Emerging out of these key questions about speaking, touching, and loving, the stories also, then, necessarily elaborate a story about language itself. Irigaray's interpretation of the problem of evil, elaborated through these stories, is intimately related to questions of reading, since it works both to diagnose and to reenvision in a continual movement of transformation, a movement that calls for the participation of the reader. As we read these religious stories, we need to explore how the Irigarayan texts themselves invoke a certain mode or strategy of reading. If we attend to this invocation, what particular story emerges out of this strategic reading? The relationality invoked throughout Irigaray's project includes the reader. What relations do we ourselves perform, as her readers? Are there risks that we as participants in this process need to discern and negotiate?

If we read relationally, we will learn how to read from the very stories and concepts at work within the text. In her critical readings of G. W. F. Hegel (1975, 1977), Catherine Malabou demonstrates such relational reading.[1] She enacts a methodology that attends to the very invocation of reading at work within Hegelian concepts. Focusing especially on the concept of "plasticity" in Hegel's texts (see, e.g., 1975 and 1977), Malabou seeks to follow the ascriptions of reading called for by Hegel. Her own texts enact this philosophical reading, "obeying Hegel's insistence that we philosophize in the language itself" (2000b, 208). She states, "It is thus Hegel the reader, Hegel the interpreter of his own posterity that I shall try to put in view" (2000a, 132). Beyond merely identifying Hegel himself as a reader, Malabou extends this analysis by calling for a reading of Hegel that in turn enacts his philosophy: "Far from merging purely and simply into the content of what is read, in order to disappear into it, the reader must express in turn that content and, to do so, can only formulate new propositions, transform what he/she reads, interpret it" (2000a, 139). Malabou's reflections on her methodology challenge us to enter into the very logic of the text that we are reading. Lisabeth During, Malabou's English translator, calls this movement of plasticity "a sign of generous reading" (2000, 193). I would like to explore this generosity of reading, not only as a challenging methodology in itself but also as a potentially enriching strategy for reading Irigaray.

Malabou reads Hegel through the concept of plasticity, a concept in which she identifies both a structure and a condition of intelligibility. In exploring the motif of plasticity as it emerges within the Hegelian text, Malabou points to multiple meanings of the word itself: being able to both receive and give form; the aptitude for formation in general; the healing of wounds; explosive materials (2000a, 134). As well as locating the meanings of plasticity solely within Hegel's writing, she notes that the meanings of plasticity continue to evolve today. Malabou's reading strategy emphasizes and enacts the concomitancy of reading both with and within the text.

According to Malabou, Hegel understood philosophical plasticity as characterizing both the philosopher as reader and the mode of being of philosophy itself. By focusing on this double task of plasticity in philosophy, Malabou opens up the radical possibility of philosophy itself as transformative and healing, carrying out the properties of plastic itself. According to Malabou, reading plastically extends beyond the deconstruction of a text, enacting a procedure that "announces, as every convalescence does, the fragile miracle of survival and which allows the philosophical text to continue to work, in every sense of the term" (2000a, 140).[2] The Hegelian text resists its own deconstruction by invoking a mode of reading that plastically undoes one's own habit of reading. Malabou argues that Hegel's philosophical plasticity calls for the participation of both text, enacted within the dialectical movement, and reader, enacted within interpretation, to reconstitute the text on the basis of its very defect, remedying the formal failure of the philosophical proposition (2000a, 138–39). Plasticity thereby enacts regeneration, a moment of repair that Malabou suggests is not thematized by deconstruction.

In reading Irigarayan texts, I would like to think through the possibilities proffered by Malabou's methodology for attending to both the logic and meanings of the incarnation story. The incarnation and its relations to divinity, sin, and touch invoke a mode of reading that corresponds intimately with the story being enacted. If we read the incarnation as a concept similar to plasticity in Malabou's reading of Hegel, we will be able to enter into the incarnational process articulated by Irigaray.[3] Perhaps, then, the incarnation itself will come to resemble a form of plasticity: a process of moving and becoming that invokes the radical participation of the reader.

Malabou portrays plastic reading as a strategy that extends beyond deconstruction. This methodology proffers resources for us as readers of Irigaray to engage with the overall movement of the Irigarayan project. Given the shift within Irigaray's work from deconstructive to more politically applied writing, plasticity enables us to be aware of the continuities at work within her project without failing to attend to its trajectory itself. Plasticity, as theorized by Malabou, operates on multiple levels, opening up the concept, the story, and the methodology of a text. By focusing on the incarnation within Irigaray, and reading this incarnation plastically, we can follow Malabou in reading beyond deconstruction.

The incarnation occupies an integral position, theoretically and practically, within Irigaray's project. Literally "en-flesh-ment," the incarnation recalls the becoming-human of the second person of the Trinity. Numerous relationships are figured by this story. The canonical biblical text, which states that "the Word became flesh" (John 1:14, New Revised Standard Version) points to an embodiment of this becoming-divine that is discursive as well as bodily. The canonical story points to an original Adam, whose fallen sinfulness is redeemed by the second Adam, the incarnated Christ. When read as a story, the incarnation provides us with a logic with which to read, similar to Malabou's plasticity. An originary sin, the conditions of possibility for redemption, and the ongoing possibility of redemption are all at work within the incarnational trope or narrative, constituting one particular elaboration of the problem of evil.

It is important to recognize, however, that Irigaray demonstrates an increasing awareness of, and commitment to, Eastern as well as Western spiritual traditions.[4] The story of the incarnation in Irigaray's work does not occupy a foundational role that excludes other stories, traditions, or practices, but rather it constitutes a narrative site at which to glimpse complex interrelated problems of Irigaray's project. The Irigarayan incarnation enacts both Eastern and Western religious traditions. She calls for a process of *becoming* divine as well as developing relations with the divine. "Evil" itself, then, becomes a complex of relations, signifying neither solely the "moral" evil of defiance against God nor the "natural" evil of cosmic violence not attributable to the acts of God. While divinity is elaborated as a revelatory source of potential healing, the divine is also figured as an internal and singular becoming, invoked as an especially critical process for women. The overall problematic of evil cannot be fully identified without acknowledging both of these critical conceptions of the divine.

Alison Martin claims that the notion of the divine motivates Irigaray's entire oeuvre: "[I]f taken in the broadest possible sense, it is the notion which animates, informs and structures all her writing" (1998, 102). The absence of a female divine in phallocentrism, exposed by Irigaray, points to the need for thinking through the conditions of possibility for such a divine. Tracing the traditional christological story, Irigaray identifies the colonizing potential of divinity within this particular narrative: "This is not a secondary matter. It is very important. Without divine power, men could not have supplanted mother-daughter relations and their attributions concerning nature and society. But man becomes God by giving himself an invisible father, a father language. Man becomes God as the Word, then as the Word made flesh. Because the power of semen isn't immediately obvious in procreation, it's relayed by the linguistic code, the *logos*. Which wants to become the all-embracing truth" (Irigaray 1993b, 68).

Irigaray's elaboration of the divine points to the critical stakes at work within both the identity of God and any discourse in the name of God. For example, in her essay on Maurice Merleau-Ponty, she moves through the various integral components of any relationship with God, posing several key questions: What is the nature of God and what are the implications of this nature for woman's relations with her own body? Who is speaking in God's name, giving themselves the authority to sell indulgences and secure redemption? Is it possible to redeem discourse on and in the name of God? She writes:

> What kind of God is this? One who corresponds to a transcendental that is metaphysical but not physical (except prior to the first sin?). A God who would have created me as man or woman to make me guilty of my *body*? . . . Who is this God? And who has, since the beginning, committed the sin of simony vis-à-vis God? While speculating on the text of the law? But above all while exploiting (consciously or unconsciously) the meaning of the word. This is a difficult question; but more and more it seems to me that God has always been a victim of simony. Were it otherwise, would grace come to pass more easily? Whoever writes a truth or makes a pronouncement, above all concerning God, should always add: *open [overt(e)]*. (1993a, 162)

This compelling invocation to openness seems to call, not for a displacement of the possibility for an active divinity, but rather for radical transformation and healing in and through the divine.

The incarnation operates within Irigaray's oeuvre as one specific embodied story of this engagement with the divine, thereby constituting a useful traversal of Irigaray's interpretation of the problem of evil. Martin explains the theoretical usefulness of the incarnation for Irigaray's project: "Irigaray's subject has to be known differently, she is one who is known through and by her representations which are always in a state of becoming. The impetus to adopt Christianity for this purpose derives in part from a theorized preference for evolution from the basis of where you are, thus from the historical significance of Christianity in the West and from Irigaray's own acknowledged Catholicism. But equally significant is the potential offered by the notion of a God made man, who, after being modified through Irigaray's adoption of certain concepts of Eastern thought, becomes a sexed embodied subject" (1998: 105). Irigaray explicitly identifies the importance of retelling the incarnation story: "Christian patriarchal order seems indeed nearer to gloomy and repressive reason than to a celebration of the joy of a human incarnation of the divine" (1989: 62). Her own story, then, attempts to open up this celebration both in the questioning of the existing conceptions of the incarnation and in the actual performance of this questioning in and through incarnational discourse.

In order to attend carefully to the incarnational logic at work within Irigarayan texts, we must continually recognize the integral connections to sexual difference. As one example, Irigaray's reading of Hegel through sexual difference, calling for a more radical dialectic, occurs through an incarnational process: "The process whereby gender might become perfect is lacking in Hegel, and indeed in ourselves. If gender were to develop individually, collectively, and historically, it could mark *the place where the spirit entered human nature,* the point in time when the infinite passed into the finite, given that each individual of a gender is finite and potentially infinite in his or her relation to gender" (1993c, 139). The awareness of sexual difference is inseparable from the call for an incarnation of the spirit within human nature. Gender itself becomes the source of infinity, actualized within a finite and singular relation to each individual.

We can again look to Malabou for a critical explication of this logic at work within the incarnational invocation, a logic that operates both synchronically and diachronically. Also reading Hegel, Malabou describes the temporality of the dialectic as both synchronic, emerging out of the system as a whole, and diachronic, differentiating itself from itself in time (2000b, 211). Reading through this logic actualizes both this retrospective and prospective temporality: "In the present time in which reading takes place, the reader is drawn to a double expectation: waiting for what is to come (according to a thought which is linear), while presupposing that the outcome has already arrived (according to the teleological ruse)" (2000b, 212). Reading Irigaray though the logic of the incarnation extends the regeneration at work within her project, synchronically in relation to the structure of her problematic, and diachronically as we ourselves participate in the transformative process. The incarnational event, spirit entering human nature, requires the participation of readers so that it continues to figure both an actual event and an ongoing process of rereading. While this process invokes the infinity of spirit, it is also necessarily limited by the finite and singular moment of reading.

We need to read Irigaray's analysis of evil, then, through the incarnational logic of her project, thereby avoiding interpretations that could restore dogma to Irigaray's rereadings of religious stories. For example, Martin cautions us to avoid reductive theological readings of Irigaray's texts: "Only a gross misinterpretation could return Irigaray's 'sins' and 'graces' to the doctrines of good and evil. They have to be understood in the context of a proposal for a female divine which is an ideal for the self in the process of becoming" (1998, 117). The register in which we read "sin" becomes one of feminist theoretical possibilities rather than theological doctrine. Religious words employed by Irigaray, such as "sin," do not refer to definitive moral principles, but operate as loci of continually transformative conditions for rethinking religious narratives. The problematic of evil, by extension, explicates and enacts this ongoing critical process. If we take up the word "evil" in this context, then, we are referring to this imperative to reread and transform the tradition.

Rereading theological words such as "sin" opens up the possibility of rethinking salvation as well. For example, Serene Jones (1995) explains how "sin" is reconceptualized in contemporary feminist theology. As opposed to traditional conceptions of sin as pride, feminist theologians propose that a woman's sin "is better described as the sin of fragmentation, of subjective dissolution. Once her sin is identified in this manner, it then becomes apparent that her salvation rests not in a vision of the Divine who breaks through the wall of her narcissistic gaze, but of a God who inscribes borders within which she might begin to conceive of herself as a coherent self, capable of relation and yet contained enough not to let the relation dissolve her" (1995, 61). Reading Irigaray through this paradigm calls for the reader to participate in this process of discovering new relations with ourselves and with the divine. Kelly Oliver explains that Irigaray, as well as Emmanuel Lévinas (see, e.g., 1989), elaborates relationships that take us beyond ourselves and toward otherness: "Through relationships humanity gives birth to divinity" (2001, 183). The divine is integral not only to the exploration of relationality and difference, but to the very enactment of renewed and healthy relations.

In a critical and creative assessment of how stories of "sin" can be told, Irigaray's theoretical project retells several religious narratives, repositioning the status of both the stories themselves, and more significantly, the actual narration of these stories. If, following Malabou's methodology, we attend to the concepts and logic at work within these stories—and the very nature of "story" itself in Irigaray—we will be able to participate in Irigaray's traversal of her problematic of evil. While the incarnation provides a helpful site at which to elaborate this analysis, it remains inseparable from other religious stories, especially the creation story and the annunciation story.

The nature of the telling of stories occupies an explicitly integral role in Irigarayan texts. For example, in *I Love to You* (1996), Irigaray points to the dire risks inherent in how the creation story has traditionally been imparted:

> As our tradition dictates, man originates from God, and woman from man. As long as the female generic—woman—is not determined as such, this will be true. Women will remain men's or Man's creatures. With respect to themselves, and among themselves, they are unable to create, create (for) themselves, especially an

ideal, for want of an identity and of mediations. They will be able to criticize their condition, complain, reject themselves or one another, but not establish a new era of History or of culture (1996, 64).

The chronology of the story—woman, originating from man, originating from God—prescribes a logic that continually delimits the conditions of possibility for female identity, as well as the very conditions of history and culture. Continuing the work performed in *I Love to You*, Irigaray explores the status of history and culture in *To Be Two* (2001b), pointing both to the potential and the critical need for resituating formative stories about creation and sin, allowing for new ways of living out these stories.

In *To Be Two*, another rereading of the creation story points to the motivating logic at work within the philosophical tradition and the critical need to rethink its assumptions. Irigaray points to the emergence of the god of phallocentrism, a divine that reflects man's dominance, as foundational to the logic of male mastery: "Does not, perhaps, the key to or the beginning of the world's mystery lie in man's desire to keep the center of the whole in himself? . . . [H]e cannot endure the mystery of the other and, instead, conceives a god made in his own image in order to encircle, if not to dominate, the horizon of every mystery" (2001b, 73). Rather than allowing this story to continue governing the tradition both in its prevalence and in its performative significance for affecting how men and women understand their own identities and relations, Irigaray points to the imperative of thinking through creation in terms of sexual difference. Irigaray characterizes our culture's approach to sexual difference as based on two types of exteriority that, once acknowledged, need to be reenvisioned: "[W]oman seeks herself in man, who, in turn, seeks himself in the mother. In order to escape this infernal circle, logic has imagined an original causality, philosophy has imagined the univocal nature of truth, and our religious tradition—sustained by the dogmas which fix the evolution of faith—has imagined the authority of a God-Father" (2001b, 56).

In order to rethink this originary story, we need to resituate the emergence of both interiority and exteriority of our own origins—looking to our parents and to ourselves, and also, significantly, looking to the sexual other. Relations of fidelity to our own gender enable the possibility of necessary, creational connections with the other: "My life as woman, the interiority which I also receive from the other-man, is made fecund and grows beginning from the encounter between I-woman and you-man if we are each faithful to our own gender" (2001b, 56). The conditions of possibility for growth and fecundity depend upon this invocation of fidelity to oneself as well as to relations with the other.

A new creation story emerges, with an inner logic that resists the unitary beginnings of the traditional narrative, for, as Irigaray writes, "a single origin does not exist, nor is there an origin common to many: a *logos*, a civilization, a religious or civil authority" (2001b, 56). Rather, the role of the divine shifts, as Irigaray's call to "be two" elaborates transformed relations with both God and our families: "To maintain the two is to give up the sort of infancy which places the omnipotent parental One above, as well as the familial relationship which returns it below" (2001b, 57). This call to "maintain the two" becomes a site at which the story of sin is retold. The problematic of evil is thereby actualized as a rejection of the unitary logic of the tradition and its radical transformation into being-two.

Following Malabou's methodology of reading with the logic of a text, as Irigaray's readers, we need to attend to the different conceptions of divinity at work within these stories. Irigaray continually invokes both relations with the divine itself as well as the process of becoming divine. Martin argues that "it is the notion of the divine which is pivotal for Irigaray since she deploys it for its philosophical association with the absolute, as that which constitutes a prerequisite to subjectivity and upholds the female imaginary and its modalities" (2000, 104). This characterization by Martin points to the divine as a source of subjectivity as well as to divinity as this very actualization of sexual difference. Not only must the story of originary divinity be reinscribed within our discourse in order to displace the patriarchal God of creation, but the incarnational possibility of becoming divine must be opened up to women as well as men in order to continue this displacement within everyday lives and relationships.

Just as Malabou reads "plasticity" within the Hegelian project as a concept that directly challenges the reader to participate in its own logic and practice, the incarnation operates not only narratively as an integral concept within Irigaray's project but also as an invitation to the reader to share in the incarnational process. Grace Jantzen, in her explorations of a feminist philosophy of religion, elaborates this process, stating that "as Jesus, a flesh-and-blood man, was said to be the living manifestation of God for all to follow, so it is laid upon each of us, in our flesh-and-blood sexuate existence, to become divine, to incarnate the divine ideals as (differently) gendered subjects" (1999, 93). The incarnation recounts a historical and theological event as well as a continuous encounter with divinity.

Graham Ward elaborates an understanding of the incarnation that explains the necessity of its nature as an ongoing process. He states that we must engage with Christology in terms of the interpersonal and intersexual: "Christology reveals itself in the reconciliation 'between' us" (1996, 231). Ward's Christology invokes intimately our relation to Christ, the need to stand in Christ; Christology becomes an ongoing event, an action rather than a defined state. This understanding of process resonates directly with Irigaray's project. Ward also calls for the imperative of acknowledging and working from an understanding of sexual difference: "There can only be salvation with Christ, through Christ, if there is sexual difference" (232). Bringing together an awareness of sexual difference with his understanding of the incarnation, Ward asks, "Can we really speak of incarnation if we castrate Christ?" He states, "What Christ did not take, he did not redeem" (228). By pointedly bringing together the sexuality of Christ and the incarnation itself, Ward sets out a premise that is also at work within Irigaray's analysis: the critical necessity of elaborating sexual difference in order to open up the possibility of regenerating the tradition.

Irigaray's use of the word "incarnation" exemplifies the direct relations between sexual difference and her call "to be two." She describes an approach to language that will effect an incarnation: "Sharing the word does not mean believing: incarnation prevents blind faith, and requires that each person is present and speaking. It is up to us to be faithful to this crossing: body and word. The universal becoming of the word distances itself from such fidelity while speaking to each other accomplishes it, refusing every manner of speaking which is not also word. Neither body nor language simply, but incarnation between us: the word being flesh and the flesh word" (2001b, 12).

Indeed, the relationship itself, "which is realized by flesh and words," is incarnational (2001b, 28). Relations between the two perform and embody the incarnational process. Irigaray writes, "I look at you as at the passage of the word into flesh, of the flesh into word, a lasting incarnation, the fulfillment of which is not perceptible by whoever does not keep his or her gaze upon the invisible" (2001b, 42). The other becomes a manifestation of this word-and-flesh intimacy, as the incarnation becomes an ongoing process of embodiment and relationality.

Rejecting a disincarnate neuter language, Irigarayan incarnation depends upon discourse itself. She characterizes this incarnating language in *I Love to You:* "Thus it is important for it [speech] to touch and not become the alienation of the tactile in possession, in the elaboration of a truth or a disincarnated beyond, in the production of an abstract and supposedly neuter discourse. Speech must stay as word and flesh, language and sensibility, at the same time" (1996, 126). Rather than the traditional story of the Word-made-flesh, Irigaray's incarnation becomes the word-and-flesh, a relation continually in process.

Irigaray's confessional stories of sin and creation enact her problematic of evil. She tells her own stories of originary sin to indicate specific sites at which the tradition must be interrogated. For example, Irigaray rereads Merleau-Ponty's essay, "The Intertwining—The Chiasm" (1997), charging his valorization of visibility over touch with ignoring or erasing the primary touch of the womb, a valorization that she points to as potentially originary sin: "The chiasmus of the visible and the tangible is inversed in time. Is this what is at stake in the first sin? The tangible is primary and the visible claimed to equal it, even to surpass it" (1993a, 163). In this reading, Irigaray mobilizes the conception of originary sin in order to point to the need for an incarnated word-and-flesh paradigm of language. As another example, Irigaray indicts the Western tradition as being male-centered, while operating as universal. This universalizing domination, then, becomes diagnosed by Irigaray as originary sin: "And the whole of his tradition is marred by an original sin: to have mistaken the reason of man for the universal" (1996, 147). The stakes are high, then, since recognizing dangerous or "sinful" conceptions allows for the deployment of transformed stories; these stories then serve as conditions of possibility for ethical, healthy relations and subjectivities.

As Martin explains, this Irigarayan call to faithfulness to the self emerges out of a renewed feminist understanding of sin: "Sin in the feminine is, then, not to be who I am, that is, to subject oneself to the desire of the other without returning to the self" (1998, 114). According to Martin, Irigaray offers conceptions of sin and grace appropriate for women that are "not offered in the form of commandments, nor are they suggested as rules to control or deny the self; they appear, rather, to offer guidelines for the development of the self" (1998, 114). The problematic of evil itself involves attending to the judgment of the tradition's sinfulness in neglecting sexual difference as well as the restorative invocation of healing and growth, both of which are indicated, whether implicitly or explicitly, in Irigaray's religious narratives. The mobilization of "sin" language thereby both indicts and proclaims.

Taking up "originary sin" as an operative philosophical strategy, Irigaray examines the complicity of traditional conceptions of the divine in sustaining blindness toward sexual difference: "Doesn't 'original sin' consist in dissociating human and divine? In making God into a distinct and transcendent entity. . . . God—Different? And this would be the source of evil, in the beginning. A sin against the incarnation into which woman would lure man? Eve would incite the being she was created out of to reveal himself as God?" (1991, 173). How the divine is understood and described in foundational stories holds paramount significance for even the possibility of elaborating a problematic of evil: "As things stand, how can we ask a priest to absolve us of a sin defined as such by a so-called Christian religion unless he himself is aware of the harm done to a woman who is preached to about God the Father and God made man alone, about a masculine Holy Spirit and about her function as the mother of sons?" (1989, 72). Stories of originary sin and the divine can enact violence against women and against relations between men and women, thereby constituting sources of sin themselves.

Another component to the Irigarayan story of the incarnation involves the recognition of sin as violence against the earth. Irigaray declares, "I think that any sermon on the salvation of the soul, on love of the poor, any so-called Eucharistic ritual, any Evangelical discourse that doesn't concern itself with saving the earth and its natural resources, is perverted. How can certain men and women repeat the words 'This is my body, this is my blood' over the fruits of the earth without worrying about how long that earth will remain fruitful?" (1989, 75). In *To be Two*, Irigaray points to the violence at work within the phallocentric tradition, exploring this violence as inflicted directly against nature. "Is History not simply the other name for man's intolerance towards nature?" (2001b, 70), she asks. Her analysis elaborates both the emergence of this violence and the devastating ramifications, not only on nature, but also on man himself:

> Man thus appears surrounded by a double power: the power of the universe around him and that of the world created by him which he does not recognize as his work, in particular as the work of his violence which is concealed in the everyday. Man lives in the uncanny, believing that he has tamed it. For him, the familiar is his violence become History. But in such a place, generated by his dominion, he is an exile. Man has become estranged from his to be and thinks in an improper

fashion. He considers himself to be the master of the very thing which dominates him. (2001b, 70)

As Martin points out, "To lack respect for nature is also one of Irigaray's 'sins'" (1998, 115) because this demonstrates a lack of respect for the conditions of life. To go further, this lack of respect results in actually sinning against nature. Irigaray declares, "All thinking that misunderstands its natural roots and resources is not true thinking but rather a threat to life" (1993c, 86). Through the logic of mastery and intolerance, man himself lives as an "exile," needing critically to acknowledge the conditions of domination that affect his own possibility of being.

The epilogue of *To Be Two* performs an alternate relation to nature, one that invokes "healing," "faithfulness," "freshness," "love." This epilogue recalls the poetry at the end of *This Sex Which Is Not One* (1993d), with notable differences. In *To Be Two,* Irigaray elaborates a deep harmony with nature that emerges out of her ethics of "being two." The very trajectory of her project perhaps appears in the movement from *This Sex Which Is Not One* to *To Be Two.* This sex "which is not one," the focus of her loving and sensual words in the early text, is joined in the call "to be two" by relations with both the other sex and with nature itself.

As Malabou indicates in her reading of Hegel, if we examine the logic at work within a text's invocation—how a text calls for a particular mode of reading in order to actualize that text's own project—we can glimpse the stakes of that very project and of our engagement with the text. If we carry this theoretical insight to our readings of Irigaray, we can begin to discern how Irigaray is not only retelling the story of sin as it appears philosophically in canonical texts, but is also opening up the possibility of understanding how sin can be actualized within language itself. Discourse itself can be acknowledged as sinful; language itself can be a site at which sin is at work.

The story of sin, then, becomes a story about language itself. In her explication of feminist Christianity, Catherine Keller proposes that we can understand divinity in terms of a specific trope of language itself. She writes that the divine operates tropologically as catachresis: "Let me suggest somewhat metatheologically that in its feminist deconstructions, 'God' produces a version of what Gayatri Spivak calls 'catachresis'. . . . [I]t is 'brought to crisis'" (1998, 226). Keller identifies this level of elaborating the divine as "metatheological," pointing to the work performed by the divine within language itself. Through the trope of catachresis, a story is being enacted both within and about language. Andrzej Warminski elaborates this double nature of catachresis. According to Warminski, catachresis, the abuse or misuse of language, figures the syntax of tropes, operating at a metatropological level. Warminski writes, "As the abuse of all tropes, catachresis threatens to open up the tropological system and keep it from constituting itself, closing itself off, *as* a system. That is, as a nontrope, catachresis is outside the system of tropes, but as an always possible 'outside'—there will always be at least as many forced uses or abuses of trope as there are tropes that we can classify—it has nevertheless to be accounted for in terms of that system; it is also 'inside' it" (1987, liv). If we take up Keller's suggestion that the divine be read as catachresis, divinity then constitutes a site of a metatropological story, invoking the always-possible conditions for misuse both inside and outside the system. Catachresis opens up the possibility of thinking through language itself as sinful, necessitating, then, a careful exploration of how sinful language can be redeemed.

Reading the divine as it appears in Irigaray's writing in and through this conception of catachresis points to the necessity of such a redemption. In *To Be Two*, Irigaray reflects on the possible emergence of the divine "between us," exemplifying the paradigm that she continually strives to both invoke and model in her text: "Only your existence helps me to be born, to move out of my placenta. I discover the divine between us, conceived by us but not combined with us, existing between each of us. We give birth to it, adults at last. Arriving at another stage of our history, God reveals himself as the work of man and woman" (2001b, 13). The divine emerges out of a relationship between the two sexes. Martin asserts that, ultimately, Irigaray "wishes to celebrate and affirm the possibilities of a reconstituted heterosexual difference as divine" (1998, 117). Relationship itself becomes divine.

How one reads this invoked relationship between men and women becomes the critical hermeneutical question, not only for understanding the nature of divinity within Irigaray's work but also for understanding the nature of her overall invocation of sexual difference. Martin states, "Given the emphasis she gives to the two, especially in the second and third stage of her work, I believe that Irigaray is better understood as an advocate of the two rather than as an advocate of multiplicity" (2000, 121). If we read according to incarnational logic, however, this relationality is not and should not be delimited by heterosexual boundaries. In contrast to Martin, Oliver (2001) argues that the insistence on two sexes throughout Irigaray operates strategically to open up multiplicity. We must first have two in order to create conditions for multiplicity (2001b, 209). Indeed, Irigaray writes that love between women "is essential if we are to quit our common situation and cease being the slaves of the phallic cult, commodities to be used and exchanged by men, competing objects in the marketplace" (1993c, 20).

The incarnation invokes a radical intersubjectivity. Rather than the binary relationship between subject-object, traditionally understood as the appropriate paradigm for understanding the concept and emergence of intersubjectivity, Irigaray's incarnational relationality enacts a different logic altogether: "It is not, therefore, in the fusion or in the ecstasy of the One that the dualism between subject and object is overcome, but rather in the incarnation of the two, a two which is irreducible to the One: man and woman" (2001b, 59). Irigaray's words are radical and highly contentious, pointing to the "destiny" of our bodies' relations with the other: "To be born woman, before signifying to be humanity's reproducer, means to incarnate woman's to be with the other-man, together with man's to be" (2001b: 33). This relationship, however, resists the possibility of being owned or dominated by the other: "No manner of speaking about desire is valid without this muted question: 'Who are you who will never be me or mine, you who will always remain transcendent to me, even if I touch you, since the word is made flesh in you in one way, and in me an another?'" (2001b, 19).

Reenvisioning divinity suggests a response to Irigaray's passionate desire to learn how to say "I love you" differently. Irigaray asks, "Is not God the name and the place that holds the promise of a new chapter in history and that also denies this can happen? Still invisible? Still to be discovered? To be incarnated? Archi-ancient and forever future" (1993c: 72). The possibility of invoking the name of God as a way to say "I love you" differently requires integral and direct links between divinity and love. Ward persuasively describes the work of love itself as deconstructive, declaring that "love deconstructs any notion of hierarchy; it deconstructs 'Father' as the divine name for origin or source" (1996, 233). Irigaray characterizes the process of loving as both divine and redemptive: "Love, even carnal love, is therefore cultivated and made divine. The act of love becomes the transubstantiation of the self and his or her lover into a spiritual body. It is a feast, celebration, and a renaissance, not a decline, a fall to be redeemed by procreation. Love is redemption of the flesh through the transfiguration of desire *for* the other (as an object?) into desire *with* the other" (1996, 139). Following Malabou, this love extends beyond deconstruction to relationships of healing and transformation.

How, then, do we as readers learn to say "I love you" differently?

In *I Love to You*, Irigaray answers, "I am listening to you" and "I give you a silence" (1996, 116–17). Integral to this listening and gift of silence is the space between ourselves and our beloved: "It is a silence made possible by the fact that neither I nor *you* are everything, that each of us is limited, marked by the negative, non-hierarchically different. A silence that is the primary gesture of *I love to you*. Without it, the 'to,' such as I understand it, is impossible. This silence is the condition for a possible respect for myself and for the other within our respective limits" (1996, 117). The grammatical repositioning of the beloved, displaced from its usual place of object in the phrase "I love you," opens up the possibility of an intersubjective relationality. In *To Be Two*, Irigaray writes, "Far from wanting to possess you in linking myself to you, I preserve a 'to,' a safeguard of the in-direction between us—*I Love to You*, and not: I love you. This 'to' safeguards a place of transcendence between us, a place of respect which is both obligated and desired, a place of possible alliance" (2001b, 19).

How do we read Irigaray's words, which themselves invoke a continual process of relationality and becoming? As Margaret Whitford has written, "The important thing is to engage with Irigaray *in order to go beyond her*" (1991, 6). How we understand this "going beyond" might allow us to respond to critics such as Ellen Armour (1999), whose insightful reading of Irigaray forces us to acknowledge the stakes involved with proclaiming sexual difference as the central problem of philosophy. Armour writes, "If one thinks that only men are likely to confuse neutrality with sameness, then one might not view this leaning as problematic. If, however, one remembers that feminism has shown itself to be as vulnerable to an economy of sameness as any other aspect of western culture, one is disturbed by this slippage" (1999, 107). Armour goes on to point out the erasure of race from sexual difference in Irigaray's writings, referring, for example, to the fact that "all women are not *legitimate* objects of exchange to all men" (128). She concludes, then, that the "power of her [Irigaray's] insistence that women resist the form of oppression that most affects them is undercut by her own failure to attend to any salient difference in oppression" (133). According to this critique, the analysis of sexual difference can become complicit with the problem of evil, enacting blindness toward other systemic forms of oppression that it excludes as equally fundamental. However, responding to a similar critique by Judith Butler in a published conversation between Butler and Rosi Braidotti, Braidotti argues, "You must not confuse the diagnostic function of sexual difference with its strategic or programmatic aims" (1994, 39). Braidotti urges us to understand "sexual difference" as a critically rigorous project that starts with "the political will to assert the specificity of the lived, female bodily experience" (40). In responding to both Armour's and Braidotti's concerns, we can perhaps turn back to Malabou's strategy of reading in order to think through the need to both take up Irigaray's project, and in turn, discern its own limitations.

Describing the histological property of plasticity as regenerative and healing, Malabou opens up the possibility that reading plastically reconstitutes a text on the basis of its very defect (2000, 139). According to Malabou, this regeneration carries a text beyond its deconstruction to a new configuration. Through Braidotti's reading of sexual difference as diagnostic, a plastic reading will take up Irigaray's philosophy as a critical theory for rereading and reconfiguring the Western tradition. Following Armour, we will need to apply this regenerative strategy back to the Irigarayan text itself, identifying the limits of Irigaray's texts for theorizing race in relation to sexual difference. Armour's critique points to the need for the Irigarayan texts themselves to be healed through careful and critical readings.

The problematic of evil elaborated by Irigaray, then, is not only traversed within her own texts but is also effected by an ongoing critical negotiation by her readers with her project. We bring our own sexed identities and subjectivities to the Irigarayan text. Irigaray herself points to the difficulties of creating relations with both men and women through her writing when she asks, toward the end of *To Be Two*, "How do I speak to you at the same time, my female and male readers?" (2001b, 103). If Irigaray's language itself is incarnational, as she indicates in *I Love to You* and *To Be Two*, are we opening ourselves to the work of divinity when we read Irigaray's texts? Perhaps both men and women are critically necessary as readers in order to effect this incarnational performativity, since the incarnation occurs in between the two, always in relationality and in difference. As well, since the divine invoked by Irigaray includes both a relationship with the divine and an incarnational process of becoming divine, it seems that our own individual and singular faith stories need to be at work within our own reading practices. How we carry out the incarnational logic of Irigaray's texts will depend on our own critical relations with the divine as a trope, as a story, and as an ongoing revelatory encounter. The problem of evil, then, will both shift and remain continuous as a movement of repair, plastic transformation, and confessional storytelling.

Notes

1. In this chapter, I rely on Lisabeth During's translations of Malabou, which have recently been published in book form (Malabou 2005).
2. Malabou explicitly situates her project of reading plastically, the "metamorphic procedure" that she is invoking and enacting, as "beyond deconstruction" (2000a, 140). She describes this relationship of reading, one that attends to how a text repairs and regenerates itself, as carrying the text beyond its deconstruction or disjunction to its convalescence. Especially if we learn from Malabou's reflections on her methodology in order to read Irigaray in a similarly regenerative mode, we may be also positioning Irigaray's project as "beyond deconstruction." This positioning suggests a strategy for attending to the continuities as well as the differences performed by Irigaray's various texts. Given that Irigaray's texts have shifted significantly in style from an earlier deconstructive mode to a more visionary and directly political approach, Malabou's methodology may provide us with theoretical resources for engaging with the transformative logic at work within the overall movement of Irigaray's thinking. I see enormous potential here to respond to critics who claim that Irigaray's later texts are less deconstructively rigorous than her earlier work.
3. Irigaray's own readings of Hegel resemble and contrast with Malabou's methodology in significant ways. She too attends to the logic of Hegelian concepts, for example, thinking through the Hegelian ethical from the position of sexual difference in order to renew the dialectic itself. She employs the dialectical logic to envision a productive confrontation that would actualize a sexual dialectic: "Respect for the negative, the play of the dialectic between us, would enable us to remain ourselves and to create an oeuvre with the other. And thus to develop, building a temporality instead of believing in eternal promises. We can construct a History on the basis of an interiority without power" (1996, 148). However, Irigaray ultimately prioritizes the logic of sexual difference over the logic of the Hegelian dialectic: "Hegel's method is based on contradiction, on contradictory propositions. Yet sex does not obey the logic of contradiction. It bends and folds to accommodate that logic but it does not conform" (1993c, 139).
4. Irigaray concludes her essay, "From *The Forgetting of Air* (1999) to *To Be Two*" (2001b), by describing the actualization of her project of thinking

through sexual difference as a new epoch for both the East and West: "This new stage of a historial destiny would probably permit us to enter into a new epoch of the unfolding of being, faithful to Western and Eastern traditions" (2001a, 314).

References

Armour, Ellen T. 1999. *Deconstruction, Feminist Theology, and the Problem of Difference: Subverting the Race/Gender Divide*. Chicago: University of Chicago Press.

Braidotti, Rosi, and Judith Butler. 1994. Feminism by any other name: Interview. *Differences: A Journal of Feminist Cultural Studies* 6 (2 & 3): 27–61.

During, Lisabeth. 2000. Catherine Malabou and the currency of Hegelianism. *Hypatia* 15 (4): 190–95.

Hegel, G. W. F. 1975. *Aesthetics: Lectures on Fine Art*. Trans. T. M. Knox. Oxford: Clarendon Press.

———. 1977. *The Phenomenology of Spirit*. Trans. A. V. Miller. Oxford: Oxford University Press.

Irigaray, Luce. 1989. Equal to whom? *Differences: A Journal of Feminist Cultural Studies* 1 (2): 59–76.

———. 1991. *Marine Lover of Friedrich Nietzsche*. Trans. Gillian C. Gill. New York: Columbia University Press.

———. 1993a. *An Ethics of Sexual Difference*. Trans. Carolyn Burke and Gillian C. Gill. Ithaca, N.Y.: Cornell University Press.

———. 1993b. *Je, tu, nous: Toward a Culture of Difference*. Trans. Alison Martin. New York: Routledge.

———. 1993c. *Sexes and Genealogies*. Trans. Gillian C. Gill. New York: Columbia University Press.

———. 1993d. *This Sex Which Is Not One*. Trans. Catherine Porter with Carolyn Burke. Ithaca, N.Y.: Cornell University Press.

———. 1996. *I Love to You: Sketch of a Possible Felicity in History*. Trans. Alison Martin. New York: Routledge.

———. 1999. *The Forgetting of Air in Martin Heidegger*. Trans. Mary Beth Mader. Austin: University of Texas Press.

———. 2001a. From *The forgetting of air* to *To be two*. Trans. Heidi Bostic and Stephen Pluháček. In *Feminist Interpretations of Martin Heidegger*, ed. Nancy J. Holland and Patricia Huntington. University Park: Pennsylvania State University Press.

———. 2001b. *To Be Two*. Trans. Monique M. Rhodes and Marco F. Cocito-Monoc. New York: Routledge.

Jantzen, Grace M. 1999. *Becoming Divine: Towards a Feminist Philosophy of Religion*. Bloomington: Indiana University Press.

Jones, Serene. 1995. Divining women: Irigaray and feminist theologies. *Yale French Studies* 87: 42–67.

Keller, Catherine. 1998. Christianity. In *A Companion to Feminist Philosophy*, ed. Alison M. Jaggar and Iris Marion Young. Malden, Mass.: Blackwell Publishers.

Lévinas, Emmanuel. 1989. *The Lévinas Reader,* ed. Séan Hand. Malden, Mass.: Blackwell Publishers.
Malabou, Catherine. 2000a. Deconstructive and/or "plastic" readings of Hegel. *Bulle-
tin of the Hegel Society of Great Britain* 41 (2): 132–41.
——. 2000b. The future of Hegel: Plasticity, temporality, dialectic. Trans. Lisabeth
During. *Hypatia* 15 (4): 196–219.
——. 2005. *The Future of Hegel: Plasticity, Temporality, Dialectic.* Trans. Lisabeth
During. New York: Routledge.
Martin, Alison. 1998. Luce Irigaray and the adoption of Christianity. *Paragraph* 21 (1):
101–20.
——. 2000. *Luce Irigaray and the Question of the Divine.* Leeds, England: Maney Pub-
lishing for the Modern Humanities Research Association.
Merleau-Ponty, Maurice. The intertwining—the chiasm. Trans. Alphonso Lingis. In
The Visible and the Invisible, ed. Claude Lefort. Evanston, Ill.: Northwestern
University Press.
Oliver, Kelly. 2001. *Witnessing: Beyond Recognition.* Minneapolis: University of Minne-
sota Press.
Ward, Graham. 1996. Divinity and sexuality: Luce Irigaray and Christology. *Modern
Theology* 12 (2): 221–37.
Warminski, Andrzej. 1987. Prefatory postscript: Interpretation and reading. In *Read-
ings in Interpretation.* Minneapolis: University of Minnesota Press.
Whitford, Margaret. 1991. *Luce Irigaray: Philosophy in the Feminine.* New York: Rout-
ledge.

4   Genocide and Social Death

Claudia Card

This essay develops the hypothesis that social death is utterly central to the evil of genocide, not just when a genocide is primarily cultural but even when it is homicidal on a massive scale. It is social death that enables us to distinguish the peculiar evil of genocide from the evils of other mass murders. Even genocidal murders can be viewed as extreme means to the primary end of social death. Social vitality exists through relationships, contemporary and intergenerational, that create an identity that gives meaning to a life. Major loss of social vitality is a loss of identity and consequently a serious loss of meaning for one's existence. Putting social death at the center takes the focus off individual choice, individual goals, individual careers, and body counts and puts it on relationships that create community and set the context that gives meaning to choices and goals. If my hypothesis is correct, the term "cultural genocide" is probably both redundant and misleading—redundant, if the social death present in all genocide implies cultural death as well, and misleading, if "cultural genocide" suggests that some genocides do not include cultural death.

1. What Is Feminist about Analyzing Genocide?

The question has been asked, what is feminist about this project?[1] Why publish it in a book of feminist philosophy? The answer is both simple and complex. Simply, it is the history behind the project and the perspective from which it is carried out, rather than a focus on women or gender, that make the project feminist. Some of the complexities are as follows.

The evil of genocide falls not only on men and boys but on women and girls, typically unarmed, untrained in defense against violence, and often also responsible for care of the wounded, the sick, the disabled, babies, children, and the elderly. Because genocide targets both sexes, rather than being specific to women's experience, there is some risk of its being neglected in feminist thought. It is also the case that with few exceptions (such as Schott 1999; Card 1996 and 1997) both feminist and non-feminist philosophical reflections on war and other public violence have tended to neglect the impact on victims. Philosophers have thought mostly about the positions of perpetrators and decision-makers (most of them men), with some feminist speculation on what might change if more women were among the decision-makers and if women were subject to military conscription. The damage of war and terrorism is commonly assessed in terms of its ruin of individual careers, body counts, statistics on casualties, and material costs of rebuilding. Attention goes to preventing such violence and the importance of doing so, but less to the experience and responses of the majority of victims and survivors, who are civilians, not soldiers. In bringing to the fore the responses of victims of both sexes, Holocaust literature stands in sharp contrast to these trends. Central to Holocaust literature is reflection on the meaning of genocide.

Women's Studies, in its engagement with differences among women, has moved from its earlier aim to train a feminist eye on the world and all kinds of issues (such as evil) to the more limited aim of studying women and gender. I return here to the earlier conception that recognizes not only the study of women, feminism, or gender, but feminist approaches to issues of ethics and social theory generally, whether the word *feminist* is used or not. My interests move toward commonalities in our experiences of evil, not only commonalities among women differently situated but commonalities shared with many men as well. Yet my lens is feminist, polished through decades of reflection on women's multifarious experiences of misogyny and oppression. What we notice, through a feminist lens, is influenced by long habits of attending to emotional response, relationships that define who we (not just women and girls) are, and the significance of the concrete particular.

Centering social death accommodates the position, controversial among genocide scholars, that genocidal acts are not always or necessarily homicidal. Forcibly sterilizing women or men of a targeted group, or forcibly separating their children from them for re-education for assimilation into another group, can also be genocidal in aim or effect.[2] Such policies can be aimed at or achieve the eventual destruction of the social identity of those so treated. It may appear that transported children simply undergo change in social identity, not that they lose all social vitality. That may be the intent. Yet, parents' social vitality is a casualty of children's forced re-education, and in reality, transported children may fail to make a satisfying transition.

The Holocaust was not only a program of mass murder but an assault on Jewish social vitality. The assault was experienced by hidden children who survived as well as by those who died. Hitler's sterilization program and Nuremberg laws that left German Jews stateless were parts of the genocide, not preludes to it. Jews who had converted to Christianity (or whose parents or grandparents had done so) were hunted down and murdered, even though one might think their social identities had already changed.[3] This pursuit makes a certain perverted sense if the idea was to extinguish in them all possibility of social vitality, simply on grounds of their ancestral roots. Mass murder is the most extreme method of genocide, denying members of targeted groups any degree or form of social vitality whatever. To extinguish all possibility of social vitality, child transportation and re-education are insufficient; it may be necessary to commit mass murder or drive victims mad or rob them of self-respect, all of which were done to Holocaust victims.

Although I approach genocide from a history of feminist habits of research and reflection, I say little here about the impact of genocide on women and girls as opposed to its impact on men and boys. I would not suggest that females suffered more or worse than males. Nor am I especially interested in such questions as whether lifelong habits of caregiving offer survival advantages to segregated women. (Evidence appears to be that no one survives without others' care and help.) My interest here is, rather, in what makes genocide the specific evil that it is, what distinguishes it from other atrocities, and what kinds of atrocities are rightly recognized as genocidal. Feminist habits of noticing are useful for suggesting answers to these questions.

2. Genocide, War, and Justice

Genocide need not be part of a larger war, although it commonly is. But it can be regarded as itself a kind of one-sided war. Precedents for regarding one-sided attacks as wars are found in the idea of a "war on drugs" and in the title of Lucy Dawidowicz's *The War against the Jews* (1975). If genocide is war, it is a profoundly unjust kind of war, perniciously unjust, an injustice that is also an evil.

John Rawls (1999) opened his first book on justice with the observation that justice is the first virtue of institutions as truth is of systems of thought. No matter how efficient and well-arranged, he wrote, laws and institutions must be reformed or abolished if they are unjust (3). Like critics who found these claims overstated, even Rawls noted that although "these propositions seem to express our intuitive conviction of the primacy of justice," "no doubt they are expressed too strongly" (4). Not all injustices, even in society's basic structure, make lives insupportable, intolerable, or indecent. Reforms are not always worth the expense of their implementation. Had Rawls made his claim about abolishing unjust institutions in regard to *pernicious* injustices, however, it should not have been controversial: laws and institutions must be abolished when they are evil.

Not all injustices are evils, as the harms they produce vary greatly in importance. Some injustices are relatively tolerable. They may not impact people's lives in a deep or lasting way, even though they are wrong and should be eliminated—unjust salary discriminations, for example, when the salaries in question are all high. An injustice becomes an evil when it inflicts harms that make victims' lives unbearable, indecent, or impossible, or that make victims' deaths indecent.[4] Injustices of war are apt to fall into this category. Certainly genocide does.

3. The Concept of Genocide

"Genocide" combines the Greek *genos* for race or tribe with the Latin *cide* for killing. The term was coined by Raphael Lemkin (1944), an attorney and refugee scholar from Poland who served in the United States War Department. He campaigned as early as the 1930s for an international convention to outlaw genocide, and his persistence resulted in the United Nations Genocide

Convention of 1948. Although this convention is widely cited, it was not translated into action in international courts until the 1990s, more than forty years later. The first state to bring a case to the World Court under the convention was Bosnia-Herzegovina in 1993. It was not until 1998 that the first verdict interpreting that convention was rendered, when the Rwanda tribunal found Jean-Paul Akayesu guilty on nine counts for his participation in the genocide in Rwanda in 1994 (Orentlicher 1999, 153). The United States did not pass legislation implementing ratification of the 1948 genocide convention until 1988 and then only with significant reservations that were somewhat disabling (Lang 1992, 1:400). Such resistance is interesting in view of questions raised during the interim regarding the morality of U.S. conduct in Vietnam. By the time the United States ratified the convention, 97 other UN members had already done so.

The *term* "genocide" is thus relatively new, and the Holocaust is widely agreed to be its paradigmatic instance. Yet Lemkin and many others find the *practice* of genocide ancient. In their sociological survey from ancient times to the present, Frank Chalk and Kurt Jonassohn (1990) discuss instances of apparent genocide that range from the Athenians' annihilation of the people of the island of Melos in the fifth century B.C.E. (recorded by Thucydides) and the ravaging of Carthage by Romans in 146 B.C.E. (also listed by Lemkin as the first of his historical examples of wars of extermination) through mass killings in Bangladesh, Cambodia, and East Timor in the second half of the twentieth century (Chalk and Jonassohn 1990). Controversies are ongoing over whether to count as genocidal the annihilation of indigenous peoples in the Americas and Australia (who succumbed in vast numbers to diseases brought by Europeans), Stalin's induced mass starvation of the 1930s (ostensibly an economically motivated measure), and the war conducted by the United States in Vietnam.

The literature of comparative genocide—that historian Peter Novick (1999) calls "comparative atrocitology"—so far includes relatively little published work by philosophers. Here is what I have found. Best known is probably Jean-Paul Sartre's 1967 essay, "On Genocide" (Sartre 1968), written for the Sartre-Russell International War Crimes Tribunal, which was convened to consider war crimes by the United States in Vietnam. In 1974 Hugo Adam Bedau published a long and thoughtful essay, "Genocide in Vietnam?" (1974, 5–46), responding to Sartre and others who have raised the question of whether the United States was guilty of perpetrating genocide in Vietnam. Bedau argues for a negative answer to that question, relying primarily on intent as an essential factor in genocide. His view is that the intent of the United States in Vietnam was not to exterminate a people, even if that was nearly a consequence. Berel Lang's essay "The Concept of Genocide" (1984/85) and the first chapter of his book *Act and Idea in the Nazi Genocide* (1990) are helpful in their explorations of the meanings and roles of intent in defining "genocide."

Other significant philosophical works include Alan S. Rosenbaum's anthology *Is the Holocaust Unique? Perspectives on Comparative Genocide* (1996), which discusses the Nazi assault on Jews and Romani during World War II, the Atlantic slave trade, the Turkish slaughter of Armenians in 1915, and Stalin's induced famine. Legal scholar Martha Minow (1998) reflects philosophically on measures lying between vengeance and forgiveness taken by states in response to genocide and mass murder. Jonathan Glover's *Humanity: A Moral History of the Twentieth Century* (2000), in some ways the most ambitious recent philosophical discussion of evils, includes reflections on Rwanda, Stalin, and Nazism. The Institute for Genocide Studies and the Association of Genocide Scholars (which holds conventions) attract an interdisciplinary group of scholars, including a small number of philosophers. And the Society for the Philosophic Study of Genocide and the Holocaust sponsors sessions at conventions of the American Philosophical Association.

On the whole, historians, psychologists, sociologists, and political scientists have contributed more than philosophers to genocide scholarship. Naturally, their contributions as social scientists have been empirically oriented, focused on such matters as origins, contributing causes, effects, monitoring, and prevention. Yet, philosophical issues run throughout the literature. They include foundational matters, such as the meaning of "genocide," which appears to be a highly contested concept, and such issues of ethics and political philosophy as whether perpetrators can be punished in a meaningful way that respects moral standards. If adequate retribution is morally impossible, and if deterrence is unlikely for those who are ideologically motivated, then what is the point in punishing perpetrators? If there is nevertheless some point sufficient to justify doing so, then who should be punished, by whom, and how?

Controversies over the meaning of "genocide" lead naturally to the closely related question of whether genocide is ethically different from non-genocidal mass murder. The practical issue here is whether and, if so, why it is important to add the category of genocide to existing crimes against humanity and war crimes. Crimes against humanity were important additions to war crimes in that, unlike war crimes, they need not be perpetrated during wartime or in connection with a war, and they can be inflicted against citizens of the same state as the perpetrator. But given that murder of civilians by soldiers is already a war crime and a human rights violation, one may wonder whether the crime of genocide captures anything they omit.

If the social death of individual victims is central to genocide, then, arguably, genocide does capture something more. What distinguishes genocide is not that it has a different kind of victim, namely, groups (although it is a convenient shorthand to speak of targeting groups). Rather, the kind of harm suffered by individual victims of genocide, in virtue of their group membership, is not captured by other crimes. To get a sense of what is at stake in the hypothesis that social death is central, let us turn briefly to controversies over the meaning of "genocide."

The definition of "genocide" is currently in such flux that the Association of Genocide Scholars asks members on its information page (printed in a members directory) to specify which definition of "genocide" they use in their work. A widely cited definition is that of the 1948 UN Convention on the Prevention and Punishment of the Crime of Genocide:

> Genocide means any of the following acts committed with the intent to destroy, in whole or in part, a nation, ethnical [sic], racial or religious group, as such: (a) killing members of the group; (b) causing serious bodily or mental harm to members of the group; (c) deliberately inflicting on the group conditions of life calculated to bring about its physical destruction in whole or in part; (d) imposing measures intended to prevent births within the group; (e) forcibly transferring children of the group to another group. (in Robinson 1960, 147)

Every clause of this definition is controversial.

Israel Charny (1994) and others criticize the UN definition for not recognizing political groups, such as the Communist Party, as possible targets of genocide. Political groups had been, in fact, recognized in an earlier draft of the genocide convention, and Chalk and Jonassohn (1990) do recognize political groups as targets of genocide in their historical survey. Some scholars, however, prefer the term "politicide" for these cases and reserve the term "genocide" for the annihilation of groups into which one is (ordinarily) born—racial, ethnic, national, or religious groups. Yet one is not necessarily, of course, born into one's current national or religious group, and either one's current or one's former membership can prove fatal. Further, some people's political identity may be as important to their lives as religious identity is to the lives of others. And so, the distinction between "genocide" and "politicide" has seemed arbitrary to many critics. A difficulty is, of course, where to draw the line if political groups are recognized as possible victims. But line-drawing is not a difficulty peculiar to political groups.

The last three clauses of the UN definition—conditions of life intended to destroy the group "in whole or in part," preventing births, and transferring children—count as genocidal many acts that are aimed at cultural destruction, even though they are not homicidal. "Preventing births" is not restricted to sterilization but has been interpreted to include segregation of the sexes and bans on marriage. Social vitality is destroyed when the social relations—organizations, practices, institutions—of the members of a group are irreparably damaged or demolished. Such destruction is a commonly intended consequence of war rape, which has aimed at family breakdown. Although Lemkin regarded such deeds as both ethnocidal and genocidal, some scholars prefer simply to call them ethnocides (or "cultural genocides") and reserve the term "genocide" (unqualified) for events that include mass death. The idea is, apparently, that physical death is more extreme and therefore, presumably, worse than social death. That physical death is worse, or even more extreme, is not obvious, however, but deserves scrutiny, and I will return to it.

Even the clauses of the UN definition that specify killing group members or causing them serious bodily or mental harm are vague and can cover a wide range of possible harms. How many people must be killed in order for a deed to be genocidal? What sort of bodily harm counts? (Must there be lasting disablement?) What counts as "mental harm?" (Is post-traumatic stress sufficient?) If the definition is to have practical consequences in the responses of nations to perpetrators, these questions can become important. They become important with respect to questions of intervention and reparations, for example.

Although most scholars agree on including intention in the definition of genocide, there is no consensus regarding the content of the required intention. Must the relevant intention include destruction of all members of a group as an aim or purpose? Would it be enough that the group was knowingly destroyed, as a foreseeable consequence of the pursuit of some other aim? Must the full extent of the destruction even be foreseeable, if the policy of which it is a consequence is already clearly immoral? Bedau (1974) makes much of the content of the relevant intention in his argument that whatever war crimes the United States committed in Vietnam, they were not genocidal, because the intent was not to destroy the people of Vietnam as such, even if that destruction was both likely and foreseeable.

Charny (1994, 64–94), however, objects to an analogous claim made by some critics who, he reports, held that because Stalin's intent was to obtain enough grain to trade for industrial materials for the Soviet Union, rather than to kill the millions who died from this policy, Stalin's famine was not a genocide. Charny argues that because Stalin foresaw the fatal consequences of his grain policies, those policies should count as genocidal. As in common philosophical criticisms of the "doctrine of the double effect," Charny appears to reject as ethically insignificant a distinction between intending and "merely foreseeing," at least in this kind of case.

The doctrine of double-effect has been relied on by the Catholic Church to resolve certain ethical questions regarding life and death issues (Solomon 1992, 1:268–69). The doctrine maintains that under certain conditions it is not wrong to do something that has a foreseeable effect (not an aim) which is such that an act *aiming* at that effect would have been wrong. The first condition of its not being wrong is that the act one performs is not wrong in itself, and the second condition is that the effect at which it would be wrong to aim is not instrumental toward the end at which the act does aim. Thus, the Church has found it wrong to perform an abortion that would kill a fetus in order to save the mother but, at the same time, not wrong to remove a cancerous uterus when doing so would also result in the death of a fetus. The reasoning is that in the case of the cancerous uterus, the fetus's death is not an aim; nor is it a means to removing the uterus but only a consequence of doing so. Many find this distinction troubling and far from obvious. Why is the death of a fetus from abortion not also only a consequence? The aim could be redescribed as "to remove the fetus from the uterus in order to save the mother," rather than "to kill the fetus to save the mother," and at least when the fetus need not be destroyed in the very process of removal, one might argue that death due to extrauterine nonviability is not a means to the fetus's removal, either.

The position of the critics who do not want to count Stalin's starvation of the peasants as a genocide would appear to imply that if the peasants' deaths were not instrumental toward Stalin's goal but only an unfortunate consequence, the foreseeability of those deaths does not make Stalin's policy genocidal, any more than the foreseeability of the death of the fetus in the case of a hysterectomy performed to remove a cancerous uterus makes that surgery murderous. Charny's position appears to imply, on the contrary, that the foreseeability of the peasants' mass death is enough to constitute genocidal intent, even if it was not intended instrumentally toward Stalin's aims.

Some controversies focus on whether the intent was "to destroy a group as such." One might argue with Bedau, drawing on Lang's discussion of the intent issues (1990, 3–29), that the intent is "to destroy a group as such" when it is not just accidental that the group is destroyed in the process of pursuing a further end. Thus, if it was not just accidental that the peasant class was destroyed in the process of Stalin's pursuit of grain to trade for industrial materials, he could be said to have destroyed the peasants "as such," even if peasant starvation played no more causal role in making grain available than killing the fetus plays in removing a cancerous uterus. Alternatively, some argue that the words "as such" do not belong in the definition because, ethically, it does not matter whether a group is deliberately destroyed "as such" or simply deliberately destroyed. Chalk and Jonassohn (1990) appear to take this view.

Further, one might pursue the question of whether it is really necessary even to be able to foresee the full extent of the consequences in order to be accurately described as having a genocidal intent. Historian Steven Katz argues in *The Holocaust in Historical Context* (1994) that the mass deaths of Native Americans and Native Australians were not genocides because they resulted from epidemics, not from murder. The suggestion is that the consequences here were not reasonably foreseeable. David Stannard, American Studies scholar at the University of Hawaii, however, finds the case less simple, for it can be argued that the epidemics were not just accidental (Stannard 1992, 1996). Part of the controversy regards the facts: to what extent were victims deliberately infected, as when the British, and later Americans, distributed blankets infected with small pox virus?[5] And to what extent did victims succumb to unintended infection stemming from ordinary exposure to Europeans with the virus? But, also, part of the controversy is philosophical. If mass deaths from disease result from wrongdoing, and if perpetrators could know that the intolerably destructive consequences had an uncontrollable (and therefore somewhat unpredictable) extent, then, does it matter, ethically, whether the wrongdoers could foresee the full extent of the consequences? One might argue that it does not, on the ground that they already knew enough to appreciate that what they were doing was evil.

What is the importance of success in achieving a genocidal aim? Must genocide succeed in eliminating an entire group? An assault, to be homicide, must succeed in killing. Otherwise, it is a mere attempt, and an unlawful attempted homicide generally carries a less severe penalty than a successful one. Bedau and Lang point out, however, that "genocide" does not appear to be analogous to "homicide" in that way. There may still be room for some distinction between genocide and attempted genocide (although Lang appears not to recognize any such distinction) if we distinguish between partially formed and fully formed intentions, or if we distinguish among stages in carrying out a complex intention. But in paradigmatic instances of genocide, such as the Holocaust, there are always some survivors, even when there is clear evidence that the intention was to eliminate everyone in the group. There is general agreement that at least some mass killing with that wrongful intention is genocidal. The existence of survivors is not sufficient to negate fully formed genocidal intent. There may be survivors even after all stages of a complex genocidal intention have been implemented. Bedau observes, however, that there is a certain analogy between "genocide" and "murder," which enables us to contrast both with homicide. Both genocide and murder include wrongfulness in the very concept, whereas a homicide can be justifiable. Homicide is not necessarily unlawful or even immoral. In contrast, genocide and murder are, in principle, incapable of justification.

On my understanding of what constitutes an evil, there are two basic elements: (1) culpable wrongdoing by one or more perpetrators; and (2) reasonably foreseeable intolerable harm to victims, resulting from that wrongdoing.[6] Most often the second element, intolerable harm, is what distinguishes evils from ordinary wrongs. Intentions may be necessary to defining genocide. But they are not always necessary for culpable wrongdoing, as omissions—negligence, recklessness, or carelessness—can be sufficient. When culpable wrongdoing *is* intentional, however, its aim need not be to cause intolerable harm. A seriously culpable deed is evil when the doer is willing to inflict intolerable harm on others even in the course of aiming at some other goal. If what is at stake in controversies regarding the meaning of "genocide" is whether a mass killing is sufficiently evil to merit the opprobrium attaching to the term "genocide," a good case can be made for including assaults on many kinds of groups inflicted through many kinds of culpable wrongdoing. Yet that leaves the question of whether the genocidal nature of a killing has special ethical import, and if so, what that import is and how, if at all, it may restrict the scope of "genocide." I turn to these and related questions next.

4. The Specific Evils of Genocide

Genocide is not simply unjust (although it certainly is unjust); it is also evil. It characteristically includes the one-sided killing of defenseless civilians— babies, children, the elderly, the sick, the disabled, and the injured of both genders along with their usually female caretakers—simply on the basis of their national, religious, ethnic, or other political identity. It targets people on the basis of who they are rather than on the basis of what they have done, what they might do, even what they are capable of doing. (One commentator says genocide kills people on the basis of *what* they are, not even *who* they are.)

Genocide is a paradigm of what Israeli philosopher Avishai Margalit calls "indecent" in that it not only destroys victims but first humiliates them by deliberately inflicting an "utter loss of freedom and control over one's vital interests" (1996, 115). Vital interests can be transgenerational and thus survive one's death. Before death, genocide victims are ordinarily deprived of control over vital transgenerational interests and more immediate vital interests. They may be literally stripped naked; robbed of their last possessions; lied to about the most vital matters; witness to the murder of family, friends, and neighbors; made to participate in their own murder; and, if female, they are likely to be also violated sexually.[7] Victims of genocide are commonly killed with no regard for lingering suffering or exposure. They, and their corpses, are routinely treated with utter disrespect. These historical facts, not simply mass murder, account for much of the moral opprobrium attaching to the concept of genocide.

Yet such atrocities, it may be argued, are already war crimes, if conducted during wartime, and they can otherwise or also be prosecuted as crimes against humanity. Why, then, add the specific crime of genocide? What, if anything, is not already captured by laws that prohibit such things as the rape, enslavement, torture, forced deportation, and the degradation of individuals? Is any ethically distinct harm done to members of the targeted group that would not have been done had they been targeted simply as individuals rather than because of their group membership? This is the question that I find central in arguing that genocide is not simply reducible to mass death, to any of the other war crimes, or to the crimes against humanity just enumerated. I believe the answer is affirmative: the harm is ethically distinct, although on the question of whether it is worse, I wish only to question the assumption that it is not.

Specific to genocide is the harm inflicted on its victims' social vitality. It is not just that one's group membership is the occasion for harms that are definable independently of one's identity as a member of the group. When a group with its own cultural identity is destroyed, its survivors lose their cultural heritage and may even lose their intergenerational connections. To use Orlando Patterson's terminology, in that event, they may become "socially dead" and their descendants *"natally alienated,"* no longer able to pass along and build upon the traditions, cultural developments (including languages), and projects of earlier generations (1982, 5–9). The harm of social death is not necessarily less extreme than that of physical death. Social death can even aggravate physical death by making it indecent, removing all respectful and caring ritual, social connections, and social contexts that are capable of making dying bearable and even of making one's death meaningful. In my view, the special evil of genocide lies in its infliction of not just physical death (when it does that) but social death, producing a consequent meaninglessness of one's life and even of its termination. This view, however, is controversial.

African American and Jewish philosopher Lawrence Mordekhai Thomas argues that although American slavery natally alienated slaves—that slaves were born severed from most normal social and cultural ties that connect one with both earlier and later generations—the Holocaust did not natally alienate Jews (1993, 150–57). He does not explicitly generalize about genocide and natal alienation but makes this judgment in regard to the particular genocide of the Holocaust. Yet, the apparent implication is that a genocide no more successful than the Holocaust (an accepted paradigm of genocide) is not natally alienating, because enough victims survive and enough potential targets escape that they are able to preserve the group's cultural traditions. Thomas's analyses of patterns of evil in American slavery and the Holocaust are philosophically groundbreaking and have been very helpful to me in thinking about these topics. Yet I want to question this conclusion that he draws. I want to consider the Nazi genocide in light of the more fundamental idea of social death, of which natal alienation is one special case, not the only case.

Thomas's conception of natal alienation is more specific and more restricted than Patterson's conception of social death. Thomas seems not to be thinking of lost family connections and lost community connections, the particular connections of individuals to one another, but, rather, of the connections of each individual with a culture in general, with its traditions and practices. He finds members of an ethnic group natally alienated when the cultural practices into which they are born "forcibly prevent most of them from fully participating in, and thus having a secure knowledge of, their historical-cultural traditions" (1993, 150). He notes that after seven generations of slavery, the memories of one's culture of origin are totally lost, which is certainly plausible. Patterson used the term "natal alienation" for the extreme case of being *born* to *social death,* with individual social connections, past and future, cut off from all but one's oppressors at the very outset of one's life. Hereditary slavery yields a paradigm of natal alienation in this sense. Slaves who are treated as non-persons have (practically) no socially supported ties not only to a cultural heritage but even to immediate kin (parents, children, siblings) and peers. As a consequence of being cut off from kin and community, they also lose their cultural heritage. But the first step was to destroy existing social ties with family and community, to "ex-communicate them from society," as Patterson puts it. In Rawlsian terms, they were first excluded from the benefits and protections of the basic structure of the society into which they were born and in which they must live out their lives. Loss of cultural heritage follows.

Those who are *natally* alienated are *born* already socially dead. Natal alienation might be a clue to descent from genocide survivors (although not proof, insofar as genocide depends also on intent). Thus, the natal alienation of slaves and their descendants, when slavery is hereditary, is one clue to a possible history of genocide committed against their ancestors.

Thomas recognizes that alienation is not "all or nothing." A lost cultural heritage can be rediscovered, or partially recovered, later or in other places. Those who were alienated from some cultures may become somewhat integrated into others. Still, he denies that the Holocaust natally alienated Jews from Judaism "because the central tenets of Judaism—the defining traditions of Judaism—endured in spite of Hitler's every intention to the contrary" (1993, 153).

The question, however, should be not simply whether the traditions survived but whether individual Jewish victims were able to sustain their connections to those traditions. Sustaining the connections meaningfully requires a family or community setting for observance. Many Jews, of course, escaped being victimized, because of where they lived (in the United States, for example) and because the Axis powers were contained and defeated. They were able to maintain Jewish traditions with which survivors might conceivably connect or reconnect. But many survivors were unable to do so. Some found family members after the war or created new families. Many did not. Many lost entire families, their entire villages, and the way of life embodied in the *shtetl* (eastern European village). Some could not produce more children because of medical experiments performed on them in the camps. Many survivors lost access to social memories embodied in such cultural institutions as libraries and synagogues.

Responding to the observation that entire communities of Jews were destroyed and that the Yiddish language is on the way out, Thomas argues that members of those communities were destroyed not "as such" (as *shtetl* Jews, for example) but more simply "as Jews," and that the entire community of Jews was not destroyed.[8] He concludes that "the question must be whether the Holocaust was natally alienating of Jews as such, without regard to any specific community of Jews" (1993, 153). In answering negatively, he is apparently thinking of survivors who re-established a Jewish life after the war, rather than of non-European Jews who were potential victims and whose positions might be regarded as somewhat analogous to those of unhunted and unenslaved Africans at the time of the African slave trade.

Some European Jews survived, however, only by passing as Christians. Some hidden children who were raised by strangers to be Christians only discovered their Jewish heritage later, if at all. If they were full members of the societies in which they survived, Thomas does not consider them natally alienated. Those who pass as members of another religion need not be socially dead, even if they are alienated from their religion of origin. Still, if they were originally connected in a vital way with their inherited religion and if they then experienced no vital connection to the new one, arguably, then, they do suffer a degree of social death. More clearly, those who were made stateless before being murdered were certainly treated, socially, as non-persons. National Socialist decrees robbed them of social support for ties to family, peers, and community; stripped their rights to earn a living, own property, attend public schools, even ride public transportation; and on arrival at the camps they were torn from family members. Although they were not *born* to social death, they were nevertheless intentionally deprived of all social vitality before their physical murder.

For those who survive physically, mere knowledge and memory are insufficient to create social vitality, even if they are necessary. Those who cannot participate in the social forms they remember do not have real social vitality but only the memory of it. Further, from 1933 to 1945 many children were born to a condition that became progressively more *natally* alienating.

Contrary to the apparent implication of Thomas's hypothesis regarding the differences between American slavery and the Holocaust, social death seems to me to be a concept central to the harm of genocide, at least as important to what is evil about the Holocaust as the mass physical murder.

Although social vitality is essential to a decent life for both women and men, the sexes have often played different roles in its creation and maintenance. If men are often cast in the role of the creators of (high?) culture, women have played very central roles in preserving and passing on the traditions, language, and (daily) practices from one generation to the next and in maintaining family and community relationships. Where such generalizations hold, the blocking of opportunities for creativity (being excluded from the professions, for example) would fall very heavily on men. But disruptions of family and community, such as being alienated from one's family by rape or being suddenly deported without adequate provisions (or any means of obtaining them) into a strange environment where one does not even know the language, would also fall very heavily, perhaps especially so, on women.

Most immediate victims of genocide are not born socially dead. But genocides that intentionally strip victims, prior to their murders, of the ability to participate in social activity do aim at their social death, not just their physical death. In some cases it may appear that social death is not an end in itself but simply a consequence of means taken to make mass murder easier (concentrating victims in ghettos and camps, for example). When assailants are moved by hatred, however, social death may become an end in itself. Humiliation before death appears often to have been an end in itself, not just a means. The very idea of selecting victims by social group identity suggests that it is not just the physical life of victims that is targeted but the social vitality behind that identity.

If the aim, or intention, of social death is not accidental to genocide, the survival of Jewish culture does not show that social death was not central to the evil of the Holocaust any more than the fact of survivors shows that a mass murder was not genocidal. A genocide as successful as the Holocaust achieves the aim of social death both for victims who do not survive and, to a degree and for a time, for many survivors as well. Thomas's point may still hold that descendants of survivors of the African diaspora produced by the slave trade are in general more alienated from their African cultures of origin than Holocaust survivors are from Judaism today. Yet it is true in both cases that survivors make substantial connections with other cultures. If African Americans are totally alienated from their African cultures of origin, it is also true that many Holocaust survivors and their descendants have found it impossible to embrace Judaism or even a Jewish culture after Auschwitz. The survival of a culture does not by itself tell us about the degree of alienation that is experienced by individual survivors. Knowledge of a heritage is not by itself sufficient to produce vital connections to it.

The harm of social death is not, so far as I can see, adequately captured by war crimes and other crimes against humanity. Many of those crimes are de-

fined by what can be done to individuals considered independently of their social connections: rape (when defined simply as a form of physical assault), torture, starvation. Some crimes, such as deportation and enslavement, do begin
to get at issues of disrupting social existence. But they lack the comprehensiveness of social death, at least when the enslavement in question is not hereditary
and is not necessarily for the rest of a person's life.

Still, it is true that not all victims of the Holocaust underwent social death
to the same extent as prisoners in the camps and ghettos. Entire villages on the
Eastern front were slaughtered by the *Einsatzgruppen* (mobile killing units)
without warning or prior captivity. Yet these villagers were given indecent
deaths. They were robbed of control of their vital interests and of opportunities
to mourn. Although most did not experience those deprivations for very long,
inflicted en masse, these murders do appear to have produced sudden social
death prior to physical extermination. The murders were also part of a larger
plan that included the death of Judaism, not just the deaths of Jews. Implementing that plan included gradually stripping vast numbers of Jews of social
vitality, in some places over a period of years, and it entailed that survivors, if
there were any, should not survive as Jews. The fact that the plan only partly
succeeded does not negate the central role of social death within it or the importance of that concept to genocide.

If social death is central to the harm of genocide, then it really is right not to
count as a genocide the annihilation of just any political group, however heinous. Not every political group contributes significantly to its members' cultural
identity. Many are fairly specific and short-lived, formed to support particular
issues. But then, equally, the annihilation of not just any cultural group should
count, either. Cultural groups can also be temporary and specialized, lacking in
the continuity and comprehensiveness that are presupposed by the possibility
of social death. Some mass murders—perhaps the bombings of September 11,
2001—do not appear to have had as part of their aim, intention, or effect the
prior soul murder or social death of those targeted for physical extermination.
If so, they are mass murders that are not also genocides. But mass murders and
other measures that have as part of their reasonably foreseeable consequence,
or as part of their aim, the annihilation of a group that contributes significantly
to the social identity of its members are genocidal.

Notes

1.   This question was raised by anonymous reviewers of an earlier draft of this
     essay.
2.   Unlike Native American families whose children were forcibly transported for
     re-education in the United States, many Jewish families during the Holocaust
     sought to hide their children in gentile households. Loss to the children of

Jewish social vitality was hardly the responsibility of their families' decisions to do this but, rather, the responsibility of those whose oppressive measures drove families to try to save their children in this way.

3. An example well known to philosophers is Edith Stein, student of and later assistant to Edmund Husserl. Her doctoral dissertation on the topic of empathy was originally published in 1917 (Stein 1964). She became a Catholic nun but was nevertheless deported to Auschwitz from her convent in the Netherlands.

4. For elaboration, see Card 2002, which includes chapters on war rape and on terrorism in the home. There is not a chapter on genocide, although genocide figures throughout as paradigmatic of atrocities.

5. See Stiffarm with Lang (1992, 32–33).

6. See Card (2002, chap. 2) for development of this conception of an evil.

7. Men are sometimes also violated sexually (usually by other men), although the overwhelming majority of sex crimes in war are perpetrated by men against female victims of all ages and conditions.

8. It is commonly estimated that two-thirds of European Jews died. That leaves not only one-third of European Jews but also Jewish communities in other parts of the world, such as Israel (to which some European Jews fled), the Far East, Australia, and the Americas.

References

Bedau, Hugo Adam. 1974. Genocide in Vietnam? In *Philosophy, Morality, and International Affairs,* ed. Virginia Held, Sidney Morgenbesser, and Thomas Nagel. New York: Oxford University Press.

Card, Claudia. 1996. Rape as a weapon of war. *Hypatia* 11 (4): 5–18.

———. 1997. Addendum to "Rape as a weapon of war." *Hypatia* 12 (2): 216–18.

———. 2002. *The Atrocity Paradigm: A Theory of Evil.* New York: Oxford University Press.

Chalk, Frank, and Kurt Jonassohn, eds. 1990. *The History and Sociology of Genocide: Analyses and Case Studies.* New Haven, Conn.: Yale University Press.

Charny, Israel. 1994. Toward a generic definition of genocide. In *Genocide: Conceptual and Historical Dimensions,* ed. George Andreopoulos. Philadelphia: University of Pennsylvania Press.

Davidowicz, Lucy W. 1975. *The War Against the Jews, 1933–1945.* New York: Holt, Rinehart, and Winston.

Glover, Jonathan. 2000. *Humanity: A Moral History of the Twentieth Century.* New Haven, Conn.: Yale University Press.

Katz, Steven. 1994. *The Holocaust in Historical Context,* Vol. I: *Mass Death before the Modern Age.* New York: Oxford University Press.

Lang, Berel. 1984/5. The concept of genocide. *Philosophical Forum* 16 (1-2): 1–18.

———. 1990. *Act and Idea in the Nazi Genocide.* Chicago: University of Chicago Press.

———. 1992. Genocide. *Encyclopedia of Ethics,* Vol. 1. Ed. Lawrence C. Becker with Charlotte B. Becker. New York: Garland.

Lemkin, Raphael. 1944. *Axis Rule in Occupied Europe: Laws of Occupation, Analysis of Government, Proposals for Redress.* Washington, D.C.: Carnegie Endowment for International Peace, Division of International Law.

Margalit, Avishai. 1996. *The Decent Society.* Trans. Naomi Goldblum. Cambridge, Mass.: Harvard University Press.

Minow, Martha. 1998. *Between Vengeance and Forgiveness: Facing History after Genocide and Mass Violence.* Boston: Beacon.

Novick, Peter. 1999. *The Holocaust in American Life.* Boston: Houghton Mifflin.

Orentlicher, Diane F. 1999. Genocide. In *Crimes of War: What the Public Should Know,* ed. Roy Gutman and David Rieff. New York: Norton.

Patterson, Orlando. 1982. *Slavery and Social Death.* Cambridge, Mass.: Harvard University Press.

Rawls, John. 1999. *A Theory of Justice,* rev. ed. Cambridge, Mass.: Harvard University Press.

Robinson, Nehemiah. 1960. *The Genocide Convention: A Commentary.* New York: Institute of Jewish Affairs, World Jewish Congress.

Rosenbaum, Alan S., ed. 1996. *Is the Holocaust Unique? Perspectives on Comparative Genocide.* Boulder, Colo.: Westview.

Sartre, Jean-Paul. 1968. *On Genocide.* Boston: Beacon.

Schott, Robin. 1999. Philosophical reflections on war rape. In *On Feminist Ethics and Politics,* ed. Claudia Card. Lawrence: University Press of Kansas.

Solomon, William David. 1992. Double effect. In *Encyclopedia of Ethics,* vol. 1. Ed. Lawrence C. Becker with Charlotte B. Becker. New York: Garland.

Stannard, David E. 1992. *American Holocaust: The Conquest of the New World.* New York: Oxford University Press.

———. 1996. Uniqueness as denial: The politics of genocide scholarship. In *Is the Holocaust unique?* ed. Alan S. Rosenbaum. Boulder, Colo.: Westview.

Stein, Edith. 1964. *On the Problem of Empathy.* Trans. Waltraut Stein. The Hague: Nijhoff.

Stiffarm, Lenore, with Phil Lane Jr. 1992. The demography of native North America. In *The State of Native America,* ed. Annette Jaimes. Boston, Mass.: South End.

Thomas, Lawrence Mordekhai. 1993. *Vessels of Evil: American Slavery and the Holocaust.* Philadelphia: Temple University Press.

5   Holes of Oblivion: The Banality of Radical Evil

Peg Birmingham

> Radical evil has emerged in connection with a system in which all men have become equally superfluous. The manipulators of this system believe in their own superfluousness as much as in that of all others and the totalitarian murderers are all the more dangerous because they do not care if they themselves are alive or dead, if they ever lived or never were born. The danger of the corpse factories and holes of oblivion is that today, with populations and homelessness everywhere on the increase, masses of people are continuously rendered superfluous if we continue to think of our world in utilitarian terms.
>
> Hannah Arendt, *The Origins of Totalitarianism*

In her 1945 review of Denis de Rougemont's *The Devil's Share* (1944), Hannah Arendt argues, "The reality is that the Nazis are men like ourselves; the nightmare is that they have shown, have proven beyond doubt, what man is capable of." She writes, "In other words, the problem of evil will be the fundamental question of postwar intellectual life in Europe" (1994, 134). Certainly, nearly three decades of Arendt's writing have offered readers ample arsenal for debate about whether she changes her mind on the nature of evil, whether the radical evil she attempts to comprehend in *Origins of Totalitarianism* (1951) is rejected in favor of evil as banal in *Eichmann in Jerusalem* (1963a), with some trying to show that both conceptions of evil have a place in her thought, and though distinct, are not incompatible (for example, see Berstein 1996). Strangely absent in discussions of Arendt's political thought, however, is how the problem of radical evil is Arendt's *own* fundamental and enduring preoccupation throughout her writings, and more importantly, how the problem of evil informs the key notions of her political thought, such as natality, action, solidarity, the *sensus communis,* and above all, what she calls the "predicament of common responsibility" in the face of our shared humanity (1951, 236). This absence has resulted in a general view of Arendt's notion of political action that is curiously (and falsely) optimistic—an unconditional, unhesitating celebration of action as the miracle and joy of human beginning rooted in the event of human natality (see Bowen-Moore 1989; d'Entreves 1994; and Taminiaux 1997).[1]

The human capacity for radical evil renders such optimism untenable. There is evil. This fact marks the beginning and enduring preoccupation of Arendt's thought.[2] In what follows, I propose that Arendt does not change her mind regarding the nature of evil. Already in *Origins of Totalitarianism* (1951), her analysis of the superfluousness of the modern human being grasps the banality of radical evil. Her later report on the trial of Eichmann (1963a) further elucidates this banality but does not in any way refute or alter what she has argued in the earlier work. In the second part of this chapter, I take up Julia Kristeva's recent work on Arendt (2001). Kristeva's analysis is important to this proposal insofar as her concept of abjection illuminates Arendt's claim that the superfluousness of the modern human being accounts for the emergence of radical evil. To go further, Kristeva's concept of abjection suggests that the banality of radical evil is the ever-present threat to the "fragility of human affairs" (Arendt 1958, 188), *precisely because* of the event of natality.[3] In other words, two inseparable moments comprise the event of natality: (1) the abject desolation that carries with it the ever-present threat of radical evil; and (2) the activity of beginning that allows for the transformation and fragile redemption of finitude itself, a transformation that holds at bay but never eradicates this threat. In the final part of the chapter, I argue that Arendt's "politics of natality" emerges from these two inseparable moments of the event of natality, offering the only possible remedy to the threat of radical evil by modifying our relationship to temporality, which in turn allows for a transformed sense of the "solidarity of humanity" through the affective bond of political friendship.

Radical Banality, Abjection, and the Horror of Humanity

Arendt's essay "Organized Guilt and Universal Responsibility" (1945) is her first extended analysis of the problem of evil. Here she argues that a sense of shame is all that remains of any sense of human solidarity: "For many years I have met Germans who declare that they are ashamed to be German. I have often been tempted to answer that I am ashamed to be a human being. This elemental shame, which many people of the most various nationalities share with one another is what finally is left of our sense of international solidarity; and it has not yet found an adequate political expression" (1994, 131). Arendt argues that this sense of shame is the pre-political or nonpolitical expression of the insight that "in one form or another men must assume responsibility for all crimes committed by human beings and that all nations share the onus of evil committed by all others" (131). The international solidarity of humanity lies in this almost unbearable burden of global responsibility; it is a solidarity that has its roots in facing up to the human capacity for evil:

> Those who today are ready to follow this road in a modern version do not content themselves with the hypocritical confession, "God be thanked, I am not like that" in horror of the undreamed of potentialities of the German national character.

Rather, in fear and trembling, have they finally realized of what man is capable—and this indeed is the condition for any modern political thinking. Upon them and only upon them, who are filled with a genuine fear of the inescapable guilt of the human race, can there be any reliance when it comes to fighting fearlessly, uncompromisingly, everywhere against the incalculable evil that men are capable of bringing about. (1994, 132)

Arendt, however, is not arguing that evil is an inherent trait of human beings. In her review of *The Devil's Share* (1944), she takes issue with the argument that good and evil are inherent to the human condition, involved in a gnostic fight for dominance (1944, 135). Radical evil does not point to a demonic nature; instead, it is a *capacity*.[4] The problem for Arendt is that the Western tradition has not faced up to our very real capacity for incalculable evil, preferring instead to see evil as a kind of nothingness—a lack of Being or the Good.

In her 1954 essay "Concern with Politics in Recent European Thought," Arendt has not changed her mind concerning the origin of modern political thought. While agreeing with the Greeks that philosophy begins with wonder at what is, Arendt harbors no nostalgia for recovering the Greek experience. Instead, she claims that whereas the Greek experience of wonder was rooted in the experience of beauty (*Kalon*), the experience of wonder today—if not engaged in a flight from reality—is rooted in the experience of horror at what humans are capable of, the speechless horror that philosophically must be endured and politically instituted against: "It is as though in this refusal to own up to the experience of horror and take it seriously the philosophers have inherited the traditional refusal to grant the realm of human affairs that *thaumadzein*, that wonder at what is as it is. For the speechless horror at what man may do and what the world may become is in many ways related to the speechless wonder of gratitude from which the questions of philosophy spring" (1994, 445). Speechless horror, not beauty, marks the contemporary experience of wonder. This facing up to the human capacity for evil also separates Arendt from her Enlightenment predecessors who, she argues, were too naive in their view of humanity: "Our fathers' enchantment with humanity was of a sort which not only light-mindedly ignored the national question; what is far worse, it did not even conceive of the terror of the idea of humanity" (1994, 132).

Arendt, however, makes an attempt to articulate the speechless horror of the twentieth century; she names it *hell*. The terror and total domination of the death camps is the fabrication of hell on earth: "Concentration camps can very aptly be divided into three types corresponding to three basic Western conceptions of a life after death: Hades, Purgatory, and Hell." Hades, Arendt argues, corresponds to "those relatively mild forms, once popular even in non-totalitarian countries, for getting undesirable elements of all sorts—refugees, stateless persons, the asocial and the unemployed—out of the way." She goes on to write, "Purgatory is represented by the Soviet Union's labor camps, where neglect is combined with chaotic forced labor. Hell in the most literal sense was embodied by those types of camps perfected by the Nazis, in which the whole of life was thoroughly and systematically organized with a view to the greatest possible torment" (1951, 445).

Arendt suggests that the emergence of total domination and terror is the hubristic appropriation of religious limits, specifically the belief in hell;[5] it materializes this belief by incarnating it in immanence:

> Suddenly it becomes evident that things which for thousands of years the human imagination had banished to a realm beyond human competence can be manufactured right here on earth, that Hell and Purgatory, and even a shadow of their perpetual duration, can be established by the most modern methods of destruction. Nothing perhaps distinguishes modern masses as radically from those of previous centuries as the loss of faith in a Last Judgment; the worst have lost their fear and the best have lost their hope. Unable as yet to live without fear and hope, these masses are attracted by every effort which seems to promise a man-made fabrication of the Paradise they had longed for and of the Hell they had feared. The one thing that cannot be reproduced is what made the traditional conceptions of Hell tolerable to man: the Last Judgment, the idea of an absolute standard of justice combined with the infinite possibility of grace. (1951, 446–47)

In this passage, Arendt points to the symbolic function that images of heaven and hell have played in political thought since Plato's *Republic* (1968): they arouse both our longings and our fears. Religion, however, puts heaven and hell beyond the reach of human fabrication. Although the modern political space is marked by an abyss opened by the loss of its theological underpinnings and a loss of belief in the Last Judgment, Arendt suggests that these representations still continue to play a political role at the level of our hopes and fears (see Lefort 1988). In other words, the separation of the theologico-political opens the way for the possibility of these representations to be brought down to earth: "The totalitarian hell proves only that the power of man is greater than they ever dared to think, and that man can realize hellish fantasies" (1951, 446). In her essay "Religion and Politics" (1953), Arendt reiterates this insight: "In totalitarian states we see the almost deliberate attempt to build, in concentration camps and torture cellars, a kind of earthly hell" (1994, 383).

Indeed, in a 1951 letter to Karl Jaspers (see Kohler and Saner 1992), Arendt clarifies the above point, suggesting that the totalitarian vision of hell is an attempt to establish an *omnipotent* presence on the earth itself:

> What radical evil is I don't know, but it seems to me it somehow has to do with the following phenomenon: making human beings as human beings superfluous. This happens as soon as all unpredictability—which, in human beings, is the equivalent of spontaneity—is eliminated. And all this in turn arises from—or, better, goes along with—the delusion of the omnipotence (not simply the lust for power) of an individual man. If an individual man qua man were omnipotent, then there is in fact no reason why men in the plural should exist at all—just as in monotheism it is only God's omnipotence that makes him ONE.

Arendt calls this desire for omnipotence the "madness for the superlative," a madness that brings God down to earth in the figure of a particular omnipotent individual. Arendt is clear in her letter to Jaspers that this "madness for the superlative" is very different from the desire for power that is found in Hobbes; for Hobbes, she argues, the desire for power remains comparative, relative to the power of other human beings (Kohler and Saner 1992, 166). On the other hand, the desire for omnipotence is a rejection of plurality altogether in favor of "being one," a godlike power on earth that desires absolute rule.

The hell of radical evil lies in the refusal of symbolic transcendence, represented by religious and moral limits, substituting instead the fantasies of immanent ideologies and omnipotent dreams. Here we grasp the full import of Arendt's insistence that radical evil requires a move from "everything is permitted" to "everything is possible" (1951, 303). Facing the death of God, "everything is permitted" still recognizes the exigency of judgment, of making a distinction between the permissible and the impermissible, even if the impermissible is emptied of any absolute measure. "Everything is possible" refuses *both* the death of God *and* the exigency of judgment. In other words, it reestablishes an omnipotent presence on earth without any hope of pardon or grace.

The rage against the symbolic, the collapse of transcendence into immanence, is also true of totalitarianism's relation to the law. Arendt insists that these regimes are not lawless. A totalitarian regime, she argues, "claims to obey strictly and unequivocally those laws of Nature or of History from which all positive laws always have been supposed to spring" (1951, 461). Raging against the constraining and absent symbolic law, totalitarian politics "promises justice on earth because it claims to make mankind itself the embodiment of the law" (1951, 462). Totalitarianism substitutes another law, a law that would be incarnate and reassuring because the law can now be known—it literally dwells among us, having been brought down to earth.

This is evident in the trial of Eichmann. Arendt reports that Eichmann suddenly declared that he had lived his whole life according to the Kantian moral imperative (1963a, 135). At first Arendt is affronted at such an outrage against Kant. Upon further examination, however, she grasps that what Eichmann actually did was to pervert the Kantian law, substituting the will of Hitler for the universal and *transcendent* law of reason: "[Eichmann] had not simply dismissed the Kantian formula as no longer applicable, he had distorted it to read: Act as if the principle of your actions were the same as that of the legislator or of the law the land—or, in Hans Frank's formulation of the 'categorical imperative in the Third Reich,' which Eichmann might have known: Act in such a way that the Fuhrer, if he knew your action, would approve it" (1963a, 136). Facing Eichmann, Arendt is confronted with the specificity of the general claim she first made in *Origins of Totalitarianism* (1951): the terror of radical evil and total domination is possible through the perversion of the symbolic dimension of the law, that is, a human being becomes its embodiment, its sovereign will: "In Kant's philosophy, that source [of the law] was practical reason; in Eichmann's household use of him, it was the will of the Fuhrer" (1963a, 137).

The perversion of the law is accompanied by a perversion of desire. While attention has been paid to Arendt's analysis of the role of duty for the law-abiding citizen, it is not often noticed that her analysis of the dutiful citizen concludes with a discussion of the inseparability of Eichmann's sense of duty from his resistance to the *temptation* to do good: "Evil in the Third Reich had lost the quality by which most people recognize it—the quality of temptation. Many Germans and many Nazis, probably an overwhelming majority of them, must have been tempted *not* to murder, *not* to rob, *not* to let their neighbors go off to their doom. But, God knows, they had learned how to resist temptation" (1963a, 150). The resistance to desire occurs through the fascist imperative of obedience and sacrifice; it is an imperative delivered most forcefully by what Eichmann terms the "winged words" of Heinrich Himmler, who was the most gifted, Arendt argues, at solving the problem of conscience—the desire to resist evil (1963a, 105). The effect of these winged words on Eichmann was one of *elation* in which the slogans and watchwords were no longer felt to be issued from above but instead self-fabricated: "and you could see what an 'extraordinary sense of elation' it gave to the speaker the moment it popped out of his mouth" (1963a, 53). Indeed, Arendt points out that whenever the judges "tried to appeal to his conscience, they were met with 'elation,' and they were outraged as well as disconcerted when they learned that the accused had at his disposal a different elating cliché for each period of his life and each of his activities" (1963a, 53).

Eichmann's voice of conscience was not silenced—it was carried away, caught up in the voice of another; his voice had literally been "voiced over" with the voice of Himmler. His elated voice of conscience not only identifies the law with the will of Hitler, but at the same time, Eichmann's desires and fantasies become identified with Hitler's. The elated voice of conscience tells Eichmann to ignore his own desire and dutifully carry out the law of the land: "And just as the law in civilized countries assumes that the voice of conscience tells everybody, 'Thou shalt not kill,' even though man's natural desires and inclinations may at times be murderous, so the law of Hitler's land demanded that the voice of conscience tell everybody: 'Thou shalt kill,' although the organizers of the massacres knew full well that murder is against the normal desires and inclinations of most people" (1963a, 150).

Citing the court's judgment, Arendt points out that for justice to be based on the voice of conscience, "orders to be disobeyed must be 'manifestly unlawful'" and unlawfulness must "be like a black flag above them as warning: 'Prohibited!'"—as the judgment pointed out (1963a, 148). She goes on to argue, however, that in Hitler's regime "this black flag" with its "warning sign" flies as "manifestly" above what normally is a lawful order—for instance, not to kill innocent people just because they happen to be Jews—as it flies above a criminal order under normal circumstances. "To fall back on an unequivocal voice of conscience—or in the even vaguer language of the jurist, on a 'general sentiment of humanity' (Oppenheim-Lauterpacht in *International Law*, 1952)—not only begs the question, it signifies a deliberate refusal to take notice of the central moral, legal, and political phenomena of our century" (1963a, 148). The moral, legal, and political phenomena of our century are the fragile status of both the law and its subject. The transformation of the transcendent law into perverse immanence attests to the fragility of the law in modernity. Eichmann's all too easily "voiced over" voice of conscience, an elated voice in which he identifies with both the law and the desires of the Fuhrer, points to the fragile identity of the modern subject.

In Eichmann's case, the sacrifice of his desire through the elated voice of conscience is accomplished, Arendt argues, by turning basic instincts such as the instinct of pity, whereby we recoil at the suffering of others, back upon the self: "The trick used by Himmler consisted in turning these instincts around, as it were, in directing them toward the self. So that instead of saying: What horrible things I did to people! the murderers would be able to say: What horrible things I had to watch in the pursuance of my duties" (1963a, 106). Himmler's trick, accomplished through slogans and stock phrases (for example, "My honor is my loyalty"), is effective because it promises the *unity* of the subject if only the subject gives way on its desires. In other words, sacrificing desire for duty, the subject has the fantasy of a stable and fixed identity. In a perverse departure from Jean-Jacques Rousseau, self-pity allows for a united *amour propre* only on the condition that the subject becomes an elated and at the same time a dutiful instrument of the other's fantasies. In other words, Rousseau argues that pity is the move from the *amour de soi* to the *amour propre*. *Amour de soi,* the level of need, becomes the *amour propre* through the awakening of desire in which the sentiment of pity becomes socialized. To turn pity back on the self is to move from desire back to need. In Eichmann's case, this has the effect of a "post-desire" need, which explains why he is able so easily to give up his desire (see Rousseau 1979, 222). I will return to this issue in the next section when addressing Kristeva's notion of phobia.

Scant attention has been paid to how the fragile identity of the modern subject informs Arendt's analysis of radical evil. Arendt understands radical evil as the attempt to eliminate spontaneity from the human race; it is the attempt to reshape human nature itself by doing away with the very unpredictability that lies at the root of human freedom and action; it is the attempt to stabilize human behavior in order to allow the law of history or the law of nature to progress: "The camps are meant not only to exterminate people and degrade human beings, but also serve the ghastly experiment of eliminating spontaneity itself as an expression of human behavior and of transforming the human personality into a mere thing, into something that even animals are not; for Pavlov's dog, which, as we know, was trained to eat not when it was hungry but when a bell rang, was a perverted animal" (Arendt 1951, 438). Again, the terror of totalitarianism is involved in the inseparable perversion of both the law and human subjectivity: (1) it perverts humanity by eliminating the capacity for action, the capacity for new beginnings; and (2) it perverts the very meaning of the law, transforming the law from its traditional sense as that which provides limits and boundaries to human action into that which is itself is limitless and constantly on the move. The movement of the law now requires human beings to be static and fixed.

Indeed, Arendt locates the appeal of totalitarian ideology with its claim of carrying out the law of nature or history in the longing for a fixed and stable identity:

> Just as fear and the impotence from which fear springs are anti-political principles and throw men into a situation contrary to political action, so loneliness and the logical-ideological deducing the worst that comes from it represent an anti-political solution and harbor a principle destructive for all human living-together. The "ice-cold reasoning" and the mighty tentacle of dialectics which "seize you as in a vise" appears like a last support in a world where nobody is reliable and nothing can be relied upon. It is the inner coercion whose only content is the strident avoidance of contradictions that seems to confirm a man's identity outside all relationships with others (1951, 478).

Fascist ideology promises a ready-made, united identity—fixed, static, without contradiction and utterly reliable. In still other words, the "madness for the superlative," Arendt argues, is mirrored in the desire of the individual desolate human being who also wants to reject the plurality (the two-in-one) at the very heart of the self in favor of a completeness, an integrity promised in submitting to a fantasy of omnipotence.

For Arendt, the appeal of this promise of unity has its roots in the modern phenomenon of superfluousness. Radical evil, she writes in *Origins* (1951), "has appeared in connection with a system in which all men have become superfluous in some way" (475). It is the desolation of individuals who are economically superfluous and socially uprooted that provides the conditions for radical evil. A peculiar kind of loneliness is key to understanding this evil: "Loneliness, the common ground for terror, the essence of totalitarian government, and for ideology and logicality, the preparation of its executions and victims, is closely connected with uprootedness and superfluousness which have been the curse of modern masses. To be uprooted means to have no place in the world, recognized and guaranteed by others, to be superfluous means not to belong to the world at all" (475). While Arendt argues that superfluousness is a peculiarly modern phenomena, nevertheless, "we have only to remind ourselves that one day we shall have to leave this common world which will go on as before and for whose continuity we are superfluous in order to realize loneliness, the experience of being abandoned by everything and everybody" (476).

In other words, a radical superfluousness or abandonment marks human finitude itself. Banality comes from the same root as abandon: *banumm.* Something was said to be banal when it was no longer under the jurisdiction of the lord, but instead abandoned, given over to the use of the entire community. Banality is the condition of humanity who has been forsaken, banished—we are "holes of oblivion" (459). In the past, this desolation or banality has been covered over by the tripartite structure of authority, tradition, and religion. Modernity, Arendt argues, is marked by the splintering of this structure, a splintering in which our desolation appears at the very center of our existence (see Arendt's essay "Tradition and the Modern Age" in *Between Past and Future*

1961). This oblivion or banality is the secular ordeal of modernity. The banality of radical evil is the refusal to endure this ordeal.

Here we arrive full circle to Arendt's claims as laid out at the beginning of this chapter, namely, that the idea of humanity is terrifying. Arendt argues against the popular notion that the more we know about each other, the more we will come to like each other. On the contrary, Arendt writes, "The more peoples know about one another, the less they want to recognize other peoples as their equals, the more they recoil from the ideal of humanity" (1951, 235). Arendt's insistence that the element that most unites us, humanity, is also the element that causes terror and a recoiling is important. The ideal of humanity, purged of all sentimentality, demands that human beings assume political responsibility for all crimes and evils committed by human beings. At the same time, she argues, this demand is terrifying; this is "the predicament of common responsibility" (1951, 236). Our predicament lies in the double face of humanity: our humanity is at once that which unites us in common responsibility *and* what causes us to recoil in terror. The recoil, Arendt suggests, is in the face of our banality, our desolation. Still further, our terror lies in facing up to our lack of being, our being "holes of oblivion." In a letter to Gershom Scholem, Arendt argues that radical evil is not demonic because it is not "deep"; instead, it spreads like a fungus on the surface of human existence (1978a, 251). The horror of the banality of radical evil is precisely this fungus-like quality that attempts to fill in the cracks and holes of human finitude with dreams and deliriums of fabricating the absolute on earth; it necessarily lies on the surface insofar as it attempts to cover over the abyssal nature of human existence. Critical of the Western tradition's understanding of evil as nothing—a lack of the good—Arendt suggests that the banality of radical evil lies in the disavowal of our own nothingness, our own desolation and impossibility of being. Of utmost importance here is Arendt's insight that the event of natality itself carries with it this desolation and, therefore, the ever-present threat of radical evil as the refusal of this desolation.

Radical Evil and the Event of Natality

In *The Human Condition* (1958), Arendt writes, "With word and deed we insert ourselves into the human world, and this insertion is like a *second birth,* in which we confirm and take upon ourselves the naked fact of our original physical appearance" (176; italics added). This second birth, argues Arendt, allows human beings to appear, and without this birth humans would be dead to the world: "A life without speech and without action is literally dead to the world, it has ceased to be a human life because it is no longer lived among men" (176). Through this *linguistic* birth, humans become political kinds of beings. Arendt cites Aristotle's definition of man as *zoon logon ekhon,* one for whom exists "a way of life in which speech and only speech made sense" (27). This linguistic birth is the birth of the "who," the unique self, insofar as the event of linguistic natality is the being—born of the unexpected and the new.

In other words, the birth of the political self, the "who," is the birth of the un-expected word.

It would be easy, but also a mistake, to think of this second birth as the birth of a kind of heroic individuality, distinct in the sense of being "a word unto itself." Arendt rejects any notion of the self as a "singular word," arguing that the unexpected word is always already immersed in a web of relationships and plurality of enacted stories (181). The Arendtian notion of a "web" reveals that the unexpected word erupts from within a plurality of discourses that are en-tangled and interwoven in their sedimented histories. At the same time, Arendt makes only a brief reference to the unexpected word as tied to an *embodied* web: "To be sure, this web is no less bound to the objective world of things than speech is to the existence of a living body, but the relationship is not like that of a facade or, in Marxian terminology, of an essentially superfluous super-structure affixed to the useful structure of the building itself" (183).

The above passage suggests that Arendt's all-too-tidy distinction between the first birth, the "naked fact of our physical appearance" and the second, the lin-guistic birth of the "who," is eventually rejected in her thought. Linguistic natality cannot be "laid over" physical natality, suggesting that both births must be thought of as intimately connected. Yet it is striking that Arendt does not develop her account of the first birth and its connection with the second. At this point Kristeva's reading of Arendt, particularly Kristeva's notion of abjection, is helpful, insofar as her notion of abjection points to a "primary natality" that provides further insight into the banality of radical evil. In *Powers of Horror* (1982), Kristeva argues that abjection is "the result of a primary natality, the birth pangs of a body becoming separated from another body in order to be" (10). Our desolation, our banality, is due to the very first birth pangs of em-bodiment, the traces of which we carry with us into linguistic natality. Prior to linguistic natality, the subject is "located" in processes that cannot be named. In other words, the identity/nonidentity of the subject as a signifying process ex-ists prior to "birth" into the symbolic order of language under the "father's law." Kristeva claims that abjection rises from a primal repression when the infant struggles to separate from the mother's body that nourishes and comforts, from the ambivalent struggle to establish a separate bodily schema, still seeking a continuity with the mother's body which it seeks to incorporate (1982, 10). Thus, the subject enters into language from a background of conflict between attraction and repulsion with an image of the pre-oedipal archaic mother.

The subject that emerges from this unnamable point of division is a split subject, identifying its previous fragmentary experience, which only "exists" as affect—bare want, loss that is unrepresentable—with the mother's body. Before desire—the movement out from a self to the objects on which it is directed—there are drives that involve pre-oedipal semiotic functions and energy dis-charges that connect and orient the body to the mother. Abjection is the mo-ment of separation, the border between the "I" and the other, before an "I" is formed; it is want itself—an unassimilable nonunity experienced by one who is neither in the symbolic order nor outside of it.

Abjection is the place between signs; it is a trace, a rhythm, an excess or disturbance that destabilizes and threatens to undermine all signifying processes. Abjection, therefore, is that place "where the subject is both generated and negated, the place where his unity succumbs before the process of charges and stases that produce him" (Kristeva 1984, 105). Thus, the emergent subject is infused with a negativity, an alterity that is definitive of its emergent subjectivity. And this negativity is both pleasurable and painful; it is the source both of creation and meaning and of absence, estrangement, desolation. The latter is important insofar as Kristeva stresses that abjection ought not to be "designated as such, that is, as other, as something to be ejected, or separated" (1982, 127). Abjection, therefore, is associated with the disintegration, or perhaps more precisely, the heterogeneity that exists at the very heart of the self.

Important here is the affective dynamic of attraction and repulsion with the mother's body in the labor pains of emerging subjectivity. For Kristeva, abjection as the moment of separation is always double; it is the feeling of loathing and disgust the subject has in encountering certain matter, images, and fantasies—the horrible, to which it can only respond with aversion, with nausea and distraction—and it is at the same time the feeling of fascination, drawing the subject toward it in order to repel it. Kristeva argues that "abjection is above all ambiguity. Because, while releasing a hold, it does not radically cut off the subject from what threatens it—on the contrary, abjection acknowledges it to be in perpetual danger. But also because abjection itself is a composite of judgment and affect, of condemnation and yearning" (1982, 10–11). Kristeva points out that while Arendt is aware of Hitler's fascination with the protocols of the *Elders of Zion* (it is said that he knew them by heart), she misses the abjection that drives Hitler's interest. In her analysis of Arendt, Kristeva argues: "Nazi propaganda proceeded by negatively identifying with an enemy slated for death while at the same time imitating him with a hateful fascination" (2001, 138). Thus, Hitler does not denounce the protocols but seeks instead to establish an exact replica in reality, designating the Jew as his worst enemy in a delirious and yet fascinated revulsion.

Moreover, Kristeva insists that abjection is a historically and culturally specific response to the fragility of the law; in modernity, it is tied to the secular ordeal of the collapse of the religious foundation of the political order (1982, 68). Kristeva agrees with Arendt's analysis of the immanent status of the law in totalitarian regimes, but she criticizes her for not taking into account the sadomasochistic dimension that accompanies the fragility of the law and contributes to the fabrication of hell on earth: "Arendt touches upon the theme of sadomasochism when she delves into the Christian concept of authority, particularly the fear of hell that is its basis. Nor does Arendt analyze the specific fate of the alchemy between fear and authority that operates at the heart of the secularized modern world, which has clearly left the fear of hell behind but which has in no way diffused the sadomasochistic spirit of what Arendt cautiously refers to as the 'frailty of human affairs'" (2001, 181). Certainly Arendt is not unaware of the "instinct for submission," the alchemy between fear and authority, at the heart of the human psyche. In *On Violence* (1970), Arendt observes, "If we were to trust our own experiences in these matters, we should know that the instinct of submission, an ardent desire to obey and be ruled by some strong man, is at least as prominent in human psychology as the will to power, and, politically, perhaps more relevant" (39). Yet Arendt does not explore this instinct or articulate its political relevance.

Kristeva, on the other hand, suggests that in modernity the political relevance of this desire for submission (what she is calling the sadomasochistic dimension) lies in the instability of the symbolic dimension of the law that manifests itself in abjection: the permeability of the inside and the outside boundaries, the weakness of cultural prohibitions, and the crisis of symbolic identity. The fragility of the law exposed in abjection is linked specifically to a crisis of authority. This crisis manifests itself in phobia, an elaboration of want and aggression: "In phobia, fear and aggessivity come back to me from the outside. The fantasy of incorporation by means of which I attempt to escape fear threatens me nonetheless, for a symbolic, paternal prohibition already dwells in me. In the face of this second threat I attempt another procedure: I am not the one that devours, I am being devoured by him" (1982, 39).

To offset the fear associated with the weakness of the symbolic order, the phobic subject regresses to the narcissistic fantasy of fusion with the maternal body; yet this fantasy is threatening because the subject is always already in the symbolic order governed by the paternal prohibition of incest. Thus the fantasy is inverted—rather than devouring the mother (the fantasy of incorporation that promises *jouissance* and the escape from fear), the subject fantasizes that it is being devoured. This phobic fantasy then constructs an imaginary other who becomes the metaphor of the subject's own aggression. Insofar as the phobic fantasy is always culturally and historically specific, fascist regimes are able to mobilize these phobic fantasies onto the social body. Kristeva argues: "The imaginary machinery is transformed into a social institution—and what you get is the infamy of fascism" (1982, 25).

Most important, the phobic fantasy operates at the level of drive rather than desire—it is the unleashing of the death drives onto the social body. However, insofar as the subject is already in the symbolic (the paternal prohibition is in effect), these drives *postdate* desire. Kristeva's analysis of phobia allows us to better understand Himmler's successful trick of inverting basic instincts such as the instinct of pity. Recall the earlier discussion in which we saw that Himmler successfully inverts the instinct of pity for the suffering of the other into self-pity. Reading this inversion through Kristeva's analysis, Himmler's "winged words" produce phobic fantasies at the level of drives incorporated by a subject who has the double fantasy of incorporation and unity (fusion with the maternal/social body) and projection that displaces aggression onto the imaginary other (the Jew), who now seems to threaten from without. Elatedly, Eichmann is caught up in the phobic fantasy which demands only that he sacrifice his desire (the temptation to do good) and carry out his duty to the law; however, it is a law that mobilizes at the level of drives and fantasies rather than at the level of the symbolic. The phobic fantasy is mobilized by "winged words" that hollow out language with its infinity of significations, substituting instead clichés and slogans that operate at the level of drives—"phobia is a metaphor that has mistaken its place, forsaking language for drive and sight" (Kristeva 1982, 35).

In an age where power and the symbolic "exclusionary prohibition" no longer belong to the ultimate Judge—"God who preserves humanity from abjection while setting aside for himself alone the prerogative of violence," Kristeva argues that the "exclusionary prohibition" now belongs to discourse itself (1982, 132). Discourse itself is now the location of the "prohibition that has us speak." The fascist and *racist* discourses of Céline (1934) and Hitler give legitimacy to hatred as they rage against the monotheistic symbolic law (itself infused with negativity and loss) and substitute in its place another law that would be "absolute, reassuring, and fully incarnated" (1982, 178). At the same time, seeking to resecure the boundaries of the immanent law, this discourse turns the Jewish body, which is deliriously viewed by Céline and Hitler as the embodiment of the monotheistic symbolic law, into the rejected site of all forces of negativity, loss, and dissolution.

Reading Céline's pamphlets, Kristeva (1982) shows how his writings transform an experience of abjection and the fragility of the law into the phallic ambition to name the unnamable. Céline's anti-Semitism and fascism can be seen, therefore, as "a kind of parareligious formation" into a fantasy of "the immanence of substance and meaning, of the natural/racial/familial, of the feminine and the masculine, of life and death—a glorification of the Phallus that does not speak its name" (179). Raging against the symbolic law, Céline substitutes an immanent substantial law in the phantasmatic revitalization of the social body: "Again carrying out a rejection, without redemption, himself forfeited, Céline will become body and tongue, the apogee of that moral, political and stylistic revulsion that brands our time. A time that seems to have, for a century now, gone into unending labor pains" (23). Like Arendt, Kristeva gives the name "hell" to the horror of the fascist discourse: "This is the horror of hell without God: if no means of salvation, no optimism, not even a humanistic one, looms on the horizon, then the verdict is in, with no hope of pardon" (147).

Kristeva, therefore, provides a much-needed supplement to Arendt's understanding of the "event of natality," a supplement that allows us to see the ambiguous and fragile status of this event. The frailty of human affairs arises first out of the abjection of a "primary natality," an abjection that means we must face the ever-present threat of the banality of radical evil, a banality that can be traced to a radical abandonment—a desolation inherent in embodiment itself. Kristeva reminds us that the Arendtian "second birth" (linguistic natality) is not only inseparable from this first birth but bears within it the traces of these primary birth pains. At the same time, it would be a mistake to think of the abjection of "primary natality" as itself inherently delirious or evil. Kristeva agrees with Arendt: evil is a capacity, not an inherent trait, of human beings. Evil is our capacity for self-deception that is fundamentally a denial of abjection. More precisely, the banality of radical evil lies in our inability to live with the abject—to live with the ambiguity, abandonment, and negativity that in-fuses the event of natality at both its levels: bodily and linguistically.

Radical Evil and a "Politics of Natality"

In her reading of Arendt, Kristeva asks: "If we resist the traditional safe-guard of religions, with their focus on admonishment, guilt, and consolation, how can our individual and collective desires avoid the trap of melancholic destruction, manic fanaticism, or tyrannical paranoia?" (2001, 129). I want to argue in this final section that Arendt answers Kristeva's question by argu-ing for a transformation of temporality. In other words, given the human ca-pacity for evil, rooted, as I have tried to show, in our banal denial of abjection, Arendt suggests that the only possible remedy for the modern, secular world is to change our relationship to time through a *politics* of natality.

In *The Human Condition* (1958), Arendt begins her analysis of the *vita activa* with a distinction between eternity and immortality. While her discussion of immortality is often read as an argument for heroic deeds and speech that dis-tinguish the actor in the public realm and thereby ensure through remembrance his or her endurance in time, close examination of Arendt's argument reveals that she is not so much interested in the endurance of individual deeds as in the endurance of humanity itself. Immortality, she argues, is the concern of those beings who are mortal: "Imbedded in a cosmos where everything was immortal, mortality became the hallmark of human existence. Men are 'the mortals,' the only mortal thing in existence, because unlike animals they do not exist only as members of a species whose immortal life is guaranteed through procreation. The mortality of men lies in the fact [that] the individual life, with a recogniz-able life-story from birth to death, rises out of biological life" (18–19). Mortality marks the division between life and death; it marks a cut in time whereby hu-man beings move "along a rectilinear line in a universe where everything, if it moves at all, moves in a cyclical order" (19). This transformation of linear into rectilinear time distinguishes the human being from other animal species. To put it more strongly: to be fully human requires a transformation of time. This transformation, Arendt argues, is accomplished only insofar as mortality is linked to a concern with immortality, the latter inseparable from a political life: "Without this transcendence into a potential earthly immortality, no politics, strictly speaking, no common world and no public realm is possible. But such a common world can survive the coming and going of the generations only to the extent that it appears in public. It is the publicity of the public realm which can absorb and make shine through the centuries whatever men may want to save from the natural ruin of time" (55). In negative terms, Arendt argues that the decline of modern humanity is inseparable from the decline in a concern with immortality and the public world: "There is perhaps no clearer testimony to the loss of the public realm in the modern age than the almost complete loss of authentic concern with immortality" (55).

Immortality, therefore, is a political achievement that institutes an enduring, common world. Neither a religious sentiment nor founded in the fear of death, the desire for immortality is the desire for a common world that delivers us from obscurity; it is the desire to be visible—to be seen and recognized by equals; it is the desire for our own image granted only through the perspectives of others. Far from celebrating a politics of heroic individualism, Arendt's emphasis on immortality is rooted in the desire to appear; that is, the desire to *be:* "The term 'public' means, first, that everything that appears in public can be seen and heard by everybody and has the widest possible publicity. For us, appearance—something that is being seen and heard by others as well as by ourselves—constitutes reality" (50). The fulfillment of this desire depends on there being a plurality of others who share a common world. Citing Aristotle, she argues, "To men the reality of the world is guaranteed by the presence of others, by its appearing to all; 'for what appears to all, this we call Being,' and whatever lacks this appearance comes and passes away like a dream" (199). Indeed, our very sense of reality "depends utterly upon appearance" in a common world, the re-ality of which "relies on the simultaneous presence of innumerable perspec-tives and aspects in which the common world presents itself and for which no common measurement or denominator can ever be devised" (57). (It is clear in these passages that Arendt is thinking of the solidarity of humanity not as a solidarity that identifies with the other or as one established in a reciprocity of identifications; rather, solidarity emerges out of the irreducible nonintegration of different standpoints wherein there is equality, not identification, in differ-ence: "sameness in utter diversity" [57].)

Arendt (1978b) goes so far as to call this desire to appear an "innate impulse" as compelling as the fear that accompanies the urge for self-preservation: "It is indeed as though everything that is alive—in addition to the fact that its surface is made for appearance, to be seen and meant to appear to others—has an *urge to appear,* to fit itself into the world of appearances by displaying and show-ing, not its 'inner self' but itself as an individual" (29). Looking to the research of the Swiss biologist and zoologist Adolf Portmann, Arendt argues that this "urge to appear" cannot be explained in functional terms; instead, she suggests, the "urge to appear" is gratuitous, having to do with the sheer pleasure of self-display (29). Human beings, who have a concern with an *enduring* image, trans-form this urge to self-display into a desire for self-presentation that she argues involves a "promise to the world, to those to whom I appear, to act in accordance with my pleasure" (36). The hypocrite, on the other hand, is one who breaks his or her promise to act in accordance with his or her pleasure.[6]

The division between the natural and mortal/immortal being, therefore, co-incides with the first division between the private and public realm. To return to Kristeva's question posed at the outset of this section: for Arendt the only way our individual and collective desires can avoid the fanaticism and madness of radical evil is for the *political institution* of a different form of time—the time of immortality—rooted not in religion or fear, but in the desire for an enduring image and mode of appearance. This is a desire met only in a public space with an irreducible plurality of others with whom we promise our pleasures rather than assert our needs.

Indeed, Kristeva (2001) herself suggests that Arendt's highly controversial distinction between the social and the political be understood against the background of this transformation of temporality. Kristeva asks whether Arendt's distinction between *zoe* and *bios* is not another way to articulate the distinction between needs that link the subject to an archaic realm and its dependence on the mother and desires that afford the dangerous freedom of bonds with other people in the space of appearance: "To transform the nascent being into a speaking and thinking being, the maternal psyche takes the form of a passageway between *zoe* and *bios*, between physiology and biography, between nature and spirit" (47). Quoting Arendt, "The 'nature' of man is 'human' only to the extent that it gives him the possibility of becoming something highly unnatural, that is, a man" (1994, 455), Kristeva argues that Arendt's distinction between *zoe* and *bios* is rooted in her analysis of the death camps wherein the metamorphosis of human beings into nature serves to transform them into "living cadavers" (2001, 140). Emerging from the event of natality, the human being is a beginner, which means that the "nature" of the human being is inherently flexible and open-ended. At the same time, this capacity can all too easily be foreclosed. Arendt is fond of quoting Montesquieu's Preface to the *Spirit of the Laws* (1977): "Man, this flexible being who submits himself in society to the thoughts and impressions of his fellow-men, is equally capable of knowing his own nature when it is shown to him and of losing it to the point where he has no realization that he is robbed of it" (e.g., see Arendt 1994, 408). As we have seen throughout this essay, the loss of the human occurs whenever the attempt is made to stabilize the "nature" of the human being: to make it united, complete, without contradiction or heterogeneity.

Finally, Arendt suggests that the political institution of the temporality of immortality must be accompanied by an affectivity that provides an animating or dynamic basis for the political bond, or what Arendt calls "the solidarity of humanity."[7] Here I want to argue that Arendt goes much further than Kristeva in understanding the need for a *political* remedy for the fantasies and deliriums that accompany the banality of radical evil. In other words, Kristeva seems still to appeal to fear and authority when thinking about the affectivity of the political bond. In her reading of Arendt, she argues:

> She [Arendt] delves into the Christian concept of authority, particularly the fear of hell that is its basis. She correctly considers the interplay between rewards and punishments, as well as the arousing fear that stems from its being a substratum of faith, to be "the only political element in traditional religion" (Arendt 1961, 133). And yet she concerns herself with neither the psychological foundation of this dynamic nor the indispensable support that it offers the political bond as such. "*Are perhaps all political bonds based on an arousing fear?*" (2001, 180–81; italics added).

With this last question, Kristeva seems still too close to a kind of Hobbesian position wherein the dynamic of fear and authority found in religion is transposed into the fear of the sovereign with the introduction of the modern Leviathan. It should not go unnoticed that in Hobbes's *Leviathan*, chapter 12, "On Religion," directly precedes the all-important chapter 13, "Natural Condition of Mankind as Concerning Their Felicity and Misery." While Kristeva would certainly not follow Hobbes in the direction of the sovereign (indeed, her work on abjection as well as on the stranger directly calls Hobbes into question), it does seem that she is not able to think of something other than fear as the animating political bond.

Arendt clearly rejects fear as the affect capable of instituting the political bond, arguing, as we saw in an earlier passage cited above, that fear is a *nonpolitical* emotion rooted in the isolating self-interest of the individual human being (1951, 478).[8] While Arendt agrees that fear can be used as a political tool for dominating individuals, it cannot be the animating or affective bond of a "we" (1994, 337). Indeed, one could read her "politics of natality" and its insistence on the move from the natural to the mortal/immortal, from *zoe* to *bios*, as adding another properly *political* chapter to Hobbes's understanding of the human being. Contrary to Hobbes's natural position, Arendt's political understanding of the human being insists on the transformation of the time of self-interest to the temporality of public happiness with its promise of shared pleasures. This, in turn, allows her to reformulate the "solidarity of humanity" and its predicament of common responsibility.

In her essay *On Violence* (1970), Arendt takes up the issue of whether "enlightened self-interest" can adequately resolve conflict and prevent violence. Using the example of a rent dispute between tenant and landlord, Arendt argues that "enlightened interest would focus on a building fit for human habitation; however, the argument that '*in the long run* the interest of the building is the *true* interest of both the landlord and the tenant' leaves out of account the time factor which is of paramount importance for all concerned" (78). Because of mortality, she argues, the self *qua* self cannot calculate in long-term interest: "Self-interest, when asked to yield to 'true interest'—that is, the interest of the world as distinguished from that of the self—will always reply, 'Near is my shirt, but nearer is my skin.' It is the not very noble but adequate response to the time discrepancy between men's private lives and the altogether different life expectancy of the public world" (78). To move from self-interest to "world-interest" requires a move from fear to love of the "public thing."

Love of the "public thing" occurs only through the vigilant partiality of political friendship, which rejects from the outset any notion of truth, engaging instead in the practice of questioning and doubt that marks the secular ordeal of modern humanity: "If the solidarity of mankind is to be based on something more solid than the justified fear of man's demonic capabilities, if the new universal neighborhood of all countries is to result in something more promising than a tremendous increase in mutual hatred and a somewhat universal irrita-

bility of everybody against everybody else, then a process of mutual understanding and progressing self-clarification on a gigantic scale must take place"
(Arendt 1968, 84).

For Arendt, Gottfried Lessing (1955) is the figure who embraces this secular
ordeal: "He was glad that—to use his parable—the genuine ring, if it had ever
existed, had been lost; he was glad for the sake of the infinite number of opinions that arise when men discuss the affairs of this world. If the genuine ring
did exist, that would mean an end to discourse and thus to friendship and thus
to humanness" (Arendt 1968, 26). Lessing rejoices in that very thing that has
caused so much distress, namely, "that the truth once uttered becomes one opinion among many, is contested, reformulated, reduced to one subject of discourse
among others" (27). Arendt goes on to suggest that Lessing was a "completely
political person" because of this understanding of the relation between truth
and humanity: "He insisted that truth can exist only where it is humanized by
discourse, only where each man says not what just happens to occur to him at
the moment, but what he 'deems truth.' But such speech is virtually impossible
in solitude; it belongs to an arena in which there are many voices and where the
announcement of what each 'deems truth' both links and separates men, establishing in fact those distances between men which together comprise the world"
(30–31). This does not amount to tolerance; instead, "it has a great deal to do
with the gift of friendship, with openness to the world, and finally with a genuine love of mankind" (30–31).

Lessing's antinomy between truth and humanity provides Arendt with a
kind of thought experiment. She asks the reader to assume for a moment that
the racial theories of the Third Reich could have been proved: "Suppose that a
race could indeed be shown, by indubitable scientific evidence, to be inferior;
would that fact justify its extermination?" (1968, 29). She asks the reader not to
make the experiment too easy by invoking a religious or moral principle such
as "Thou shalt not kill"; she asks this in order to show a kind of thinking governed by neither legal, moral, nor religious principles (she asks this in the sober
recognition that legal, moral, and religious principles did not prevent the worst
from happening). This way of thinking without recourse to transcendent principles paradoxically gives rise to a fundamental political principle by which to
judge our "truths": "*Would any such doctrine, however convincingly proved, be
worth the sacrifice of so much as a single friendship between two men?*" (1968, 29;
italics in original).

The political principle is friendship: any doctrine that in principle barred the
possibility of friendship must be rejected.[9] Political friendship retreats from a
notion of truth as "objective"; nonetheless, Arendt argues, it has nothing to do
with a kind of subjective relativism where everything is viewed in terms of the
self and its interests. Instead, "it is always framed in terms of the relationship
of men to their world, in terms of their positions and opinions" (1968, 29). Lessing's understanding of friendship, therefore, has nothing to do with the warmth
of fraternity that desires above all to avoid disputes and conflicts. The excessive
closeness of brotherliness, Arendt claims, obliterates all distinctions, and Less-

ing understood this: "He wanted to be the friend of many men, but no man's brother" (1968, 30). Finally, while political friendship does not recognize any ultimate arbiter for its disputes and disagreements, nonetheless, it is guided by a fundamental exigency: we must assume responsibility for what is just and what is unjust, answering for our deeds and words. Our only remedy for radical evil, Arendt suggests, are these fragile friendships that in the face of humanity's demonic capabilities provide the animating or affective dimension of the solidarity of humanity.[10] These friendships are animated by the willingness to endure the burden of questioning and doubt inherent in the very event of natality itself, characterized at once by a desolation and abandonment that makes the banality of radical evil an ever-present threat even as it allows for the miracle of new beginnings and rebirth.

Notes

1. For a more cautious analysis of Arendt's notion of action, one that insists on taking into account the negative side of action, that is, violence, see McGowan 1997. McGowan's account of violence, however, does not consider Arendt's understanding of evil. Indeed, he argues that "Arendt consistently refused throughout her career to attempt any explanation of evil while persistently calling our attention to the relevance of its existence as a political fact" (269). McGowan does give an account of Arendt's understanding of evil, but he views it entirely through the Arendtian lens of thinking and judging, neglecting altogether her notion of radical evil. While I do not disagree that Arendt's later analyses of thinking and judging add to our understanding of evil, I want to argue that her understanding of the banality of evil is rooted in her account of radical evil and the radical superfluousness of human beings, a superfluousness that itself can only be understood through Arendt's account of natality. Steven Aschheim's (2001) work on Arendt is to my mind the least optimistic about action as the promise of new beginnings. Arguing that Arendt's analysis of radical evil rejects understanding evil in terms of particular national and historical categories, instead favoring more general historical and psychological categories (120), he implicitly suggests that Arendt's insight into the psychological roots of evil would yield a far less optimistic reading of Arendt's notion of action. Aschheim, however, does not develop Arendt's psychological insights. This chapter attempts to do this through an analysis of Arendt's understanding of the event of natality. (See note 3 below.)

2. I am indebted to George Kateb's seminal work (1984) on Hannah Arendt's understanding of evil, particularly his discussion of the "pseudomoral" at the conclusion of his long analysis of totalitarian evil. Kateb argues that Nazism was the enactment of a myth of punishment in which Jews and Gypsies were punished for the worse possible *sin* (not crime)—the sin of being unclean and hence unfit to live or to share the earth (80). Kateb points out that the pseudomoral myth of punishment is a myth of exorcism, which he points out is a self-exorcism: "To kill the Jew in oneself, one must kill all Jews" (81). Kateb

raises several urgent questions concerning the nature of this exorcism: "What is the Jew that must be exorcised? And by extension, what groups might one day be assigned the role of victim in a new ideology, a new myth of punishment? Most of the human race? The best counsel is to remain in perplexity" (81). This essay takes seriously Kateb's questions even as it does not follow his counsel; it seeks to clarify the pseudomoral (or pseudoreligious) myth that animates Nazism and radical evil through an analysis of Arendt's imagery of the death camps as "hell on earth" (1951, 445), an analysis illuminated by Kristeva's notion of abjection (see Kristeva 2001). This notion provides clarification of Kateb's insight that a radical exorcism is at work in the pseudomoral myth while avoiding (as does Kateb) the theory of the eternal scapegoat—a theory Arendt rejects at the outset of the *Origins of Totalitarianism* (1951).

3. For a groundbreaking analysis of how Kristeva's notion of abjection provides crucial illumination of Arendt's thought, see Moruzzi (2000). Moruzzi's analysis focuses on the ways in which Arendt's political thought attempts to exclude the abject from political life while at the same it recognizes the force of the abject in her analysis of the worldly achievement of artifice and her understanding of political performance as requiring the actor to assume the masquerade of individual self-representation. Moruzzi devotes an entire chapter to an analysis of the banality of evil, arguing that it is rooted in the thoughtless refusal of this masquerade (2000, 114–35). She ends her analysis of evil emphasizing the hopefulness inherent in new beginnings. My focus in this chapter is to render problematic the promise of beginning granted in the event of natality, arguing that the event of natality carries its abjection with it, and thereby the promise of beginning is tempered by the threat of radical evil. Unfortunately, Moruzzi is not able to consider Kristeva's work on Arendt, which only appeared in French in 1999 and was not available before Moruzzi's book went to press.

4. We must be careful, therefore, not to jump to the conclusion that Arendt changes her mind on radical evil. She agrees with Jaspers that radical evil cannot be attributed to a demonic nature. Later, in her exchange with Gershom Scholem, she argues that evil is not radical if by that is understood "deep." Rather, she writes, evil is like a fungus that spreads on the surface of things (1978a, 251). That it spreads like a fungus, however, does not make it any less radical or horrible. As I shall argue later in the chapter, the fungus of radical evil points to its banality—it is an attempt to fill in the cracks and holes that characterize human finitude. Arendt's use of the metaphor of fungus indicates that she disagrees with Kant's argument that radical evil has a *root* in human nature.

5. See also "Social Science and Concentration Camps" in *Essays in Understanding* (1994). Arendt writes, "The concentration camps are the laboratories in the experiment of total domination, for human nature being what it is, this goal can be achieved only under the extreme circumstances of a *human-made hell*" (1994, 240; italics added).

6. For a detailed analysis of Arendt's understanding of the hypocrite, see Moruzzi 2000, 32–37. Confining her analysis to Arendt's *On Revolution* (1963b), Moruzzi emphasizes the hypocrite's refusal to understand the self as artifice, a multiple and changing appearance among a multiplicity of appearances. While entirely in agreement with Moruzzi's reading of the hypo-

crite in *On Revolution*, I want to suggest that Arendt in *Life of the Mind* (1978b) adds significantly to her own understanding of the hypocrite by introducing the hypocrite's "broken promise to pleasure." While it is beyond the scope of this chapter, Arendt's notion of the "broken promise to pleasure" further illuminates those like Eichmann who were all too ready to sacrifice desire for duty.

7. Insisting on an affective dimension to political life, Arendt is in the tradition of Montesquieu, who argues that the laws and institutions (the form) of any political regime are always animated by an *affective principle* (the spirit of the laws) that establishes the political bond. Thus, the laws and institutions of a monarchy are animated by the love of honor, while the laws and institutions of a republic are animated by love of virtue. For Montesquieu's argument, see *Spirit of the Laws*, especially Part I. For Arendt's reading of Montesquieu on this point, see Arendt 1994, 331–33.

8. Indeed, in "Philosophy and Religion," Arendt argues that the remedy to totalitarian evil is to embrace the *doubt* that characterizes the modern secular world rather than belief in heaven or fear of hell (1994, 384).

9. For an extended analysis of Arendt, Lessing, and the ways in which friendship might provide a bulwark against radical evil, see Disch (1994). Disch and I do not disagree on the centrality of friendship for confronting the evil of totalitarianism. Her analysis, however, concentrates on how given identities can be challenged by the "vigilant partisanship" of friendship. My focus differs from Disch's analysis in that I argue that political friendship is the affective principle that animates the political bond or what Arendt calls the "solidarity of humanity." The "predicament of common responsibility" in which this solidarity is both terrifying and unifying is able to be borne through this type of friendship.

10. Following Montesquieu, I want to emphasize that in arguing for political friendship as a remedy for radical evil, it is also the case that this affective dimension of political life cannot be divorced from the institutions and laws that form governments. It is outside the scope of this chapter to raise the further question, What would the form of institutions and laws look like if animated by these fragile friendships that insist on the burden of questioning and doubt? While this may seem to provide a "weak remedy" to radical evil, it seems to me that such weakness or lack of guarantees is endemic to what Arendt calls the "fragility of human affairs."

References

Arendt, Hannah. 1951. *The Origins of Totalitarianism*. New York: Harcourt Brace.
———. 1958. *The Human Condition*. Chicago: University of Chicago Press.
———. 1961. *Between Past and Future: Six Exercises in Political Thought*. New York: Viking.
———. 1963a. *Eichmann in Jerusalem: A Report on the Banality of Evil*. New York: Viking.
———. 1963b. *On Revolution*. New York: Penguin Books.

——. 1968. *Men in Dark Times.* New York: Harcourt Brace.

——. 1970. *On Violence.* New York: Harcourt Brace.

——. 1978a. *The Jew as Pariah.* Ed. Ron H. Feldman. New York: Grove Press.

——. 1978b. *The Life of the Mind.* New York: Harcourt Brace Jovanovich.

——. 1994. *Essays in Understanding: 1930–1954.* Ed. Jerome Kohn. New York: Harcourt Brace.

Aschheim, Steven E. 2001. *In Times of Crisis: Essays on European Culture, Germans, and Jews.* Madison: University of Wisconsin Press.

Berstein, Richard. 1996. *Hannah Arendt and the Jewish Question.* Cambridge: MIT Press.

Bowen-Moore, Patricia. 1989. *Hannah Arendt's Philosophy of Natality.* New York: St. Martins Press.

Calhoun, Craig, and John McGowan, eds. 1997. *Hannah Arendt and the Meaning of Politics.* Minneapolis: University of Minnesota Press.

Céline, Louis-Ferdinand. 1934. *Journey to the End of the Night.* Trans. John H. P. Marks. Boston: Little, Brown.

d'Entreves, Maurizio Passerin. 1994. *The Political Philosophy of Hannah Arendt.* New York: Routledge.

de Rougemont, Denis. 1944. *The Devil's Share.* Trans. Haakon Chevalier. New York: Pantheon Books.

Disch, Lisa Jane. 1994. *Hannah Arendt and the Limits of Philosophy.* Ithaca, N.Y.: Cornell University Press.

Kant, Immanuel. 1956. *Critique of Practical Reason.* Trans. Lewis White Beck. Indianapolis: Bobbs-Merrill.

Kateb, George. 1984. *Hannah Arendt: Politics, Conscience, Evil.* Totowa, N.J.: Rowman and Allenheld.

Kohler, Lotte, and Hans Saner, eds. 1992. *Hannah Arendt—Karl Jaspers Correspondence: 1926–1969.* Trans. Robert and Rita Kohler. New York: Harcourt Brace Jovanovich.

Kristeva, Julia. 1982. *Powers of Horror: An Essay on Abjection.* Trans. Leon S. Roudiez. New York: Columbia University Press.

——. 1984. *Revolution in Poetic Language.* Trans. Margaret Waller. New York: Columbia University Press.

——. 2001. *Hannah Arendt.* Trans. Ross Guberman. New York: Columbia University Press.

Lefort, Claude. 1988. *Democracy and Political Theory.* Trans. David Macey. Minneapolis: University of Minnesota Press.

Lessing, Gottfried. 1955. *Nathan the Wise.* Trans. Bayard Quincy Morgan. New York: Frederick Ungar.

McGowan, John. 1997. Must politics be violent? Arendt's utopian vision. In *Hannah Arendt and the Meaning of Politics,* ed. Craig Calhoun and John McGowan. Minneapolis: University of Minnesota Press.

——. 1998. *Hannah Arendt: An Introduction.* Minneapolis: University of Minnesota Press.

Montesquieu, Baron de. 1977. *Spirit of the laws.* Ed. David Wallace Carrithers. Berkeley: University of California Press.

Moruzzi, Norma Claire. 2000. *Speaking Through the Mask: Hannah Arendt and the Politics of Identity.* Ithaca, N.Y.: Cornell University Press.

Plato. 1968. *Republic.* Trans. Allen Bloom. New York: Basic Books.

Rousseau, Jean-Jacques. 1979. *Emile.* Trans. Allen Bloom. New York: Basic Books.

Scholem, Gershom. 1976. *On Jews and Judaism in Crisis: Selected Essays.* New York: Schocken Books.

Taminiaux, Jacques. 1997. *The Thracian Maid and the Professional Thinker: Arendt and Heidegger.* Trans. and ed. Michael Gendre. Albany: State University of New York Press.

6 Banal Evil and Useless Knowledge: Hannah Arendt and Charlotte Delbo on Evil after the Holocaust

Jennifer L. Geddes

Three related divisions currently mark scholarship on evil. The first is the divide between studies of perpetrators and studies of victims. In the field of Holocaust studies, this division is a matter of principle for some scholars, who focus solely on the testimonies and histories of the victims. One rationale behind refusing to study the perpetrators of the Nazi horrors is the belief that they do not deserve the dignity even of being made objects of study. Behind the work of those who study the perpetrators is the idea that unless we understand how it was that humans came to do such evil, we will not be in a position to prevent it from happening again. The second division—one that is closely associated with the first—is the split between viewing evil either in terms of intention or in terms of effects. Behind this division is a debate about what constitutes evil: Is an event evil because of the intention of the actor to inflict harm, or because the event results in great suffering? A third division is the divorce between theoretical and empirical studies of evil. Theoretical studies take up the problem of evil in general. Empirical studies focus on particular historical events. This is often a disciplinary divide, with philosophers and theologians debating the problem of evil—Kant's struggle with the concept of radical evil is an example of this (see Kant 1960)—while historians, sociologists, and psychologists focus on empirical cases, either institutional or individual.

This chapter argues that these divisions in the study of evil are artificial and can be pernicious. First, perpetrators commit acts that make people victims; we should not ignore the relational aspect of evil. Second, intentions and effects must be looked at together, both because intentions when enacted produce effects and because, as Hannah Arendt (1964) shows us, the absence of evil intentions does not necessarily imply that a person is not responsible for evil. If we look merely at intentions, we might miss numerous instances of evil. If we look only at effects, we may miss intentions to do evil that have so far been unsuccessful but may not always be so. Finally, the abstract concept of evil is worthy of our attention precisely because of the empirical realities to which it refers, but we are able to see those realities more clearly, at times, with the help of theoretical insights. This chapter attempts to bridge the gaps between these scholarly foci, divided discourses, and methodologies in the context of thinking about the Holocaust by bringing together the writings of Hannah Arendt and Charlotte Delbo.

One reason why a study of evil that focuses only on the perpetrators of evil or their intentions is problematic is that evil is relational and does not merely exist in the minds of "evildoers." For evil occurs between people: one or more persons *do* evil (and are thereby understood to be evil or connected to evil) and someone else, or some other group, *suffers* evil. As Paul Ricoeur notes, "To do evil is always, either directly or indirectly, to make someone else suffer. In its dialogic structure evil committed by someone finds its other half in the evil suffered by someone else" (1995, 250).

In the attempt to understand the horror of the Holocaust, we need to look at the perpetrators' intentions and actions *and* at the victims' experiences, as well as at theoretical discussions of evil and analyses of empirical events deemed evil. If we fail to study the perpetrators and look only to the victims, we run the risk of forgetting the agents of their suffering, those who are morally responsible for the suffering inflicted by evil. We run the risk of forgetting the task of justice. However, if our understanding of evil is limited to a study of the perpetrators, we can lose sight of the main reason that evil is such a persistent concern—the extreme suffering inflicted on the victims of evil.[1] Another danger of failing to attend to the experiences of the victims of evil is that we run the risk of seeing evil through the distorted eyes of the perpetrators.

Separately, Arendt and Delbo each bridge the gap between theoretical and empirical (or particular) approaches to evil. Brought together, they move us to a better understanding of evil—one that resists both the temptation to mythologize evil (or the person who does evil) and the temptation to find something redeeming in, or to impose meaning on, the suffering that results from evil.

People speak of evil geniuses or demonic monsters as if there is an extraordinary quality to those who do evil (Shattuck 1996). Evil takes on a mythical quality in these ways of speaking, making it less a problem for humanity than a mysterious aberration. The evildoer who is a monster is removed from us, placed in a category outside of the human; for if evildoers are demonic monsters, they can be accounted for by jettisoning them from the category of "human beings," from the "we." Thinking of those who do evil as monsters renders them as dissimilar from us as possible. But as Arendt shows us, and as much research on the perpetrators of the Holocaust has revealed, thoughtless bureaucrats and "ordinary people" were responsible for extreme cruelty and inflicted evil of the sort it is hard even to imagine (see Arendt 1964; Browning 1993; Goldhagen 1996).

The other temptation we face is the impulse to "redeem" suffering, to find something useful or some good that has come out of it. This is a more subtle process and may seem, at first glance, to be not a temptation but a constructive response to suffering. But as Delbo shows us, there are subtle ways in which we fail to listen to the stories of those who have suffered evil, fail to face suffering *as* suffering, fail to acknowledge the extremity of suffering undergone as a result of evil actions (Delbo 1995). Sometimes we sentimentalize extreme suffering, glossing over the sheer destructiveness of it. Sometimes we sanitize extreme suffering, ignoring the unpleasant, harsh, or even disgusting elements associated with it. We want to think of the experience of extreme suffering as at least being useful—in other words, as not being completely suffering but as somehow leaving the victim with something that can be of use. This is an understandable response to the horror of the stories that many survivors of evil have to tell, but it is one that we need to learn to move beyond. Sometimes suffering is "for nothing." Sometimes suffering is useless. Sometimes nothing good comes from evil. It is important to listen to the stories of those who have suffered evil and to recognize those points at which we bring erroneous presuppositions or imaginings of the suffering of evil to the table, to recognize those points at which we may be trying to impose our "version" of suffering onto their experiences. For whether or not an experience of suffering has meaning or is "useful" is a question that only the sufferer, not an observer or outsider, can decide (Levinas 1998).

These two temptations—to mythologize evil and to "clean up" suffering—arise out of the understandable desire to avoid the outrage of evil and the suffering it inflicts, but as scholars of evil, we need to recognize these temptations and resist them. Arendt and Delbo help us to do just this. Brought together, Arendt's *Eichmann in Jerusalem* (1964) and Delbo's *Auschwitz and After* (1995) trouble our preconceptions about those who do evil and those who suffer evil. Each writer does so, in part, by presenting us with a counterintuitive and jarring term: Arendt's "banal evil" and Delbo's "useless knowledge." Immediately we might ask: How can evil be banal? What does it mean to call knowledge useless? In seeking to understand these terms, we "unlearn" hindering preconceptions and open up space to learn about evil from those who have a different knowledge of it than we as scholars can have.

While Arendt and Delbo had very different relations to the events of the Holocaust, each was profoundly affected by it. A young German-Jewish woman during the rise of the National Socialist Party, Arendt left Germany in 1933 and subsequently emigrated to the United States, where she spent the remainder of her life as a leading intellectual and scholar. Delbo, a non-Jewish woman who was part of the French Resistance, was captured in 1942 with her husband (who was executed shortly thereafter) and sent with 230 other women to Auschwitz, which she barely survived (Langer 1995, ix). Both women's interest in, approach to, and understanding of evil were shaped by their experiences during the Holocaust.

Arendt and Delbo, this chapter argues, move us toward new ways of thinking and speaking about evil that do not shy away from the challenges that concrete evil presents to thought and language. Arendt shows us that evil can be banal. Delbo shows us that the knowledge gained from extreme suffering can be useless. Arendt shows us that evil can be much more ordinary than we imagine—

and this fact makes evil more horrifying, not less so. Delbo reveals that the suffering of evil is much more unfamiliar than we imagine—and this makes it even more disturbing. In other words, Arendt helps us to resist mythologizing evil, and Delbo helps us to resist domesticating suffering.

By thinking about evil with the help of *both* Arendt and Delbo, we are also able to steer away from the dangers implicit in demythologizing evil and defamiliarizing suffering. The danger of demythologizing evil, as Arendt does for us, is that we then domesticate it; we become too familiar, perhaps even complacent in the face of it. Reading the accounts of those who have suffered extreme evil serves as an antidote to our complacency. The danger of revealing the unfamiliarity of extreme suffering is that we thereby distance ourselves from it, lose our connection to the sufferers, and begin to isolate them. Reading about the perpetrators reminds us of the extreme dangers in allowing that distance to remain and underscores the necessity of seeking ways to respond to those who have suffered evil.

The "Banality of Evil": A New Kind of Evil, A New Kind of Perpetrator

Ever since Arendt connected the words "evil" and "banal," any work on the nature of evil has had to grapple with this counterintuitive understanding of evil. Arendt was criticized for essentializing evil as banal and disregarding the experience of the victims of evil. For what could be *less* banal than the experience of physical injury, pain, and violation at the hands of the torturer, rapist, or death-camp guard? What could Arendt possibly mean by calling evil "banal," particularly in the context of reporting on the trial of a Nazi official responsible for the implementation of the "Final Solution," a person responsible for the deaths of millions of Jewish women, men, and children? After the book came out, some critics suggested that evil may be "banal" when it is sitting behind glass (as Eichmann was throughout the trial), but quite another thing when felt on one's flesh (see, e.g., Améry 1980, 25).

Arendt's "banality of evil" thesis is a direct result of the puzzle Nazi criminal Adolf Eichmann presented to her thinking about evil. The sort of person that Eichmann appeared to be did not square either with the deeds for which he was being tried or with the traditional preconceptions about the kind of person who does evil. Instead of a monster intent on inflicting harm, she found an efficient bureaucrat who thoughtlessly sent thousands to their deaths and considered it a day's work. Eichmann displayed little of the demonic intelligence associated with "moral monsters" or "evil geniuses." What Arendt faced was the "dilemma between the unspeakable horror of the deeds and the undeniable ludicrousness of the man who perpetrated them . . . everybody could see that this man was not a 'monster,' but it was difficult indeed not to suspect that he was a clown" (1964, 54). In fact, the intention to do evil was replaced with a thoughtlessness that enabled him to do evil in the guise of doing his job. Arendt writes:

Eichmann was not Iago. . . . Except for an extraordinary diligence in looking out for his personal advancement, he had no motives at all. . . . He *merely*, to put the matter colloquially, *never realized what he was doing.* . . . He was not stupid. It was sheer thoughtlessness . . . that predisposed him to become one of the greatest criminals of that period. . . . That such remoteness from reality and such thought-lessness can wreak more havoc than all the evil instincts taken together which, perhaps, are inherent in [humans]—that was, in fact, the lesson one could learn in Jerusalem . . . the strange interdependence of thoughtlessness and evil. (1964, 287–88)

It is important to recognize that in noting Eichmann's thoughtlessness, Arendt is in no way suggesting that he is not responsible for the deeds he committed, nor is she suggesting that our moral judgment of him be lessened in any way. His thoughtlessness is in no way a mitigating factor. While Larry May rightly sees in Arendt a focus on "the institutional factors that socialized Eichmann, as well as so many other petty bureaucrats, into believing that their highest moral duty was to follow their superiors' orders" (May 1996, 84), it is important to note that Arendt's account of evil is not deterministic. She places a strong emphasis on moral responsibility and agency throughout *Eichmann in Jerusalem*. While this new form of evil was made possible by the emergence of the modern bureaucratic state, individual actors were responsible for the acts they committed.

Many readers of *Eichmann in Jerusalem* misinterpret its subtitle, *A Report on the Banality of Evil*, thinking it proposes that banality is the essence of evil. However, the evil that Arendt writes about in this book is of a particular kind. It is specifically connected to a particular kind of perpetrator; it is also connected to a particular time period. Banal evil is a new form of evil in the modern world. Arendt's subtitle should not, then, be read as "A Report on Banality as the Essence of Evil," but rather as "A Report on the Banality of the Evil of which Eichmann is an Example." Implicit in this idea is the suggestion that evil has many forms, that these forms may change over time, and that historical/sociological contexts may produce new forms of evil and evildoers. In other words, Arendt's thesis points to an understanding of evil as particular, evolving, and nonessentialist. In fact, that she arrived at her thesis about evil by attending a historical event and focusing on a particular perpetrator suggests that Arendt herself resisted essentialist understandings of evil. Her method reveals the importance of attending to the particular and of continually attending to the possibility of new forms of evil.

Arendt's focus on one new form that evil has taken in the modern world implicitly suggests both that there are multiple forms of evil and that these forms are not a static set of unchanging elements. Evil occurs in different ways at different times. Because of this, we need to be wary of failing to recognize evil. As Arendt notes: "Evil in the Third Reich had lost the quality by which most people recognize it—the quality of temptation" (1964, 150). By thinking that evil has an unchanging, abstract essence, we may fail to recognize the particular, unfamiliar form that evil has taken right in front of us. In other words, *Eich-*

mann in Jerusalem, rightly understood, moves us in the direction not of essentializing evil or reducing all of evil (including the suffering of evil) to banality, but rather of specifying what we are talking about each time we use the multivalent term "evil."

Jean Améry, who was tortured at the hands of SS officers, argues that the very use of the term "banality" in the context of evil betrays an insensitivity to the realities of suffering that the person who does evil inflicts (1980). He suggests that it is only someone who has not suffered at the hands of evil who could make such a connection. Améry writes: "For there is no 'banality of evil,' and Hannah Arendt, who wrote about it in her Eichmann book, knew the enemy of [hu]mankind only from hearsay, saw him only through the glass cage. When an event places the most extreme demands on us, one ought not to speak of banality" (1980, 25).

Améry's point is a strong one, and that evil may appear to be a very different thing from the perspective of the sufferer than from the perspective of a scholar looking at it after the fact is something we should keep in mind as scholars of evil. However, while Améry is right in saying that the victim's experience of evil is certainly not banal, Arendt's banality of evil thesis is not thereby wrong if it is rightly understood—that is, if it is understood in context. She does not argue that banality is the essence of evil, nor does she suggest that the *experience* of evil is banal. Arendt's writing was occasioned by a particular, concrete event—Eichmann's trial; she did not set out to write a treatise on the nature of evil and conclude that its nature was banality. Arendt's book is a report on a trial that challenged her understanding of evil, that suggested a new and shocking form that evil had taken in the modern world. However, her report needs to be supplemented by the reports of those who, like Améry and Delbo, saw evil up close, who experienced in their bodies the results of the decisions people such as Eichmann made.

In the years since the publication of *Eichmann in Jerusalem,* scholars have begun to see the need to include the study of suffering in the study of evil. Twenty-five years after the publication of his book *The Symbolism of Evil* (1967), Paul Ricoeur confessed: "The problem which haunts me more and more—and which is taking the place of the problem of evil or of guilt: [is] the evil of suffering. . . . There is a language to be found. It is the problem of Auschwitz" (in Reagan 1996, 135). One place this language can be found is in the testimonies of survivors who have undergone that evil. What emerges from the perspective of the survivor is a recognition of our outsider position as scholars of evil—a recognition that cautions us against presumptuous knowledge when it comes to thinking and speaking about evil. As Ricoeur notes, "the problem of evil offers at the same time the most considerable challenge to think and the most deceptive invitation to talk nonsense, as if evil were an always premature problem where the ends of reason always exceed its means" (1967, 165).

Delbo's *Auschwitz and After,* a testimony of her experiences in and after the camps, offers a phenomenology of suffering that questions the outsider's ability to know or comprehend that suffering. Her phenomenology of the evil of suffering disrupts our understanding of how evil is suffered and shows us the limits of our knowledge of evil.

"Useless Knowledge" and the Phenomenology of Suffering

Whereas Arendt moves us to think about the varied, changing, and historically specific forms evil can take—and specifically one form it took in Nazi Germany—and challenges us to resist the temptation to essentialize or mythologize evil, Delbo's work challenges us to consider the limitations in our ability to understand evil, to acknowledge the gap between the knowledge we scholars have of evil and the knowledge one has of evil when one has suffered because of it. Her work also reveals our temptation to find something redeeming about the suffering inflicted by those who do evil.

Delbo's account of the suffering that she and her "comrades" experienced at the hands of the Nazis and its long-term aftereffects provides a stark yet thick description of the experiences of non-Jewish women prisoners in Auschwitz. By showing us the ways in which these women suffered, formed bonds with each other, and, in a few cases, survived, Delbo's testimony offers an important portrait of the particularity of women's suffering during the Holocaust.

In doing so, Delbo also interrogates the shape and extent of our knowledge of suffering. She asks her reader: "O you who know / did you know that you can see your mother dead / and not shed a tear. . . . / Did you know that suffering is limitless / that horror cannot be circumscribed / Did you know this / You who know" (1995, 11). We philosophers and scholars of evil, did we know this? Did we know that "suffering is limitless, that horror cannot be circumscribed" before we read the testimonies of those who have suffered evil? The suffering of evil is not circumscribed by the facts of the events of harm. To know that someone was stripped, shaved of all her body hair, and beaten is one kind of knowledge. To know that you have seen your mother dead and not shed a tear is quite another. The latter is "useless knowledge." By this Delbo means that the knowledge one acquires from extreme suffering is not useful for life. It does not teach the sufferer anything that will be of help after the suffering is over. The sufferer has not gained anything through suffering. In fact, the knowledge itself is a liability: "a knowledge / born from the depths of despair / You find out soon enough / you should not speak with death / for it is useless knowledge. / In a world / where those who believe they are alive / are not / all knowledge becomes useless / for the one possessed of that other knowledge / it is far better to know nothing" (1995, 225). For Delbo, the knowledge acquired through suffering is costly and not useful, a liability not an asset, and it is "far better to know nothing" of this kind of knowledge.

"Useless knowledge" is a difficult concept to grasp. To say that the knowledge acquired through extreme suffering is useless seems to condemn sufferers to having gone through a meaningless experience, to having suffered "for nothing." Doesn't this add to their suffering by denying that their suffering might have meaning, that the knowledge gained through their suffering might be useful? It is important to note, however, that the term "useless knowledge" is not one to be used by an outsider looking at someone else's suffering, but rather by the sufferer herself. Only the sufferer herself can make use of her own suffering or can deem the knowledge gained from suffering useful; an outsider doing so imposes meaning onto the suffering of another. As Emmanuel Levinas (1998) notes, the only suffering we can make use of is our own suffering; to make use of someone else's suffering is to co-opt that suffering for one's own purposes and to fail to respond to the sufferer.

By highlighting the uselessness of the knowledge acquired in extreme suffering, Delbo is resisting efforts by outsiders to redeem suffering ("Well, at least you learned something out of the experience"), to make it "good" for something ("At least something good came out of it"). These efforts seek to make the extremity of suffering less extreme, to grasp hold of the knowledge gained as a reason for hope; they shut our ears and eyes to the extreme nature of suffering that results from evil.

If anything "useful" is to come out of Delbo's experience in Auschwitz, it is not from the knowledge acquired through suffering, for that knowledge is part of the infliction and ongoing effects of suffering. The knowledge, like the memories, is part of the haunting past that the survivor lives with in the present. The knowledge gained from suffering is part of the suffering itself, not a good that can be extracted from it. To know one has seen one's mother dead and not shed a tear is to know the extent of one's own degradation, to know how unlike oneself one can be made to become, and that knowledge is part of the devastating destructiveness of evil.

This is not to say that Delbo writes out of despair or a nihilistic sense that all of life is "for nothing." Her accounts of the many ways that the women around her formed a community of support that enabled her to survive point to the possibility of hope, to the possibility that helping and healing connections can be made between women, between sufferers, and even between those who have suffered and those who have not. But these connections will not be based on the redemption of extreme suffering as something that gives us useful knowledge.

For the possibility of connections between outsiders and sufferers to happen, it is important that we outsiders begin to "unlearn" some of our presumed knowledge of evil. Delbo tries to bring about this process of unlearning in her writing. In particular, she challenges our sentimentalized and sanitized representations and imaginings of suffering, and she does so in the starkest of language. Again and again in *Auschwitz and After*, Delbo shows us the limits of our knowledge of evil: "You may say that one can take away everything from a human being except the faculty of thinking and imagining. You have no idea. One can turn a human being into a skeleton gurgling with diarrhea, without time or energy to think. Imagination is the first luxury of a body receiving sufficient nourishment, enjoying a margin of free time, possessing the rudiments from which dreams are fashioned. People did not dream in Auschwitz, they were in a state of delirium" (1995, 168). Clichés about it not being possible to destroy the human spirit fail to recognize the facts of extreme suffering as a result of evil and the degradation it can inflict.

Rosette C. Lamont, the translator of Delbo's writings, tells us: "As I was working I recalled her impassioned tone as she explained that she had to transmit the knowledge she acquired in *l'univers concentrationnaire*. 'Je veux donner à voir!'[2] she kept on repeating. She was referring to the moral obligation she felt to raise the past from its ashes, to carry the word (the title of one of her plays)" (Lamont 1995, vii). This transmission of "knowledge" is not one of passing on information but of helping us to see what extreme suffering is really like, as opposed to how we might imagine it to be. Delbo wants us to "see." She presents us with bodily images and pungent details that call to our senses to see, feel, hear the physicality of her suffering and that of the other women with her in Auschwitz. She uses all the power she has as a writer of spare and painful prose, and yet there is a gap between her experience of extreme suffering and our ability to understand that experience.

For example, Delbo describes her inability to speak due to extreme thirst: "I'd been thirsty for days and days, thirsty to the point of losing my mind, to the point of being unable to eat since there was no saliva in my mouth, so thirsty I couldn't speak, because you're unable to speak when there's no saliva in your mouth. My parched lips were splitting, my gums swollen, my tongue a piece of wood" (1995, 142). Notice the interweaving repetitions that carry the prose along in a delirious rush: "thirsty . . . thirsty . . . so thirsty," "days and days," "to the point of . . . to the point of," "no saliva . . . no saliva." Notice the brilliant clarity of her last image: "my tongue a piece of wood." The reader can feel it in her mouth. Or, can she? Delbo continues: "There are people who say, 'I'm thirsty.' They step into a café and order a beer" (145). What does it mean to know a thirst that turns your tongue into a piece of wood? Delbo shows us what we do not know (for example, a thirst that renders one's tongue a piece of wood), and in so doing helps us unlearn what we have presumed to know or to be able to imagine. And yet, in doing so, Delbo gives us a glimpse (a taste almost) of what we cannot really know and brings us closer to "seeing" her suffering and those of the women with her, even though our seeing is merely a glimpse.

Knowing that our abilities are limited, Delbo struggles to make us see by pointing out the ways in which our preconceptions blind us to the realities of extreme suffering. She reveals our temptation to sentimentalize suffering: "So you believed that only solemn words rise to the lips of the dying. . . . Naked on the charnel house's pallets, almost all our comrades said, 'I'm going to kick the bucket.' They were naked on a naked board. They were dirty and the boards were soiled with pus and diarrhea" (1995, 108). Like Terrence Des Pres in his essay on "excremental assault" (1976), Delbo does not retreat from the physical details of suffering that may arouse our disgust—there is no sterilization of suffering, no glorification of what it means to be a victim. Our knowledge will always be partial and inadequate, and we should allow our "knowledge" of suffering to be thoroughly interrogated by those who have another kind of knowledge of suffering, a "useless knowledge" that haunts them.

By acknowledging the limitations to our knowledge of suffering due to the fact that we are outsiders, by recognizing our temptations to "redeem" suffering —to find something good that can come out of it—and by listening to those who have suffered evil in ways that allow our preconceptions to be reshaped, we begin to "see" in the way that Delbo strove to make us see.

Conclusion

Calling into question our preconceptions about what kind of person a perpetrator of evil can be, what the suffering of evil is really like, and what kind of knowledge of evil is available to us who are outsiders, Arendt and Delbo lead us away from discourses of mastery, that is, ways of speaking about evil that suggest a knowledge of evil from on high. Our knowledge is always from a distance but not from on high, and we need to listen to survivors' testimonies, to those who have a view from up close. Because evil can take on new forms with the emergence of new historical and social contexts, we will never have solved the problem of evil once and for all. Our knowledge of evil is always partial, always in process, always in need of interrogation. We need to pay ongoing attention to the particular forms evil takes and to move away from the thoughtlessness that is sometimes linked to the infliction of harm. That evil can be banal, that knowledge can be useless, should give us pause—pause enough to look around to see what unfamiliar shapes evil might be taking in our present world and pause enough to listen to the testimonies of those who have suffered evil.

Notes

Thanks are due to Mitchel Gerber, Beth Hawkins, Husain Kassim, Charles T. Mathewes, Michael Popich, John Roth, Julius Simon, and Mark Stern for comments on drafts of this essay, and to the Institute for Advanced Studies in Culture and the Center for Advanced Holocaust Studies at the United States Holocaust Memorial Museum for their financial and intellectual support.

1. Primo Levi goes so far as to propose that if it were possible to contain evil in one image, it would be the image of the victim: "If I could enclose the evil of our time in one image, I would choose this image which is familiar to me: an emaciated man, with head dropped and shoulders curved, on whose face and in whose eyes not a trace of thought is to be seen" (1993, 90).
2. This phrase might be translated as "I want to make it seen" or "I want to make them see."

References

Améry, Jean. 1980. *At the Mind's Limit: Contemplations by a Survivor on Auschwitz and Its Realities.* Trans. Sidney Rosenfeld and Stella P. Rosenfeld. Bloomington: Indiana University Press.

Arendt, Hannah. 1964. *Eichmann in Jerusalem: A Report on the Banality of Evil.* New York: Viking.

Browning, Christopher R. 1993. *Ordinary Men: Reserve Police Battalion 101 and the Final Solution in Poland.* New York: HarperPerennial.

Delbo, Charlotte. 1995. *Auschwitz and After.* Trans. Rosette C. Lamont. New Haven, Conn.: Yale University Press.

Des Pres, Terrence. 1976. *The Survivor: An Anatomy of Life in the Death Camps.* New York: Oxford University Press.

Goldhagen, Daniel Jonah. 1996. *Hitler's Willing Executioners: Ordinary Germans and the Holocaust.* New York: Knopf.

Kant, Immanuel. 1960. *Religion within the Limits of Reason Alone.* Trans. Theodore M. Greene and Hoyt H. Hudson. New York: Harper and Row.

Lamont, Rosette C. 1995. Translator's preface. In Charlotte Delbo, *Auschwitz and After.* Trans. Rosette C. Lamont. New Haven, Conn.: Yale University Press.

Langer, Lawrence L. Introduction. In Charlotte Delbo, *Auschwitz and After.* Trans. Rosette C. Lamont. New Haven, Conn.: Yale University Press.

Levi, Primo. 1993. *Survival in Auschwitz: The Nazi Assault on Humanity.* Trans. Stuart Woolf. New York: Collier Books/Macmillan.

Levinas, Emmanuel. 1998l. Useless suffering. In *Entre Nous: On Thinking-of-the-Other.* Trans. Michael B. Sith and Barbara Harshav. New York: Columbia University Press.

May, Larry. 1996. Socialization and institutional evil. In *Hannah Arendt: Twenty Years Later.* Ed. Larry May and Jerome Kohn. Cambridge: MIT Press.

Reagan, Charles E. 1996. *Paul Ricoeur: His Life and His Work.* Chicago: University of Chicago Press.

Ricoeur, Paul. 1995. *Figuring the Sacred: Religion, Narrative, and Imagination.* Trans. David Pallauer. Ed. Mark I. Wallace. Minneapolis, Minn.: Fortress Press.

———. *The Symbolism of Evil.* 1967. Trans. E. Buchanon. Boston, Mass.: Beacon Press.

Shattuck, Roger. 1996. *Forbidden Knowledge: From Prometheus to Pornography.* San Diego: Harcourt Brace.

7 February 22, 2001: Toward a Politics of the Vulnerable Body

Debra Bergoffen

February 22, 2001

On February 22, Marlise Simons of the *New York Times* reported that the United Nations International Criminal Tribunal for the former Yugoslavia (ICTY) found three Bosnian soldiers guilty of crimes against humanity. Their offense? Rape. The court's ruling opens a new chapter in international law. In Simons's words: "In its first trial dealing exclusively with sexual violence, the United Nations war crimes tribunal today found three former Bosnian Serb soldiers guilty of raping and torturing Muslim women and girls. It also convicted two of the three men of enslaving their captives, the first time that an international tribunal has prosecuted and condemned sexual slavery. . . . [It] also identified rape for the first time as a crime against humanity" (2001b).

Three factors make this a landmark event: first, the decision to prosecute; second, the condemnation; and third, the classification of rape as a crime against humanity in its own right rather than as a crime against humanity only insofar as it is identified as a species of torture. Of these three factors, the condemnation is the most dramatic. Had the decision gone the other way, the story might not have made headlines. It might not have become the topic of numerous editorials, commentaries, and news releases. Surely, women's groups would not have been elated. The judgment is important. It signals that the traditional defense of rape in times of peace and war, "Boys will be boys," and the specific wartime defense, "I was only following orders," are no longer acceptable. Two principles are articulated in the court's verdict. One refers to men and their responsibility to women; the other refers to women and their rights. The first, elegantly put by Judge Florence Mumba, states, "In time of peace as much as in time of war, men of substance do not abuse women" (in Simons 2001b). The second, more radical, links women's dignity to their "fundamental human right to sexual self-determination" (Trial Chamber 2001, 6).

These principles and the verdict that activates them, however, depend on a prior event: the decision to prosecute. Without this prior decision, the raped and enslaved Muslim women and girls would have found themselves in the situation of the women who were used by the Japanese as comfort women. Their stories would remain untold, or if told, would never come before the court. The rapes of the Muslim women and girls, like the war rapes of women and girls before them, would have been classified as pillage. They would have been dismissed as an inevitable (and of course regrettable) aspect of war, and excused as collateral damage.

The decision to prosecute is grounded in the determination that a raped woman's body is not analogous to a misappropriated piece of goods. It rejects the idea that women's sexual and reproductive bodies are the property of men. The decision to prosecute the accusations of rape, in other words, established women, *qua* sexually embodied, as persons. *Qua* sexually embodied, they must be given the respect due a human being. In framing its guilty verdict in such a way that rape was identified as a crime against humanity, the court affirmed the principle of embodied subjectivity. It goes beyond past rulings on torture, however. In insisting that violating a woman's sexual integrity constituted a crime against humanity, "the second most serious category of international war crimes after genocide" (Landmark Ruling 2001), the court attended to the sexed realities of embodiment, something ignored in previous crimes against humanity judgments.

Before this ruling, the standard against which evidence for or against the charge of a crime against humanity was the normative "neutral" body. Using this body as a measure, torture, understood through the criteria of physical pain, was identified as a crime against humanity. Appealing to this criteria, rape was equated with torture, and by virtue of this equivalency was classified as a crime against humanity. Working with this understanding of rape, however, to be convicted of rape, and to establish that a crime against humanity had occurred, evidence of physical violence was necessary. If such evidence was established, the rape victim, like the torture victim, could be recognized as having her humanity violated, for like the torture victim, she too could establish that having suffered physical pain and injury, her humanity was criminally abused.

The ICTY took a different position. It identified an act as rape, a crime against humanity, *whether or not* there was evidence of violence or physical pain and injury. It decoupled the idea of forced entry from the idea of painful entry. In doing this, it exposed the injustice of judgments that claim to speak to the issue of human rights but that ignore the relationship between the universal right to be respected as human and the specificity of the sexed body through which we live our humanity. What may be true for men: a crime against humanity occurs when the body is subjected to violence, injury and pain, may not always be true for women. Women's humanity, the court ruled, can be criminally abused even if they have not been subjected to physical violence, injury, or pain.

The court makes it clear that it does not come to this conclusion lightly or arbitrarily. It spends considerable time showing that the basic underlying principle common to domestic rape laws concerns the matter of consent. It establishes itself as following customary understandings. Drawing on the principle of consent, the court refused to define rape as an act of sexual penetration accompanied by coercion or force or threat of force against the victim or a third person. It found this definition to be too narrow. It does not, the court says, "refer to other factors which would render an act of sexual penetration nonconsensual or non-voluntary, on the part of the victim" (Trial Chamber 2001, 438). According to the court, "sexual penetration will constitute rape if it is not truly voluntary or consensual on the part of the victim" (Trial Chamber 2001, 440). To arrive at this definition of rape, the court appeals to what it calls "a common sense understanding of the meaning of genuine consent" (Trial Chamber 2001, 461).

According to the court, distinguishing submission, the appearance of consent, from genuine consent is a matter of common sense. Bringing this common sense to bear on its legal reasoning, the court stipulates that only apparent consent exists "where the victim is subjected to or threatened with or has reason to fear violence, duress, detention or psychological oppression or reasonably believed that if she did not submit another might be so subjected, threatened or put in fear" (Trial Chamber 2001, 464). In cases of apparent consent, the raped woman's body may not be the object of physical violence. In dismissing the apparent consent defense and in insisting on proof of genuine consent, the court determined that the situation of the woman, her capacity to give consent, not the quota of violence inflicted on her body, determines whether or not a rape occurred.

A crime against women identified as a crime against humanity; a violation of a woman's body as a crime against humanity—stunning. The woman's body not only not property, not only a mark of *her* subjectivity, but the site of humanity, the species, the universal. This in a world where rape, identified as a war crime since the American Civil War and mentioned in the 1949 Geneva Convention as an outrage upon personal dignity, remained a crime that, so long as men were responsible for deciding what crimes to prosecute and who to charge, remained an unprosecuted crime; this by a United Nations that only decided to expand the list of war crimes to include abuses of women in the mid-1990s (Landmark Ruling 2001); this by a United Nations that in its first four years of investigating war crimes in Rwanda almost completely ignored rape.

We need to attend to the implications of the judgment that male soldiers who rape civilian women are guilty of crimes against humanity, whether or not it is established that their violation of the women caused physical pain or suffering. Reading the court's decision, we discover that in order to arrive at this conclusion, the court had to rework current understandings of torture and crimes against humanity. Until the court's ruling, a crime against humanity had been identified with the pain and suffering of the unsexed (that is, the unmarked male) body. Appealing to this understanding, the defense counsel argued that the prosecution did not prove that the alleged victims of rape were exposed to any severe physical or psychological suffering: that rape in itself is not an act that inflicts severe bodily pain and therefore that no crime against humanity occurred (Simons 2001a). In effect, the defense argued that if the court wished to include rape in the category of crimes against humanity, it would have to identify rape with violence and pain, and that if the court defined rape without reference to violence and pain, it could not establish rape as a crime against humanity. Given accepted definitions of rape as torture and familiar understandings of crimes against humanity, there was nothing amiss in the defense lawyer's logic. The argument failed, however, not because the court refused the defense lawyer's reasoning, but because it refused traditional definitions of rape and of crimes against humanity. It determined that the data of pain and suffering, essential ingredients of torture, are not the defining characteristics of either rape or a crime against humanity. To do this, it had to pay particular attention to the way in which rape is a violation of the humanity of the body. It appealed to the criteria of consent.

In focusing on the matter of consent and in using criteria of consent rather than criteria of violence or pain for determining whether or not a crime against humanity occurred, the court took note of the relationship between a woman's humanity and her sexual integrity.[1] Read through the lens of Luce Irigaray's *je, tu, nous* (1993), the court may be seen as embarking on the project of women's sexed rights; for though it is the case that men can be raped, this case concerned the matter of the heterosexual rape of civilian women by military men. In its judgment, the court made it clear that it was a woman's bodily violation that was at issue. When it determined that rape is not limited to cases where there has been outrageous force and physical threat but includes cases marked by a lack of consent by the victim or cases where victim consent is secured under pressure for fear of prosecution of self or a third party, when it determined that penetrating a woman's vulva without her consent, whether or not that penetration is painful, violates her personal dignity, the court effectively ruled that a woman's sexual integrity is inseparable from her human integrity and that this integrity can be violated without evidence of physical violence. Though the court does not cite Irigaray's argument for the legal codification of virginity as the basis of "the free consent of women to sexual relationships" (1993, 87), it appeals to her ideal of female sexual autonomy when it insists that evidence of consent, not violence, determines whether or not rape has occurred. In arguing for sexed rights, Irigaray argues that recognizing the sexual difference between women and men is a necessary condition for establishing equity between the sexes (1993, 82). Irigaray's equity politics veers away from the ideal of equality to preserve the specificity of the sexual difference. The court moves in another direction. It takes up the sexual difference in the name of a crime against humanity. It invokes the idea of universality. Its ruling addresses the way in which women's bodies, signified by patriarchy as the uniquely vulnerable body, signifies the vulnerability of all human bodies. The court did not rule that the rapes were a crime against the sexed rights of women. It ruled that rape, a criminal violation of women's sexed rights, was a crime against humanity.

In finding that rape does not have to be represented as a species of torture to be condemned as a crime against humanity, the court spoke to the issue of sexual difference. The effect of its speech is threefold. First, it exposed the fallacy of treating the masculine body as the universal/neutral body. Second, it directed us to identify the woman's body in its difference as the mark of the universal. Third, it directed us to the intersections of difference and universality; for it is not as the neutral/universal body, but as the specifically sexed body, that the court sees the woman's body as speaking of our shared human condition.

Does this ruling inaugurate a politics of the body where the particularity of a woman's sexed body replaces the man's "neutral" body as the standard of the human body—humanity? If so, how would this politics be something other than a reversal of the status quo? How would it not repeat the mistake of allowing one sexed body to stand for the universal to the exclusion of the other? How does defining rape as an intrusion into a woman's body without her consent get us to a politics of the body that speaks to the shared human condition of embodiment? Could it get us to see that though patriarchy identifies vulnerability as a unique feature of the woman's body, all bodies are vulnerable? Could it get us to understand that seeing women as singularly vulnerable is both right and wrong: right in that women's vulnerability is specific to their lived bodies; wrong in that vulnerability is a human, not a sexed condition? Men's bodies, too, are vulnerable. Their humanity may also be violated absent physical pain and suffering.

In adopting the standards of pain and suffering, we have set the bar too low. Uncritically accepting patriarchal myths of male and female bodies, establishing the mythical male body as the normal human body, and establishing that a violation of this normal human body occurs only when its "natural" invulnerable borders are "unnaturally" forcibly breached, courts have made it difficult for the charge of rape to stick. The ICTY verdict should change this; for its judgment leads us to challenge the myth of the male invulnerable body and to interrogate the ways in which this mythical body has come to represent the human ideal.

The court's ruling deals with a specific category of rape: the violation of a civilian woman's rights as a noncombatant to be respected in her humanity by men who are enemy soldiers. It is concerned with upholding what it sees as the agreed-upon rules of heterosexuality: "Men of substance do not abuse women." Also specific to these cases is that some of the raped women were also enslaved. The court does not limit its convictions to circumstances where rape was either a prelude to slavery or part of a strategy of enslavement. It singles rape out as a crime against humanity in its own right.

Two things strike me as important here. One is the distinction between heterosexual rape and slavery. The other is the relationship between heterosexual rape and slavery—the fact that the military rapes often set the stage for the army's use of women as domestic and sexual slaves. As distinct from slavery, heterosexual rape engages the specific vulnerability of a woman's body. As related to slavery, it shows the way in which a woman's specific vulnerability speaks of a bodied vulnerability that is not unique to women. Not only is it not the case that only women can be raped; it is also not the case that only women can be enslaved. All human bodies are vulnerable. The violation of humanity occurs, not at the point of pain, for consensual pain relationships are neither uncommon nor criminal; not at the point of objectification, for no human offense occurs when one person agrees to be objectified by another (as, for example, in the case of the model and the artist, or the sex worker and her client); but at the point of consent. It is at this point, the point where my intentionality is negated, the moment when my vulnerability is used against me, that the crime against my humanity occurs.

Determining that a crime against humanity occurs sometimes but not always when pain is inflicted, but always when consent is denied or coerced, the court identifies the animality of our humanity, the body and its capacity for pain, and the limits of referencing this animality. The concept of consent speaks to the unique vulnerability of the human body. It identifies the ways in which our intentionalities constitute the meaning of our animality. These rape case convictions, specifically those which found the Bosnian Serb soldiers guilty of a crime against humanity because they violated the right of consent (whether or not there was evidence of inflicted pain) point us to the phenomenon of the humanly constituted body. They show us that though we cannot ignore our animality by dismissing the criminality of violent bodily abuse, we cannot forget that human bodies are abused when their intentionalities are violated. The woman's right to sexual integrity is a specific instance of this intentionality. In speaking of this right as a human right, and in tying this right to the right of consent, the court brings the phenomenologically lived body into the halls of justice.

In a trial concerned with wartime rape between a soldier and a civilian, the ICTY must notice what domestic rape trials often fail (refuse?) to notice: the inequality of the man and the woman. This is not to say that the court addressed the inherent inequalities of women and men in patriarchal societies, but rather to indicate that the status of the accused as a soldier and the position of the victim as a civilian established their inequality at the outset. Given that the equality of the power and position of the rapist and his victim could not be presumed, as it often is in civilian trials, the court did not get involved in disputes about whether and when her "no" means "yes." It immediately identified the difference between submission and consent (Pateman 1989, 78–83). During times of war civilians are subordinate to soldiers. They are expected to submit; their "no" has no standing. They are powerless to ward off physical assault. They become women.

Had the court presumed the possibility of consent and resistance, it might have accepted "evidence of physical force" criteria of rape. It might not have convicted the Bosnian Serb soldiers. Often there were no signs of struggle. Instead of presuming the possibility of consent and resistance, however, the court asked whether the women could have resisted. Asking whether the conditions of consent existed, the court found the soldiers guilty, not of ignoring the women's "no" (sometimes the women did not refuse), but of putting the women in a position where they could not exercise their right of refusal. The soldiers were guilty of violating the rule of consent, not because they physically overpowered the women, not because they heard the women's "no" as "yes" or refused to hear it at all, but because they abused the women's status as civilians to destroy the conditions that make consent a meaningful political and moral concept. Their crime against humanity consisted in destroying the conditions under which a woman may exercise her right to assert her human sexual dignity.

News accounts attribute this dramatic trial and verdict to the pressure of women's groups and to the fact that this war crimes tribunal had one woman judge who insisted on investigating and prosecuting the stories of mass rape. These accounts are concretely correct. The concrete importance of the women who came forward to testify and of the women's groups who insisted that the rape charges be investigated cannot be underestimated; for it is through this work in the concrete that soldiers, who for centuries were permitted to rape civilian women without fear of prosecution, were now prosecuted as criminals and sentenced for their crimes. In celebrating the concrete, however, we must not lose sight of the principle at the heart of this unfolding drama, for it is with this principle that the future of justice lies, and it is in probing the meanings and implications of this change of principle regarding the relationship between the woman's body, its vulnerability to being raped, and the status of humanity, that the hope of a politics of democracy lies. That, at least, is the hypothesis of this chapter.

The Court and the Philosopher

Postmodern critiques of the Cartesian subject and humanist narratives have been criticized for discrediting democratic discourse, for stealing subjectivity from women just as they were on the brink of securing it, and for undermining the politics of rights necessary for securing women's social, economic, and political well-being. Jacques Derrida's *The Politics of Friendship* (1997) responds to the criticism that postmodernism is politically bankrupt and strategically irresponsible. Dramatically declaring, "No deconstruction without democracy. No democracy without deconstruction" (1997, 105), Derrida applies the deconstructive scalpel to democracy's narratives of friendship, fraternity, and equality. He claims to speak in the name of a democracy to come—a "democracy of the perhaps." According to Derrida, this democracy of the perhaps is the thought of the event (29). It calls for an excess of freedom and a surplus of democracy that breaks with the reign of right and vengeance (40, 69). It requires thinking of alterity without hierarchal difference (232). It rejects the phallogocentricism of contemporary democracy that equates political courage with the willingness to kill (158–59). Derrida envisions this democracy of the perhaps as a politics of responsibility of/before the other, where political practices of speaking to/with the other replace current practices of speaking for others (69).

The Politics of Friendship, like ICTY rape convictions, confronts the violence embedded in modern democratic traditions. Where the court appeals to traditional liberal democratic categories of consent to contain this violence and attends to the unique vulnerability of women's bodies in the face of this violence, Derrida appeals to the power of deconstructive strategies to expose the violence of the democratic ideal of fraternity and to challenge it. He, too, is aware of the relationship between democratic violence and patriarchy. Like Carol Pateman (1989), he is not taken in by the "neutral" language of democratic discourses. He hears the patriarchal timbre of the democratic rallying cries of liberty, equality, fraternity. He knows that they exclude women. Confronting this exclusion, the court issues a verdict that takes up Pateman's call for concrete legal changes. Derrida, suspicious of democracy's juridical discourses, offers searching analyses and asks for women's patience. The problem of masculine friendship's legacy to/for democracy must be worked through before the question of woman can be raised.

The court and the philosopher challenge each other. The philosopher exposes the limits of relying on the legal categories of rights and consent. The court pushes the envelop of these limits. It exposes the ways in which the philosopher both addresses and evades his responsibility to women when he takes up the question of woman/women and the possibility of friendship/politics with the sister, the wife, the (m)other, only to postpone it. Its decision indicates that Derrida is correct in identifying the link between Western discourses of friendship and fraternity and those Western democratic practices that direct us to deal with the other violently and with women unjustly. Its decision also shows us, however, that Derrida repeats the patriarchal gesture embedded in the discourses of democracy when he analyzes the relationship among questions of friendship, fraternity, and politics.

For Derrida, "describing friends as masculine neuter . . . [is] a laborious way of letting a question furrow deeper. . . . What is a friend in the feminine and who in the feminine is her friend?" (1997, 56). For me, describing friends as masculine neuter buries the question of the feminine. The ICTY decisions unearth the violence at the heart of the strategy of considering friendship in the masculine neuter. They probe the possibilities of an other politics. They mark the bodies of women as the parchment on/through which the justice of Derrida's democracy to come will be inscribed.

Engaging the Universal

Like the court, the philosopher Derrida reads the future of democracy through the lens of crimes against humanity. Both the court and the philosopher find current inscriptions of these crimes wanting. Facing the violation of the violence against women, the court struggles to decode its principles. Confronting this violence, the philosopher finds himself formulating a sphinx's question: "What would be today in a new system of law, a crime against humanity? Its recent definition is no longer sufficient. It will be said that the question is very old and this is true, but it is also as new, still intact, pregnant, replete, heavy with a future whose monstrosity by definition, is nameless" (Derrida 1997, 273).

By "recent definition," Derrida seems to mean "the categorical imperative: not to betray humanity" (1997, 273), where betraying humanity is identified with falling short of the virtue of fraternity. This categorical imperative only recognizes the betrayal of the brother as criminal. Thus, "only the brother can be betrayed. Fratricide is the general form of temptation, the possibility of radical evil, the evil of evil" (273). The ICTY verdict identifies the betrayal of the sister as a radical evil and gives the monstrosity of the question, "What constitutes a crime against humanity?" a figure, face, and body: woman. In interrogating the democratic tradition that Derrida deconstructs, however, the court endorses the tradition's legitimacy.

At issue between the court and the philosopher is the role and meaning of the universal. In passing judgment, the court subsumes the particular under the universal. The rape convictions may be read as a corrective to a misdefined universal (the universal of an invulnerable body that is only dehumanized when physically assaulted). It cannot be read as a rejection of the procedure of appealing to universals as absolute standards. Derrida's *Politics of Friendship,* however, identifies the violence of the democracy of fraternity with the invocation of the universal as absolute. What for the court is a misunderstanding of the meaning of a particular universal, is, for Derrida, a misunderstanding of the way in which all universals work. The court believes that establishing proper universals will eradicate the violence. Derrida argues that any appeal to a universal entails violence. For him, there are no proper (universally inclusive) universals. How, then, are we to understand Derrida's concern with crimes against humanity? What violence lies in the court's appeal to the universal right to human dignity? A detour through Judith Butler's work may help to clarify these issues.

As I turn to the ICTY ruling to give Derrida's questions regarding crimes against humanity, evil, and the meanings of humanity and democracy a material referent, Judith Butler (2001, 414–34) looks to the 1995 UN Beijing resolutions on the status of women to anchor these questions in concrete political realities. Butler reads the Beijing resolutions as a lesson in the continued political potency of the universal concepts developed by Europeans in response to the particular historical circumstances of the Enlightenment. The Beijing Conference appealed to the concept of universal human rights to assert the rights of women. The ICTY ruling invoked the universal concept of human dignity/integrity to establish rape as a crime against humanity. The conference and the case demonstrate the ways in which the appeal to these Enlightenment universal categories continues to carry political weight. They seem to show that at this point in our history we cannot do without them. It would be a mistake, however, to say that these universal categories work today in the same way as they worked in the past. In Beijing and at the ICTY, the concept of human rights was scrutinized, pushed, and meaningfully transformed. Instead of questioning the very concept of a universal, these UN bodies demanded that those excluded from its protections be included.

Derrida and Butler argue, however, that if we continue to use Enlightenment categories in their traditional forms, we will repeat their violent history. They ask us to do more than adjust the content and context of the universal. They ask us to restructure it. For Derrida, it is a matter of aligning the universal with the idea of the perhaps; for Butler, it concerns understanding the universal through the ideas of undecidability and performative contradiction. The ideas of the perhaps, of undecidability, and of the performative contradiction demystify the universal concepts of "humanity," "consent," and "human" rights. Dethroned from their position as absolute Platonic realities, universals become embedded in material realities—sites where the tension between the specificity of those articulating the universal appeal and the absolute resolution articulated in the particulars of the appeal become politically productive. In Butler's words: "What is permitted within the term universal is understood to be dependent on a consensus [and] . . . presumes that what will and will not be included in the language of universal entitlement is not settled once and for all, that its future shape cannot be fully anticipated at this time" (2001, 430). Butler calls this unsettledness of entitlement, this undecidability of the universal, the performative contradiction. We must, she argues, reformulate our understanding of the universal by taking the relationship between the performative particular enactment and the universal claims of the enactors into account.

The ICTY verdict and the effect of the Bosnia rape convictions exemplify Butler's politics of performative contradiction. The trial is a response to a specific war. The conviction represents the judgment of particular judges. These judges, however, claim the right to articulate universal, absolute, and enduring obligations. The judges do not wish to call attention to their specificity. Butler, however, argues that it is in remembering the identity of the judges and the specificity of their judgment that we guarantee the future of democracy. Rather than align the universal with an absolute unerring content, rather than ignore the disjunction between the historicity of the judgment and its affirmation of a universal principle, Butler identifies the universal with the "not yet." She calls the "that which remains unrealized" the essence of the universal, and identifies all appeals to the universal as challenging its existing formulations (2001, 431). The Enlightenment foundations of today's democracies are stripped of their status as natural or divine laws. They are not, however, abandoned. They become the human, finite, unstable ground of the not-yet-but-possible of the political.

Butler uses the concept of the performative contradiction to align traditional democratic principles with the idea of an undecidable future. According to Butler, the performative contradiction engages the thought of "a modernity without foundationalism . . . [where] the key terms of its operation are not fully secured in advance, one that assumes a futural form for politics that cannot be fully anticipated, a politics of hope and anxiety" (2001, 421).

Neither Butler not Derrida cites each other. They are, however, engaged in similar projects. Both privilege the future as the time of the possible and the promise. Both link the possibility of justice to a thinking that frees the thought of the future from its betrayal either by already determined concepts of universality or by the necessities imposed by the idea of progress. By unhinging the future from these determinations, Butler opens it to the hope and anxiety of the not yet of the universal (2001, 431). Derrida, also invoking the categories of promise and uncertainty, aligns the future with the thought of the event (1997, 29). Derrida's "event, perhaps" and Butler's "that which remains to be realized" direct us to envision the possibilities of a democracy to come.

If we examine the ways in which the court both appealed to and undermined social contract criteria of consent, we can, I think, understand the ways in which its judgment gives Derrida's ideas of the perhaps and the event, and Butler's thought of the hope and anxiety of the not yet of the universal, concrete form. The relationship between rape laws, democratic theories of consent, and patriarchy has been a matter of concern to feminist political theorists for some time. These feminists have exposed the "double speak" of social contract consent theory. They have documented the ways in which "women's silence or even their express 'no' has been taken to mean 'yes'. . . . [as] women have been forced to 'consent' to marriage, to motherhood and to the activities, work, and roles that these have entailed for different classes and races of women" (Hirschmann 1996, 160). They have detailed the ways in which the emphasis on consent relies on a masculine concept of the self as an autonomous, independent being. They have examined the ways in which this concept of self runs counter to women's experience of the self as a relational being with responsibility to/for others (Hirschmann 1996, 162).

Given these feminist critiques of consent and the court's reliance on consent, the hope of the ICTY judgment carries certain anxieties. Insofar as the idea of consent is bound up with the ideals of fraternity, invoking the justice of consent may perpetuate the violence of today's democracies. Pateman alerts us to this danger when she writes:

> Consent must always be given to something; in the relationship between the sexes it is always women who are said to consent to men. The "naturally" superior, active and sexually aggressive male makes an initiative or offers a contract to which a "naturally" subordinate passive woman "consents." An egalitarian sexual relationship does not rest on this basis; it cannot be grounded in consent. Perhaps the most telling aspect of women and consent is that we lack a language through which to help constitute a form of personal life in which two equals freely agree to create a lasting association together (1989, 84).

What consent theory identifies, however, and what is particularly relevant in these and all rape cases, is our need to "find areas and modes of connection that are safe, that can provide for needs without risking the loss of self" (Hirschmann 1996, 170). Given our current historical location, we cannot, I think, abandon consent theory. For if it is the case that consent theory presumes that choices create relationships and obligations, and if it is the case that women's experiences speak to the fact that relationships and obligations are given rather than consciously chosen, it is also the case that there are times when relationships ought to be governed by the rules of choice (for example, sexual relationships). There are also times when we want to invoke the right to challenge our presumed obligations (for example, the obligation to become a mother). Here I find myself agreeing with Patricia Williams (1991). However flawed the democratic system of rules and rights may be, so long as rules and rights are the keys to power, I, like Williams, do not think that feminists can abandon the pursuit of rights in their quest for justice. Everything depends, I think, on the way in which the rules of consent are articulated and applied.

The court's ruling identifies the feminist hope of the rule of consent, for when it appealed to the way in which consent is invoked to protect self-integrity, it did not equate self-integrity with the integrity of the unmarked autonomous self. Instead, it spoke of the integrity of the sexed vulnerable self. Its judgment, in marking out the category of consent from the category of physical violence/ violation, recalls us to our obligations to respect and respond to each other's vulnerability. Like the work of Susan Okin (1989) and Robert Goodin (1985), it prompts us to argue for the rule of consent in the context of a theory of justice where the humanity of the political subject is articulated through their vulnerability rather than their autonomy.

War Crimes

Butler addresses the "that which remains to be realized" of democracy through the concept of performative contradiction. Derrida takes up "the perhaps of the democracy to come" through the question of translation. Can the heteronomies of friendship become the principles of citizenship? In Derrida's words: "Does not the heteronomic disproportion of sovereign friendship, *once translated into the political realm*, endanger the principle of equality, mutuality and autarky which, it would seem, inspires Aristotle? But our question at every moment concerns *political translation*. It is indeed a question of knowing the rules of translation, but first of all of making sure that translation is possible and that everything can be translated into politics. Is the political a universal translating machine?" (1997, 196).

Reading Derrida's discussion of war and the enemy, we find that the heteronomy of friendship has already been translated into politics. We find that the translation resides in the political decision that creates the heteronomy of the enemy. This translation establishes the parameters of violence. It limits it to the enemy and deflects it from the friend. The enemy is the one against whom I may declare war, the only one I may legitimately kill. The possibility of war crimes resides in this friend/enemy distinction. All of this is familiar terrain. The law of the enemy is codified in the accepted rules of war. As Derrida describes it: "The death of a *human being*, thus implied in this concept of the enemy—that is, in all war, exterior or civil war—is neither natural death since the enemy must be killed, nor murder, for wartime killing is not seen as a crime. The war crime is something else again; it would consist in transgressing this law to revert to the savageness of a violence that no longer respect the laws of war and the rights of people" (1997, 122).

War, then, is that state of affairs where killing a human being is justified if and only if the law of the enemy is respected. Not to respect this law is to be guilty of savagery—of an uncivilized violence. The Bosnia rape convictions challenge the current political translations of the heteronomy of friendship. In identifying rape as a crime against humanity, the court directs us to another translation of the heteronomy of friendship. In this translation, heteronomy would become the ground of a radical politics where the killing of another human being would always be called murder and where the concept of vulnerability and the rights of trust would expose the injustice embedded in the law of justified violence.

Read in this way, the judgment is, in Derrida's word, an event. It is the political "perhaps." It takes up Derrida's challenge to the traditional political translation of friendship. It "addresses itself to the possible" by reformulating the criteria of a crime against humanity (1997, 67). As a judicial ruling, however, it establishes a "steadfast determination" (67). It provides the calculability necessary for law but destroys the "perhaps" that made the decision possible. Here we are confronted with the tension between the event, the disruptive advent of the possible, and the decision—the instantiation of the possible as the real. In Derrida's words: "Without the opening of an absolutely undetermined possible, without the radical abeyance and suspense marking a *perhaps*, there would never be either event or decision. Certainly. But nothing takes place and nothing is ever decided without suspending the *perhaps* while keeping its living possibility in memory. . . . In the order of law, politics or morality, what would rules and laws, contracts and institutions indeed be without steadfast determination, without calculability and without violence done to the *perhaps*, to the possible that makes them possible" (67).

Friend Wanted: Gods Need Not Apply

Confronting the problem of suspending the "perhaps" while keeping its living possibility in memory, I begin again. Veering away from the heteronomy of the friend and the enemy, I turn to Derrida's discussion of friendship as a virtue unique to human beings. Among the gods, Derrida, following Aristotle, tells us, friendship is neither necessary nor possible. A god is by definition an autonomous self-sufficient being. He, she, or it needs no other. Derrida writes:

> In sum, it is of God (or man in so far as he should or would want to resemble Him) that one must think in saying "there is no friend." . . . Friendship *par excellence* can only be human but above all, and by the same token there is thought for man only to the extent that it is thought *of the other . . . qua thought of the mortal.* . . . Translated into the logic of a human and finite *cogito,* this gives the formula: I think, therefore I am the other; I think, therefore I need the other (in order to think); I think therefore the possibility of friendship is lodged in the movement of my thought in so far as it demands, calls for, desires the other. (1997, 223–24)

I think, therefore you are. I think, therefore I am the other. Is this the way to the "we" of friendship? Is this the route to a political translation? Yes and no.

For if it is a necessary way to the "we" insofar as it inaugurates a critique of the fantasy of autonomy, the "we" arrived at may be the "we" of a paternalism that justifies authoritarian politics. It will not necessarily be the "we" of the friendship of the anticipated democracy to come. To get to the "we" of democracy's "perhaps," we need to think of the other/otherness *qua* the thought of the mortal. This thinking probes the meaning of finitude. It ponders the relationship between finitude and friendship and turns to the lived vulnerabilities of the mortal body.

For Derrida, to mark the distinction between the human and the gods through the thought of mortality is to invoke the category of the vulnerable. A god is invulnerable. That is the secret meaning of autonomy. To be mortal is to be vulnerable. That is the secret of friendship. That is the law of the enemy. That is the terrain of human rights. The we of humanity is the we of vulnerability. It is the fact of our vulnerability to the violence of the other. The law of the enemy and of war codifies this vulnerability and circumscribes the violence. The virtue of trust speaks of this vulnerability differently. Here, instead of becoming the trigger for the politics of war, the passion of uncertainty provoked by our dissymmetry precipitates the gamble of vulnerability. I take the chance that you will befriend my finitude rather than abuse it. I trust you. Derrida puts it this way: "The bond uniting me to the soul of the friend . . . places me under the law of the other. It disjoins and disproportions me, inspiring a confidence, a faith, a 'fidence' *greater in the other than in myself,* and this dissymmetry itself alone, marks the rupture . . . between knowledge and the heart—or the body and the 'entrails.' . . . The knowledge we have of each other may be symmetrical and reflective, equally shared in the glass of a mirror; it is nevertheless autonomous on both sides. As for trust, it could never be measured in this way; in truth it cannot be measured. . . . I must trust the other more than myself. . . . Passion and heteronomy" (1997, 194–95).

The lines are drawn. The knowledge of the other operates under the laws of symmetry and autonomy. In this knowledge we evade our vulnerability to each other by positioning ourselves as each other's autonomous equals. Thus, the law of autonomous equality under which we emulate the gods (and delude ourselves into thinking that we can produce a political translation through this ruse?). Friendship is not taken in by the mirrored cogito. It escapes the trap of the ego-imago *méconnaissance.* It lives the passion of finitude through the law of the other—the law of the vulnerable body. It risks the we of dissymmetry by counting on the incalculable (Derrida 1997, 197).

The risks of this incalculability are made clear in Jean Améry's account of being tortured by the Nazis (1986). Améry tells us that what is dehumanizing about being tortured is not the physical pain and abuse but the sudden understanding that the other is impervious to his cry for help—that there is no one he can trust. The essence of torture, he concludes, is the destruction of the trust in the other that makes the concept of humanity possible. From this perspective, the court's decision to invoke the criteria of consent is not an appeal to the rights of an autonomous subject but a political translation of friendship's virtue of trust—a virtue only necessary to, and possible among, those who are vulnerable to each other because they are not autonomous.

Do Derrida and Améry get us far enough? I think not. If the problem of the perhaps of the democracy to come is the problem of "inegalitarian heteronomy," if it must save a certain equality "in respect of dissymmetrical and heteronomic singularities" (Derrida 1997, 196–97), if it is a matter of politically translating the virtue of trust, the virtue of the passionately lived body, then we cannot avoid noticing that our passionate bodily vulnerabilities are never lived asexually. In speaking of dissymmetry without noting that in our current historical circumstances the sexual difference is the crucial site of the dissymmetrical and heteronomous, Derrida, despite his talk of dissymmetry, repeats the gesture of the blind spot of symmetry.

The dissymmetry of the fraternal friend, the fraternal violations of trust, will not get us to the ruling that rape is a crime against humanity; for this ruling speaks of the violation of trust as a crime against humanity, not in the name of a nameless neutered body, but in the name of the concretely sexed woman's body. It speaks to the flaw in the fact that at this point in our history the matter of dissymmetry and trust is translated from friendship into politics through the medium of patriarchy. It points to the fact that under these conditions, when such translations occur, there are some bodies that are left untranslated because they are rendered untranslatable. The court takes note of these bodies and provides a lexicon for their speech.

Judith Butler, in her most recent works, *Precarious Life* (2004a) and *Undoing Gender* (2004b), traces a route from the vulnerable mortal body to the promise of democracy similar to that of Derrida. Where he speaks of friendship, she speaks of mourning and grief. Where he skirts the questions of embodiment and women, however, she invokes and multiplies them. She conjures up the bodies of other others, transsexed, transgendered, raced, disabled, ambiguously sexed others, whose vulnerability renders them less than human, ungrievable. Between Derrida and Butler we seem to be converging on a political translation of the risks of vulnerability where the law of the vulnerable body and the requirements of trust become the ground of moral, legal, and political accounts of human rights.

The Bosnian Serb army employed rape as a military strategy. Despite the fact that this was a war fueled by the dissymmetry of ethnicity and religion, the Bosnian Serb command determined that the sexual difference as structured by patriarchy could be used as a powerful weapon against its enemies. It determined that if its armies raped Muslim women with impunity, they would disarm Muslim men, strip them of their masculinity, and destroy their ability to resist. In adopting this strategy, the Bosnian Serb military demonstrated its understanding of the way in which patriarchal men are gendered as *man* through their relationship to women and revealed the ways in which patriarchy mistranslates the trust of friendship into a politics of protection. I doubt that this was their intent.

Within patriarchy, the sexual dissymmetry of the human body is marked as crucial. Thus, the question of trust is translated into the question of the sexual relationship. It then gets perverted. Instead of recognizing a mutual vulnerability between men and women that throws them both before each other in the passion and heteronomy of a trust that can neither be determined nor measured, it establishes the law of patriarchal dissymmetry. According to this law, men are established as the protectors of women: "In times of war as in times of peace, men of substance do not abuse women" (Simons 2001b). Women must rely on men for their safety and security. The sexual difference, instead of revealing our shared human vulnerability, instead of throwing us all before each other in our embodied finitude, instead of opening us to the passions, uncertainties, and necessities of trust, becomes the structure through which only one sex lives the humanity of vulnerability. The vulnerable human body is feminized. Men's lived vulnerable bodies are encased/erased in imaginary, god-like, invulnerable bodies.

Following the law of desire's *méconnaissance,* this imaginary body becomes the standard by which human rights were established. In being charged with the obligation to protect women, men are allowed to see themselves as invulnerable. Their reliability as soldiers depends on this self-perception. Men who cannot protect "their" women are unfit. Thus the rape of women aimed at the men. Thus the rape of the women intended to remind them of their vulnerability to men, of their need of protection, of the fact that they cannot depend on the kindness of strangers. Thus the rape of the women, exposing the latent violence of a system that recognizes only one sexed body as vulnerable and allows the other sexed body to enjoy the fantasy of autonomy. Thus the rape of the women, alerting us to the injustice of a politics that speaks of humanity (the universal) from the position of the fantasmatic autonomous male body that refuses its human vulnerability.

In judging that the rape of the women was a crime against humanity because it violated the dignity of the women, not because it disarmed the men, and not only because it was part of a strategy of ethnic cleansing, the ICTY identified women *qua* woman *qua* uniquely sexed and vulnerable as human. The details of its ruling challenged the right of the fantasmatic male body to determine the sphere of the human. Whether or not the convictions undermine the (in)justice of a politics of protection, however, is less clear. For example, the court reprimands the civilian authorities for not carrying out their duty to protect the women and girls (Trial Chamber 2001, 3). It does not, however, formulate its legal judgment in the language of protection. Instead, it speaks of sexual exploitation as a violation of a woman's fundamental, sexed, bodily right to self-determination. This language is crucial. It exposes the violence at the heart of the concept of protection.

A Conclusion by Way of a Beginning

The social contract tradition that grounds liberal democratic politics appeals to the body politic metaphor to advance a narrative of justice wherein autonomous bodies consent to become part of another body, a body politic, so long as their singular autonomy is recognized. Caught in the structures of patriarchy, the social contract principles of justice only apply to a specific category of human beings, those who fit the model of the autonomous citizen—a model grounded in the masculine imaginary. This tradition finds the inequalities of the sexual difference natural and necessary. It cannot, therefore, speak to the possibilities of justice between autonomous men and dependent women (or others) whose "nature" renders the injustice of their inequality invisible. In this silence, the social contract tradition evades the question of justice between those who have nothing in common save the vulnerability of their shared humanity.

Derrida credits Friedrich Nietzsche with being one of the first thinkers of the twentieth century to speak to this question of justice. He notes that in speaking of the justice of the community without community, we are forced to speak "in the language of madness . . . by the most rigorous necessity, to say things as contradictory, insane, absurd, impossible, undecidable as 'X without X', community of those without community, 'inoperative community', 'unavowable community' . . ." (1997, 42). The idea of a community of those with nothing in common is abhorrent to Enlightenment thought. From the perspective of Enlightenment discourse, our heteronomy is an obstacle to justice. The efforts of Enlightenment politics are directed toward erasing the differences among us so that we may, in our homogeneity, exist as each other's equals. From the perspective of *Politics of Friendship*, however, heteronomy is the secret of humanity. Here we discover that our humanness consists in the fact that we are neither autonomous nor homogenous—that justice concerns the heteronomy of our mutual vulnerability.

We have, to date, lived our heteronomy violently and sacrificially. Derrida urges us to live it virtuously through friendship. In friendship, heteronomy is lived through the risk of trust. The securities and fantasies of autonomy and protection are rejected. If we took it upon ourselves to translate this understanding of heteronomy from the domain of friendship into the field of the political, the other could never be my enemy, that is, the one whose trust I can legitimately violate, the one I can kill. The crime against humanity would occur when the killing of another human being is honored rather than called murder, when that human being's otherness is identified with the threat of the enemy.

The perhaps of democracy lies in testing the limits of a politics of friendship. As I read them, the ICTY rulings reject translating our mutual vulnerability into a politics of protection and in this way lead us in the direction of a politics of friendship. Instead of finding the soldiers guilty of not fulfilling their role as women's protectors, it finds them guilty of violating the laws of heteronomy and trust, of not respecting the humanity of a woman's heterogeneous sexual dignity. The court ruled that this lack of respect is a breach of the fundamental trust that we owe to each other and thus constitutes a crime against humanity.

Patriarchy marks the woman's body as definitively other and as uniquely vulnerable in its otherness. The court's ruling identifies woman's otherness and vulnerability with a universal human obligation to acknowledge and abide by the virtue of trust. It translates this virtue into the political law of consent. If we pursue the logic of this ruling, we discover that the politics of the vulnerable body leads us to speak of justice in terms of the community of those with nothing in common. Nothing in the ruling suggests that the difference of the woman's sexual integrity could or should be erased. The point of the ruling is to insist that the difference be recognized and respected. In this the court brings the Enlightenment's universal principles of humanity, equality, and dignity to the hope and anxiety of a politics of the body—perhaps.

Note

1. In identifying rape as a violation of a woman's sexual and human integrity, the court's position reflects women's experience of rape. See, for example, Hankey 1997 and Herrera-Sobek 1977.

References

Améry, Jean. 1986. At the mind's limits, In *Contemplations by a Survivor on Auschwitz and Its Realities.* Trans. Sidney Rosenfeld and Stella P. Rosenfeld. New York: Schocken Books.

Butler, Judith. 2001. The end of sexual difference? In *Feminist Consequences: Theory for the New Century,* ed. Elisabeth Bronfen and Misha Kavka. New York: Columbia University Press.

———. 2004a. *Precarious Life: The Powers of Mourning and Violence.* New York: Verso.

———. 2004b. *Undoing Gender.* New York: Routledge.

Derrida, Jacques. 1997. *Politics of Friendship.* Trans. George Collins. New York: Verso.

Hankey, Leone Sandra. 1997. Women write patriarchal wrongs: Narrative resistance to the rape culture. In *Beyond Portia: Women, Law and Literature in the United States,* ed. Jacqueline St. Joan and Annette Bennington McElheney. Boston: Northeastern Press.

Herrera-Sobek, María. 1977. The politics of rape: Sexual transgressions in Chicana fiction. In *Beyond Portia: Women Law and Literature in the United States,* ed. Jacqueline St. Joan and Annette Bennington McElheney. Boston: Northeastern Press.

Hirschmann, Nancy J. 1996. Rethinking obligation for feminism. In *Revisioning the Political,* ed. Nancy J. Hirschmann and Christine Di Stefano. Boulder, Colo.: Westview Press.

Irigaray, Luce. 1993. Why define sexed rights? In *je, tu, nous: Toward a Culture of Difference.* Trans. Alison Martin. New York: Routledge.

A landmark ruling on rape. 2001. Editorial. *New York Times,* 24 February.

Pateman, Carol. 1989. Women and consent. In *The Disorder of Women.* Stanford, Calif.: Stanford University Press.

Simons, Marlise. 2001a. Bosnian war trial focuses on sex crimes. *New York Times,* 16 February.

———. 2001b. Three Serbs convicted in wartime rapes. *New York Times,* 22 February.

Trial Chamber. 2001. Judgment of trial chamber II in the Kunarac, Kovac and Vukovic case. February 22. http://www.un.org.icty.

Williams, Patricia. 1991. *The Alchemy of Race and Rights: Diary of a Mad Law Professor.* Cambridge, Mass.: Harvard University Press.

8 Obscene Undersides:
Women and Evil between the
Taliban and the United States

Mary Anne Franks

> What you engender in the mode of production will never be anything but the
> image of yourselves. Only what comes to pass in the mode of disappearance is
> truly other.
>
> Jean Baudrillard, *The Perfect Crime* (1996, 85)

A Note on Good and Evil

This chapter was originally written in November 2000, almost a year
before the World Trade Center attacks took place. Since then, the international
perception of the Taliban has shifted greatly. Formerly perceived as a largely
irrelevant, though brutal, foreign regime, the Taliban became the subject of intense international focus after September 11, 2001. More recent events compelled me to alter aspects of my argument that were based on the West's seeming indifference to Afghanistan and to examine the dramatic changes in policy
and rhetoric that the United States effected in the months following the WTC
attacks.

The concept of "evil" has figured prominently in the rhetoric of both the U.S.
government and of Islamic extremists, though to very different ends. The Bush
administration declared the war against Afghanistan a war between good and
evil, that the terrorists who carried out the attacks are "evil," that governments
that harbor terrorists are "evil," and, perhaps most notoriously, that the United
States faces an "axis of evil" consisting of Iran, Iraq, and North Korea. For their
part, Islamic extremists, and especially their now most famous representative,
Osama bin Laden, often pronounce America, and Western culture in general, to
be "evil."

This chapter originally did not deal with the concept of evil directly, but
rather attempted to focus on hidden affinities between the Taliban and Western
(especially American) culture as regards the "place" of women. My purpose in

highlighting these affinities was to provoke a radical revision of an "us against them" mentality and to challenge Western indifference to the sufferings and resistances of "other" peoples. This was motivated by the belief that the West is politically and historically implicated in the crisis in Afghanistan and that a rigid assertion of Western cultural and moral superiority insulates countries such as the United States against self-critique in a dangerous and hypocritical way.

In November 2000 I did not anticipate that the United States and the Taliban would become embroiled in a direct conflict and that the Taliban would receive the wrath, instead of the indifference or even tacit support, of "the world's only superpower."[1] It seems to me that the affinities that bind the two together became all the more significant after the WTC attacks, and that a reading of the Taliban as (to use psychoanalytic terminology) the "obscene superego underside" of the United States is all the more credible in light of recent events. This sentiment is voiced in a recent article by Slavoj Žižek, who writes that nothing in the United States' conception of the "Other" is not already at work in the United States itself:

> Every feature attributed to the Other is already present in the very heart of the U.S.: murderous fanaticism? There are today in the U.S. itself more than two millions of the Rightist populist "fundamentalists" who also practice the terror of their own, legitimized by (their understanding of) Christianity. . . . What about the way Jerry Falwell and Pat Robertson reacted to the bombings, perceiving them as a sign that God lifted up its protection of the U.S. because of the sinful lives of the Americans, putting the blame on hedonist materialism, liberalism, and rampant sexuality, and claiming that America got what it deserved? The fact that the very same condemnation of the "liberal" America as the one from the Muslim Other came from the very heart of the *Amerique profonde* should give as [sic] to think. America as a safe haven? When a New Yorker commented on how, after the bombings, one can no longer walk safely on the city's streets, the irony of it was that, well before the bombings, the streets of New York were well-known for the dangers of being attacked. (Žižek 2002)

One should add, for reasons I will develop further, to the list of similarities Žižek enumerates a high incidence of sexual violence and a lucrative sex industry. Despite this, the current U.S. administration explicitly renders the coordinates of the present "war against terrorism" as good against evil. If it had not done so before, the United States after 9/11 distinctly asserted its position as the diametrical opposite of Taliban-controlled Afghanistan. This patriotic self-identity allows for no similarity with the enemy; it is a rhetoric of absolute contrast, an archetypal civilization-versus-barbarism construction, intended to divide the world into opposing camps: "You are with us or against us."

Within this reinterpretation of the world as a battle between good and evil, the issue of women's oppression was (rather suddenly) brought up. Policies of gender apartheid that once provoked no more than indifference in the West became a key element of a crusade. Suddenly the Bush administration had a lot to say about Taliban atrocities; the First Lady is now famous for making speeches about the violation of women's rights in Afghanistan. After years of silence and indifference to the Taliban's gender policies, the United States declared that they are, in fact, evil.

At the same time, women began to receive renewed attention from the other side of this conflict: Islamic extremists often point to the sexual liberation of women as one of the most pernicious sins of the West because it leads to immorality and evil. Rape, prostitution, and AIDS, so this logic goes, are the fruit of Western "sexual liberation." For this reason and others, America is called the Great Satan and a country of infidels. While this particular rhetoric of evil is easily recognizable to Westerners as "fundamentalist" and "backward," U.S. rhetoric about the Taliban revolves around a very similar instrumentalization of "evil." In fact, one could suggest that this new American discourse of evil is precisely the expression of what is called fundamentalism.

One might be led to think that in this "war" women were finally *present,* as both sides declared their respective opinions as to women's status, place in society, and equality. But this impression is illusory. It was precisely in this realm of escalated rhetoric and assured contrasts that women were more absent than ever—instrumentalized within a discourse of evil that masks an ideology of internal hatred and aggression. Women were invoked, but not present, in the war in Afghanistan. One need only look at the alliances America forged in order to fight this war: cooperation with the Northern Alliance (or United Front), largely composed of the very soldiers who led campaigns of rape, torture, and slaughter in the country before the Taliban came to power; and with the military dictator of Pakistan, a country that holds one of the worst records on women's rights in the world. On the other side, it is obvious that the Islamic extremist view of women (disguised in rhetoric of "honor" and "morality") inevitably leads to women's disenfranchisement, subjugation, and oppression.

This chapter, then, attempts to read both sides against themselves and to examine the way both American and Taliban ideology deployed "evil" as a political concept in the "war against terrorism." It does so via an ideological critique based on the theoretical works of Slavoj Žižek, Jean Baudrillard, and Luce Irigaray. Each of these contemporary authors has contributed significantly to the analysis of cultural discourse in unique and yet complementary ways—the theorist Žižek applies the insights of Lacanian psychoanalytic theory to political situations, such as the breakup of the former Yugoslavia; the philosopher Baudrillard critically interrogates the technological and cultural transformations within contemporary Western civilization; and the feminist psychoanalyst/philosopher Irigaray re-marks the decisive and divisive significance of gender in the analysis of politics or culture.[2]

Let us begin with a brief historical summary of women's rights in Afghanistan.[3] Until the twentieth century, Afghanistan's government, like that of many Islamic countries, greatly restricted women's roles in society. But under the rule of King Amanullah (1919–1929), many significant changes took place. King Amanullah feared that Afghanistan would become an unsuccessful, backward country because of its summary rejection of Western ideas and institutions. He thus made several reforms concerning the position of women and girls in society and gender-related customs, banning child marriage, outlawing polygamy among civil servants, and allowing women to discard the veil (Marsden 1999). In 1928 the queen led a group of a hundred unveiled women at a public function. When Amanullah's reign ended, however, these reforms were speedily annulled, and this situation lasted for more than twenty years. Peter Marsden writes that it was only in 1953, when Muhammad Daoud Khan became prime minister, that "any further initiatives were taken to improve the position of women" (1998, 94). In 1957, female singers and presenters were heard on Kabul radio. In 1958 the government sent a female delegate to the United Nations in New York. Women were employed as hostesses and receptionists at the national airline and were unveiled (Marsden 1998, 93–94).

The global intellectual movements of the 1960s helped Daoud to maintain his reforms despite virulent protests from the *Ulema*, the group of male scholars who interpret the *Shari'a*, or Islamic law. The idea that women should benefit from secondary and higher education alarmed Islamic traditionalists, who believed that the spread of nontraditional education eroded morals and undermined social values. Nonetheless, the People's Democratic Republic of Afghanistan, set up through the Soviet coup of April 1978, pushed the reform process even further, seeking to make female education mandatory throughout the country.[4] The resistance to the Soviet invasion was thus, Marsden writes, "presented as a resistance to both Western and socialist influences" (1998, 95). "The socialist system was seen as potentially undermining Islam through its secular nature. Western society was viewed in a similar light, in part because of the distinction drawn between the state and religion, with religion being relegated to the private sphere, and in part because Western society had been presented to the public as decadent. On both counts it was feared that women would, at the very least, abandon their Muslim values and, at worst, slide into immoral behavior" (Marsden 1999, 95).

As the war of resistance against Soviet occupation raged, women gradually achieved the right to full participation in social, economic, cultural, and political life. They continued to do so even when Afghanistan fragmented into warring fundamentalist groups, known as *jehadin* or *Mujahidin*, each of whom sought to take control of the country. By the late 1980s, at least half of working professionals and those enrolled in higher education were women. In many Afghan cities (though not all), women enjoyed freedom of movement and relative equality with their male counterparts. There was a price, however: the *jehadin* focused much of their violence and aggression on the women of Afghanistan, and mass rape and torture became common.

Dramatic changes came with the Taliban regime. Progressive reforms and accommodation of "secular" ideas had long enraged Islamic traditionalists. As the country was torn apart first by the war of resistance and then by the civil war amongst the different religious militias, the economy plummeted, poverty and famine soared, the number of people forced into refugee camps rose into the millions, and the rape and killing of women became rampant. "Western" reforms became the scapegoat. It became very easy to associate, and then to attribute, the cause of all sufferings to "Western" or "socialist" influence, even though it was the *jehadin* themselves who propagated the violence against the people of Afghanistan in the years following the Soviet occupation (albeit with arms provided by various other countries, including the U.S.). Thus when the Taliban, a group of Islamic fundamentalist militants who promised to lead the country back to morality and stability—back to the true meaning of Islam—made a bid for power in 1994, their message fell on fertile ground.

In September 1996, when the Taliban controlled 90 percent of Afghanistan, including the capital city of Kabul, it made the following restrictions official policy (this is only a partial list):

- Women may not work outside the home, except for a few health workers, or attend any kind of educational institution.
- Women are not allowed to leave their houses at all unless accompanied by a *mahram* (a close male relative).
- Women are not allowed to be treated by male doctors.
- Women must wear a *burqa* (a garment that covers the body completely, with only a piece of mesh around the eyes) at all times.
- Women may not gather for any public functions or festivities.
- Women are not allowed to use cosmetics.
- The windows of women's houses must be painted over, so that women cannot be seen from the outside.
- Women must not talk or laugh loudly, must not wear high-heeled shoes or any shoes that make noise, must not wear bright colors, or at any moment allow any part of their flesh to show, wash clothes in public, or appear on the balcony of their houses, so as not to incite the lust of men.
- The names of places which include a reference to women must be changed; for example, "women's garden" is renamed "spring garden."[5]

Women who did not comply with these restrictions were beaten, tortured, and sometimes executed. Women with painted fingernails had their fingers cut off. Widows, who had no male relatives to accompany them in public, starved to death in their homes. The rate of female suicide rose dramatically: the most common method was the ingestion of caustic soda, which as one doctor explained, "burns away the throat. It takes three days to die."[6]

On December 6, 1996, the Taliban's Department for the Promotion of Virtue and Prevention of Vice announced that it had punished 225 women the previous day, in accordance with the *Shari'a* (Islamic law), for violating its rules on clothing. It stated: "As the dignity and honour of a Muslim woman is ensured by observing *hejab* [seclusion from society] as requested by Shari'a, all honourable sisters are strongly asked to completely observe *hejab* as recommended by Shari'a. This can be achieved only if our dear sisters wear *burqas,* because full *hejab* cannot be achieved by wearing only a *chador* [a large piece of material that envelops the body and covers the head but leaves all or part of the face uncovered, at the discretion of the wearer]. In case of violation, no one will have the right of complaint" (Marsden 1999, 63).

Back in 1935, before anything like the Taliban existed, Virgilio Martini wrote a book called *Il Mondo senza Donne,* or *The World Without Women.* In this book, a mysterious disease strikes all women of childbearing age. The disease is eventually discovered to have been created by men in order to exterminate all the females of the human species. It succeeds, and in due course all adolescent girls and young women disappear, and the world is threatened with extinction. A few decades later, Jacques Lacan enigmatically declared: "la Femme n'existe pas"—Woman does not exist (1998, 7). In the 1990s Žižek wrote that "Woman" is a "phantasmatic specter," and that "the specter gives body to that which escapes (the symbolically structured) reality" (1996, 123). In 1996 Jean Baudrillard revisited the novel *The World Without Women* and wrote that its central idea is "an extermination of femaleness—a terrifying allegory of the extermination of all otherness, for which the feminine is the metaphor, and perhaps, more than the metaphor" (1996, 111).

Indeed, it seems that the extermination of femaleness is much more than a metaphor, and that under the Taliban it became a literal reality. Women were forced into invisibility as their traces (voices, faces, names) were erased. Afghanistan literalized the pronouncements of Western theorists on the disappearance of women. Under the Taliban, women were literally reduced to specters.

The situation in Afghanistan, pre–September 11, attracted attention from some Western feminists, humanitarian agencies, and the United Nations, or at least it did for a little while. But Western (especially feminist) outrage against what was perceived to be the Taliban's primitive disregard for basic human rights and an archaic devaluation of women was often itself criticized in the name of multiculturalism. Many Muslims, for example, protested against what they saw as a Western, especially American, assumption of moral and cultural superiority. Westerners were taken to task for their ignorance of Islamic tradition and familiar arguments were raised about the irreducibility of cultural differences and multiculturalism.[7] However, while multicultural debates did check protest against the Taliban's practices before September 11, Western condemnation of its oppression of women *after* September 11 became almost unanimous.

But it was not very long before that—four years after the Taliban took over the capital city of Kabul—that the mainstream Western media had all but let the matter of gender apartheid drop. While the United Nations was still active in its investigation and reporting of human rights abuses—its Special Report on violence against women in Afghanistan appeared in March 2000—and humanitarian agencies continued their work, popular support to stop the oppression of women dwindled, and the media paid the Taliban little attention.[8] While some feminists critiqued the multiculturalism argument and called for recognition of the oppression of women under extremist regimes, very little of this was reflected in popular debate and discussion.[9] Prior to the events of September 11, most of the political action against the Taliban took the form of UN sanctions that often did more harm than good for the captive population. The situation for women and girls continued largely unabated.

What is the explanation for this extended period of Western indifference, which appeared all the more strange when the Taliban's treatment of women became part of the rationale for bombing of Afghanistan? Surely, multicultural arguments, public indifference, and complicated political interests all helped neutralize the response to the Taliban's atrocities. The same Clinton administration that considered deals with Taliban representatives concerning oil and gas resources likely found it difficult or perhaps merely inconvenient to condemn that regime's practices toward women. But this is not the full story.

There is a *supplement* to these reasons for American inaction, a supplement that becomes even more clear in light of America's sudden and apparent change of heart after 9/11. As mentioned previously, a genuine concern for women's welfare in Afghanistan is little served by cooperation with the notoriously misogynist and violent Northern Alliance.[10] Discussion of how to better Afghan women's situation faded into the background as soon as the Taliban had been subdued. In short, the West's explicit condemnation of the violation of women's rights seems to have been a rhetorical, and short-lived, tool. The hidden supplement here is that, despite all appearances and rhetoric to the contrary, an implicit ideological affinity exists between the oppression of women in Afghanistan and Western "liberal" gender equality, an affinity that prevented the West from recognizing and countering certain oppressive practices until it became in its interest to do so, and that allowed the West to disregard them once again when its aims had been achieved.

To clarify this, let us examine some particular, little-known aspects of the Taliban's gender policy that seem inconsistent with its overall claims and that received little attention from the West, even from feminist advocacy organizations. Even as the Taliban strictly enforced its dress, mobility, and behavioral restrictions on the majority of Afghani women, it acknowledged and supported a burgeoning prostitution industry and was implicated in the abduction and international trafficking of women. The Taliban demonstrated a paradoxical logic regarding prostitution, declaring it on the one hand a crime punishable by death but patronizing and encouraging it on the other. The *Sydney Morning Herald* reported that brothels were protected by the Taliban (RAWA Web site), and a RAWA report from 1999 maintained that the Taliban has "increased the flesh trade by leaps and bounds" (RAWA Web site). The UN Special Report on Afghanistan (March 2000) provided testimony from refugees of mass abductions, rape, and forced prostitution (Coomaraswamy 2000). Several Taliban officers have been accused of rape and sodomy, and in September 2000, Taliban officials authorized the release of a convicted serial rapist—even as a woman accused of adultery (based merely on the word of a man) could be stoned to death.[11]

The Taliban's success in Afghanistan was due in no small part to the dire situation for women under the *jehadin*. As mentioned previously, these were soldiers in what is now called the United Front or Northern Alliance, America's "helpers" throughout the recent conflict, who were notorious for gang rapes, sex murders, and abductions of young women. The Taliban's initial popularity was based on their seeming ability to restore order and stamp out the rampant violence of the warring factions. One must reflect on just how unbearable civilian existence must have been under the *jehadin* for the Taliban to be welcomed as a great improvement. But as RAWA reported, while the Taliban "initially made a show of piety and of abhorring sexual crimes against women . . . recent reports of their depravity are growing with each passing day. In this, like other atrocities, they have surpassed their fundamentalist brethren" (RAWA Web site). The Taliban ultimately shared the brutal *jehadin's* views of women, but used other means to express them.

The Taliban, like many other fundamentalist groups, claimed that the restrictions placed on women were for the protection of women's own honor and dignity. According to this logic, women should be spared the dangerous and degrading prospect of the company of men, whether that be in working alongside them, walking around unattended, or revealing any flesh, because it could (and did) lead to rape or other violence. Women inevitably provoke uncontrollable lust in men, and must therefore be carefully guarded lest a man be unable to restrain himself. Of course, this logic does not seek to correct or reform the criminal behavior of men, but rather attempts to restrict women in such a way as to provoke this behavior as little as possible. Moreover, if one looks at the Taliban's policy on rape, for example, the idea that women are an honored and protected group does not hold up: a rape victim must produce four male witnesses to testify that the rape occurred, and if she fails to prove that the sexual relation was forced, she can be stoned to death for fornication. This, along with the prostitution, abduction, and trafficking of women in Taliban-controlled Afghanistan, suggests that what underlies the purported injunction to "protect" women is actually the desperate attempt to be protected *from* them. Women must be feared; they threaten order and morality and control. Their sexuality is so fearsome that it must be harnessed and marketed along very specific guidelines, namely either completely denied or indulged exclusively according to patriarchal dictates. A woman, according to this ideology, must truly be either a mother/madonna, or a whore.

The thriving sex industry in Afghanistan reveals the hypocrisy of the Taliban's self-proclaimed allegiance to Islam. According to Islamic tradition, women are invested with the charge of guarding culture; they produce the next generation of Muslims and safeguard the passing along of beliefs. But the Taliban apparently also had other, secret uses for women, as the thirty brothels in the capital city of Kabul alone attested (Khan 1999). The Taliban, through their patronization of prostitution, demanded that women (*some* women) serve another function—not as partners in the workplace or equals in intelligence, but as whores. Though the two functions—mother and whore—seem to be opposites, the absolute domination over women, the positioning of them as empty-object-vessel, is the same in both. In neither case do women exist—only the fantasy of women exists, to be either erased or exposed as men see fit. Women in Taliban-controlled Afghanistan were explicitly meant to be "women on the market," to borrow a concept from Irigaray: "The division of 'labor'—sexual labor in particular—requires that woman maintain in her own body the material substratum of the object of desire, but that she herself never have access to desire" (Irigaray 1985, 188). Irigaray writes that both "mothers" and "whores" are emptied out of their own bodies by patriarchal regulation: "Mothers, reproductive instruments marked with the name of the father and enclosed in his house, must be private property, excluded from exchange," whereas the prostitute's body is valuable "because it has already been used . . . its nature has been 'used up,' and has become once again no more than a vehicle for relations among men" (1985, 185–86).

Irigaray's analysis of the equalization and containment of extremes within patriarchal societies bears much similarity to what Žižek describes as the two sides of the Law: the law itself, and the law's "obscene superego underside," its built-in contradiction, the inherent transgression that paradoxically ensures its existence (1996: 101). This underside is typically embodied by a fantasized Other, who is then held responsible for the ultimate failure of a racist or sexist ideology to fully actualize itself. Žižek illustrates the way this law functions in his discussion of anti-Semitism, emphasizing that that the fantasized Other has *nothing to do* with the reality of a particular oppressed group. Žižek writes that the fantasy of the Jew, the "conceptual Jew," does not exist. The conceptual Jew is not, as anti-Semites claim, the cause of a social antagonism, but rather is a figure who embodies an inherent antagonism within an ideological system itself. Because all ideologies aiming at totality continually fail, their adherents must *create* an Other to blame for this failure. This is why Žižek writes that *"fantasy is a means for an ideology to take its own failure into account in advance"* (1989, 126). Because this fantasy of the Other has no coordinate in reality, it can never be contradicted or undermined by a "real" Jew or, in the case of the Taliban, a "real" woman, but can remain ever functional as a phantasmatic support. As a fantasy construction, it can simultaneously lay claim to various contradictory perceptions: in the case of patriarchal, misogynist ideology, woman is weak and pure and needs protection to maintain her purity, but at the same time she is dangerous, contaminating, and powerful, and must be severely restrained so as not to contaminate the purity of men.

Continuing the example of anti-Semitism, Žižek writes that because the fantasy-Jew does not really exist, it is for that reason that the anti-Semite fears him "even more—in short, *the very nonexistence of the Jew in reality functions as the main argument for anti-Semitism.* That is to say, the anti-Semite constructs the Jew as a phantomlike entity that is to be found nowhere in reality" (1996, 108). Irigaray's description of how women are produced as commodities within patriarchal societies parallels the way that anti-Semites produce the fantasy Other: "When women are exchanged, woman's body must be treated as an *abstraction . . . woman has value on the market by virtue of one single quality: that of being a product of man's labor.* On this basis, each one looks exactly like every other. They all have the same phantom-like reality" (Irigaray 1985, 175). In the Taliban's ideology, a fantasy of woman was constructed to disguise the fundamental impossibility of the actualization of a society according to its interpretation of Islam. In this radical interpretation, the place of the woman— her desire, her sexuality, her action—is overdetermined, a static, impossible state of utter transparency and subject to complete control. She must be only a mother and a cultural receptacle, devoid of all desire except for what will please her husband and what is best for her children. She *must not exist* in any other way; hence she must become invisible to all others. But this attempt to anticipate and dictate the totality of woman's desire, as well as the desire for woman, is doomed to failure. The Taliban's law was thus necessarily always two laws. The official, written Islamic law proscribed women's roles as wives and mothers, whose sexuality is restricted to servitude to their husbands, while its "obscene" underside is evidenced in the opposite extreme, the woman who is nothing but sexuality and belongs to all men, the prostitute.

Reporters in Afghanistan wrote that certain prostitutes in Kabul wore the same long, covering robes like the *burqa* over their revealing attire so as not to be detected by the Taliban (RAWA Web site). This stemmed not from a general fear that the Taliban would arrest them for offending morality but from the fact that the Taliban was selective in protecting some prostitutes while punishing others. These distinctions, according to the prostitutes, were based on the extent to which the prostitutes complied with Taliban demands for extremely humiliating sexual acts, often accompanied by beating and certainly without payment. Under the Taliban, then, both the "madonnas" and the "whores" moved silently under long robes, their faces hidden and their mouths covered: phantom-like entities.[12]

Veiled women, public beatings, bans on women working or being seen in public—these ideas startle and horrify Westerners, and the U.S. government in particular condemned them (although belatedly, and then only briefly). They are ideas from which Westerners feel at the same time a very comfortable distance, things which could "never happen here." And it is certainly true that Western women enjoy freedoms denied to women in many Islamic countries. In many contexts this point should be repeated and re-emphasized; for all of its flaws, American democracy in principle allows for basic freedoms, such as the freedom of speech, which make it possible to formulate and express criticism of those flaws. However, it is distressing how claims of "freedom and democracy" can be used as shields against debate, as a means of closing down discussion rather than opening it. The fanatical patriotism that has stricken America since the bombing campaign began in Afghanistan, the inflated rhetoric that the Bush administration has employed to justify its actions, and the self-righteous (again belated) concern for women's rights under the Taliban attest to a self-complacent, if not self-congratulatory, constriction of thought and reflection that is anything but democratic. Moreover, the fact of sexual violence and the commodification of women that exists in both countries points to a much more complex relation between the two than either side would like to acknowledge.

The Law is always two laws, and not just under the Taliban. In the United States too there is the written Law, which grants many rights to women and in theory protects them from sexual assault and other violations; but there is equally an unwritten law that remains indifferent to or encourages violence against women, evidenced by a lucrative and violent prostitution industry and by shockingly high statistics of rape and sexual homicides, all of which works to impede those rights taken for granted in the West. In America, a woman is free under the law to walk down any street she wishes, at any time she wishes, unattended by a male escort, but often cannot or will not for fear of rape. There is no restriction under the law as to what a woman can wear in public, but a woman who wears "suggestive" clothing is often perceived as inviting sexual advances. These unwritten codes of violent subjugation of women in the West were explicitly written into the Law of the Taliban: whereas the Taliban hides the explicitly sexual aspect of this subjugation and justifies its repressive dicta on the basis of "respect" for women, in the United States women are compelled to formulate their identities as ever-available sexual beings under the guise of "sexual liberation."

Many Americans, feminists included, seem to have few problems with the interpretation of "good and evil" in the current "war on terrorism" even when, and sometimes especially when, one refers to the treatment of women in Afghanistan. What could be more evil than the Taliban's oppressive policies? How could we be any more secure in our superiority than when we see the way women are treated as second-class citizens in some Islamic countries, denied access to education, health care, or employment? America may have its problems, but surely they pale in comparison to the atrocities that take place in Afghanistan. Why not leave it at this—even if concern for women's rights is being instrumentalized in a greater political scheme, aren't the women of Afghanistan nonetheless better off for it? Even if bombing the war-racked, ravaged country multiplies suffering and starvation for the civilian population, won't it be worth it in the end, when a "friendly" Western-supported government is established in place of the relentless Taliban?

This "things might be bad here, but they're better than over there" attitude is dangerous precisely because it posits real horror as being eternally "over there," and intervention from "here" becomes the only possibility of salvation. The West becomes, as it were, transfixed by the suffering of the Other and by the idea of its own heroic status: as Žižek writes, our "compassion" for victims of international warfare and oppression "presupposes that *in it, we perceive ourselves in the form that we find likeable:* the victim is presented so that we like to see ourselves in the position from which we stare at her" (1994, 211). He argues that constant images of the other's suffering—starving children, victimized women, or in the case of Afghanistan, women shrouded in burqas—are fantasy-images that actually serve to eternalize the victimized status of the other and to evade the possibility of the ethico-political *act* (a concept to which we will return later).

Žižek's critique is echoed in an essay by Sonali Kolhatkar, vice president of the Afghan Women's Mission, titled "'Saving' Afghan Women" (2002). Kolhatkar relates her experience of being interviewed by feminist and anti-nuclear campaigner Helen Caldicott, a woman Kolhatkar had long admired for her activist work. Expecting intelligent, thoughtful questions, Kolhatkar relates how shocked she was when Caldicott aggressively questioned her as to why Afghan men treated their women so badly, and then seemed uninterested in her replies. Caldicott lectured Kolhatkar about FGM—female genital mutilation—which she had learned about from the Feminist Majority Foundation (FMF) and which she claimed was a common practice among the women of Afghanistan. Kolhatkar, who is Indian, had never heard of FGM being practiced in Afghanistan, but in the face of Caldicott's angry assertions, left the interview shaken and unsure. Upon researching the issue, she discovered that Caldicott was in fact mistaken—she could find no evidence of the practice of FGM in Afghanistan. Kolhatkar was forced to conclude that "feminists like Helen Caldicott and the Feminist Majority, approach the women of the Global South with short-sighted preconceptions of feminism and their superiority. Helen Caldicott was more interested in exploring the fascinating desire of Afghan men to treat women like dirt, than in examining those forces (most often Western male-dominated governments) that have fostered misogynist religious extremism at the expense of women's rights" (2002). Kolhatkar continues,

It is easy to condemn the "barbaric" men of Afghanistan and pity the helpless women of Afghanistan. It is this very logic that drives the Feminist Majority's "Gender Apartheid" campaign for Afghan women. Far more interested in portraying Afghan women as mute creatures covered from head to toe, the Feminist Majority aggressively promotes itself and it's [sic] campaign by selling small squares of mesh cloth, similar to the mesh through which Afghan women can look outside when wearing the traditional Afghan burqa. The post card on which the swatch of mesh is sold says, "Wear a symbol of remembrance for Afghan women," as if they are already extinct. An alternative could have been "Celebrate the Resistance of Afghan Women" with a pin of a hand folded into a fist, to acknowledge the very real struggle that Afghan women wage every day, particularly the women of the Revolutionary Association of the Women of Afghanistan (RAWA), who are at the forefront of that struggle. . . . On almost every image of Afghan women in the Western mainstream and even alternative media, images of shapeless blue-clad forms of Afghan women covered with the burqa, dominate (Amnesty International's poster of Afghan women, the cover of Cheryl Bernard's new book on RAWA, etc.). We all know and understand the reactions which the image of the burqa brings, particularly to Western women and feminists. That horror mixed with fear and ugly fascination like knowing the site [sic] of a bloody car wreck will make you want to retch but you do it anyway. Whose purpose does this serve? (Kolhatkar 2002)

Kolhatkar knows the answer as well as Žižek does. "How 'effective' would the Feminist Majority's campaign be," she asks rhetorically, "if they made it known that Afghan women were actively fighting back and simply needed money and moral support, not instructions?" (2002). Kolhatkar's indictment of the FMF's determination to present Afghan women as helpless victims, rather than as active individuals fighting for their freedom, illustrates Žižek's point. Both he and Kolhatkar reject the notion of the "innocent gaze" that perceives Evil all around, and acknowledge, as Žižek reminds us constantly, "Hegel's dictum that true Evil resides . . . in the innocent gaze that perceives Evil all around" (1994, 212). This is the reason, argues Kolhatkar, that for all the West's claims to "help" Afghan women, RAWA—which has existed since the Soviet occupation, and whose members have risked their lives to provide equal rights, education, and health care for women and girls for decades—was shut out of the Bonn conference and has had no official Western governmental support. If humanitarian organizations focused on "images of Afghan women marching militantly with fists in the air, carrying banners about freedom, democracy and secular government . . . we may gather that Afghan women are perfectly capable of helping themselves if only our governments would stop arming and empowering the most violent sections of society" (Kolhatkar 2002). In short, the West might recognize its own implication in the terrible situation in Afghanistan, "traverse the fantasy" (see Žižek 1997, 32) of the eternalized victim "over there," and approach the *act*—or at the very least facilitate Afghan women's attempt to act. Simply put, in Žižek's sense the "act" is real political action, action that changes the coordinates of a given ideological situation. It exposes "the inherent limitation of the standpoint of social totality itself" (Žižek 1994, 148). Such an act involves what he calls "striking at oneself," here in the sense of striking at the transfixing image of the victim that an ideology creates and re-creates (2000, 150). It means giving up on the support of the phantasmatic image of the other.

Žižek's criticism of the Western response to the conflict in Kosovo is illuminating in this context: Žižek argued that Western governments are invested in helping victims as long as they remain victims—hence their eagerness to dwell on the suffering of Kosovar women and children, while refusing to support the armed soldiers of the KLA. A victim who takes up arms to escape his victimhood is suddenly viewed as a terrorist, drug runner, and so forth.

But the situation in Afghanistan does not quite fit this mold. The United States allied itself with the Northern Alliance—again, the same murderous, raping bands of "resistance" fighters that carried out campaigns of torture prior to the Taliban takeover. The cooperation between the Northern Alliance and the United States presents a complicated situation: on a superficial level, the Northern Alliance is a kind of KLA, made up of ethnic groups disempowered by Taliban rule who armed themselves in order to oppose it. If the United States only wants to deal with victims, as Žižek suggests, how does one explain this support? To answer this, it is necessary to revise Žižek's assessment—to "gender" it. The recent history of Afghanistan seems at first to attest that power shifted from one group to another—the Soviets, then one or another or the jehadin groups, then the Taliban. But this overlooks a very important fact: in each of these power shifts, women were consistently targeted for violence and oppression. The conflict in Afghanistan must be seen as more than a struggle among differing religions or ethnicities: it has been at least as much a struggle of men against women, or for women to have both their rights and the freedom from violence. In a sense, what the United States has done by aligning itself with the Northern Alliance (and Musharraf in Pakistan) is exactly what Žižek would expect it to do: perpetuate victimhood—of *women*. It is the *women* who continue to be victimized, regardless of what group seizes or is given power. The United States has *not* lent official support (or, perhaps more importantly, money) to an organization like RAWA. Instead, it "saves" Afghan women, American-style: allowing a few token females into the puppet government set up in the Taliban's place.

By supporting the Northern Alliance, the United States does not break with the fascinating image of the victim, at least not with the image of women as victims. It provides only alternative versions of the same story of violence and oppression, but can also congratulate itself for helping to set up a "democratic" government. In other words, the United States at most alters the situation in Afghanistan so that it will no longer function as the United States' obscene underside, but as its twin—reversing the status of the written/unwritten law so that Afghanistan will eventually resemble nothing so much as the United States itself. For example, as reports from Afghanistan demonstrate, women are "freed from the burqa" but they continue to wear it out of fear of violence (Paterson 2002). The written law of violence may become the unwritten, but will be no less effective for that.

Hegemonic ideologies must be interrogated constantly for their failures. It should never be forgotten that women's right to self-determination, their right to an existence free of exploitation and violence, is not exclusive to Western civilization. The progressive situation that existed for women in Afghanistan prior to the takeover of the Taliban was due, significantly, to the work of women within Afghanistan itself, women who may have benefited from the influence of certain Western ideas, but who chose for themselves, within their own cultural and religious context, the existence they wished to have. As the Egyptian feminist Dr. Nawal el-Saadawi pointed out in a recent lecture (2002), women's rights to an existence free of violence or oppression is not a Western invention, and it is patronizing and antifeminist to suggest that it is. RAWA, as mentioned before, has existed since the Soviet occupation, and its members have risked their lives to provide equal rights, education, and health care for women and girls for decades.

Good-versus-evil rhetoric is predicated on a model of absolute difference, but this model is false. The Taliban should be seen as America's own specter, its obscene underside, because the Taliban's policies explicitly played out elements implicitly at work in the West. Perhaps this is made clearest by Sahar Saba's statement, "They are two sides of one coin, the Taliban and the Northern Alliance." [13] As the United States has aligned itself with the Northern Alliance, one may also say that by extension, the Taliban and the United States are two sides of the same coin.

On the surface, America and Afghanistan could not seem more different, especially as far as women's sexuality is concerned. After all, what more of an opposite could there be to society under the Taliban, where women were covered from head to toe, images of humans were banned, and even the sound of female footsteps had to be muffled, than the United States, where sexually explicit images saturate public space, where women can wear what they choose, where strip clubs and brothels are commonplace? Where, in short, woman is everywhere displayed, completely, unashamedly, explicitly? But that is precisely the point: in both America and Afghanistan, women's bodies are on the market; female flesh is bought and sold by men who reap enormous profits; "clients" become abusive and force prostitutes to perform acts against their will, beat them up, and leave without paying; teenage and prepubescent girls sell themselves on the street; women are raped by the thousands each year; domestic violence is omnipresent, and no one wants to talk about it. In the United States, these issues are not part of public consciousness; instead, public space and discourse is saturated by images of compulsive consumerism that explicitly grounds itself in women's bodies and women's sexuality. In any given major U.S. city, one will confront hundreds of images of women in a day—but none of these will be images that seek to highlight rampant problems of violence and sexual exploitation facing women. The average New Yorker probably knows what the latest cover of *Hustler* looks like, or what the newest beauty product from Estée Lauder is. But the average New Yorker doesn't know the current statistics of rape and domestic violence in his or her own city. In both Afghanistan and in the United States the *fantasy* of women reigns supreme; a constructed and artificial femininity is everywhere on display, while the facts of violence and exploitation remain hidden.

The clandestine sex trade under the Taliban, and the sexual violence that is re-emerging under the Northern Alliance, is a side of Afghanistan that the mainstream West did not and does not look into very much, and with good reason. It calls into question the West's own distance from a repressive and brutal regime, its clear assurances of what it is and what it is not. It suggests that the United States has its own specters. By examining this very disturbing affinity of sexual violence, the West risks the consistency of its own liberal ideological system, risks exposing a fissure within its perception of itself, the traumatic antagonism within its own cultural identity.

One probing examination of Western cultural identity is provided by the philosopher Jean Baudrillard, whose book *The Perfect Crime* (1996) offers a critical examination of contemporary Western culture's obsession with the visible. Baudrillard writes that technological progress has produced the phenomenon of what he calls "hyperreality"—excessive reality—and questions whether its consequences are in fact as progressive and positive as they are often proclaimed to be (1996, 4–7).

Baudrillard finds particular significance in the proliferation of the "sex industry" within this presumably advanced culture, which primarily focuses on the bodies of women. He critiques the view that omnipresent pornography, for example, offers genuine sexual liberation, and instead argues that it may in fact exacerbate the already unequal and resentful relations between men and women. "Obscenity may be sublime or grotesque, if it shatters the innocence of a natural world," he writes. "But what can porn do in a world pornographied in advance? Except bring an added ironic value to appearances? Except tip a last paradoxical wink—of sex laughing at itself in its most exact and hence most monstrous form, laughing at its own disappearance beneath its most artificial form?" (1996, 129).

Though Baudrillard can hardly be called a feminist, his assessment of the history of sexuality is not so far from Irigaray's: he argues that because men have historically constructed women as sexual objects, "woman" as such is always-already trapped in fantasy-projections of a sexuality marked out, as it were, on her body. Irigaray has written that the woman is always-already a commodity, and that "in order to be able to incorporate itself into a mirror of value, it is necessary . . . that the body of a commodity be nothing more than the materialization of an abstract human labor. That is, [it must] have no more body, matter, nature, but . . . be objectivization, crystallization as visible object, of man's activity" (1985, 179).

What is often called the Western "liberal" view of sexuality is "liberal" only with regard to the proliferation and marketing of women's bodies, which, far from opening itself to the possibilities and potentialities of female or nonpatriarchal sexuality, of *other* sexuality, rather produces and re-produces only the same, the infinitely repeatable, ready-made patterns of "spectacular" sex. This is ironically so far from "liberalism" as to resemble instead what Roland Barthes (1998) called *inoculation*. In his essay on Parisian striptease, Barthes writes of inoculation in the sense of a controlled, carefully measured, and manufactured dosage of "sexuality" whose ultimate purpose is to keep a full-edged threat of Other-sexuality at bay (1998, 85). As Irigaray writes, "woman serves as reflection, as image of and for man, but lacks specific qualities of her own. Her value-invested form amounts to what man inscribes in and on its matter: that is, her body" (1985, 187). "Feminine sexuality" in Western society is predicated on the fascination with the visible and the consumable. Baudrillard writes, "By the invention of a femaleness which makes woman superfluous, makes her a supplemental incarnation, woman really has disappeared—if not physically, then at least beneath a substitute femininity" (1996, 116–17). This substitute femininity of which Baudrillard speaks points to the more subtle but no less violent tendency of Western culture to transform "women" into fantasized others—indifferently consuming, ahistorical, compulsively enjoying others—and to maintain that condition at all costs.

By none of this do I mean to suggest that the Taliban regime should not have been scrutinized and challenged for its oppression of women. The effort to bring the oppression of women to the attention of the international community is one that should and must continue. But this cannot truly be accomplished so long as the West maintains its blind spot toward its own ideological system, so long as it grants itself a false distance from such oppression. Afghanistan must not serve only as an example of the brutality of Islamic fundamentalism, but as the obscene underside of Western liberal society: a society in which in many ways women also do not exist.

The women of Afghanistan, and their specter-like, ghostly appearances on the international stage must alarm and disturb the comfortable perceptions of the West and point to the erasure of women within the United States' own borders as well as without. The situation in Afghanistan presents a dual challenge of recognition, of breaking with structures of repression and oppression even when, and especially when, those structures are hidden deep within a liberal ideology that does its best to convince us such things do not exist. It means that women, especially, must confront the fantasy of deeply cherished beliefs about Western enlightened society. As Žižek writes, "the crucial precondition for breaking the chains of servitude is . . . to 'traverse the fantasy' which structures our *jouissance* in a way that keeps us attached to the Master—makes us accept the framework of the social relationship of domination" (1997, 48). For this is what the dominant ideology fears: the irruption of the Other within the familiar and secure terrain of the same.

In *This Sex Which Is Not One* (1985), Irigaray allows herself to imagine what the world would be like free of the exploitation of women, free of the internalized violence that passes for liberation, free of the blindness to the enormity and omnipresence of the violation of women's rights, free of the tyranny of the visible and the consumable. She muses, "Without the exploitation of women, what would become of the social order? What modification would it undergo if women left behind their condition as commodities—subject to being produced, consumed, valorized, circulated, and so on, by men alone—and took part in elaborating and carrying out exchanges? Not by reproducing, by copying the 'phallocentric' models that have the force of law today, but by socializing in a different way the relation to nature, matter, the body, language, and desire" (1985, 191). This sentiment, I suggest, supplements the Lacanian/Žižekian concept of the socio-political "act" specifically in terms of gender. If one situates Irigaray's statement within the field of Žižek's admonition to "include oneself in the picture" (2002) and to break with the fantasy that keeps us in servitude to a master ideology (1997, 48), the urgency of a cultural and political self-interrogation of continuing patriarchal structures—even when disguised as "liberalism"—becomes apparent. This is the way that Westerners might begin to approach the question of evil and women's oppression in "the other."

In a slightly different context, Baudrillard (1996) writes that the "others"—those who have been suppressed and repressed and erased—are beginning to stir and to resist: "Their *ressentiment* may be impotent, but from the depths of their virtual extermination a passion for revenge is infiltrating and dislocating the Western world, just as the ghost of the excluded is beginning to haunt our conventional societies" (147). "So, everywhere, objects, children, the dead, images, women, everything which serves to provide a passive reflection in a world based on identity, is ready to go on the counter-offensive. Already they resemble us less and less" (149). In many ways this statement reads like an eerie premonition of September 11; however, it can also be read as another incitement to break with the phantasmatic images of the "other" that underpin the ideology of good and evil, and as an affirmative observation that these "others"—many of the women in Afghanistan, for example—may be fighting back in ways that the West is not yet able to recognize.

Notes

1. This term has been applied to the United States in a variety of circumstances and for a variety of effects; it is used pejoratively, for instance, in the title of William Blum's highly critical book *Rogue State: A Guide to the World's Only Superpower* (2000).

2. In this chapter I refer to Irigaray's early works, particularly *This Sex Which Is Not One* (1985).

3. Much of this information is drawn from Peter Marsden's *The Taliban: War, Religion and the New Order in Afghanistan* (1999).

4. Afghani perception of Soviet occupation is varied and complicated: see, for example, the Revolutionary Afghan Women's Association (RAWA) Web site (www.rawa.org), from which much of the information regarding the Taliban and women's rights in Afghanistan cited in this article is taken. The Web site describes the martyrdom of the organization's founder, who was apparently killed by a KGB operative.

5. See the RAWA Web site.

6. RAWA Web site.

7. See, for example, the remarks made by Taliban Ambassador Designate to the United Nations Abdul Hakeem Mujahid, as cited in Kushal Dave and Alan Schoenfeld (2000).

8. An exception to this was the Campaign to Stop Gender Apartheid led by the Feminist Majority Foundation. The Foundation worked consistently throughout the crisis to bring attention and raise support and awareness for the plight of women in Afghanistan and continues to do so today. However, see the critical remarks below by Sonali Kolhatkar in her essay "'Saving' Afghan Women" (2002).

9. The tensions between multiculturalism and feminism are lucidly mapped out by the debate between Susan Okin and Homi K. Bhabha (among others) in the anthology *Is Multiculturalism Bad for Women?* (Okin et al., 1999). See also the works of Valentine M. Moghadam, particularly "Revolution, Religion, and Gender Politics: Iran and Afghanistan Compared" (1999); also Bronwyn Winter, "Fundamental Misunderstandings: Issues in Feminist Approaches to Islamism" (2001).

10. See the 19 November 2001 CNN interview with Sahar Saba of RAWA: "They are two sides of one coin, the Taliban and the Northern Alliance. The only difference is that one was in power, and the other was trying to be in power. They are against women, against civilization, against democracy. How can we forget that groups in Northern Alliance called democracy an infidel, gateways to hell? So now, when they talk about women's rights or education, or rights to work, it's really just like a joke, insulting those women."

11. The article "Taliban release a rapist commander" (Khan 2000), as well as other related articles, can be found on RAWA's Web site.

12.   In addition to RAWA's Web site, information about the Taliban's paradoxical endorsement/condemnation of prostitution can also be found in Keerthi Reddy's article, "Taliban: A Perfect Islamic Society," www.swordoftruth.com/swordoftruth/archives/byauthor/keerthireddy/tapis.html, accessed May 5 2005; "Violence against women within the personal and public spheres," by Farida Naccache, www.macmag-glip.org/joussour_stance.htm; "Heaping Indignities on Afghan Women" by Rasheeda Bhagat, Business Line Internet Edition, 27 September 2001, www.blonnet.com/businessline/2001/09/27/stories/042744ra.htm; Amnesty International's 2001 report on Afghanistan, www.web.amnesty.org/web/ar2001.nsf/webasacountries/AFGHANISTAN?OpenDocument.

13.   See note 10.

References

Barthes, Roland. 1998. Striptease. In *A Barthes Reader,* trans. and ed. Susan Sontag. New York: Hill and Wang.

Baudrillard, Jean. 1996. *The Perfect Crime.* Trans. Chris Turner. London, New York: Verso.

Bhabha, Homi K. 1999. Liberalism's sacred cow. In *Is Multiculturalism Bad for Women?* ed. Susan Okin, Joshua Cohen, Matthew Howard, and Martha Nussbaum. Princeton, N.J.: Princeton University Press.

Blum, William. 2000. *Rogue State: A Guide to the World's Only Superpower.* Monroe, Maine: Common Courage Press.

Coomaraswamy, Radhika. 2000. *UN Special Report on Afghanistan.* E/CN.4/2000/68 Add. 4. Integration of the Human Rights of Women and the Gender Perspective.

Dave, Kushal, and Alan Schoenfeld. 2000. War of words: East and West clash at Master's Tea. *Yale Herald Online.* Retrieved 21 September 2005 from www.yaleherald.com/archive/xxix/2000.01.28/news/p4taliban.html.

Irigaray, Luce. 1985. *This Sex Which Is Not One.* Trans. Catherine Porter and Carolyn Burke. Ithaca, N.Y.: Cornell University Press.

Khan, M. Ilyas. 1999. Beyond good and evil. *Herald Magazine.* Cited on RAWA Web site. Retrieved 21 September 2005 from www.rawa.org/ilyas.htm.

Kolhatkar, Sonali. 2002. 'Saving' Afghan women. *Znet.* Retrieved 21 September 2005 from www.zmag.org/content/showarticle.cfm?ItemID=1534

Lacan, Jacques. 1998. *On Feminine Sexuality: The Limits of Love and Knowledge: The Seminar of Jacques Lacan Book XX: Encore 1972–73.* Trans. Bruce Fink. Ed. Jacques-Alain Miller. New York, London: W. W. Norton.

Marsden, Peter. 1998. *The Taliban: War, Religion and the New Order in Afghanistan.* London, New York: Oxford University Press.

Martini, Virgilio. 1969. *Il mondo senza donne.* Lido di Iesolo: Tritone.

Moghadam, Valentine M. 1999. Revolution, religion, and gender politics: Iran and Afghanistan compared. *Journal of Women's History* 10 (4): 172–95.

Okin, Susan Moller. 1999. Is multiculturalism bad for women? In *Is Multiculturalism*

Bad for Women? ed. Susan Okin, Joshua Cohen, Matthew Howard, and Martha Nussbaum. Princeton, N.J.: Princeton University Press.

Paterson, Maggie, ed. 2002. A new freedom? *Amnesty* 112 (March/April): 6

Revolutionary Afghan Women's Association. 1997. Retrieved 21 September 2005 from www.rawa.org.

Saadawi, Nawal el. 2002. Globalisation, fundamentalism, and feminism. Lecture given May 13 at St. Antony's College, Oxford University.

Saba, Sahar. 2001. CNN interview. Retrieved 21 September 2005 from: www.cnn.com/2001/COMMUNITY/11/19/saba.cnna.

Winter, Bronwyn. 2001. Fundamental misunderstandings: Issues in feminist approaches to Islamism. *Journal of Women's History* 13 (1): 9–41.

Žižek, Slavoj. 1989. *The Sublime Object of Ideology.* London, New York: Verso.

———. 1994. *Metastases of Enjoyment: Six Essays on Woman and Causality.* London and New York: Verso.

———. 1996. I hear you with my eyes. In *Gaze and Voice as Love Objects,* ed. Renata Salecl and Slavoj Žižek. Durham, N.C., and London: Duke University Press.

———. 1997. *Plague of Fantasies.* London and New York: Verso.

———. 2000. *On Belief.* London and New York: Verso.

———. 2002. Welcome to the desert of the real. *The Symptom: Online Journal for Lacan.com* (spring/summer) 2. Retrieved 14 September 2005 from www.lacan.com/desertsymf.htm.

9 Cruelty, Horror, and the Will to Redemption

Lynne S. Arnault

> In time, every sad ending will become a happy story. The sad ending is only because the author stops telling the story. But it still goes on. It's just untold.
>
> Francis Falls, *Twin Falls Idaho*

> A diamond is a chunk of coal that is made good under pressure.
>
> Anonymous, *The Book of Positive Quotations*

> Deep, unspeakable suffering may well be called a baptism, a regeneration, the initiation into a new state.
>
> George Eliot, *Adam Bede*

The Will to Redemption

In U.S. American mainstream popular culture, the idea that meaning can be reclaimed from even the cruelest of circumstances is highly cherished. For a myriad of reasons, many Americans are deeply invested in believing that there must be some good purpose and final ending to the suffering caused by cruelty. In Charles Taylor's words, "We want our lives to have meaning, or weight, or substance, or to grow towards some fullness. . . . But this means our *whole* lives. If necessary, we want the future to 'redeem' the past, to make it part of a life story which has sense or purpose, to take it up in a meaningful unity" (1989, 51, in Langer 1996). Not surprisingly, given our commitment to the idea that good always arises from the wreckage of cruelty to restore meaning and purpose to our lives, moral formulas such as "Every cloud has a silver lining," "Suffering is good for the soul," and "Everything happens for a purpose" are staple forms of consolatory rhetoric.

A particularly striking illustration of the belief that victory over cruelty is inevitable occurred in 1995 shortly after the bombing of the Alfred P. Murrah Federal Building in Oklahoma City—an act of domestic terrorism that resulted in the death of 168 children and adults. As reported by Ron Rosenbaum in the *New York Times Magazine*, Oklahomans repeatedly insisted that "the real meaning of the whole murderous episode was how it was really about good, about the manifestation of the goodness of Oklahoma to the world" (1995, 15). In the words of a preacher who ministered to the families of the bomb victims and who handed out "angel pins" to rescue workers, "Even if the man [the bomber] . . . meant to do evil, he managed to accomplish some good. . . . All he did was cause the genuineness of Oklahoma to come alive" (Rosenbaum 1995, 15).

Public officials in Oklahoma used rhetoric whose tone was similarly triumphant. According to Governor Frank Keating, to emerge from the bombing incident "muscular, attractive and lionized is something quite candidly that surprised people. . . . Oklahoma has an opportunity to step into the first tier of states. The good will generated by this tragedy . . . is a door-opening opportunity for us and one we fully wish to enjoy" (Linenthal 2001, 45). The mayor of Oklahoma City, Ronald Norick, echoed these sentiments by proclaiming that the bombing had given the city "an opportunity to expand its horizons. It's a terrible way to do it," he admitted, "but we do end up getting a real opportunity" (Rosenbaum 1995, 15). Three years later, revitalization was still on the minds of public officials. In an interview with author Edward Linenthal, Charles Van Rysselberge, the president of the Oklahoma City Chamber of Commerce, expressed the hope that widespread respect for Oklahomans' outpouring of generosity in response to the bombing "would transform what many in Oklahoma believed was an enduring national image of 'ignorant Okies' and that the same civic energies evident in response to the bombing would spark a revitalization of the city" (Linenthal 2001, 41).

It is interesting to compare discourse after the Murrah Building bombing with that after the September 11, 2001, terrorist attacks on the World Trade Center in New York. To my knowledge, city and state officials have simply spoken about rebuilding; they have not used the idiom of economic boosterism. On the other hand, much was made about how patient and friendly New Yorkers were being with one another, about how deep the wellsprings of generosity had proven to be in the city, and about how the perception of the city as consisting of balkanized neighborhoods had been exploded—demonstrating, I suppose, that every locale has its own particular image problems. Given the magnitude of the local damage and devastating economic projections on every level, as well as its reputation as one of the most famous cities in the world, apparently New Yorkers could not, or did not, console themselves with discourse about silver linings.[1]

This is not to say, however, that the rhetoric of redemption was absent: talk about good triumphing over evil was ubiquitous. According to pundits, unprecedented national unity, a rebirth of patriotism, and renewed confidence in our ability to take an enemy's best shot "on the chin" helped redeem the devastation wrought by the terrorists' attacks. In an interview on September 28, 2001, with Dan Rather on the CBS television newsmagazine *48 Hours*, Mayor Rudy Giuliani declared that New York "is a better city now than it was before the attack took place in terms of its spirituality and its understanding of what it means to be an American, its understanding of unity."

Cruelty, Horror, and the Will to Redemption 161

As one would expect, popular discourses of redemption find a comfortable home in Hollywood. Thus, in *Twin Falls Idaho,* a haunting 1999 film directed by Michael Polish about conjoined twins, it seems natural that the sadness that envelops the characters is brushed aside by the reassuring words of the dying twin, Francis Falls, who explains (and who is later quoted as saying) that every sad ending eventually becomes a happy story: "The sad ending is only because the author stops telling the story. But it still goes on. It's just untold."[2]

The will to happy endings is pervasive even in American narratives about the Holocaust. For example, Steven Spielberg's 1993 blockbuster movie *Schindler's List* tempers the harrowing and seemingly meaningless brutality of the Holocaust by offering a story about a flawed protagonist—a member of the Nazi party, a womanizer, a war profiteer—who ultimately redeems himself through acts of heroism. Given the unimaginable horrors, moral chaos, and sheer loss that make up the Holocaust and that challenge what we had previously imagined as humanly possible, one might suppose—Francis Falls notwithstanding— that a movie on the Holocaust could not provide a happy ending or leave us with the optimistic belief that cruelty brings out the good in people. And yet *Schindler's List* does just that: it transforms the frightening reality of the Holocaust into an uplifting message of hope. In the words of Harold Schulweis, *Schindler's List* seems to have become "the defining symbol of the Holocaust . . . not because of its artistry alone, but because it enables the viewer to enter the dark cavern without feeling that there is no exit" (1994, 157, in Rosenfeld 1997).[3]

In seeking to tell a story about the Holocaust that leaves us with an essentially optimistic view of the potential of humans to do good, Spielberg's movie about Oskar Schindler is not unusual. This, of course, is just my point—many people cherish the idea that good eventually triumphs over evil, thereby restoring meaning and purpose to our lives. In what follows, I want to raise the question of why we find redemptive explanations of suffering so compelling. After briefly arguing that a proper understanding of the moral harm of cruelty calls into question the credibility of redemptive logic, I will suggest that the frequent insistence that cruelty ultimately ennobles the human spirit or that something good always emerges from cruelty is due, in part, to the epistemic dynamics of horror, that is, to the capacity of horror to generate a certain kind of knowledge.[4] As I shall argue, reason abhors the horrible, not—as we commonly believe—because being horrified is the opposite of being rational, but because horror is an ordeal of practical reason. During or after the experience of horror, we tend to be attracted to the logic of redemption because horror signals violation—the fact that the world is not as we think it should be. As creatures who are committed to things existing in the way we conceive them to exist, when our expectations are violated, we want to see things set or made right. Committing ourselves to the prescription that the future will redeem the past is one way of expressing our resolve to see the world conform to our universalizing prescriptions. We will the world back on course—but, I shall argue, sometimes at a considerable cost. In the final section of my paper, I will raise questions about the status of redemptive explanations of suffering.

Before proceeding with my argument, I should make several further prefatory remarks. The first is that I am not trying to argue that there is no such thing as redemptive suffering: my objective is to show that victory cannot always be snatched from the jaws of cruelty, no matter how long the story goes on, and that insistence on this consolatory construction is sometimes morally problematic.

Secondly, because many cruelties are a form of evil and because my focus is mostly on extreme forms of cruelty, much of what I have to say about cruelty and the will to redemption could also be said of evil. However, while I cannot argue for this here, I think it is a mistake to hold that *all* cruelties have the moral gravity that characterize acts, practices, or social forces that are evil. Moreover, I do not want to preclude the possibility that the components that make up cruelty are not identical to those that comprise evil. Thus, while my paper may have the beneficial "side effect" of shedding some light on issues concerning evil in general, I am only claiming to elucidate cruelty, horror, and the will to redemption.

In addition to the above points, I also want to preface my essay with the explicit recognition of the heterogeneity of the meanings and modes of the experience of suffering. The ways people suffer vary across time and space as well as within communities. For example, because American parents of all economic classes generally tend to view the death of one of their own children as a horrifying anomaly, losing a very young child is experienced as being one of the greatest sorrows that can befall a parent. In parts of the Brazilian northeast, on the other hand, indifference to the death of poor young children is so seamlessly socially produced that feelings of sorrow, sadness, and grief are seen as misplaced, if not pathological. In fact, if we take poor mothers at their word, these feelings are simply absent (see Scheper-Hughes 1992, chap. 9).

Just as there is no universal form of suffering, so too there is no universal way in which redemptive longing takes shape. Thus, for the purposes of this essay, I am limiting my analysis of redemptive longings to the context of contemporary American mainstream popular culture. While I presume that we can meaningfully speak, in many contexts, of collective or shared modes of responding to suffering, I also recognize that local social variables—for instance, gender, economic class, race/ethnicity, and religion—shape people's expressions of suffering and make social influences partial and multifaceted.[5]

Undoubtedly, Christian ideology has been one of the most important influences on common redemptive explanations of suffering in American mainstream popular culture. One reason, then, that redemptive explanations have such a commanding hold on the popular imagination is that the United States is a highly Christianized nation. My objective in this paper, however, is not to chart the (complex) history of Christian thinking on notions of redemptive suffering or to chronicle the influence of Christian and other religions' doctrines of divine providence on popular discourses of redemption in the United States. I simply assume these religious influences on popular manifestations of the will to redemption.[6]

Obviously, then, I do not purport to give a comprehensive or exhaustive analysis of popular understandings of redemption, especially since, in addition to religion, other factors account for the grip of meaning-seeking explanations of cruelty on the popular imagination. I will be addressing only one of them—the epistemic dynamics of horror.

The Moral Harm of Cruelty

As a first step to explaining the role that horror often plays in redemptive logic, it is useful to ask the question of what makes cruelty morally problematic. Let us approach this question by looking briefly at torture, domestic battery, and terrorism, three paradigmatic forms of cruelty. My argument is the relatively simple one that the very feature of an action, practice, or social condition that makes it cruel—providing a person with a sound reason to consider her sense of self and world seriously violated or nearly seriously violated—is also the feature that makes it morally harmful.

Torture, domestic battery, and terrorism are forms of cruelty, I submit, because of what the infliction of severe bodily pain does to the personhood, as well as to the body, of the victim. What is transpiring when torture takes place, for example, is not just a torturer producing blood and gore, but a victim undergoing the destruction (or near destruction) of meaning, the loss of dignity and agency, the fragmentation and disintegration of subjectivity, and an assault on her memory of herself in spaces of selfhood outside of the world in which she is being brutalized. The torture victim's agony, in other words, encompasses much more than the sensations or materiality of physical pain: a blow is not just a blow. In the words of Jean Améry, a torture victim of the Nazi regime, as soon as the very first blow descends on the prisoner, he loses "trust in the world":

> Trust in the world includes all sorts of things . . . [among them] the certainty that by reason of written or unwritten social contracts the other person will spare me—more precisely stated, that he will respect my physical, and with it also my metaphysical, being. The boundaries of my body are also the boundaries of my self. My skin surface shields me against the external world. If I am to have trust, I must feel on it only what I want to feel. . . . But with the first blow from a policeman's fist, against which there can be no defense and which no helping hand will ward off, a part of our life ends and it can never again be revived. (Améry 1995b, 126–27)

From Améry we learn that cruelty involves the undermining, if not destruction, of subjectivity. To be reduced to the status of an object, to have another's will literally inscribed on one's body, to become merely a thing in the eyes of another—this, according to Améry, is what the torturer's blows do to cause the one being tortured to lose "trust in the world." Now it is worth noting that Améry's rhetoric does not acknowledge the multiplicity of the self and of social reality. He does not speak of inhabiting multiple "worlds of sense," that is, different, co-temporaneous, lived constructions of the social that stand in tense or contested relations of power to one another and that produce plural and ambiguous selves (Lugones 2003, 20–26). By referring to the expectation of having the boundaries of his body and therefore of his self respected, Améry seems to be talking about having lost trust in a world many people rarely get to inhabit, at least materially. This does not change the fact, however, that cruelty involves dispossession in the world or worlds of sense that one inhabits.

Améry's rhetoric is worth noting for another reason: he says that the torture victim's sense of self and world is destroyed *with the first blow*. This raises an interesting question: are people who occupy privileged worlds more vulnerable to losing trust at the very first blow than those who experience dispossession regularly, that is, who occupy social locations where their subjectivity is routinely disrespected, violated, or severely circumscribed? Are the relatively dispossessed—especially those who are dispossessed in official worlds of sense—relatively immunized, not from utter dispossession, but from overwhelming shock when, to use Susan Brison's words, "the tormentor says with his blows: You are nothing but a body, a mere object of my will—here, I'll prove it!" (1997, 18) This is a provocative (and ultimately empirical) issue. What should nonetheless not get overlooked is that Améry describes a process of dispossession that, whatever its speed, all victims of traumatic violence seem to have in common.[7]

The subject of how severe bodily pain harms the basic structures of the victim's self and world is insightfully discussed by Elaine Scarry in her book *The Body in Pain: The Making and Unmaking of the World* (1985). As she points out in chapter 1, the intense bodily pain inflicted by the torturer "unmakes" or nearly "unmakes" the victim's self and world: the contents of consciousness disintegrate; the self that is formed and sustained in relation to others is shattered; the belief systems that give meaning to human experience are undermined; one's sense of continuity with the past is lost; the realm in which one's will can operate contracts; and one's extension out into the world shrinks—even one's capacity for speech, a major source of our self-extension, is altered.[8] In Scarry's words, "the created world of thought and feeling, all the psychological and mental content that constitutes both one's self and one's world, and that gives rise to and is in turn made possible by language cease to exist" (1985, 30).

Another illustration of the ways in which the infliction of unbridled pain has the potential to unmake the basic structures of an individual's self and world can be found in the example of battered women.[9] Severe, chronic battering produces profound deformations in consciousness, identity, agency, and connection with others. A battered woman's agency becomes seriously compromised because battering is a process of forcing the victim to do the will of the victimizer. During a beating, almost by definition, the battered woman's point of view, interests, and needs count for nothing.

Not only does the victim of severe battering lose meaningful control over the world she inhabits with her batterer, she loses the sense of this being a meaningful world. To borrow a phrase from Lawrence Langer, she experiences a "reversal of expectations" (1996, 54). The old beliefs that gave meaning to her life and that linked her to worlds outside herself are jeopardized or undermined. As her assumptions about such things as family, home, community, justice, truth, God, and love crumble, her created world of meaning is unmade as well, and with that comes not only a severing of the past from the present, but often an increasing inability to envision a future of meaningful possibilities in that world. As she grows silent, or as language in this world ceases to have meaning for her, her world contracts. Scarry points out that through our ability to project words and sounds out into our environment, we human beings inhabit, human-ize, and "possess" spaces much larger than those occupied by our bodies alone (1985, 49). Because the voice is an important—sometimes final—source of self-extension, nearly losing the ability to speak or having one's voice silenced or appropriated by the batterer means that the perimeter of the severely battered woman's world shrinks until it nearly becomes coterminous with the edges of her body (1985, 33). Nothing matters but avoiding, or at least surviving, another round of blows.

Severe, chronic battering has the power to annihilate the victim's sense of self as well as world. There is, first of all, the experience of self-alienation and self-betrayal that occurs when one's own body is made a weapon against oneself: the "ceaseless, self-announcing signal of the body in pain, at once so empty and undifferentiated and so full of blaring adversity, contains not only the feeling 'my body hurts' but the feeling 'my body hurts me'" (Scarry 1985, 47).

More profoundly, perhaps, are the deep alterations the severely battered woman experiences in her relations with others and in her images of herself in relation to others. She will lose a sense of her own separateness within her re-lationship with the batterer. Inasmuch as the self is formed and sustained in relation with others, she will often literally feel as though she has lost her self. Engulfed in pain and fear, lacking effective recourse, cut off from family and friends, and having developed considerable disassociative powers in order to survive, a battered woman may experience the sensation of watching herself be a "false self." Battered women who end up in prison because they have resorted to killing their batterer will frequently make statements such as "I feel like my-self again" or, more ironically, "I feel free again."[10]

Judith Herman's words about prolonged captivity help to illuminate the pro-found alterations in the self that battered women experience: "All the psycho-logical structures of the self—the image of the body, the internalized images of others, and the values and ideals that lend a person a sense of coherence and purpose—have been invaded and systematically broken. . . . Even after release from captivity, the victim cannot assume her former identity. Whatever new identity she develops in freedom must include the memory of her enslaved self. Her image of her body must include a body that can be controlled and violated. Her image of herself in relation to others must include a person who can lose and be lost to others. And her moral ideals must coexist with knowledge of the capacity for evil, both within others and within herself" (1992, 93).[11]

In this description, Herman is emphasizing how prolonged captivity, as a form of cruelty, has the potential to unmake or deform the basic structures of the victim's self and world. According to Bat-Ami Bar On, violation of self and world is also what happens to people who have been subjected to the cruelty of terrorism: "Terrorism interrupts the causal relation between what people do and what happens to them. . . . The terrorized's sense of a continuous experience and memory weakens and even breaks down. This in turn leads to a shrinking or breakdown of personality. . . . The terrorized too will experience an alienation from self and a loss of the sense of oneself as an agent capable of acting on her or his own behalf and deserving of respect. The sense of alienation from self together with the lack of a sense of agency and dignity constitute a dissolution of the individual self" (1991, 111–12).

The September 11 attacks on the World Trade Center and the Pentagon illustrate this characterization of the harmful effects of terrorism. In the months immediately following the terrorist assaults, many Americans showed signs of being less confident about their ability to have meaningful control over the "connection between what they do and what happens to them." Thus, discourse was sprinkled with the phrase "the day the world changed, "[12] and, not surprisingly, people began to demand that the government provide foolproof security measures at airports, the country's borders, facilities such as nuclear plants, and mass gatherings. Rather ominously, fear and loss of confidence also yielded almost immediate calls for using torture against enemies of the state (see, e.g., Alter 2001, 45) and the uncommonly swift passage of the U.S. Patriot Act with its very questionable violations of civil liberties and human rights. Furthermore, while it is undoubtedly an overdetermined phenomenon, the ostentatious displays of patriotism engendered by the terrorist attacks seem, in part, to be symptomatic of terrorism's potential to challenge, if not shatter, people's sense of self-possession, agency, and strength of will.

It is worth noting that Bar On's comments on terrorism are specifically focused on how sustained terrorist campaigns such as those in Israel affect the formation of a person's self. In her discussion, she reminds us that "in *The Demon Lover: On the Sexuality of Terrorism,* Robin Morgan claims that terrorism democratizes violence and brings men to experience the world in relation to each other similarly, though not identically, to how women experience the world in relation to men" (in Bar On 1991, 110). According to Morgan, in many contexts sudden, rapid footsteps produce immediate fear in women if they think they are hearing a man's footsteps, but a man does not feel the same way if he suddenly hears a woman's rapid footsteps behind him (Morgan 1989, 23–24; 49–50). In making this observation about the gendered phenomenon of fear,[13] Morgan is implicitly relying on our recognition of a well-established *history* of gendered violence.[14] Her point would not hold water if it were based on a few isolated incidents of male violence against women.

Morgan's observation about the gendered nature of fear raises an interesting question: have the events of September 11 brought Americans to experience the world similarly to how people in other countries, who are subject to ongoing campaigns of terrorization, experience the world? It has seemed to me that previous terrorist attacks on American property (here and abroad) have hitherto engendered anger, outrage, and horror on the national level, but not really a nation of terrorized people. Perhaps this is partly due to these incidences having been perceived by most Americans as anomalous occurrences in (mostly) distant lands.[15] Perhaps, also, it is attributable to the fact that many (but not all) Americans live lives where the boundaries of what they hold to be unthinkable, unimaginable, or inviolable are rarely violated. It remains to be seen, I think, whether the United States has really become a nation of terrorized people or whether this country is a nation of temporarily terrorized people, whose expectations and defenses against threats to their well-being and peace of mind are being (and can be) relatively rapidly and easily repaired.

Having said this, I am also mindful of the fact that because of social hierarchies and personal circumstances, Americans are by no means equally protected from, or defended against, unpleasant realities, truths, and injustices, and would not, therefore, react identically to the events of September 11. It is possible that the episodic nature of the terrorist attacks has had the effect of producing more deeply terrorized selves among those who occupy privileged social locations than among those whose expectations about what is possible or thinkable have suffered numerous reversals. When terrorists strike, purportedly "out of the blue," how well, one wonders, do the psychological structures of people who have previously experienced little moral dislocation and dispossession hold up, as opposed to the psychological structures of the already dispossessed?[16]

Ultimately, this is an empirical question. Bar On's words about the process of becoming terrorized do suggest that, as with torture and domestic battery, part of what makes acts of terrorism cruel is that they cause, or have the potential to cause, the serious diminution or deformation of a person's self and world. This characterization still leaves open the question of what distinguishes cruelty such as terrorism from other phenomena—for example, catastrophic illnesses and earthquakes—that can have similar negative effects.

Because the salient difference between cruelty and these harms seems to lie in agent intentionality, that is, in the fact that cruelty is the result of choices agents make, I believe we should define cruelty as any sort of behavior, practice, or social condition that constitutes a sound reason for a person to consider her world and self seriously (or nearly seriously) violated. So long as we understand violations as the result of actions or omissions by human beings, this characterization of cruelty enables us to distinguish the self- and world-shattering power of cruelty from that of other natural harms.[17] Moreover, it has the merit of allowing us to recognize that cruelty is concretely manifested in social set-ups as well as in personal relationships, and it accounts for the sense of betrayal and inability to trust people that victims of cruelty typically experience (Brison 1999, 201). This particular characterization of cruelty permits us, furthermore, to recognize that a person's feeling violated is not sufficient for an attribution of cruelty, and on the other hand, that an act or situation may be cruel even if a person does not actually feel violated. Finally, because culpable harm-doing is built into the concept of violation, this characterization of cruelty allows us to take into account the complexity of some situations, in particular, those cases of cruelty in which the wrongdoer uses others as instruments of her wrongdoing (see Levi 1989; Card 1999) or in which the wrongdoer's behavior issues from both "a resistant and an oppressed motivational structure" (Lugones 2003, 13).

Now it seems to me that how we respond to the suffering of others, especially suffering as serious as that of shattered selves, is significant in terms of the moral content of our character and of our communities. In my opinion, having people who care about alleviating suffering and having institutions dedicated to the care of suffering people are necessary characteristics of a good society—whatever the cause of the suffering. With respect to cruelty, I would want to add that a good society is also one whose institutions do not subject people to cruelty, whose institutions protect people as much as possible from cruel individuals and from conditions that unmake or deform the basic structures of an individual's self and world, and whose institutions produce individuals not disposed to act cruelly.

Needless to say, this ideal is a distant reality: widespread cruelty is a sad fact of life. One typical American way of responding to suffering is to invoke the rhetoric of redemption. This idiom is not unique to the context of cruelty, but because human agency is involved in the suffering caused by cruelty, I am particularly interested in considering how redemptive rhetoric intersects with cruelty. I do not believe that only the suffering caused by cruelty calls the credibility of redemptive logic into question or that everything I mention in the following sections is entirely unique to the context of cruelty. Nevertheless, because the suffering caused by cruelty bears human fingerprints, I think a compelling case can be made for maintaining that in the context of cruelty, popular forms of redemptive rhetoric sometimes incur some special costs.

Preempting Cruelty

Once we recognize that cruelty, like other serious harms, involves the unmaking or near unmaking of a person's sense of self and world, we are well positioned to question the conventional wisdom that "suffering is good for the soul." Admittedly, identifying discontinuity, disruption, and disintegration as among the central characteristics of cruelty does not logically entail rejecting the rhetoric of redemption. But this understanding of the nature of cruelty does at least clear space for recognizing that cruelty may result in diminishing and dividing the self, not in paving the way for a greater self, and that, more often than not, the rhetoric of redemption "preempts" cruelty.[18]

When we recognize that the moral harm of cruelty is in the violating of a person's sense of self and world, we are less apt to see cruelty as a point or discrete time period in a storehouse of consecutive moments in time, and we are poised to view serious cruelty as a process that can so divide and disorder time that the person who experiences the cruelty moves from life to a kind of death. Similarly, when we recognize that what is morally problematic about cruelty is that it violates the basic structures of a person's self and world, we become less inclined to regard survival as the moment when the blows stopped and more open to understanding that survival is itself an ordeal, a problem in which the survivor may find that *she* is the problem—that her experience of cruelty back *then* is no less an experience of loss, dispossession, and dissolution *now*. We are better equipped to see, particularly in extreme cases, that cruelty can so interrupt "the stream of time" that people not only experience the loss of their particular way of being in the world but also endure a way of living that promises no resolution to suffering, that dispels the dream of making the past "part of a [unified life] story which has sense or purpose" (Taylor 1989, 51), and that mocks the very idea of closure.

It is true that people often talk about "picking up the pieces and moving on"—rhetoric that seems to acknowledge that survival is a process. However, this characterization is generally used in a way that belies the fact that in many cases doing this would be even harder than putting Humpty Dumpty back together again: no "old" self exists to be pieced together again, and any illusions we may have harbored of having a stable, unified, and coherent self have been shattered as well. Because the basic structures of the victim's self and world have been assaulted, restoration may not be possible: in a very real sense, the victim may have outlived herself. Just as cruelty is a process in which the victim's sense of self and world is seriously violated, so also is survival a process—one in which the person may have to undergo profound, personal transformation.

One of the strengths of this analysis of cruelty, I would suggest, is that it enables us to recognize not only that previous meanings do not reassert themselves just because the blows (or other sources of the suffering) have stopped, but also that the victim of cruelty can become alienated even from the meaning-seeking dimension of her being. Not only are the victim's former meanings shattered; sometimes even meaning itself is destroyed. We tend to think of cruelty and survival as processes that are discrete—that occur in two distinct periods in time. But the very feature of an action, practice, or social condition that makes it cruel—being dispossessed—also characterizes the aftermath of cruelty. If cruelty is essentially the violating of a person's core sense of self and world, not the blows per se (or the other sources of the suffering), then the suffering that begins with the blows can continue long after the blows have stopped. As I quoted above from Jean Améry's essay on torture, "with the first blow . . . a part of our life ends and it can never again be revived." I might also have quoted these other famous words from his essay: "Torture has an indelible character. Whoever was tortured stays tortured. Torture is ineradicably burned into him, even when no clinically objective traces can be detected" (1995b, 131).

Thirty-three years after his liberation from Bergen Belsen, Jean Améry committed suicide. Whatever his reasons for killing himself, I would object to saying that Améry preempted the possibility of giving his story a happy ending. Pace the film character Francis Falls, I would argue that not all stories have happy endings, no matter how long they last. The self that arises from the ashes may be a lost or shattered self, sometimes even one whose will and character have become infected by cruelty. Cruelty can be "senseless," not in the (mistaken) sense of being motiveless, but in the sense of resisting the victim's attempts to make it part of a reality that makes any sense. Henry Greenspan describes the profound duality with which some Holocaust survivors must contend: "For survivors, [Elie] Wiesel has written, 'The problem is not: to be or not to be, but rather: to be *and* not to be'. . . . Other survivors similarly speak both of having died during the Holocaust yet continuing to live. . . . As contrary as it is to our usual logic and experience, this simultaneity of being and not-being should be understood literally. The copresence of ongoing death and ongoing life—without resolution or higher synthesis—is, for survivors, embodied reality" (1992, 148).

I would note, moreover, that even when a happy ending occurs, the person's suffering might not have been redemptive. Happy endings, in other words, do not always mean renewal or a restored connection with the past: the self that arises from the ashes may be a divided self. As Charlotte Delbo, a Nazi concentration camp survivor, replied when asked if she lives with Auschwitz, "No—I live beside it. Auschwitz is there, fixed and unchangeable, but wrapped in the impervious skin of memory that segregates itself from the present 'me.' Unlike the snake's skin, the skin of memory doesn't renew itself" (Delbo 1985, quoted in and translated by Langer 1991, 13).

By referring to the impervious skin of memory wrapped around her former "self," Delbo is rejecting the rhetoric of redemption, which would assign a higher or transcendent meaning to the cruelties she endured at Auschwitz. From Delbo we learn that it is possible to live beside ruin that is impossible to undo. We are made aware that for some people "life after atrocity . . . [is] only a form of private and communal endurance" (Langer 1996, 63). We are forced to recognize that unlike chronological time, where "the present appears to follow the past and precede the future" (Langer 1996, 55), for some victims of extreme cruelty the present lives beside the past because their experiences in the past are toxins with an eternal half-life that cannot be reconciled with life as it goes on.[19] I am not denying that many victims of cruelty reconnect with their former selves or come to discern parts of a life pattern; this is especially true for those subjected to circumscribed traumatic events rather than to prolonged, repeated trauma (see Herman 1992) and for those fortunate to have strong, empathic listeners with whom to reverse "the privatization of memory" (Greenspan 1992, 163) and to rebuild a self (see Brison 1997 and 1999). Nor am I disavowing the possibility that some victims can genuinely say that their experiences have produced better selves. Some victims are able to reconcile their pasts and experience liberatory growth into the future. The point I am trying to make here is simply that positive developments in a victim's life do not necessarily redeem her suffering. If we are to believe survivors such as Charlotte Delbo, suffering can give way to a measure of happiness without having redemptive value. Thus, some suffering is useless and fruitless.

This observation, of course, brings us back to the question, "Why do we insist upon meaning-seeking explanations of cruelty?" In the following sections,

I argue that one explanation lies in recognizing that the will to redemption is an antidote to the horror that cruelty often generates.

The Epistemic Dynamics of Horror

As an emotion that is often elicited by cruelty, horror plays a dominant role in our normative constructions of cruelty.[20] The more horror that an event or act of cruelty generates in us, the more cruel the situation seems to be and the more certain we tend to be about our diagnosis of cruelty. Thus, when a man uses his pregnant wife's abdomen as a punching bag, or when an interrogator hacks off the ears of a prisoner, or when a suicide bomber blows up a school bus filled with young children, our horror is the alarm that signals cruelty.

Needless to say, most of us in the West are not accustomed to thinking of horror as an emotion that does salutary work in the moral domain. Love, compassion, forgiveness, benevolence—when we think of emotions having positive epistemic value, these are some of the more usual candidates. When we reel in horror, it seems as though reason has taken leave: for some of us, our thoughts "freeze" and our mind seems to become paralyzed; for others, the mind may start racing, and thoughts become chaotic and disorderly. However we experience horror, we seem to be in a state that is nearly the opposite of being rational in the normative sense. Given the importance we tend to attach to the image of reason as calm, imperturbable, and steady—as immune to subjective influences or "intrusions"—we are liable to think that horror is unsuitable for work in the moral domain.[21] Appearances and prejudices notwithstanding, however, horror plays an important role in our moral lives, particularly by disclosing strong normative sentiments in the face of cruelty.

To understand the epistemic dynamics of horror, we must recognize that no emotion is just a bodily impulse or a blind surge of affect cut off from cognition and judgment. Any particular emotion is a feeling *about* something. It is directed toward an object and depends upon our way of perceiving that object, as well as upon the sorts of beliefs and judgments that are intimately connected with the object.[22] As Martha Nussbaum points out, our emotions involve cognitive appraisals (whether linguistic or nonlinguistic) that implicitly acknowledge our vulnerability and lack of self-sufficiency vis-à-vis external things we view as being highly salient to our projects and goals (see Nussbaum 1994; 1995; 2001).

In the case of horror, I would argue, what is involved is the apprehension that we can do little or nothing to prevent or undo the violation of conceptual norms that we take to be very important. The cognitive content of horror, then, involves fundamental presuppositions about the way we think things are or should be. As beings with the capacity to make judgments about the way things are or should be, we have "trust in the world"—here, not in Améry's sense, but in the sense that we believe that we can and should be able to understand the nature or order of things well enough to make appropriate prescriptions to live by.[23] This expectation has no single, timeless form, but as individuals we tend to believe that we can understand the basic order or nature of things and conduct ourselves accordingly. When we are horrified, our feelings of fear, incredulity, and recoil involve the apprehension that one or more of our conceptual norms has been violated. Horror signals that the norm whose violation we are witnessing or imaging is a prescription to which we are deeply committed. Thus, when a young child is sexually molested by her father, most of us in this country feel horror because incest is an act that offends deep-seated normative beliefs about the nature of humanity, parenthood, and love, among other things. Our horror rests on the belief that there is something "sick," "unnatural," or "perverted" about the father's behavior.

Similarly, torture elicits horror in many Americans[24] because it challenges our sense of the way persons should be treated. Like Jean Améry, many of us presume that the boundaries of the body are also the boundaries of the self, and we tend to believe that the people and institutions that populate our world are committed, or should be committed, to respecting and protecting the integrity of our beings. When we witness or imagine a person being physically tortured, most of us experience horror because we believe that by violating the boundaries of the victim's body, the torturer is also violating that which we hold particularly sacrosanct—the subjectivity of the person being tortured (Améry 1995, 126).

Horror, then, discloses truths that we hold about the nature of reality, but this does not mean, of course, that as individuals we experience horror at the same things. Needless to say, the meanings and modes of the experience of horror are heterogeneous: horror is a richly social and cultural phenomenon, one whose content is open to wide variations across cultures and time. The horror that grips us on any given occasion is always a particular historical formation.

Moreover, because cultures are far from being homogeneous "spaces" whose inhabitants possess a uniform and consistent understanding of the world, the events and situations that trigger horror will vary among people in any given cultural context, as will the expression of horror.[25] Thus, while some of us recoil in horror in a particular situation, others may not be horror-stricken—either because they do not hold the conceptual norms upon which our horror is based or because they do not attach as much importance to them as we do. For example, in order to experience horror when a husband batters his wife, one must believe, among other things, that a man's masculinity does not depend on his willingness and ability to physically dominate the woman or women with whom he is intimate; that men are not entitled to disrespect the bodily integrity of women, including spouses; that women do not undergo pain and suffering dumbly but have the same sensitivities that men have; and that the intentional infliction of pain and suffering on women is a serious wrongdoing.

I would emphasize that the events and situations that trigger horror in individuals will vary, not only because people have different convictions, but also because situations do not have prepackaged descriptions or "people-independent" constructions. The issue of police brutality illustrates this point well. It is one (important) thing to believe, for example, that police officers can and should respect the bodily integrity of suspects. It is yet another—equally important—thing to believe that in any particular case, the police officer's handling of a suspect actually violated this expectation. Thus, even when there is agreement that police officers should respect the bodily integrity of suspects, we may find that in any given situation some people do not experience our horror because they do not perceive the incident as constituting a violation of that norm. Social location, social experiences, personal history and circumstances—all of these influence how an individual defines what a situation is.[26]

Now it seems to me that because the cognitive content of horror involves fundamental presuppositions about the way things are or should be, and because some modes of interpretation and understanding are "more equal" or dominant in a culture than others, what routinely grips individuals in a cultural context as horrific will tend to reflect the perspectives of those who occupy privileged social locations. We may also want to consider the possibility that while occupying privileged social locations may often help to indemnify individuals from the *consequences* of a reversal of expectations, thereby muting their experiences of horror, in some situations—paradoxically—it may also make them liable to experience horror more acutely than would be the case for people whose trust in the world is routinely violated and whose lived experiences are regularly marked—and marred—by reversals of expectations and/or the constant need to lower expectations. As we might expect, for example, horror, not "death without weeping," is experienced when wealthy rather than impoverished mothers in northeast Brazil lose one of their own children at a young age (see Scheper-Hughes 1992, 326-30).

What is clear, I think, is that a key epistemic aspect of horror is its capacity to reveal truths, however inchoately, that one holds about the world. It bears emphasizing at this point that horror is not simply the apprehension of violated norms. As beings with the desire to understand the nature or order of things so as to make appropriate prescriptions to live by, we are committed to things existing in the way we conceive them to exist. If this were not true—if I could just be completely unconcerned about my conceptions of the world—I would have no reason, when confronted by a violation of my norms, not to set my world right by simply revising pertinent concepts or reclassifying relevant objects. For instance, in cases where a father sexually molests his child, I could just alter my normative concepts of humanity and fatherhood to accommodate sexual molestation, or I could stop applying these concepts to men who sexually molest their children. But I am not indifferent, especially about my more fundamental concepts, and I cannot be indifferent unless I become radically stoical about my inability to control things in the external world, including the prescriptions of other people and their interpretations of those prescriptions: my concepts about the nature or order of things are my way not only of understanding the world but of having projects and goals—of being engaged in and with the world. Both my moral and nonmoral prescriptions are wishes (usually tacit wishes) for things to assume and maintain a relatively certain and stable order conducive to the realization of my projects and goals.

Thus, because we have a vested interest in believing that the world has an understandable order, we recoil when we discover that people and things have not cooperated with our conceptual norms. Furthermore, in instances where we recognize that our *moral* prescriptions have been violated, we experience fear, incredulity, and possibly revulsion[27] because we want our moral prescriptions, at least our most fundamental moral prescriptions, to be universal—to apply to others as well as to ourselves. This means, for example, that if I am horrified by incest, I not only believe that incest is wrong for me, but I also want or will everyone to see incest as taboo, and I do not want to try to adjust my beliefs to accommodate its existence in the world. The question for me is not only, "How *can* he want to have sex with his child?" but also "How *dare* he have sex with his child?"

I may also ask, "What kind of a person does such a thing?" Paradoxically, the will to prescribe universally is most evident when I claim that the perpetrator of incest is "just an animal" or "a monster." Calling a person a beast or a monster carries no moral force if I really believe what I am saying. Why condemn a beast for acting beastly or a monster for acting monstrously? Granted, we find it difficult to accept what cannot be changed. But if I accuse a perpetrator of being an animal or a monster, it is not that I have mistaken a human for a beast or a monster, but that I believe that there are humans who act *as if* they were beasts or monsters, that is, *as if* they were creatures or moral aliens that could not have acted otherwise. Calling a perpetrator of incest an animal or monster is an indication, therefore, that I am deeply invested in applying my prescription forbidding incest to others as well as to myself. Because most Americans are heirs to the Enlightenment view that human beings are essentially good, rational, and capable of self-governance, the common American tendency to regard people who commit serious transgressions as "animals" or "monsters" indicates that our reactions of horror to incest often involve the premise that only categorically transgressive creatures would violate the "natural order" of things. At best, however, ascribing animality or monstrosity to the perpetrator of incest provides a psychologically satisfying way of expressing moral condemnation: if taken literally, such ascriptions constitute a conceptually self-defeating way of insisting on the universality of our moral prescriptions, and as a result, they carry no real moral force.

Thus, horror is a regular feature of my emotional life because typically I resist the thwarting of my will. When faced with a phenomenon such as incest, I am shocked on everyone's behalf, not just my own, and I remain that way because I am invested in, or committed to, my way of seeing and carrying on in the world. The experience of horror exposes my futile aspirations to be a legislator of universal ends. I am forced to recognize my vulnerability and lack of self-sufficiency vis-à-vis the external world, for I cannot control the prescriptions of others or their interpretations of those prescriptions. When conflict occurs, I am powerless to ensure that my normative conceptions will carry the day.

Of course, if I am able to revise relevant beliefs in a given case, I am capable of overcoming my reaction of horror. Cannibalism is a case in point. Because cannibalism violates basic cultural and personal prescriptions about respect for human life and for the bodies of our dead, the report of a starving person eating the flesh of a dead companion would be horrifying to me. However, with some effort I could probably overcome my sense of horror. By learning more about the desperate particulars of the person's situation, I might be able to adjust my beliefs about the person's conduct. "Well, is there really a morally significant difference between eating human body parts and the parts of cows and pigs?" I might say to myself (assuming I am a carnivore). "If organ transplantation is morally acceptable, why—in extreme situations—isn't cannibalism?" "Some things are hard to swallow, but who am I, sitting in the comfort of my home and its well-provisioned larder, to say that cannibalism is absolutely wrong?"

Indeed, who am I? If I am open to revising the beliefs that underlie any one of my normative concepts—and I am more apt to become open as time goes by and my horror loses its "freshness" (see Nussbaum 2001, 79–85)—I can try, and perhaps should try, to overcome my horror. But if I am particularly invested in my prescription, I will resist—and perhaps should resist—the thwarting of my will. Horror is born in the yawning gap between, on the one hand, the desire to make my ends the ends of everyone's actions and, on the other hand, the powerlessness of my will to make my ends actually universal. Reason abhors horror, then, not because being horrified is the opposite of being rational, but because horror is an ordeal of practical reason.

Giving Cruelty Its Due

> Hardship and opposition are the native soil of manhood and self-reliance.
>
> John Neal, *The Book of Positive Quotations*

> Fire is the test of gold; adversity, of strong men.
>
> Lucius Annaeus Seneca, *Moral Essays: On Providence*

Having isolated the epistemic dynamics of horror and having demonstrated that cruelty threatens the basic structures of an individual's self and world, we are well-situated now to discern why many people find the rhetoric of redemption so compelling. Cruelty often generates horror. Horror elicited by cruelty not only discloses the violation of truths we hold about the way life should or might be lived but also protests their violation. The rhetoric of redemption represents an effort to rehabilitate these truths, that is, to exorcise the specter of moral indifference or defeat and to renew our commitment to the normative conceptions or prescriptions that we had previously legislated. In essence, the will to redemption is an antidote to the horror that cruelty often engenders. By believing that the suffering caused by cruelty must have some good or transcendent purpose, we implicitly express our resolve to remain faithful to our normative prescriptions.

What, then, can be problematic about this resolve—about committing our-selves to the prescription that the future will always redeem the past? Even our belief in the redemptive value of all suffering may be violated, but why is it inadvisable to refuse to be reconciled to the idea that some suffering has no redeeming value? Though we are often powerless to prevent the unmaking of things as we will them to be and though we are frequently unable to undo what has already been done to others or to ourselves, shouldn't the legislation of *this* prescription, of all prescriptions, be continuously affirmed?

Without a doubt, popular idioms of redemption are appealing, and I do not want to suggest either that there is no such thing as redemptive suffering or that the will to redemption in its secularized forms lacks any redeeming value. Nevertheless, because it often authorizes a masculinized and commercialized approach to suffering, because it can be a rather frugal response to lives violated by cruelty, and because it tends to normalize cruelty and to turn victims and their suffering into "object lessons," in my opinion the will to redemption as it is typically expressed in popular culture has morally problematic features that warrant the attention of feminists.

To underscore the salutary effects of deflating the rhetoric of redemption, let us begin by noting how masculinized the discourse can be. Take, for example, some of the rhetoric that was used after the terrorist attacks in Oklahoma City and New York City. Terrorism, we were told, provides opportunities for a city or a state to become "muscular" and "lionized" and for its people to show that it is "made of the right stuff." It affords a nation the occasion to demonstrate that its people are "tough" and heroic, that its spirit cannot be broken, that it can "take it on the chin" and spring back into action—in short, that it is a nation of men with iron wills and staying power, not losers in a contest of strength.

Expressions of redemptive longing are not always imbued in our popular culture with such masculinized imagery. But when this occurs, we should be troubled, because this imagery shapes how we think about and respond to acts of cruelty. One significant effect of this imagery, for example, is that it promotes a conventionally masculine approach to grief and suffering by stressing the re-pression and denial of all emotions but the one emotion in American main-stream popular culture that most classes of men are not typically denied—anger.[28] In so doing, it not only taps into the commonly held belief that the redemption of suffering requires retribution; it also has the potential to steer us into the waters of excessive vindictiveness and revenge-seeking. Furthermore, it reflects and reinforces disdain for emotionality, which has been traditionally associated in the dominant culture with femininity and marked as a sign of inferiority. We should also note that with the possible exception of cases where anger and vindictive passions come to rule a person's life, redemptive rhetoric that is masculinized implicitly disparages victims of cruelty who have not been able to make their experiences part of a coherent life story or who have found that the negative imprint of cruelty on themselves and their lives has been in-delible: such people, it is implied, are "wimps"[29]—code for emasculated losers or women.

Another problematic aspect of masculinized idioms of redemption is that they are apt to employ a good guy/bad guy dichotomy—a bifurcation that relies on the interlocking binary oppositions of good and evil, us and them, and civilized and uncivilized. Endemic to this set of dichotomies is the fiction that the modalities presumed to make the bad guys (say, the Taliban) "bad"— intolerance, hatred, misogyny, violence against women, xenophobia, militarism, and terrorization—do not have any application to us, the "good guys." Such a fiction requires revisionist history (what about the appalling incidence of male violence against women in this nation?) as well as homogenizing and exclusionary constructions of "us" and of "them." To illustrate this latter point, it is useful to recall that when homegrown terrorists Timothy McVeigh and Terry Nichols were arrested for the Oklahoma City bombing, people rushed to deny that they were really "one of us." The two men were cast as domestic aliens: "Interpretive strategies portrayed McVeigh and Nichols as 'in' but not 'of' America, peripheral beings who did not threaten convictions of [national] innocence. . . . Portraying both men as 'animals,' 'monsters,' 'drifters,' 'loners,' 'right-wingers,' 'robots,' 'mutated creatures,' served to separate them from 'real' Americans" (Linenthal 2001, 19). As Utah Senator Orrin Hatch opined, the perpetrators "are not Americans in my book. The true Americans are the men, women, and children who were killed. . . . Americans are the rescue workers. . . . Americans are all of us who share the same moral outrage" (1995, 2).

What bears emphasizing about the good guy/bad guy dichotomy is that positing an implacably evil perpetrator also encourages us to make unnuanced judgments and assumptions of total innocence. To be sure, there are plenty of instances—for example, rape—where the victims are true "innocents" and the "bad guys" bear sole responsibility for the harm-doing.[30] But there are also instances where acts of cruelty may be partially the product of injustices or conditions that implicate "the good guys." In the wake of the September 11 terrorist attacks, for example, Americans have rushed to embrace the consolation that the United States is an innocent, peace-loving, civilized nation in a largely wicked world. As is endemic to the good guy/bad guy dichotomy, in order to retain faith in ourselves as "the good guys," too few Americans have seriously questioned whether the United States, because of its myopic foreign policies and practices, must own any responsibility for causing the conditions that engendered the terrorism and that permitted an illegitimate regime to hijack Afghanistan and to deprive its citizens, especially women, of basic civil liberties and rights. Asked frequently, but usually posed rhetorically, the question, "Why do they hate us?" has been, for most Americans, just a smoke screen for self-righteousness and for continuing indifference and ignorance about the United States' policies and actions abroad. Not surprisingly, relatively few Americans have seriously bothered to question the legitimacy of the specific actions that our government is taking in our name against "the bad guys."

In addition to helping us evade unpleasant truths, the good guy/bad guy dichotomy allows us to frame conflict in terms of one-upmanship. Take, for example, post–September 11 bumper stickers such as "Up yours, bin Laden," "Piss on you, bin Laden," and "Yo Mama, Osama." These expressions clearly evoke male competitive identity issues, and while it is tempting to dismiss them as just slang, having little or no import, I believe they indicate that the good guy/bad guy dichotomy countenances highly charged, personalized, competitive, and often sexualized emotional responses to acts of cruelty. Idioms of redemption often employ good guy/bad guy dichotomies, it would seem, because the principal players really *are* guys. Even when the victims are women who should qualify as the "good guys," what is likely to occur is that they will find themselves being relegated to the role of bit players who provide the occasion for men—both the good ones who rush to avenge, protect, or rescue them, and the bad ones—to jockey for control and dominance over one another.

This brings us to another, closely related aspect of masculinized idioms of redemption in popular culture that is problematic: this discourse encourages third parties coping with cruelties suffered by others to indulge in what feels good or right to *them*. Of course, what feels good or right to bystanders may also feel good or right to the actual victims, and we will want to acknowledge that this kind of convergence does not, in and of itself, legitimize whatever concrete measures are in the making. Having said this, we should still recognize that when rape victims, for example, find themselves consumed with the emotional turmoil of others or with worries about what others may do in their name, the central moral importance of their suffering is being subverted.

This is a point that I will revisit shortly, but first I would like to return to a previously mentioned liability of masculinized expressions of the will to redemption: excessive vindictiveness and revenge-seeking. To make good on claims that suffering is a test of our "toughness," we are liable to think that we must give back as good as we got—and then some. What I would emphasize is that even if we countenance the possibility of justified revenge, we should question whether masculinized idioms of redemption in popular culture predispose us to become infected with the desire for excessive retribution. We might also wonder whether these idioms encourage us to show only as much restraint as is needed to convince others and ourselves that our acts have not sunk to the level of the perpetrators' acts and that we, therefore, have not now turned into the "bad guys." The "rub" is that quite a bit of revenge-seeking can take place before individuals or societies deem their responses excessive or illegitimate. And it is questionable whether we should aspire to show only as much restraint or concern for "the bad guys" as we think is necessary to preserve our presumed status as "the good guys."

Popular idioms of redemption in this country should warrant the attention of feminists because they authorize not only a masculinized approach to suffering but also a commercialized approach. For example, when public officials in Oklahoma talked about the "attractive, prosperous future" of their state and about "door-opening opportunities," "expanded horizons," and the "revitalization" of Oklahoma City, they seemed to be literally, and not just figuratively, searching for a "silver lining" in the clouds. Their comments should prompt us to wonder about the connections that can be drawn between the rhetoric of redemption and the ways in which longings for connectedness and community are exploited and rendered counterfeit in a capitalist society.

As social analysts have pointed out, the dominant philosophical and political discourses in the United States reflect and reinforce a perspective that Nancy Hartsock (1985, chap. 2) calls "the standpoint of exchange": these discourses constitute human beings as fundamentally separate, prudential, interest-driven monads who pursue their own self-chosen conception of the good life and who interact with one another only when there is a momentary convergence of interest. Because of the dominance of "the standpoint of exchange" in U.S. American culture, not surprisingly we are particularly susceptible to counterfeit claims of community. According to John Freie, "lacking genuine community, yet longing for the meaning and sense of connectedness that it creates—the feeling of community—people become vulnerable to even the merest suggestion of community" and to mistaking the *feeling* of connectedness or community for the genuine article (1998, 2). Although the feeling of connectedness is necessary to communal bonds and identity, this emotional dimension is not sufficient: community is "an interlocking pattern of just human relationships in which people have at least a minimal sense of consensus within a definable territory. People within a community actively participate and cooperate with others to create their own self-worth, a sense of caring about others, and a feeling for the spirit of connectedness" (Freie 1998, 23).

What bears emphasizing here is that active participation and genuine cooperation do not happen by verbal fiat; in order for social interactions to be substantively (and not merely abstractly) dialogical and democratic, the heterogeneity of human viewpoints, interests, and desires must be recognized—and this, in turn, requires allowing for the epistemic significance of social divisions. More specifically, it necessitates acknowledging, on the one hand, the inescapably limited, partial, and socially embedded perspectives of human deliberators and, on the other hand, the role that social, political, and economic power plays in the abilities of dominant social groups to create defining discourses and in the abilities of subordinated groups to resist the use of marginalizing or subjugating discourses and to create discourses that give voice to their experiences, interests, and needs in an authentic way. Unless the concrete social and institutional conditions and constraints that govern communicative interactions are themselves subject to ongoing thematization, critique, and change, and until, therefore, members of subordinated groups are able to represent their experiences, interests, and needs in a nondistorted, nonrepressed way (Arnault 1989), whatever feelings of cohesion, solidarity, and connectedness have been generated in any given situation will ultimately be counterfeit.

Certainly, the terrorist attacks in Oklahoma City engendered the *feeling* of connectedness—and on a wide scale: people in Oklahoma and across the nation imagined themselves as part of an "extended bereaved community" (Linenthal 2001). As one might expect when intense media coverage turns an event into a social spectacle of suffering, Americans not granted the cultural status of "victims," "survivors," or "rescuers" had an intense desire to touch—at least from a safe distance—the traumatic experiences of those immersed in the world of the destruction wrought by mass murder: "People followed the search for survivors, the grim recovery of bodies, the anguish of grieving family members, the public memorial ceremonies, and in some cases even the televised funerals of those killed. Intense and enduring media coverage made it possible for millions to imagine themselves part of a worldwide bereaved community, participating in the pathos of the event and connecting with families of those murdered through a variety of fund-raising efforts, tens of thousands of letters, early memorial suggestions, music, poems, memorial services, visual arts creations, and travel to the site" (Linenthal 2002, 3).

As Americans imagined themselves as members of a nationwide bereaved community, some even insinuated that the multiple ways in which Americans are divided—by race, ethnicity, class, gender, religion, ideology, and region, for example—had been transcended and that Americans had rediscovered community. As Linenthal reports, many people were saying that "all blood ran one color that day," and that "'there is only one color in Oklahoma City these days—the color of love' . . . It was as if Martin Luther King's 'beloved community' could arise from the response to mass murder" (2001, 112–13). In the words of President William Clinton, "We were *for a moment* once again family, outraged and heartbroken" (Linenthal 2001, 111; italics added).

The operative expression here is "for a moment." When the cord that holds together a community is "an act of will" (see Sennett 1970)—born of horror, shock, outrage, and candlelight vigils—and not the communal experience of people actually and continuously having to interact and understand each other as they really are, the result is counterfeit community. This was illustrated all too well by tensions that emerged in Oklahoma City in the aftermath of the bombing: "State senator Angela Monson, state representative Kevin Cox, and Oklahoma City councilwomen Willa Johnson spoke of subterranean resentment in the African American community about national news reports that portrayed the bombing as a 'majority hurt,' with little or no discussion about the impact on African Americans. Councilwoman Johnson also cast a skeptical eye on the comforting idea that the bombing had bridged the racial divide in Oklahoma City in any enduring manner. 'There was no sea change after the bombing,' she said. 'After the crisis, most people just "went home." Not all, but most'" (Linenthal 2001, 80).

Discourse about Americans and community was as prevalent after the September 11 terrorist attacks as after the Oklahoma City bombing, and it was surely revelatory: American officials exhorted people to show community spirit by "letting their lives return to normal"—a surefire way to perpetuate counterfeit community, since life as normal for most Americans just means going about their purely personal, self-interested business, especially the business of private consumption and consumerism. When the going gets rough, governmental officials were telling the citizenry, the tough go shopping.

For those Americans who long for genuine community, the emphasis on consumerism is surely misplaced, for "genuine community," as Freie suggests, "is not traditionally an economic concept. Although communities must maintain a certain level of economic viability, the functions of community have never been solely oriented toward encouraging consumerism" (1998, 8). The 1990s, with its conspicuous consumerism and massive concentration of wealth into the hands of the few, certainly bears witness to the fact that consumerism and the pursuit of economic wealth usually keep people divided, unconnected, and lacking a more collective, cohesive, interdependent, and cooperative model of social relations.

Acts of cruelty such as terrorist bombings can obviously produce disorder and damage in civic entities as well as in individuals. Without a doubt, civic revitalization and transformation would, in the context of an event such as the Oklahoma City bombing, be "a silver lining." Unfortunately, by talking about taking advantage of "door-opening opportunities" and "stepping into the first tier of states," public officials in Oklahoma conflated civic and economic revitalization. In a society where community "has become a product to be marketed and sold" and where consumerism has become the primary way of belonging (Freie 1998, 12), not surprisingly the will to redemption is often expressed in commercialized terms. But *this* is bound to produce, not a silver lining such as genuine community, but (at best) the veneer of recovery. One benefit of resisting popular idioms of redemption is that we become less susceptible, in contexts such as the terrorist attacks on Oklahoma City and on New York City, to the delusion that something greater or better, such as the formation of genuine community, comes simply with the activities of rescue and cleanup, restoring public order, replacing destroyed buildings, creating memorials—and attracting new businesses and places of commerce.

The Oklahoma City mayor's remark that the goodwill generated by the bombing incident had afforded his city an unprecedented "opportunity to expand its horizons" illustrates another pitfall of our discourse about redemptive suffering. "*Whose* suffering will be redeemed?" we want to ask the mayor. "*Who* has been blessed with a real opportunity?" Certainly the bombing did not expand the horizons of the dead victims, and at the time that he was uttering these words, it was too premature for the living victims and for the loved ones of victims to assess the ultimate toxicity of that act of cruelty on themselves and their lives. As mentioned above, one of the problems with redemptive explanations of suffering is that they can provide a rather frugal response to lives shattered by cruelty—so frugal that they "disappear" the victims. By placing suffering in the simple context of an agenda for improving the future, this discourse can blind us to the stark realities of other people's suffering and to the central moral importance of the victims' suffering. In addition to running the risk of letting victimizers "off the hook," the idiom of redemption countenances the possibility of letting bystanders think that what tragedies are really about are themselves, not the victims. Although third parties can certainly be profoundly affected by acts of cruelty, it is a bitter irony for victims—the ones who are truly reaping the harvest of sorrow—to witness bystanders becoming "the survivors"[31] while they, the victims, become displaced and further dispossessed, mere bit players whose experiences of cruelty are appropriated, defined, and often distorted by others. Effacing the suffering of victims in this way is surely a high form of moral indifference, if not moral and epistemological arrogance. Matters are made even worse if people also attempt to impose term limits on suffering by reproaching victims for failing to find a transcendent meaning for their suffering—a consoling purpose to help them "get on with their lives."

This kind of reprimand is highly revealing. It suggests that we do not necessarily respect the victim's standpoint and that we may not really want to know that cruelty can lack redemptive value. The possibility of unredeemable suffering brings us face to face with the yawning gap between our desire to be universal legislators and our limited ability to make the world conform to our will. The desire to insist on redemption is understandable, but one benefit of not committing ourselves to the prescription that the future will always redeem the past is that we are better prepared to resist impulses to minimize the harm that cruelty can cause others and to arrogate to ourselves the prerogative of defining the suffering of those who experience cruelty.

I would note, moreover, that another problem with the idiom of redemption is that only a small leap is required of us to go from seeing an act of cruelty as part of a "higher purpose" to regarding the higher purpose as something that rights or "unmakes" the wrong. Popularized concepts of redemptive suffering lend themselves to being used to normalize cruelty: by making the suffering caused by cruelty something that can be productive or good, we open ourselves up to viewing suffering as something that ought to be, if not exalted, then accepted or, at least, not resisted. This paves the way for yet further callousness and cruelty. How many "hard beds," for example, have battered women not only been (falsely) accused of making, but heartlessly encouraged to lie in—all in the name of some higher purpose such as "saving the family" or "preserving the sanctity of marriage?"

Situating the recent terrorist attacks on U.S. soil within a narrative of patriotic sacrifice is another example of how the preference for consolation that is provided by popular idioms of redemption dilutes the realities of cruelty and virtually counsels us to accept suffering that is caused by cruelty. In his account of public reactions to the Oklahoma City terrorist bombing, Linenthal provides a number of examples of how mass murder was transformed almost immediately into a story of patriotic sacrifice:

The lyrics in Red River's country and western music video, "You Can't Break America's Heart," declared "freedom has a price," and "sometimes people have to give their lives to make sure the spirit of America survives." . . . The *Christian Science Monitor* . . . informed its readers six days after the bombing that "all Americans have a responsibility to those killed and missing in Oklahoma to ensure their sacrifice was not in vain." . . . On the fifth anniversary of the bombing, April 19, 2000, Governor Keating told a crowd of approximately 25,000 that, like Gettysburg, the Oklahoma City memorial was "another American shrine, another patch of hallowed ground." Also speaking at the dedication was President Clinton, who said "there are places in our national landscape so scarred by freedom's sacrifice that they shape forever the soul of America—Valley Forge, Gettysburg, Selma. This place is such sacred ground." (2001, 234)

As with Linenthal, I take exception to equating the taking of human lives in an act of mass murder with lives given in acts of conscious sacrifice for one's nation. So too does Pam Whicher, the wife of a Secret Service agent murdered in the bombing. In an interview with Linenthal, she explained that what makes her angry at the suggestion that her husband "gave" his life for others is that her husband "was always prepared to defend the innocent, or put his life on the line to protect. [But] he was given the opportunity to do neither in this situation. . . . This was nothing more than *a damn waste of lives.* All the more worthy of our heartbreak, and the families, all the more worthy of our sympathy" (2001, 235; italics added).

Whicher's anger is well placed. Granted, the rhetoric of redemption that underlies all the references to patriotic sacrifice is an antidote to the horror that mass murder engenders, but this antidote is not necessarily a harmless one. Why did such "a damn waste of lives" occur? A narrative of patriotic sacrifice stops the questioning before it starts: we have our answer: "to protect freedom," "to make sure the spirit of America survives." Besides enabling us to avoid difficult, unwelcome questions about this country's values and culture of violence, taking refuge in the idea that mass murder can serve a higher purpose not only implicitly fosters callousness toward the loss and suffering of victims and their loved ones by exalting their suffering, but it also opens the door to rather econometric reasoning, in this case that the loss of 168 lives is a fair price to pay for something as important as making sure that freedom or the spirit of America survives.

This leads me to one final critical observation about the belief that some good purpose and final end to the suffering caused by cruelty must exist. As I have argued, popular discourses of redemption often dilute, if not preempt, the realities of cruelty and turn victims and their suffering into "object lessons." What bears emphasizing is the special perniciousness of this dynamic in a society such as ours where, because of oppressive social institutions and ideological mechanisms, some people are subjected to particular forms and degrees of suffering from which others, who occupy more privileged social strata, find themselves relatively or totally exempt. The focus on discerning the "higher purpose" of suffering—endemic to the idiom of redemption—not only implicitly calls on members of oppressed groups to accept a construction of reality that may effectively trivialize or marginalize the cruelty they are enduring, but it also entices them to take satisfaction from self-sacrifice, acquiescence, and quietism. Self-sacrifice, acquiescence, and quietism—these are feminized phenomena in American mainstream culture that place unfair burdens of suffering on all members of socially dominated (that is, "feminized") groups. *This* phenomenon—to hark back to the words of Francis Falls—is a sad story, often untold, that has gone on way too long and that needs urgent reframing.

Notes

I would like to thank the three anonymous reviewers for *Hypatia* for their constructive criticisms and valuable suggestions. I also want to express my appreciation for all the work that Robin May Schott had to undertake in order to assemble and edit this anthology and the special volume of *Hypatia* that preceded it.

1. Linenthal writes about Oklahoma City that the "community's response to the bombing, an outpouring of generosity by tens of thousands of people, was characterized as 'the Oklahoma Standard'" (2001, 48). He further notes that pride in "the Oklahoma Standard" sometimes turned into the rhetoric of economic boosterism: in the words of Robert DeRocker, a person who had just been contracted to provide public relations services for Oklahoma City, "I think someone in the media . . . banged out 'Terrorism in the Heartland' very early in the whole process, and suddenly it became institutionalized: Oklahoma is the heartland of America. And I have to tell you that's a beautiful image. . . . If you're trying to attract distribution facilities, who wouldn't want to be in the heartland? *So that's another gift to come out of this*" (Linenthal 2001, 49; italics added). I have not come across references to "the Oklahoma Standard" in reports about the response of New Yorkers to the events of September 11. However, given the frequency with which the media reported on the generosity displayed by New Yorkers, I suspect that citizens of "the Big Apple" were being partly measured by standards presumed to exist in a mythic heartland. The notion of New Yorkers discovering their better selves as a result of the attacks on the World Trade Center is an excellent example of redemptive logic, but it is interesting that pride on this point has not seemed to turn into the rhetoric of economic revitalization, as it did so quickly in Oklahoma City.

2. Much of the melancholy enveloping the twins cannot be attributed to cruelty, because the greatest source of their sadness is that one of them is dying. However, we do see the twins being treated with cruelty by some of the characters in the movie, most especially by their mother, who has always rejected them because of their biological condition.

3. I have found that a significant number of my students express the sentiment that *Schindler's List* is the only Holocaust movie they have liked because it made them feel hopeful and good about people. I would note, moreover, that when I have presented this paper to audiences, my comments about *Schindler's List* have generated the most controversy and commentary. Typically, my rather compressed reading of *Schindler's List* is challenged, my attempt to attach any significant meaning to a Hollywood movie is questioned, and the relevance of fiction about the Holocaust to an essay on popular American discourses of redemption is interrogated. My response to these complaints is—quite briefly—as follows: (1) Lawrence Langer's work definitively establishes that a great deal of artistic and nonfiction work about the Holocaust—created by non-Americans as well as Americans, by Jews as well as non-Jews, by Holocaust survivors as well as those less immediately connected

with the Holocaust experience—is shaped by the will to redemption. Whatever the merits of my particular interpretation of the movie, I am not reluctant to admit that texts bear multiple readings. If *Schindler's List* does not seem to be a good example of the American will to redemption, people can easily find other American works about the Holocaust that illustrate the phenomenon I am discussing. (2) Although they are clearly driven by the profit motive, "blockbuster" Hollywood movies often tap into revealing cultural anxieties and tensions. What makes these movies "work" in the sense of attracting profit-generating audiences is that they ameliorate and pacify potential unpleasantness through the incorporation of familiar codes and conventions of cinematic storytelling, including redemption motifs. This dynamic seems significant to me. (3) Though the Holocaust did not take place on American soil, it is very telling, I think, that an American-made movie about the Holocaust, intended to be a "blockbuster" film, caters to the American propensity for transcendent meanings and "happy endings." To paraphrase John Bowler's words very loosely, what an American work of art has to say about the Holocaust reveals, in many ways more than anything else, what Americans typically believe the nature and purpose of suffering to be (Bowler 1970, 2; Bowler's words are an indirect quote from Langer 1996, 46).

4. Horror is often, but not always, generated by cruelty. In my unpublished paper, "Cruelty: More or Less than Torture," I argue that because of the centrality of horror in popular constructions of cruelty, we tend to overlook or misunderstand important manifestations of cruelty.

5. Thus, we should recognize the heterogeneity of redemptive explanations of suffering in American mainstream popular culture. The will to find something redemptive in suffering assumes many meanings, including such formulae as the following: something good always emerges from the ordeal of suffering; the good that arises from suffering makes things better than before; good always wins out in the end, providing a happy ending to people's suffering; the emergence of good requires suffering; suffering helps to restore good; the ordeal of suffering is never meaningless; through suffering, victory over evil is assured; those who cause suffering will get their just deserts; good reconciles past suffering and integrates the past with the present and the future. These are obviously not equivalent claims, but what they have in common is that they all "steer us into friendly harbors" by providing consolation for suffering (Langer 1996) and assurances that our prior moral values, ideals, and concepts remain essentially intact and viable.

6. Inasmuch as I argue that popular redemptive logic can be morally problematic, the thesis of my essay may conflict irreconcilably with the views of some Christians and other faith believers, depending on the specifics of their understanding of divine providence and redemption. It should not be assumed, on the other hand, that popular expressions of redemption are universally endorsed by theologians, religious thinkers, or other ecclesiastical authorities.

7. Dispossession, it seems to me, does not require the existence of a self that is fixed, unified, coherent, and/or completely self-transparent. Furthermore, we should not mistake the concept of dispossession for the notion of socially fragmented subjectivities. Still, the important question of the nature of the self that experiences annihilation or near annihilation has been left open. See Brison 1997 and Lugones 2003.

8. The intentional infliction of intense bodily pain—whether the agent takes pleasure in the other's pain or is indifferent to it—is not the only mechanism for "unmaking" or nearly "unmaking" a person's sense of self and world. Psychological abuse and serious illnesses can produce the same sort of damage, as can natural disasters such as earthquakes and tornadoes.

9. It should be noted that while the phenomenology of battering that I provide is characteristic of some cultures, including mainstream U.S. American culture, it is not applicable to all cultures or to all individuals within a culture.

10. While these statements may seem, and may be meant by the women who make them, to imply the existence of an underlying, fixed, coherent, and unified "I" that is the "true" self, the phenomenological account I am giving is compatible with the view that the self and its world are many and that personal transformation can arise through the interactions of a person's multiple selves as she navigates multiple worlds. We should not regard liberatory personal transformation as necessarily requiring a profound change from an inadequate sense of self or an old unified self to an adequate sense of self or a new unified self.

11. It is telling that in order to establish the cruelty and seriousness of male violence against women as women, feminists must demonstrate that the experiences of victims of incest, rape, and battering are comparable to those of war veterans, prisoners of war, political prisoners, and concentration camp inmates. Although not without its problems, Herman's book is noteworthy for its attempt to establish some of the relevant parallels. See also MacKinnon 2002. The idea that extreme trauma produces people who must live with the knowledge of the capacity for evil within themselves as well as within others is particularly provocative, especially given the predicaments faced by those who inhabit what Primo Levi (1989) calls "the gray zone." See also Card 1999 and Andrea Dworkin, who makes the rather poignant observation that "battery is a forced descent into hell and you don't get by in hell by moral goodness" (1997, 52).

12. Of course, for most of the much less privileged and secure world, the world did not change on September 11, 2001, and thus great reversals of expectations did not occur. In fact, one does not need to look beyond the borders of the United States for this reality check. From the perspectives of many poor people, battered women, and gay men in this country, for example, fear and violence are a routine part of their everyday lives.

13. Given the existence of enmeshed oppressions, I think Morgan is guilty of overgeneralizing. For example, most gay men in this country do not need terrorism to democratize violence for them and to bring them to experience the world in relation to other men as women experience the world in relation to men. The same point could be made about African American men during the Jim Crow era or in present-day encounters with the police.

14. Catharine MacKinnon points out that the "number of women who die at the hands of men every year in the United States alone is almost the same as the number of people who died on September 11. . . . FBI Uniform Crime Reports for the United States report 3,076 female victims of homicide in 2000" (2002, 7–8). MacKinnon goes on to note that given these statistics and the absence of a settled definition of "war" in international law, one would think that calling male violence against women "a war on women" would be

regarded as no less metaphorical than calling the events of September 11 an act of war (2002, 7–8).

15.   Undoubtedly, the magnitude of a single act of terrorism is a significant variable.

16.   I find it interesting that in the months immediately following September 11, on my side of town it was in working-class and middle-class neighborhoods, not in poor communities, that American flags, including the Revolutionary-era flag "Don't tread on me," were on ubiquitous display. A friend who is a social worker in an elementary school located in a very poor neighborhood in a city in central New York reported to me that while pupils were aware of the terrorist attacks, their concern was relatively minimal and short-lived—something I would attribute not only to their age but also to the attitudes of the adults in their homes and to the "inoculation" against reversals of expectations that everyday reality provides when fear and violence are a normal occurrence. If one lives in a neighborhood where gunfire is routine, where children "live with the thought of being shot while playing" (Nolan 2002), and where many people have at least one relative who has suffered a premature, violent death, a terrorist attack may not have the same capacity to terrorize as it does in more affluent, secure neighborhoods. According to Katie Davis (2001), because " 'normal' is often a numbing and fearful place to be," poor Americans were not as traumatized after September 11 as more privileged Americans.

17.   Although I believe that we are speaking metaphorically if we talk about a medical condition or a force of nature violating a person's sense of self and world, I also recognize that people's responses (or failures to respond) to the suffering of victims of natural harms can rise to the level of cruelty. When cruelty occurs in this fashion, many people begin to interrogate the notion of "natural harms."

18.   Langer speaks of "preempting the Holocaust" to refer to attempts to use—and perhaps abuse—"its grim details to fortify a prior commitment to an ideal of moral reality, community responsibility, or religious belief that leaves us with space to retain faith in their pristine value in a post-Holocaust world" (1998, 1). In speaking of "preempting cruelty," I am referring, somewhat analogously, to idioms or ways of talking about cruelty that many of us use in order to evade the unpleasant truth that cruelty, especially in its extreme forms, can take victims and viewers alike into "dark caverns with no exits" (Schulweis 1994, 157, quoted in Rosenfeld 1997, 146).

19.   Langer introduces the concept of "durational time" (e.g., see 1995a and 1996) to explain how the past for survivors of atrocities can colonize what we normally call "the stream of life." According to Langer, Holocaust testimonies reveal "hundreds of instances of unredeemed and unredeemable loss" (1996, 53–54). Edward Linenthal reports that while many family members of victims of the Oklahoma City bombing regard their suffering as having redemptive value, others see their experiences as a sheer, senseless happening that cannot be integrated with the present or the future (2001, 70–80).

20.   I am not claiming that horror is either a necessary or a sufficient condition of cruelty.

21.   The development of the view that the knower must be purified of all subjec-

tive "distortions," including emotional attachments, has been characterized and insightfully analyzed by Susan Bordo (1987) as a historical "flight from the feminine."

22. It is not necessary for my purposes here that I specify the precise relation between emotion and belief. For a discussion of this issue, see Nussbaum (1995, chap. 3; 1994, chap. 10; and 2001, chap. 1).

23. To varying degrees, most Americans tend to believe that the world is ordered to their good and their happiness. However, as I am defining the expression here, "having trust in the world" should not be confused with the Enlightenment-inspired belief that the world is centered on human happiness and justice.

24. As I write this chapter, inserting the qualification "in many Americans" seems to be particularly important, given the aftermath of the events of September 11, which has seen the unbridled abuse and torture of detainees in Afghanistan and at Guantánamo Bay as well as the "rendition" of prisoners to countries where it is known that they will be tortured by interrogators. The American public's willed ignorance and relative complacency about the acts of torture being committed in their name suggests that torture (at least from a safe distance) has currency in the United States. Nonetheless, this fact does not undermine my analysis of horror. It only underscores the importance of recognizing that horror is socially, culturally, and historically variable. It also raises the issue of horror's epistemological weaknesses and liabilities—a topic that space does not permit me to address here.

25. Depending upon one's views on the relation between emotion and belief, one may also want to recognize that the variability of emotionality is due to the fact that the physical sensations that accompany the beliefs that make up any given emotion differ from person to person.

26. Virtually everyone in this country who believes that the police must respect the bodily integrity of suspects was horrified by the treatment that Abner Louima received at the hands of the New York police department. (In August 1997, Abner Louima was taken into custody by the police in Brooklyn and, in a police station bathroom, was so brutally beaten and sodomized with a broken broomstick that his sigmoid colon and bladder were perforated.) Given the prevalence of racism, horror would probably not have been a virtually universal reaction from the American public had there not been overwhelming agreement that shoving a broken broomstick up a person's rectum, even a dark-skinned Haitian immigrant's rectum, constitutes police brutality. It is likely that disgust-generated homophobia was also responsible for generating many people's horror.

27. I would argue that, pace Miller (1997, 26), horror does not necessarily entail revulsion or disgust. Consider, for example, the Columbine school shootings. Since disgust tends to do its moral work on issues that involve the body, most Americans were horrified, I suspect, but not also disgusted (except metaphorically), by the images being broadcast on television on the day of the shooting massacre at Columbine High School. Until it lost its "freshness," to borrow a term from Nussbaum (2001, 79–85), through sheer repetition, one particularly horrifying sight was that of heavily armed police escorts flanking students as they ran from the building with their arms up in the air to show that

they were not carrying any weapons. The question that seemed to hang in the air, "What is the world coming to?" is just what one would expect when people experience horror.

28. I say "most classes of men" because gender, race/ethnicity, class, culture, and other differences are "enmeshed" (Lugones 2003, chap. 6). For example, imagine a black man in the Jim Crow South expressing anger at a white man. For an excellent discussion of the relationship between anger and subordination, see Spelman 1989.

29. Taken at face value, the common saying, "Life doesn't hand us more suffering than we can bear" reads an awful lot like "Don't be a wimp."

30. We should note that "innocence" is not an innocent—that is, apolitical—concept. For example, because of the interplay of gender ideologies and social politics, adult female victims of male rape in this country, as in many others, will often find ascriptions of innocence very hard to come by.

31. As an example of this phenomenon, it is interesting to note that among some mental health professionals in Oklahoma City there was "a growing sense of unease about the way in which the language of 'trauma' and 'PTSD' [Post-Traumatic Stress Disorder] was increasingly used to describe the emotions and reactions of people who had no personal ties with the actual victims of the bombing" (Linenthal 2001, 91).

References

Alter, Jonathan. 2001. Time to think about torture. *Newsweek,* 5 November, 45.

Améry, Jean. 1995. Torture. In *Art from the Ashes: A Holocaust Anthology,* ed. Lawrence L. Langer. New York: Oxford University Press.

Arnault, Lynne S. 1989. Talking 'bout a revolution: Feminism, historicism, and liberal moral theory. In *Logos* X (Special Issue on Reason and Moral Judgment): 39–55.

Bar On, Bat-Ami. 1991. Why terrorism is morally problematic. In *Feminist Ethics,* ed. Claudia Card. Lawrence: University of Kansas Press.

Bordo, Susan. 1987. *The Flight to Objectivity: Essays on Cartesianism and Culture.* Albany: State University of New York Press.

Bowler, John. 1970. *Problems of Suffering in Religions of the World.* Cambridge: Cambridge University Press.

Brison, Susan J. 1997. Outliving oneself: Trauma, memory, and personal identity. In *Feminists Rethink the Self,* ed. Diana Tietjens Meyers. Boulder, Colo.: Westview Press.

———. 1999. The uses of narrative in the aftermath of violence. In *On Feminist Ethics and Politics,* ed. Claudia Card. Lawrence: University of Kansas Press.

Card, Claudia. 1999. Groping through gray zones. In *On Feminist Ethics and Politics,* ed. Claudia Card. Lawrence: University of Kansas Press.

Cook, John, ed. 1993. *The Book of Positive Quotations.* Minneapolis, Minn.: Fairview Press.

Davis, Katie. 2001. An inner city reality check. National Public Radio. Retrieved 25 October from www.npr.org/news/specials/response/essays/ 011025. daviscommentary.html.

Delbo, Charlotte. 1985. *La mémoire et les jours*. Paris: Berg International.

Dworkin, Andrea. 1997. *Life and Death*. New York: Free Press.

Freie, John F. 1998. *Counterfeit Community: The Exploitation of Our Longings for Connectedness*. Lanham, Md.: Rowman and Littlefield.

Greenspan, Henry. 1992. Lives as texts: Symptoms as modes of recounting in the life histories of Holocaust survivors. In *Storied Lives: The Cultural Politics of Self-understanding*, ed. George C. Rosenwald and Richard L. Ochberg. New Haven, Conn.: Yale University Press.

Hartsock, Nancy. 1985. *Money, Sex and Power: Toward a Feminist Historical Materialism*. Boston: Northeastern University Press.

Hatch, Orrin. 1995. Terrorism in the United States; the nature and extent of the threat and possible legislative responses. Committee on the Judiciary Hearings, United States Senate, 104th Congress, 1st session (April 27): 2.

Herman, Judith Lewis. 1992. *Trauma and Recovery*. New York: Basic Books.

Langer, Lawrence L. 1991. *Holocaust Testimonies: The Ruins of Memory*. New Haven, Conn.: Yale University Press.

———. 1995a. *Admitting the Holocaust: Collected Essays*. Oxford: Oxford University Press.

———, ed. 1995b. *Art from the Ashes: A Holocaust Anthology*. New York: Oxford University Press.

———. 1996. The alarmed vision: Social suffering and Holocaust atrocity. *Daedalus* (Winter): 46–65.

———. 1998. *Preempting the Holocaust*. New Haven, Conn.: Yale University Press.

Levi, Primo. 1989. *The Drowned and the Saved*. Trans. Raymond Rosenthal. New York: Vintage.

Linenthal, Edward T. 2001. *The Unfinished Bombing: Oklahoma City in American History*. Oxford: Oxford University Press.

Lugones, María. 2003. *Pilgrimages/Peregrinajes: Theorizing Coalition against Multiple Oppressions*. Lanham, Md.: Rowman and Littlefield.

MacKinnon, Catharine A. 2002. State of emergency: Who will declare war on terrorism against women? *Women's Review of Books* 19 (6): 7–8.

Miller, William Ian. 1997. *The Anatomy of Disgust*. Cambridge, Mass.: Harvard University Press.

Morgan, Robin. 1989. *The Demon Lover: On the Sexuality of Terrorism*. New York: W. W. Norton.

Nolan, Maureen. 2002. Fear walks with them to school. *The Post-Standard*, 23 June.

Nussbaum, Martha C. 1994. *The Therapy of Desire: Theory and Practice in Hellenistic Ethics*. Princeton, N.J.: Princeton University Press.

———. 1995. *Poetic Justice: The Literary Imagination and Public Life*. Boston: Beacon Press.

———. 2001. *Upheavals of Thought: The Intelligence of Emotions*. Cambridge: Cambridge University Press.

Rosenbaum, Ron. 1995. Staring into the heart of the heart of darkness. *New York Times Magazine*, 4 June, 36–44, 50, 58, 61, 72.

Rosenfeld, Alvin H. 1997. The Americanization of the Holocaust. In *Thinking about the Holocaust: After Half a Century*, ed. Alvin H. Rosenfeld. Bloomington: Indiana University Press.

Scarry, Elaine. 1985. *The Body in Pain: The Making and Unmaking of the World*. Oxford: Oxford University Press.

Scheper-Hughes, Nancy. 1992. *Death without Weeping: The Violence of Everyday Life in Brazil.* Berkeley: University of California Press.

Schulweis, Harold M. 1994. *For Those Who Can't Believe.* New York: HarperCollins.

Sennett, Richard. 1970. *The Uses of Disorder: Personal Identity and City Life.* New York: Vintage Books.

Spelman, Elizabeth V. 1989. Anger and insubordination. In *Women, Knowledge, and Reality,* ed. Ann Garry and Marilyn Pearsall. Winchester, Mass.: Unwin Hyman.

Taylor, Charles. 1989. *Sources of the Self: The Making of the Modern Identity.* Cambridge, Mass.: Harvard University Press.

Part Two   *Forum on September 11,
2001: Feminist Perspectives
on Terrorism*

10 Terrorism, Evil,
and Everyday Depravity

Bat-Ami Bar On

The appropriation of the term "evil" by President George W. Bush's administration has caused me to hesitate in thinking about terrorism as "evil." Quite quickly after the Al Qaeda attacks of September 11, 2001, the Bush administration began to deploy the term "evil" in conjunction with the term "axis" and referred, with the phrase "an axis of evil," to the Al Qaeda network and the weave of individuals, organizations, and especially states that support it (Bush 2002). The connection of "evil" with "axis" in this context is probably intended to evoke memories of World War II and use them to create a parallel that equates the Bush administration's "war on terrorism" with the United States' war against the Axis forces; hence, against Nazi Germany and its retinue of associates and followers, including, perhaps in particular, Imperial Japan, a point reinforced just after the attacks of September 11, 2001, by comparisons of these attacks and the Japanese attack on Pearl Harbor.

By equating its "war on terrorism" with the United States' war against the Axis forces during World War II, the Bush administration has obviously been trying to secure for itself—and for a while was domestically relatively successful (though the actual rate of this success has been declining due to the Iraq quagmire)—an image of world leadership in what it portrays by implication as a "just" and even "good" war.[1] This leadership is not merely military. The United States has by far the world's strongest military, and its defense expenditures are designed to keep it so (see Anderson 2005). Furthermore, it projects its military capabilities and will across the world. But because it is a democracy, what the United States needs in a globalizing world in order to act, and not be just presumed to do so for selfish reasons, is ethico-political leadership. The success of the Bush administration's domestic appearance as providing the world with an ethico-political leadership (despite overwhelming evidence to the contrary insofar as worldwide popular acceptance of U.S. leadership is concerned) has to be attributed at least in part to its reliance on the idea of "evil."[2] Popularly, "evil" is an idea with religious, and in the United States, quite Christian, undertones. As such, it justifies a relentless and prolonged struggle that must be engaged not only because "evil" ought to be fought but also because it is by persevering in the struggle against "evil" that one proves one's moral mettle and worth (see Ricour 1967).

This is all quite righteous and seems awfully masculinist, requiring one to keep firm as one forges on (see Bennett 2002; Bar On 2003), which leaves me concerned about contributing to the cloak of noble rectitude being constructed by the Bush administration. If I am to discuss terrorism as "evil," especially in an analysis of it that responds to the attacks of September 11, I think that I might necessarily become complicit in a discourse that I do not condone. And yet, why should I let the Bush administration seize and control an extremely powerful ethical term, especially since it is becoming very clear that the notion of "evil" is in need of a post-Nietzschean restoration simply because of the enormous weight of human inhumanity (see, e.g., Baudrillard 1993 and Lara 2001). We are surrounded by atrocities, both old and new, and could make use of robust and potent ethical concepts to think about them. "Evil" seems to at least some to be uniquely promising in this respect.[3]

However, upon examination, the concept of "evil," secularized, might not be too promising. As "evil" sheds the mythical representations that permit its construction in "pure" terms, therefore making sense of it only in contrast to "pure goodness," it becomes less clear what might qualify as "evil" (see Baumeister 1997). In a world of complex and growing interdependencies, it is hard for evil to be as "pure" as it seems to be in a Manichean world. The debates on the Left following the attacks of September 11 about the United States' arrogance— let alone its actual role in the wretchedness of so many worldwide—and how this contributes to the background conditions behind the attacks, illustrate some of the confusions that accompany the secularization of "evil." In so intricately multifaceted a situation, the loss of the binary opposition of "pure goodness" versus "pure evil" seems to necessarily yield convoluted judgments (see Hitchens 2001).

In addition, "evil" secularized might be just a bit too abstract an idea for speaking about the specific modalities that human inhumanity takes, including terrorism, particularly of the September 11 kind, which is indiscriminate and disregards one of the most important constraints on the violence of war—the distinction between "civilians" and "combatants."[4] The abstractness of secularized "evil" is attested to, for example, in the work of Adi Ophir, who, in an attempt to think of "evil" ontologically, exactly in order to be able to comment in a secular way on outrageous brutalities, insists that "evil" is a noun rather than an adjective and declares that "evil" is part of what is, and that it "is the set of vicious wrongs and their order" (2001, 11).

Abstractness such as Ophir's removes one from the actual horrors of concrete "evil." One stops witnessing when one abstracts so much and gets away from the phenomenological experience of the suffering of real people. Abstractness, in other words, undermines the work of the imagination on which a "spectator,"[5] who is on the outside of some immediate horrendous event, depends in order to connect to embodied people in pain—as a case in point, on the morning of September 11, 2001, to the embodied people in the World Trade Center, dying instantaneously just as they register shock, or dying more slowly as they try to escape, or as they fall out of melted and broken windows.

And yet, there is something about which Ophir, despite the abstractness of his own claims, is right: "evil" is ontological and thus part of what is; or as he seems to suggest, it is actually "evils" in the plural that should be conceived ontologically. Terrorism, I think, if one wants to use this kind of moral language when thinking about it, can be counted among the many "evils" that are part of what is, not necessarily a better or worse evil than many others, even if more dramatic than some, often staged less as a military operation and more for the effects of its depiction in the media and especially its telecasted reproductions.[6]

It is important to emphasize the extent to which the "evil" of terrorism is, most of the time, quite ordinary when compared with many other "evils." There are monstrous "evils," such as genocide or the kind of wholesale chattel slavery practiced in the United States prior to the Civil War (see Thomas 1993). The still (as I write) ongoing genocide in Darfur is a reminder that the twenty-first century may have its own share of genocides and thus of monstrous evils. There are also ignoble yet petty "evils," such as social discrimination—an evil that is psychically wounding but does not necessarily have undermining effects on one's material well-being, on, for instance, one's schooling, employment, housing, or judicial treatment.[7] Ignoble "petty" evils are, I tend to believe with Freud (1930), who was profoundly aware of the sources of human aggression and the limits on the ability to affect them, an inescapable social phenomenon. Terrorism cannot be likened to either of these in any way that illuminates the kind of "evil" it is. Corresponding or analogous "evils" to terrorism might be certain war crimes (see Gutman and Reiff 1999), perhaps paradigmatically rape in war, or rape more generally considered (see, e.g., Bar On 1991, 107–25; Card 1996a, 5–18; and Card 1996b, 97–117).

The analogy between terrorism and rape can be developed in a variety of ways. Here I want to call attention only to a victimization usually suffered as a function of a group membership, and in general a basically involuntary group membership. Women, the primary victims of rape, are raped because they are women, not biologically but socially. Similarly, many terrorist attacks, though appearing random, target people because the people in question can be assigned a group identity.

The analogy that can be drawn between terrorism and rape does not, I think, testify to something essentially manly about terrorism. Violence in general has been and still is a "male" prerogative. At the same time, this is a contingent and changing fact. There have been in the past, and there currently are, women terrorists. But due to the habituated association of violence and "maleness" and the hegemony men have over the means of violence, women's participation in terrorism has not been focused on, and women continue to be suspected of terrorism less than men (see McDonald 1991; Victor 2003).

War crimes and rape are not the only "evils" that are like terrorism. There are other more prosaic "evils" that are also similar to terrorism. Israeli-Palestinian forms of violence against each other provide good examples of equivalent enough "evils" that are neither monstrous nor ignobly petty. As part of the Al Aqsa Intifada that began in September 2000 and that for some Palestinian groups, such as the Islamic Jihad, is still ongoing but that for others, such as Fattah,[8] is at least dormant, if not over, Palestinians often have engaged in suicide bombings throughout Israel. The Israeli military, which was pulled out of the Palestinian territories as part of the Oslo peace process, reentered them in April 2002. The declared aim of the massive Israeli military incursion was the curtailing of Palestinian terrorist attacks on Israeli citizens. These attacks have made life in Israel utterly miserable due to the actual suffering of people killed and wounded; the suffering of their families and friends; the fears that prevented people from conducting even the business of everyday life; and because terrorist attacks have contributed to a deep economic crisis, literally impoverishing a great number of Israelis, both Jewish and Palestinian.

I believe, however, that Israel's military response to Palestinian terrorism demonstrates how incapable Israel is, most of the time, of giving up its repression of the Palestinians and participating in an honest political dialogue whose terms it does not dictate in advance. The "evil" of Israel's repression of the Palestinians—usually not so obvious as it is in times of acute crisis, and for the past thirty-eight years appearing in many ways administratively mundane—while not deemed as such by many Jewish Israelis and not considered at all by many outside of Israel and Palestine, is not too different from the "evil" of Palestinian terrorism. It, too, creates an enormous level of suffering via death and lesser physical harm, material deprivations, and humiliation.[9]

By saying that Israel's prolonged repression of the Palestinians and Palestinian terrorism are similar kinds of "evil," I do not mean to imply that since 1967 Israel has been involved in state terror toward the Palestinians (as is claimed, for example, by Chomsky 1986), a terror, perhaps, such as that practiced by the Argentinean and Chilean juntas. While repression depends on violence, and violence can cause feelings of terror, the violence behind repression is not always of the terrorizing version; that is, a violence that targets people along an assigned identity and due to membership in some identity group, and for which in its current version, no other distinctions matter, and thus, in front of which no innocence is possible. Israeli repression has been, on the whole, sophisticated, even when Israel has unleashed its military. There are always rules of engagement that, though not necessarily and lately not even frequently complied with,[10] do restrict Israeli military personnel from terrorizing one and all Palestinians. The existence of rules of engagement, probably admixed with self-interested or indifferent bad faith, prevents Jewish Israelis and others from appreciating the parity between the "evil" of Israeli repression of the Palestinians and the "evil" of Palestinian terrorism.

The importance of noticing that moral parity, or moral equivalence, exists between the "evil" of terrorism and the "evil" of repression, and one of the reasons for a careful differentiation between kinds of violence that permits non-terrorizing and terrorizing varieties, is that this lets the term "evil" range over a diverse domain. Without the intricacy and richness arising out of the variance in the domain to which the term "evil" is applied, all "evils" become one, measured against an identical standard resulting, among other things, in absurd disavowals and repudiations as well as disturbing competitions for recognition of "evils" suffered.

Jewish Israelis and Palestinians vie with each other for such recognition and pursue their rivalry as a public relations campaign, thereby reifying the "evils" of terrorism and repression, a process that makes it so much harder to not use a single emblematic yardstick for "evil." Yet there are many "evils," and with the renunciation of the religious connotations with which the idea of "evil" is associated, it is urgent to think of "evils" as having no essence and as related to each other only by something like a Wittgensteinian "family resemblance" (1968, 32), making some comparisons possible, but no more than that. Anything else has, right now, both improper ethical ramifications and dangerous political consequences.

I did not mean to come full circle to my initial concern about complicity in an official discourse of "evil" that I believe is deployed manipulatively in order to mobilize support and silence opposition. Yet I seem to have remained ambivalent. Though I have fewer doubts than before that one could think in ethically productive ways about terrorism as "evil," I feel even more cautious than before about engaging in this kind of thinking. I am motivated by two major concerns in addition to my anxiety about discursive complicity (which may even shed a certain light on this anxiety).

First, ever since the attacks of September 11, 2001, at least in the United States, the images of terrorism, repeated so many times, have begun to stand in for "evil," therefore detracting from other "evils," big and small, and even obscuring them. I am apprehensive about this turn. I have been thinking about violence for a long time, and I have noticed a growing tendency to equate many wrongs with violence (now with terrorism as a specific kind of violence). I am afraid that the move indicates a certain mistrust of the moral sensibilities of others who are the intended audiences of the speech acts in question. It is as if the speakers are quite convinced that a different kind of linguistic performance will just not be similarly effective as one that calls attention to some moral wrong via its association with violence (or terrorism). I think that what is amiss with this is not only the assumption of moral superiority by the speakers (disturbing in itself because so undemocratic) but also the failure to appreciate the need for a nuanced ethical vocabulary (so that even if one assumes a superior moral standing as the speaker, one still educates differently). I want to emphasize this latter point by calling attention to the lack of clear-cut moral intuitions about violence (and terrorism), let alone the lack of clear-cut intuitions about what violence (or terrorism) is.[11] Both of these are necessarily elided by any attempt to assert the wrongness of something by making it be like violence (and now terrorism) since it stands for evil.

Does it make sense to talk about violence (or terrorism) as a noun? What makes sense of talking about a violent (terrorizing?) storm and a non-stormy killing as violent (or as an act of terror)? If the common element of all violence is destruction, is the process of decay violent? Is all violence like murder? Is terrorism like murder? If not all violence is like murder, then is violence morally neutral, and some performances of it morally justified while others are not? Could there be a morally neutral sense of terrorism? These and similar questions, and many questions they lead to, are reasonable questions. They have diverse answers that when looked at together begin to give one an idea of the confusions and contestations that exist about violence (and terrorism) and the morality of violence (and terrorism). When wrongness is assimilated to violence (or terrorism), it is as if there is only one correct conception of violence (or terrorism), and it is necessarily normatively negatively loaded.

Second, I have also been thinking about the relationship between ethics and politics for quite a while as a result of some of my more recent thinking about violence and terrorism as well as extensive studies of the work of Hannah Arendt. Thus far, I have been developing this chapter as if ethics and politics flow into each other effortlessly, or perhaps even more so, as if ethics flows (or should flow) into politics effortlessly. If they do (or ought to), then it makes sense to speak of "evil" in politics, or put a bit differently and more generally, it makes sense to use moral language persuasively (be the attempt at persuasion argumentative, performative, or both) in the political sphere. But ethics and politics, I have come to believe, should not be taken as seamlessly connected with each other, nor should a seamless connection between ethics and politics be assumed at the outset as desirable in all cases, at least not for liberal democracies (see Bar On 2004). I suggested above that the wrongness of violence (and terrorism) is not intuitively obvious. Let me suggest now that among the possible criteria for judging the wrongness of terrorism (though not necessarily all types of violence) there are specifically political criteria that are motivated by, for example, an uneasiness with political coercion, namely, the coercion of individuals qua citizens and their governments.

If the political sphere is seen as all-encompassing so that it has no outside, or if it is understood as a sphere of force and domination and therefore one in which coercion is the rule, then trepidations about a distinctively political kind of coercion do not make sense. However, if the political sphere is understood as one among other spheres of a complex human life and in strong liberal-democratic terms, then one can think about the coercion of individuals via violence and terror in nonpolitical yet moral terms as well as in political yet not moral terms. What follows from this for me is that it is the uniquely political wrongs (like political coercion) and the uniquely political rights (like political equality), rather than moral rights and wrongs that should be given center stage in the political sphere and by implication in political judgment and political dialogue (or what should really be a multilogue).

I think that there is a general awareness that modern (and postmodern) terrorists, insofar as they have a political agenda, engage in political coercion. At the same time, the discussion of the wrongness of terrorism has in general re-mained fixed on the acts of terrorism and their morality. What is wrong with terrorism, most people seem to agree, is its indiscriminate violence, and to the extent that its violence is not indiscriminate, some argue, it can even be morally justified (Coady 2001; Primoratz 2004; Young 2004). This is not just a moral condemnation of means rather than ends. Political coercion is also a means and not an end.

I am not sure how to account for the focus on acts of terrorism and their morality. However, I suspect that in part this focus can be explained by the hor-ror caused by common terrorist means of coercion. Just the other day, and even though I am trying to shift my own ways of thinking about and judging terror-ism from the moral to the political, I found myself stunned and dismayed by a report about a twenty-one-year-old Palestinian woman, Wafa Samir Ibrahim, who was apprehended before she had the chance to become a suicide bomber. Her intended target was a hospital, probably the Soroka hospital in Be'er Sheva (Reguler 2005). It was the targeting choice that I responded to so strongly, and it took me awhile to re-center and concentrate my attention on the targeting as part of a coercive political strategy and become dismayed by the political coer-cion itself.

Another possible element of the account might be the common conception of the relationship of individuals and the modern state. Among the important roles of the modern state—indeed, so important that it is at the center of even the "minimal state" (Nozick 1974)—is the provision of protection against vio-lence. Every terrorist strike, whatever its level of carnage and destruction, ex-poses the vulnerability of individuals as embodied beings and simultaneously the weakness of the state, since it seems to be failing to deliver its part of the Hobbesian contract in which security is the main good that the state has to give individuals in exchange for their pacification. In this context, horror increases due to magnified fears arising out of the realization of one's concrete existential condition.

Political elites have tended to capitalize on the horror, fears, and the felt need for a working security contract; and this too contributes to the focus on acts of terrorism and their morality. Political elites promise better and more protection and therefore relief from horror and fear, and they legitimate their hold on po-litical institutions with this promise. Though they risk losing their legitimacy in case of growing popular disappointment,[12] for a while at least, they can also keep two kinds of political conversations at bay. One is of the actual goals of terrorists. The other is in a sense more abstract but always with local implica-tions, and that is of political coercion and its place in domestic and international politics.

Immediately after the attacks of September 11, 2001, it was primarily Left-ists, both in and outside of the United States, who tried to respond to the attacks by engaging in a political discussion of the political aims of Al Qaeda. Inde-pendently of what one thinks of the actual claims of this or that Leftist, some of whom could be construed as justifying terrorist means and exhibiting substantial biases and even insensitivity to the suffering caused by the attacks (see Honderich 2002), Leftists, nonetheless, tried to situate the attacks and understand them politically as well as examine possible political responses to them other than war (see Kaldor 2001). But even most Leftists do not usually undertake a political examination of political coercion, mostly because they take politics, as most realists do, as a scene of struggle in which each side attempts to coerce the other(s), whose self-interests necessarily position in a relatively untransformable opposition.

I am not sure I can go as far as Hannah Arendt (1970) in my rejection of this understanding of politics. I do think that politics cannot be free of coercion. But I also think that when it becomes an accepted and central feature of politics, politics has been perverted. Terrorism is an extreme form of this perversion.

Notes

1. In the United States, World War II is taken as exemplary (see Walzer 1971; Terkel 1984).
2. Note that in the recent past the term "evil" was relied on by another conservative Republican president, Ronald Reagan, who used the term "evil empire" to refer to the Soviet Union. President Reagan appealed directly to World War II (Reagan 1982).
3. Claudia Card develops this connection quite fully in *The Atrocity Paradigm: A Theory of Evil*. What Card suggests is that atrocities provide a paradigm for understanding evil "(1) because they are uncontroversially evil, (2) because they deserve priority of attention, and (3) because the core features of evil tend to be writ large in the case of atrocities, making them easier to identify and appreciate" (2002, 9).
4. The model for the kind of attack that took place on September 11, 2001, was developed initially by the Right Wing Zionist Irgun and Lehi in their fight against the British and for an independent State of Israel. It was elaborated further, first in Algeria during its decolonizing struggles against the French, and later by the Palestinians in their fight with Israel. The Irgun/ Lehi innovation for terrorism was to attack not only combatants but also civilians (see Rubinstein 1987, 199–201; Bar On 2002). But it is important to recognize that terrorism cannot be defined as necessarily involving a violation of the just war principle of discrimination: only some forms of terrorism do so.
5. I am borrowing the term from Hannah Arendt with a nod to Guy Debord and the Situationists so as to emphasize the tension of choices that the "outsider" to suffering has (Arendt 1958, 50–58, 175–81, 199–212; Debord 1977).
6. However, as has been noted, current warfare too is an audiovisual event (see, e.g., Ignatieff 2000).
7. Linkages between social and other forms of discrimination tend to exist. Yet as the experience of Jews under modernity in Central and Western Europe

demonstrates, the relationship between various forms of discrimination is rather contingent, and social discrimination can go on at the same time that other forms of discrimination collapse (see Ben-Sasson 1976, 727–1016).

8. Excluding the Al Aqsa Martyr Brigades, which are an offshoot of the Fattah movement.

9. For reports on Israeli repression of the Palestinians, I recommend looking at www.btselem.org.

10. The violations of the rules of engagement are at times severe and involve acts that can easily be classified as war crimes. See www.gush-shalom.org.

11. There are arguments to the contrary, and Nick Fotion's position in "The Burdens of Terrorism" (originally published in 1981 and revised for a 2004 publication) provides an excellent example of this. Fotion claims that positions like mine that fail to recognize the intuitive clear-cut case against terrorism are "disturbing" and "seem to open the door wider to terrorism and violence" (44).

12. It is more likely that a liberal-democratic leadership will lose its legitimacy if it fails to provide on the security contract. And liberal democracies have known vulnerabilities as a function of their organization, so the protection tasks of their leadership is quite delicate (Heynmann 2003; Wilkinson 2005).

References

Anderson, Guy. 2005. US defence budget will equal ROW combined within 12 months. *Jane's Report*. Retrieved 4 May 2004 from www.janes.com/regional_news/americas/news/jdi/jdi050504_1_n.shtml.

Arendt, Hannah. 1958. *The Human Condition*. Chicago: University of Chicago.

———. 1970. *On Violence*. New York: Harcourt Brace.

Bar On, Bat-Ami. 1991. Why terrorism is morally problematic. In *Feminist Ethics*, ed. Claudia Card. Lawrence: University of Kansas Press.

———. 2002. "An Arendtean scaffolding for thinking about terrorism." ORD and BILD (2/3): 53–57.

———. 2003. Manly after effects of 11 September 2001: Reading William J. Bennett's *Why We Fight*. *International Journal of Women in Politics* 5 (3): 456–58.

———. 2004. Politics and the prioritization of evil. *Hypatia* 19 (4): 192–96.

Baudrillard, Jean. 1993. *The Transparency of Evil: Essays on Extreme Phenomena*. London: Verso.

Baumeister, Roy F. 1997. *Evil: Inside Human Violence and Cruelty*. New York: W. H. Freeman.

Bennett, William J. 2002. *Why We Fight: Moral Clarity and the War on Terrorism*. New York: Doubleday.

Ben-Sasson, Haiim H., ed. 1976. *A History of the Jewish People*. Cambridge, Mass.: Harvard University.

Bush, George W. 2002. State of the union. Retrieved 15 March 2002 from www.whitehouse.gov/news/release/2002/01/20020129–11.html.

Card, Claudia. 1996a. Rape as a weapon of war. *Hypatia* 11 (4): 5–18.

——. 1996b. *The Unnatural Lottery: Character and Moral Luck.* Philadelphia: Temple University.

——. 2002. *The Atrocity Paradigm: A Theory of Evil.* New York: Oxford.

Chomsky, Noam. 1986. *Pirates and Emperors: International Terrorism in the Real World.* New York: Claremont Research and Publications.

Coady, C. A. J. (Tony). 2001. Terrorism. In *Encyclopedia of Ethics,* 2nd ed., ed. Lawrence C. Becker and Charlotte B. Becker, 1696–99. New York: Routledge.

Debord, Guy. 1977. *Society of the Spectacle.* Detroit: Black and Red.

Fotion, Nick. 2004. The burdens of terrorism. In *Terrorism: The Philosophical Issues,* ed. Igor Primoratz, 44–54. New York: Palgrave McMillan.

Freud, Sigmund. 1930. *Civilization and Its Discontents.* Trans. and ed. James Strachey. New York: W. W. Norton, 1961.

Gutman, Roy, and David Rieff, eds. 1999. *Crimes of War: What the Public Should Know.* New York: W. W. Norton.

Heynmann, Philip B. 2003. *Terrorism, Freedom, and Security: Winning without War.* Cambridge, Mass.: MIT.

Hitchens, Christopher. 2001. Against rationalization. Retrieved 15 March 2002 from www.thenation.com/doc.mhtml?i=20011008&s=hitchensi=200110.

Honderich, Ted. 2002. *After the Terror.* Edinburgh: Edinburgh University.

Ignatieff, Michael. 2000. *Virtual War: Kosovo and Beyond.* New York: Henry Holt.

Kaldor, Mary. 2001. Wanted: Global politics. Retrieved 25 June 2005 from www.thenation.com/doc.mhtml?i=20011105&s=kaldor.

Lara, María Pía, ed. 2001. *Rethinking Evil: Contemporary Perspectives.* Berkeley: University of California Press.

McDonald, Eileen. 1991. *Shoot the Women First.* New York: Random House.

Nozick, Robert. 1974. *Anarchy, State, and Utopia.* New York: Basic Books.

Ophir, Adi. 2001. *Speaking Evil: Towards an Ontology of Morals.* Tel Aviv: Am Oved.

Primoratz, Igor. 2004. What is terrorism? In *Terrorism: The Philosophical Issues,* ed. Igor Primoratz, 15–27. New York: Palgrave McMillan.

Reagan, Ronald. 1982. The evil empire. Retrieved 15 March 2002 from www.townhall.com/hall offame/reagan/speech/empire.html.

Ricoeur, Paul. 1967. *The Symbolism of Evil.* Boston: Beacon Press.

Reguler, Arnon. 2005. I joined in order to defend the people and the land and there is no other reason. Retrieved 20 June 2005 from www.haaretz.co.il/hasite/pages/ShArt.jhtml?contrassID=1&subContrassID=5&sbSubContrassID=0&itemNo=590162.

Rubinstein, Richard E. 1987. *Alchemists of Revolution: Terrorism in the Modern World.* New York: Basic Books.

Terkel, Studs. 1984. *The Good War: An Oral History of World War Two.* New York: Pantheon Books.

Thomas, Laurence Mordekhai. 1993. *Vessels of Evil: American Slavery and the Holocaust.* Philadelphia: Temple University.

Victor, Barbara. 2003. *Army of Roses.* Emmaus, Pa.: Rodale.

Walzer, Michael. 1971. World War II: Why was this war different? *Philosophy and Public Affairs* 1 (1): 3–21.

Wilkinson, Paul. 2005. *Terrorism versus Democracy: The Liberal State Response.* London: Frank Cass.

Wittgenstein, Ludwig. 1968. *Philosophical Investigations.* New York: Macmillan.
Young, Robert. 2004. Political terrorism as the weapon of the politically powerless. In *Terrorism: The Philosophical Issues,* ed. Igor Primoratz, 55–64. New York: Palgrave McMillan.

11 Responding to 9/11:
Military Mode or Civil Law?

Claudia Card

Is it justifiable to set aside rules of war in responding to opponents who did the same? Can war on terrorism respond to evil without doing further evil? Such questions invite reflection on the concepts of evil, war, and terrorism. My objectives in so reflecting are: (1) to identify issues that should complicate good answers; and (2) to consider how other nations, whose security may be jeopardized, might justifiably respond to decisions of target nations who do as they see fit to protect themselves. In pursuing the second objective, I explore analogies with the responses of states to women who kill to defend themselves against rape terrorism and domestic violence.

1. Evils

Like "terrorism," "evil" is emotively laden, hurled at enemies from all sides. Some critics therefore abandon such terms for neutral ones like "conflict" and "opponent." I find the concepts "evil" and "terrorism" too important to cede to non-philosophers.

The secular theory of my book *The Atrocity Paradigm* begins with evils, plural, defining them as reasonably foreseeable intolerable harms produced by culpable wrongdoing (Card 2002, 3). So defined, evils have two irreducibly basic elements: harm and wrongdoing, connected by causality and foreseeability. Usually, what distinguish evils from other wrongs are not worse motives but worse harms. Institutions become evils when their normal operation foreseeably produces intolerable harms which people with power culpably fail to prevent.

By intolerable harms, I mean deprivations of basics required to make a life tolerable and decent (or to make a death decent). These include access to a decent amount of nontoxic air, water, and food; sleep; freedom from severe and lasting pain and humiliation; the ability to stretch (and contract) one's limbs and move about; affective ties with others; the ability to make choices and act on them; a sense of one's worth. "Decent" is a clue that my "intolerable harm" is a normative concept. Sadly, many do, because they must, tolerate the intolerable daily.

Culpable wrongdoing includes omissions (negligence, recklessness). It includes much conduct that doers believe justified. But even ideological motivation does not excuse, as long as people can be responsible for their ideological commitments. Still, evil *doers* need not be evil *people;* their deeds may not issue from commitments or culpable character traits. Popular interest is almost always in evil people; mine is in evil deeds and doers.

2. Terrorism

The 9/11 attacks were atrocities.[1] Regardless of grievances and religious beliefs, lethal mass targeting of unarmed civilians without warning is evil. That much should be uncontroversial. Less clear is whether the bombings were terrorist.

Terrorism is not just whatever terrifies, even intentionally. (Horror films and carnival rides do that.) Nor is it just any violence against innocent civilians. Michael Walzer thought *randomness* in the murder of innocent people "a crucial feature of terrorist activity" (1977, 177). But surprise, which makes defense difficult, is more basic. Random victim selection contributes to surprise. So does unpredictable timing, even if victims are not random. And more to the point than innocence is that some terrorists inflict harm on targets regardless of what those targets have done as individuals. Vulnerability to such targeting does not presuppose innocence.

Carl Wellman (1979) analyzes terrorism as coercive political violence, usually with two targets—one direct, one indirect. Harm aimed at the direct but secondary target sends a message to the indirect but primary target, threatening further harm unless demands are fulfilled. With this idea, Walzer appears to agree (1977, 203). For terrorists, terror is a means, not an end in itself. Bombings are terrorist when they carry demands, such as to release prisoners.

The 9/11 attacks were terrorist in Wellman's sense if the intent was to manipulate the United States politically. On this reading, workers directly targeted as they began their day—"throw-away victims"—were used as a means to issue demands. Yet the bombers left no explicit message stating their purpose. Osama bin Laden—the current Western icon of evil (who inevitably, in some photos, resembles European images of Jesus)—is immortalized in tapes revealing that the attacks, including the surprise element, were planned (*Der Spiegel* 2001). Further tapes indicate that a purpose was to deter the United States from activities perceived as threatening Muslim peoples.

If the bombings' intent was punitive, or to show the world the United States is not invulnerable, either the deeds were not terrorist in Wellman's sense, or terrorism can have other than coercive messages. If not terrorist, the deeds were no less evil. If punitive, there was no shred of due process. If simply to show the world it could be done, there was an ulterior motive, not to coerce but to encourage other potential attackers.

One might object that coercion defines terrorism too narrowly. Many suicide bombings in Israel, among today's paradigms of terrorism, carry no explicit message or demand. If they are good paradigms, is "terrorism" just a pejorative term for guerilla warfare? Richard Hare (1979) observed long ago that terrorism is the resort of people who lack the resources to wage conventional war, such as those who fought in the Resistance during World War II. Mary Kaldor, of the London School of Economics and Political Science, argues that distinctions between war and other violence are eroding. The "new wars" of the 1980s and 90s blur distinctions among war, organized crime, and large-scale violations of human rights; and "the term 'low-intensity conflict'," she writes, "was coined during the Cold War period by the U.S. military to describe guerilla warfare or terrorism"—suggesting that guerilla warfare and terrorism are more or less the same (Kaldor 2000, 2).

The objection that a coercive aim is not essential might be met with a distinction. When terrorist acts are backed by organizations, we should distinguish individual agents' intentions from those of sponsoring organizations that provide encouragement, support, and a context that gives individual acts meaning. Intentions of such organizations can be what make deeds terrorist.

Regarding the alleged identity of terrorism with guerilla warfare, it can be noted that guerilla warfare often includes terrorism but is not reducible to it. What makes warfare "guerilla" is indirectness, clandestine methods, avoidance of confrontation—not terror. Guerilla attacks can take non-terrorist forms, such as destruction of paperwork, that does not aim at killing, kidnapping, or bodily harm to persons or even appeal to fear, thereby lacking a manipulative element. Objectives can be to win hearts in a local population and disable enemies rather than to coerce.

Hare reminds us that "it was an act of terrorism which sparked off the first World War" and that "to some extent terrorism is a substitute for conventional war," as is guerilla warfare (1979, 244). But terrorism is also used in conventional warfare, even if it violates codes. Saturation bombings of Hamburg, Dresden, Tokyo, Hiroshima, and Nagasaki were terrorist, meant to send a message. Civilian inhabitants were throwaways.

Not all terrorizing of civilians is terror*ist*—the Columbine High School shootings, for example, or sniper shootings by a tower gunman who aims to kill as many as possible before committing suicide. Those killings may not be means to further ends. They may simply express pent-up rage. Kidnapping can be terrorist, as in the case of the Lindbergh baby. But bride-seeker kidnapping and sexual predators who kidnap children may neither have terrorist intent (many may hope the kidnapped will be given up for lost) nor serve an organization that has such an intent.

3. War

Less clear than whether the 9/11 attacks were terrorist is whether a military response is justifiable, whether it can avoid doing further evil. *Merriam Webster's Collegiate Dictionary* says "war" is "a state of usually open and declared armed hostile conflict between states or nations" (10th ed., 1993). Carl von Clausewitz defined "war" as "an act of violence intended to compel our opponent to fulfill our will" (1982, 101). That sounds as coercive as terrorism. He meant only that each side aims to make the other capitulate. A big difference from terrorism is that war has a long and continuous history of regulation by international conventions. Walzer notes that revolutionary honor codes governed nineteenth-century "terrorists" who targeted powerful individuals but also that honor codes no longer appear to govern terrorism (1977, 198 ff.).

Some find "war on terrorism" metaphorical, like "war on crime" and "war on drugs." But military force is no mere metaphor. War confers legitimacy by tacitly invoking certain norms, simultaneously dignifying the 9/11 attacks, removing them from civil jurisdiction. Yet "war on terrorism" is oxymoronic. It is unclear how war norms apply. David Luban has discussed the contrast between war norms and civil law norms, warning that despite the language of war, the reality is a hybrid approach, "selectively combining elements of the war model, and elements of the law model [i.e., civil law model] . . . to maximize . . . [the] ability to mobilize lethal force against terrorists while eliminating most traditional rights of a military adversary" (2002, 9).

This observation should lead us to ask what limits apply to a military response to attacks unauthorized by any state, which respect no international military code? What limits the range of *opponents*, for example? What less drastic measures should be exhausted? Are there *non-arbitrary* ways to combine a military and civil model? Are there good grounds for choosing between military and civil models? Let us look at both models and then see what we might learn from an analogous dilemma regarding rape and violence in the home.[2]

4. The Civil Law Approach

Luban's major concern is that the military approach takes human rights less seriously. Distinctive of civil law is its assignment of responsibility to individuals, holding them accountable for only their own conduct. Military law permits actions against individuals in virtue of their identity or position, not just their individual choices.

The civil law approach suggests that appropriate responses to 9/11 would be global hunts by international teams for individuals responsible, as well as for individuals taking steps toward further attacks, and for collaborators, such as trainers, financial backers, providers of safe harbors. The goal need not be punitive. Learning the truth may be more valuable. Yet preservation of human rights may require that individuals who refuse cooperation be charged and tried, charges depending on evidence regarding their intentions. That evidence in the case of 9/11 appears ambiguous between two interpretations.

The 9/11 attacks have been called both terrorist and hate crimes (a.k.a. bias crimes). Yet these interpretations are distinct and can compete. Disentangling terrorism from guerilla war allows us to see that civil crimes can be terrorist. Terrorists need not be treated as soldiers. Terrorist crimes also need not be motivated by bias, nor need bias crimes be terrorist. If the 9/11 attacks were terrorist, presumably they carried a message. The direct target may have been as much the physical structures of the WTC and the Pentagon and the data and equipment they contained as the human occupants. Were the attacks' timings determined by when workers would fill the offices? Or simply by flight schedules of suitably fueled aircraft? On the terrorist interpretation, timings might have been determined solely by the availability of suitably fueled aircraft. On the hate crimes interpretation, the presence of human occupants would presumably be critical.

Hate crimes target victims for their racial, religious, ethnic, national, or, sometimes, political identity.[3] If the 9/11 attacks were hate crimes, victims were targeted for their (perceived) identity, presumably as Americans, American sympathizers, or capitalists. There need be no demand or coercive intent. Like school shooters and tower snipers, perpetrators of hate crimes may simply express rage. But hate crimes can also carry a message. Cross-burnings and lynchings commonly do. It is possible, then, that the 9/11 attacks were both terrorist and hate crimes.

The hate crime interpretation provides a sufficient reason to charge suspects with crimes against humanity. The terrorist interpretation may not. Crimes against humanity, defined in at least eleven international texts, are understood as acts of violence that are "the product of persecution against an identifiable group of persons, irrespective of the make-up of that group or the purpose of the persecution" (Gutman and Rieff 1999, 107)—in other words, major hate crimes. A terrorist interpretation might be sufficient to charge a war crime, were the attacks committed in war. Since they were not, unless we count them as initiating a war, the terrorist interpretation suggests charging suspects simply with the civil crime of mass murder.

Charging a crime against humanity outside of war might combine some of the best elements of both military and civil law models. Although universal jurisdiction applies (Gutman and Rieff 1999, 108), an international court would be appropriate for 9/11 suspects, as victims were from many nations, and the deeds threaten security globally. But when war is declared, rather than a hunt for individual suspects, opportunities for fair trials diminish with the likelihood of survivors.

5. The Military Model

Internationally accepted rules of war evolved to regulate wars *with* or *between* opponents conceived as agents (historically, nations, states, or nation-states).[4] But what guidelines regulate "wars" on terrorism or drugs? Terrorist and drug *organizations* might be treated as enemy agents. Yet they may have no knowledge of rules of war. How, then, are states to engage with them?

Analogous agency problems arise in civil wars, muddying the application of rules of war. By tradition, a just war is declared by appropriate authorities, commonly taken to be states, who have authority to negotiate for peace. But for war internal to a state, who has authority to declare war or negotiate a peace? If no one, no civil war could be just, which is implausible. But neither is it obvious who justifiably speaks for the people against its government, nor against whom a government declares war when the opponent is internal to the body it governs. Similar agency questions arise for transnational war on terrorism: on whom is the war declared? When such a war is declared global, rather than focused on named organizations or territories, it is unclear who is targeted and therefore who is not. This fact should worry other nations.

Heads of state negotiate for peace. Who can do that with a state at war on terrorism? Not only does al Qaeda not speak for all terrorists, it is unclear who speaks for al Qaeda (even whether anyone does). The structure of organized terrorism makes dubious the adequacy of both a civil law approach, with its focus on individual responsibility, and a military approach, with its focus on engaging with enemy agents. Al Qaeda cells appear not to be a hierarchy or have a head. They seem anarchical, related more like knots in a net. Destroy a ladder's base, and its top falls. Destroy a hierarchy's top, and the base lacks direction. But destroy cells in a network, and the rest may simply mend the net. With no one to negotiate a peace, how must such a war end? What is to prevent a war of extermination? Luban concludes that since new terrorists will always arise, such a war never can be concluded but only abandoned (2002, 13).

Mary Kaldor notes that 100 years ago "the ratio of military to civilian casualties in wars was 8:1" but that by the end of the twentieth century that ratio "has been almost exactly reversed: in the wars of the 1990s, the ratio of military to civilian casualties is 1:8" (2000, 8). She concludes, "Behaviour that was proscribed according to the classical rules of warfare and codified in the laws of war in the late nineteenth century and early twentieth century . . . now constitutes an essential component of the strategies of the new mode of warfare" (2000, 8). Yet there are ways and ways of killing civilians. Some distinctions can still be recognized.

A discrimination principle in the *jus in bello* part of just war theory prohibits targeting noncombatants directly. Weapons of mass destruction (WMD) make it nearly impossible to target combatants without killing even more noncombatants. Some think this fact makes rules of war obsolete—at least, the discrimination principle. But one could as well draw the opposing conclusion that since wars conducted with WMD cannot be just, *war* should be obsolete. Still, the discrimination principle is not vacuous. It implies that some reasons cannot justify targeting noncombatants: revenge, demoralizing a military opponent, sport.

The main problem of how to avoid killing noncombatants in a war on terrorism is not logistical but conceptual. Who *counts* as a noncombatant? When standing armies replaced mercenaries in Europe, uniforms were introduced to identify combatants (Kaldor 2000, 16). Medical personnel, with their own uniforms, traditionally have noncom status. Likewise producers of food and goods consumed even during peace (unlike munitions producers). Abandoning uniforms, guerillas frustrate attempts to identify combatants. War against terrorism raises the question of what the distinction between combatant and noncombatant means. What relationships to terrorist acts or organizations make one a combatant? What are people responsible to know about consequences of their choices? What counts as support of enemy activity?

Such difficulties point toward the conclusion that war against terrorism cannot be fought *justly*. Whether it is nevertheless *justifiable* depends on whether there is a less unjust alternative.

6. Other Terrorisms

"Terrorists" is not a well-defined group. "Terrorist" is not an identity or proper name like American. To identify someone as a terrorist is to render a judgment, not simply make a discovery. Not all terrorists have common goals or even similar opponents. Terrorists in the United States include native-born citizens. Lynching is the most infamous U.S. domestic terrorism. Nor is such homegrown terrorism a thing of the past. The National Coalition of Burned Churches is alive today (its concerns not lightning or faulty wiring).[5] The Southern Poverty Law Center has been vigilant against such terrorism for decades.

Other domestic terrorists are less visible. The reigning stereotype of the terrorist is someone who carries out destructive acts against public institutions or in public places, seeking attention for clearly political causes. That stereotype ignores state terrorism (of Nero, Hitler, Stalin, Idi Amin, Pol Pot, for example), which is often clandestine, as noted by Emma Goldman, Jonathan Glover, and others.[6] It also ignores terrorism in the home and the terrorism of rape with which women and girls cope routinely even in states relatively secure from external attack. Poet Susan Griffin wrote in 1971:

> I have never been free of the fear of rape. From a very early age I, like most women, have thought of rape as part of my natural environment—something to be feared and prayed against like fire or lightning. I never asked why men raped; I simply thought it one of the many mysteries of human nature. (in Vetterling-Braggin et al. 1977, 313)

Although as a child she never asked why men rape, as an adult she finds an answer:

> In the system of chivalry, men protect women against men. This is not unlike the protection relationship which the Mafia established with small businesses in the early part of this [20th] century. Indeed, chivalry is an age-old protection racket which depends for its existence on rape. (in Vetterling-Braggin et al. 1977, 320)

Rape, she implies, is a terrorist practice, analogous to organized crime.[7] It secures for men the willingness of women to serve them in everything from laundry and cooking to childcare and sexuality. As with suicide bombings, we should distinguish the purposes of individual agents from those of the practice that is served by and gives meaning to their deeds.

Like rape, much violence in the home maintains heterosexual male dominance and female dependence and service. Targets are not always selected randomly by rapists and almost never by batterers. Nor need they be innocent. But the timing of attacks is often unpredictable, making self-defense difficult. As with punishment, the threat rather than actual infliction does most of the intimidating.[8] Some men assault women for sport or for revenge, not to coerce service. Yet they know others will seldom hold them accountable. Those who could but do not hold them to account are primarily responsible for rape terrorism—legislators, officers who do not investigate or prosecute, judges who go easy on rapists—and people who listen without objection to rape tales or blame survivors for "asking for it."

Assaults and threats of domestic violence often do appear directly intended to coerce targets to maintain relationships of service with perpetrators. Attorney Joyce McConnell argues that women held to services of a wife by batterers are held to involuntary servitude in the sense of the Thirteenth Amendment (1992, 207–53). They are also targets of terrorism, in Wellman's sense. As he noted about armed hold-ups, the same person here is both direct and indirect target.

A truly global war on terrorism would target the rape protection racket as well as much abuse in the home. President Bush's war ignores such terrorism. But for those who would support Bush's war, it should be an interesting question whether war is an appropriate response to rape terrorism and to terrorism in the home. An individual rape or episode of domestic battering usually has fewer direct casualties than a bombed building. Yet the number of rapes and domestic assaults is huge. Estimates are that in the United States, a woman is raped every 1.3 minutes and a woman battered every 15 seconds.[9] Effects can be lifelong, and the mobility of other women (indirect targets) is circumscribed. Should survivors regard themselves as in a state of nature—as though governments, laws, and courts did not exist—with respect to batterers and rapists? The law's record of justice here is poor. Let's see what we can learn from two women who finally did what seemed necessary to protect themselves.

In the famous Michigan "burning bed" case, one night in 1977 Francine Hughes poured gasoline on her sleeping former husband and ignited it. For years she had endured his battering. She had repeatedly appealed unsuccessfully to the law to protect her and her children (McNulty 1980). Tried for murder, she was eventually acquitted on an insanity defense. But if killing without trial is an *appropriate* response to terrorists, should she even have been tried?

And what of the equally famous case of Inez García? In 1974, after a phone call threatening her with murder, Inez García pursued and shot at two men. One had raped her minutes before while his 300-pound accomplice stood guard. Her shots killed the accomplice. She only regretted not having succeeded in killing the other one (who was never charged with any crime) (Salter 1976; Wood 1976). Tried for murder in California, she was convicted and sentenced to five years to life. On appeal, she was exonerated. Attorney Susan B. Jordan successfully argued self-defense. Should Inez García not even have been tried?

On one hand, it may be objected that these victims lack authority to make war. Yet why does that matter, if not as part of a broader understanding of rules defining conditions of fair fighting? Have not such rules been abandoned already if men can rape and batter women with impunity? Is the real objection that war is not an appropriate female response?

On the other hand, it may be objected that it is outrageous to compare the United States to raped or battered women.[10] The United States is the most powerful nation in the world (not to mention the matter of relative innocence). The point of the analogy, however, is not that their *moral* positions were the same. Rather, their options are intriguingly analogous. Anyone can be vulnerable to terrorism, as 9/11 demonstrates, regardless of their power. The relevant similarity is that they all stepped outside the law in deciding how to defend themselves. They confront us with the questions: (1) when, if ever, is it justifiable to do that? And then (2) how should others respond to a terror target who does that? Their choices confront others with urgent questions of how to respond. Courts sitting in judgment on those choices might well come to different conclusions about who was justified in doing what.

7. Justice for the Unjust

When terrorists disregard justice, victims face a hard question: how much justice should be shown those who disregard justice themselves? Criminals often disregard justice. Yet the state offers them a trial. Fair trials give the wrongly accused an opportunity to rebut charges. Striking back without trial ignores possible errors in identifying assailants or understanding what they did, why, or the conditions under which they did it.

The point applies equally to international terrorism. Without trials, what assurance have citizens of the world that they will not be wrongly identified as terrorists and summarily dispatched? Similar questions were raised regarding the creation of the International Military Tribunal at Nuremberg in 1945. The alternative (usual practice) would have been to shoot Axis leaders from a select list decided on ("pricked") by the Allies. Chief Prosecutor Telford Taylor noted that "too many people believed that they had been *wrongfully* hurt by the leaders of the Third Reich and wanted a *judgment* to that effect," and "furthermore . . . the spectacle of Joseph Stalin, who had sent uncounted thousands of his own countrymen to their deaths by his 'political decisions,' sitting as one of a triumvirate to 'prick' a list of Germans, would have made their decisions a target of mockery as long as memory endured" (Taylor 1992, 33).

Given the circumstances and existing law, there were good cases for trying Francine Hughes and Inez García. The states were surely compromised by their own prior failures to take seriously the kinds of crimes that led both women to their deeds.[11] But trials can publicize and document those very facts. Trials and hearings determine formally whether a deed was justified, thereby assuring others that they cannot be killed with impunity by just anyone afraid of them or apprehensive about what they might do. It would have been morally right to acquit Francine Hughes without the insanity defense, given her history of having exhausted less desperate responses. Legally problematic was that the man she killed was asleep, unforewarned, not attacking her at that moment. Her deed did not fit the legal understanding of self-defense, so the only way to acquit her was the insanity defense, even though she may never have been saner. She should not have been left in the position of having to defend herself by extreme means. Her batterer is the one who should have had to stand trial. Likewise Inez García's rapists.

Francine Hughes and Inez García engaged in preemptive strikes. Although asleep, Francine Hughes's batterer was a continuing threat, as were Inez García's assailants, who made a phone threat while she was physically free to walk (or run) away. It is not that these women had no other options. The question is whether they were justified in the options they chose. If preemptive strikes can in principle be justified internationally, why not in the home or on the street?[12]

A nation that makes war on terrorism takes matters into its own hands, as did Francine Hughes and Inez García. It steps outside the bounds and processes of law, here international law, instead of working within them. Like all analogies, this one is imperfect. Inez García did not make war on the institution of rape, nor did Francine Hughes on the general practice of violence in the home. Yet both women's deeds were consistent with the idea of such wars. If Michigan was justified in trying Francine Hughes and California in trying Inez García, would it not be justifiable for international tribunals to do likewise with national leaders who make "war" on terrorism?

Yet would it not be more sensible for an international team to capture and try in court individuals accused of international terrorism, rather than leaving targeted nations to take matters into their own hands (and try them for it later), just as it would make more sense for a state to pursue rapists and batterers, rather than leave women to defend themselves by whatever means necessary (and then try them for it)? An affirmative answer means that nations have serious work to do, collectively, on intervention where terrorism looms. My conclusion is not that a military response to terrorism is unjustified. Rather, targets should not be left in the position of having to make such a choice. Meanwhile, wars on terrorism may put leaders who sanction them at risk of justifiably becoming liable to international inquests or hearings, if not criminal trials, as Francine Hughes and Inez García had to stand trial by their states for murder.

Notes

I am grateful for responses to earlier work on this topic from Leonard Berkowitz, Bat-Ami Bar On, Carl Wellman, Mohammed Abed, and audiences at the 10th Symposium of the International Association of Women Philosophers in Barcelona (Oct. 2002), the Eastern Division American Philosophical Association Convention in Philadelphia (Dec. 2002), the Wisconsin Colleges Philosophy Department (Apr. 2003), the Institute for Research in the Humanities at the University of Wisconsin, Madison (May 2003), and the

Feminist Ethics and Social Theory conference at Tampa (Oct. 2003). An essay on this topic, expanded from my Forum piece in *Hypatia* 18:1, appeared as "Making War on Terrorism in Response to 9/11" in Sterba (2003, 171–85). The present essay is updated with new arguments, new sources, new organization, and omits a little of what the earlier essays contained.

1.   I refer to the suicide bombings of the World Trade Center and the Pentagon and the aborted attempt with the plane that went down in Pennsylvania on September 11, 2001.
2.   Herman 1992 and Minow (2002, 56–71) compare violence in the home to public terrorism. During the Second Wave of feminism, Barbara Mehrhof and Pamela Kearon (in Koedt, Levine, and Rapone 1973, 228–33) wrote about rape terrorism.
3.   A useful introductory pamphlet on hate crime legislation is Rosenberg and Lieberman 1999. See also Lawrence 1999.
4.   Taylor offers a useful overview of recent elements of this evolution (1992, 3–42).
5.   News report on National Public Radio, 21 June 2002.
6.   See Glover 1991, Goldman 1969, and Card 1991.
7.   For extended development of this idea, see Card (1996, 97–117).
8.   See Mabbott (1939, 152–67) for the argument, now classic, that it is the threat of punishment, rather than the infliction of punishment, that does the work of deterrence.
9.   For more statistics, see Women's Action Coalition (1993, 49), which includes among sources on rape the National Victim Center and Crime Victims Research and Treatment Center 1992; Lafferty 1991; and an unidentified author in *Newsweek* (July 1990), quoting the United States Bureau of Justice Statistics. Its sources on battering include Faludi 1991; Rix 1990; Woodward 1989; the U.S. Department of Labor Women's Bureau 1992 [specific document not cited]; and United States Department of Labor 1991.
10.   It was so objected (vigorously!) when I ran this idea by audiences at two feminist conferences.
11.   See Card (1995, 109–17) for the argument that the law should expand its understanding of battering to take account of patterns in relationship violence, as it took account in the 1990s, in making stalking a crime, of oppressive patterns of acts that were not individually illegal. The current legal understanding of battering is modeled on the paradigm of a barroom brawl, an isolated episode.
12.   Thanks to Mohammed Abed for formulating the question so aptly.

References

Card, Claudia. 2002. *The Atrocity Paradigm: A Theory of Evil.* New York: Oxford University Press.

———. 1995. *Lesbian Choices.* New York: Columbia University Press.

———. 1991. Rape as a terrorist institution. In *Violence, Terrorism, and Justice,* ed.

R. G. Frey and Christopher W. Morris, 296–313. Cambridge: Cambridge University Press.

———. 1996. *The Unnatural Lottery: Character and Moral Luck.* Philadelphia: Temple University Press.

Clausewitz, Carl von. 1982. *On War.* London: Penguin.

Faludi, Susan. 1991. *Backlash.* New York: Crown.

Frey, R. G., and Christopher W. Morris, eds. 1991. *Violence, Terrorism, and Justice.* Cambridge: Cambridge University Press.

Glover, Jonathan. 1991. State terrorism. In *Violence, Terrorism, and Justice,* ed. R. G. Frey and Christopher W. Morris, 256–75. Cambridge: Cambridge University Press.

Goldman, Emma. 1969. *Anarchism and Other Essays.* New York: Dover.

———. 1969. The psychology of political violence. In Goldman, *Anarchism and Other Essays,* 79–108. New York: Dover.

Griffin, Susan. 1971. Rape: The all-American crime. *Ramparts* (September): 26–35. Reprinted in Vetterling-Braggin et al., *Feminism and Philosophy,* 313–32. Totowa, N.J.: Littlefield, Adams and Co., 1977.

Gutman, Roy, and David Rieff, eds. 1999. *Crimes of War: What the Public Should Know.* New York: Norton.

Hare, Richard. 1979. On terrorism. *Journal of Value Inquiry* 13:240–49.

Herman, Judith Lewis. 1992. *Trauma and Recovery.* New York: Basic Books.

Kaldor, Mary. 2000. *New and Old Wars: Organized Violence in a Global Era.* Stanford, Calif.: Stanford University Press.

Koedt, Anne, Ellen Levine, and Anita Rapone, eds. 1973. *Radical Feminism.* New York: Quadrangle.

Lafferty, Shelagh Marie. 1991. Policy analysis exercise, analysis of newspaper coverage of rape 1989–1990. Cambridge, Mass.: Harvard University, Kennedy School of Government.

Lawrence, Frederick M. 1999. *Punishing Hate: Bias Crimes under American Law.* Cambridge, Mass.: Harvard University Press.

Luban, David. 2002. The war on terrorism and the end of human rights. *Philosophy and Public Policy Quarterly* 22:3.

Mabbott, J. D. 1949. Punishment. *Mind* n.s. 48:152–67.

McConnell, Joyce E. 1992. Beyond metaphor: Battered women, involuntary servitude and the Thirteenth Amendment. *Yale Journal of Law and Feminism* 4 (2) (Spring): 207–53.

McNulty, Faith. 1980. *The Burning Bed.* New York: Harcourt Brace Jovanovich.

Merriam Webster's Collegiate Dictionary. 1993. 10th ed. Springfield, Mass.: Merriam Webster.

Minow, Martha, ed. 2002. *Breaking the Cycles of Hatred: Memory, Law, and Repair.* Princeton and Oxford: Princeton University Press.

National Victim Center and Crime Victims Research and Treatment Center. 1991. Rape in America: A report to the nation. [city not given; no other publisher given].

Rix, Sarah E., ed. 1990. *The American Woman 1990–91.* New York: Norton.

Rosenberg, David, and Michael Lieberman. 1999. *Hate Crimes Laws.* [No city given] Anti-Defamation League.

Salter, Kenneth W. 1976. *The Trial of Inez García.* Berkeley, Calif.: Editorial Justa Publications.

Der Spiegel [German magazine], reporters, writers, and editors. 2001. *Inside 9–11: What Really Happened.* New York: St. Martins.

Sterba, James, ed. 2003. *Terrorism and International Justice.* New York: Oxford University Press.

Taylor, Telford. 1992. *Anatomy of the Nuremberg Trials.* New York: Knopf.

United States Department of Labor. 1991. A report on the glass ceiling. Washington, D.C.: U.S. Dept. of Labor.

Vetterling-Braggin, Mary, Frederick A. Elliston, and Jane English, eds. 1977. *Feminism and Philosophy.* Totowa, N.J.: Littlefield, Adams and Co.

Walzer, Michael. 1977. *Just and Unjust wars: A Moral Argument with Historical Illustrations.* New York: Basic Books.

Wellman, Carl. 1979. On terrorism itself. *Journal of Value Inquiry* 13:250–58.

Women's Action Coalition. 1993. *WAC STATS: Facts about Women.* New York: New Press.

Wood, Jim. 1976. *The Rape of Inez García.* New York: G. P. Putnam's Sons.

Woodward, Kenneth L. 1989. Feminism and the churches. *Newsweek,* 13 February.

12 Naming Terrorism as Evil

Alison M. Jaggar

Within days of the dramatic attacks that occurred on September 11, 2001, the editors of *Hypatia* invited several feminist philosophers to consider whether those attacks, and terrorism more generally, should be described as evil (Schott 2003, 5).[1] In the intervening four years, marked by further terrorist attacks on Western countries, references to terrorism as evil have become commonplace in the political discourse of the United States. The present discussion offers some reasons for resisting this characterization. I do not attempt to justify terrorism, but I suggest that the language of evil, because of its theological and absolutist associations, is distinctly unhelpful for understanding and figuring out how to respond to the complex and contested phenomenon of contemporary terrorism.

Robin Schott's introduction to this volume explains how Kant opened the way to a post-metaphysical conception of evil as suffering caused by human wrongdoing; this modern conception of evil replaced the earlier biblical understanding, which referred broadly to meaningless or unjust suffering resulting from natural disasters or simply from human finitude (Schott 2003, 2). In her groundbreaking book *The Atrocity Paradigm,* Claudia Card offers a secular moral theory of evil, defined as "foreseeable intolerable harms produced by culpable wrongdoing." She argues that neither intolerable harm nor culpable wrongdoing is sufficient alone to produce evil, though each is a basic component of it (2002, 3–4). Card's analysis is illuminating, and she is surely right to suggest that evils deserve more attention than they have recently been accorded in secular moral philosophy (2003, 6). In the political discourse of the contemporary United States, however, "evil" is still widely understood in Manichean, semi-religious terms. Evils may be multiple, and they may be lesser or greater, but an unbridgeable gap is still thought to separate anything evil from anything good. Evils are intrinsically and irremediably bad; they cannot be given favorable interpretations, and they are not capable of reform or conversion. People who are committed to the good cannot tolerate or coexist with evil; instead, they are morally bound to struggle against it, and, since it is evil, they may use any means necessary.

Absolutist moral language encourages political polarization and extremism. It is surely no coincidence that the language of evil is likewise used by Islamists justifying terrorist attacks on Western countries. In the United States, the term *evil* has been deployed mainly by conservative politicians wishing to defend military interventions abroad and limitations on civil liberties at home. Speaking before the National Association of Evangelicals in 1983, President Ronald Reagan called for "the evil empire" to be defeated; he used this characterization of the Soviet Union to justify support for the contras in Nicaragua and the mujahedeen in Afghanistan—both, ironically, terrorist movements. Similarly, President George W. Bush's characterization of North Korea, Iran, and Iraq as an "axis of evil," in his 2002 State of the Union Address, was widely seen as a prelude to the use of military force against these countries. In my view, characterizing terrorism as evil is likely to short-circuit moral debate and rationalize immoderate responses.

Identifying Terrorism

As with most highly charged terms, the meaning of "terrorism" is disputed by scholars, legislators, and the general public; an international treaty on terrorism has been held up for decades because the United Nations has been unable to agree on a definition. In the fall of 2005, however, the United Nations seems ready to define terrorism as "any action intended to cause death or serious bodily harm to civilians and non-combatants, undertaken with the purpose of intimidating a population or compelling a government or an international organization to carry out or to abstain from any act."[2] This definition is close to my earlier *Hypatia* account of terrorism as intentional attacks on innocent civilians carried out with the objective of promoting some political goal by creating terror in the population attacked.[3] Characterizing terrorism in this way distinguishes it both from ordinary crimes, which are committed for personal reasons rather than in the name of some larger cause, and also from acts of war. Acts of war differ from acts of terror in that they are typically part of a large-scale assault on the institutions of a state carried out by another state's official military forces or, in the case of revolutionary war, by aspirants to state power.[4]

Although the paradigm targets of terrorism are private citizens as opposed to official representatives of states, the agents of terror are not always private in the sense of non-governmental. In contemporary Western discourse, terrorists are often presented as crazed individuals, like the so-called Unabomber in the United States, or as fanatical members of groups defined by reference to ideological objectives. Members of such groups regularly carry out terrorist attacks in most countries of the world, including the United States and the European Union, and their attacks include so-called hate crimes against members of unpopular or stigmatized groups, such as religious, ethnic, racialized, sexual, or immigrant minorities.[5] However, terrorism is practiced regularly by states as well as by non-state actors.

State terrorism causes far more harm than non-state terrorism because states typically have access to resources that are far more powerful and destructive than those available to individuals or non-state groups. Governments may use their legal apparatus and even their military forces to terrorize segments of their own populations, for example by imposing apartheid-like regimes. In wartime, states may authorize their forces to attack enemy populations in state-sanctioned terror that is distinct, at least in principle, from the unauthorized terrorist acts that military personnel often commit.[6] States may engage in terrorism covertly as well as overtly, using unofficial militias such as the extrajudicial death squads with which some Latin American governments were linked in the 1970s and 1980s. Like overt terrorism, covert state terrorism may extend beyond the state's own borders. In the 1980s, for instance, the U.S. government supported terrorist Jonas Savimbi and his UNITA militia in Angola as well as the so-called contras (counter-revolutionaries) in Nicaragua, who sought to undermine the Sandinista government by attacking farms and clinics.[7]

Reaching international agreement on a definition of "terrorism" has not been easy, but applying that definition in practice is much harder. This is because, as Claudia Card remarks in this volume, to identify terrorism is to render a judgment, not simply to make a discovery (see also Card 2003, 266). For instance:

- It is often difficult to distinguish collateral damage from deliberate terror. Military activity is invariably and probably inevitably harmful to civilians, but how far particular harms were foreseeable or avoidable is likely to be disputed.
- It may be difficult to draw the line between systemic injustice and state terror. Harshly discriminatory laws or practices of law enforcement are likely to be perceived by some and not others as institutionalized state terrorism.
- Some may question whether attacks on property, as opposed to persons, are acts of terror. Contemporary mainstream media usually conflate the two, but anarchists have long distinguished assassination, or terror directed against persons, from politically motivated sabotage.
- What counts as a private target may also be debated. For instance, workers in weapons industries may be seen as integral parts of a war machine, and members of colonizing populations may be regarded as representatives of an invasive state. It is plausible to regard the World Trade Center, the Pentagon, and the Congress or White House not as private targets but rather as symbolic centers of economic, military, and political power.[8]

Because terrorism is widely condemned—and the forthcoming United Nations resolution is likely to state that it is never morally justified—debates about the extension of the term are frequently passionate. Those who kill often deny that they are murderers, perhaps by arguing that they killed by accident or in self-defense. Similarly, those who attack seemingly civilian targets often deny that they are terrorists, contending, for instance, that those attacked were not really private citizens or that the deaths were unforeseen or unavoidable. Characterizing terrorism as evil adds only heat but no light to the many conceptual, normative, and empirical questions about when the term is properly applied.

Law Enforcement versus Military Responses to Terrorism

When anything is determined to be evil, those committed to good are morally obliged to struggle against it. A common response to evils is to declare war on them, often a metaphorical war; for example, a war on crime or corruption might be waged through law enforcement, a war on illness through the provision of health care, a war on poverty through redistributive measures. The war on terror that the U.S. government declared very shortly after attacks of 2001 has been waged largely by military means, notably by bombing and invading Afghanistan and Iraq. Extreme military responses are encouraged by describing the enemy as evil, but responding to terrorism primarily by military means raises serious questions of moral and legal, as well as pragmatic, justification.

Despite significant areas of dispute, the meaning of terrorism is sufficiently agreed upon to allow its prohibition in both national and international law. All modern states have laws designed to protect the lives and property of their citizens, and people suspected of breaking those laws must be apprehended, fairly tried, and, if convicted, punished. Terrorism in wartime is prohibited by international law, so military personnel who attack private citizens and officials who order such attacks are guilty of war crimes or even of crimes against humanity. Those accused of war crimes may be tried either by courts in their own countries or in international tribunals set up for the purpose. Such a tribunal was established at Nuremberg after World War II to try Germans accused of war crimes, and another at Arusha, in Tanzania, to try those accused of genocide in Rwanda.

International terrorism is prohibited by a variety of multilateral conventions, supplemented in November 2000 by a Convention against Transnational Organized Crime, which has been ratified already by 140 countries, including the United States.[9] These agreements, as well as several articles in the United Nations Charter, oblige their signatories to deal with terrorist attacks according to the rule of law. Thus, a signatory state with reason to believe that terrorists involved in attacking its citizens have taken refuge in another signatory state may request that the suspects be extradited, presenting evidence of their involvement. If the evidence presented is plausible, the second country should extradite the suspects, so long as it can be confident that they will receive a fair trial.

The aspiration to a global rule of law is still far from reality. International conventions are not signed by all states, and many sign with reservations. Furthermore, international enforcement procedures are weak and used selectively against less powerful states. The operation of INTERPOL, the international police organization, is hampered by a small budget and by lack of cooperation on the part of many national law enforcement agencies. The International Criminal Court is only beginning its operations and is opposed by the United States, the most powerful country in the world. Some states are too weak to prevent suspected terrorists from operating on their territory, and some engage in terrorism themselves.

Given these problems, a state occasionally may need to resort to military force to implement its laws against terrorism, just as it may sometimes call on its military to fight fires or deal with natural disasters. The most likely role for the military in enforcing laws against terrorism is to capture suspects who elude or resist the police. However, a state's need for military force against its own citizens raises worries about its legitimacy, including whether the state itself may be terrorist. State terrorism is more difficult to address than non-state terrorism, because the law is both less developed and harder to enforce, and therefore it may be easier to justify responding militarily to state terrorism than to terrorism perpetrated by non-state actors. When state terrorism occurs, citizens may engage in armed resistance, and occasionally a case may be made for foreign intervention. However, current international law permits such intervention only in very few cases and only as a last resort, when authorized by the United Nations.

The terrorist attacks that occurred in the United States on September 11, 2001, were covered by several international treaties, including the 1971 Montreal Sabotage Convention, signed by both Afghanistan and the United States. Despite the existence of these treaties, legal protocols were not followed in this case. The United States demanded that Afghanistan extradite Osama bin Laden and his Al Qaeda associates, but it did not offer evidence that they were linked directly to the attacks. Afghanistan refused the extradition demands on the grounds that the United States neither presented plausible evidence of the suspects' involvement in the attacks nor provided convincing assurance that they would receive a fair trial. In fact, it is unlikely that the government of Afghanistan was able to extradite bin Laden and his associates, even had it been willing to do so. In November 2001, the United States and its allies began a massive bombing campaign directed not only against suspected terrorist bases in Afghanistan but also against the Afghan government.

Military action against suspected terrorists that goes beyond law enforcement clearly undermines the rule of law. It is also morally problematic. It is difficult to justify military action against a country in which suspected non-state terrorists have taken refuge and especially difficult to justify the aerial bombardment of that country. Terrorists currently live in most countries of the world, including the United States and Western Europe. If a government is aware that terrorists are living in and even launching attacks from its territory, that government is abetting criminal activity and shares some collective responsibility for the terrorists' crimes; but the whole country, especially its civilian population, does not thereby become terrorists or their moral equivalent. Suspected terrorists should receive a fair trial in a duly constituted court of law, but aerial bombardment is more likely to kill than to capture suspects, thus making it impossible to bring them to trial. Moreover, even the smartest bombs can be predicted to harm civilians, subjecting them to a form of extra-judicial and collective punishment that may be terrorist itself.

Military responses to terrorism are disproportionately harmful to women, especially to poor women and their children. During the twentieth century, civilians rather than soldiers came to constitute an ever-increasing proportion of the casualties of war.[10] The combatants in war are predominantly male, but the vulnerable civilians are predominantly women and children, especially women and children in the Third World, where most casualties of recent wars have occurred. Women and children also constitute 80 percent of the millions of refugees dislocated by war. Rape is a traditional weapon of war, and military action is usually associated with organized and sometimes forced prostitution. Less directly, military action is likely to rationalize public spending on war industries, from which women enjoy relatively little benefit, and women suffer disproportionately when tax revenues are diverted from social into military programs. Militarism promotes a sexist and violent culture in which men are glorified as warriors while women are either degraded or portrayed as national resources. Furthermore, women suffer disproportionately from pollution of the world's environment, of which military action is the major cause. Thus, women have a special interest in finding alternatives to military strategies against terrorism. Unfortunately, the characterization of terrorism as evil encourages heavy-handed military responses with disregard for civilian costs.

The Limits of the Law

A number of Western writers have argued that law enforcement responses to terrorism are preferable to military responses for both legal and moral reasons.[11] Such writers typically acknowledge that law enforcement, like military action, is unable to prevent future terrorist attacks, but they imply that at least law enforcement does not continue the cycle of terror. In evaluating these proposals, it is important to remember that not all laws are just and that states as well as non-state actors may be terrorist; thus law enforcement may sometimes become a cover for state-sanctioned terrorism.

In the name of war against terrorism, laws may be passed that are so repressive or permit such discriminatory application that they facilitate terror by the state. For instance, its critics claim that the Patriot Act of 2001 violates several elements of the U.S. Constitution, allowing agents of the state to terrorize some U.S. citizens and residents.[12] International laws passed in the name of combating terrorism may also be repressive, harshly burdening vulnerable populations in order to protect the privileges of the wealthy and powerful; for instance, the recent Convention against Transnational Organized Crime requires governments to restrict the smuggling of migrants, but many citizens of impoverished countries reasonably regard migration as the only available strategy for improving their lives. In a context of extreme global inequality, laws restricting migration make already vulnerable people even more vulnerable, not only to criminals, but also to corrupt and abusive government officials and to exploitative government policies.[13]

Many of the strategies used in the war on terror waged by the United States and its allies have been ruthless to the point of perpetrating further terror. These strategies have been rationalized and even made to appear inevitable by repeated assertions that terrorism, and those responsible for it, are evil.[14] Such sweeping assertions discourage further investigation of the causes of particular instances of terrorism, whose specificities are obscured by the generic condemnation. Yet terrorism does not come from nowhere; it is a tactic employed in various types of conflicts and in combination with other ways of making claims (Jaggar 2005). The various conflicts from which terrorism emerges have differing causes, but as an untitled working document of the United Nations notes, terrorism flourishes in environments of despair, humiliation, poverty, political oppression, extremism, and human rights abuses, as well as contexts of regional conflict and foreign occupation.[15] For this reason, effective opposition to terrorism requires not only vigorous and impartial enforcement of just laws; it also requires addressing the injustice, poverty, and political exclusion with which terrorism is typically associated and which we should not hesitate to name as evil.

Notes

1. I wish to thank Robin Schott for giving me this opportunity to rewrite a paper that appeared originally in *Hypatia* 18:1 (Winter 2003). My reflections on this topic have been aided by discussion with many people, especially Virginia Held and Claudia Card.
2. See www.un.org/News/dh/infocus/terrorism/sg%20high-level%20panel %20report-terrorism.htm.
3. "Responding to the Evil of Terrorism" (Jaggar 2003, 175–182). A somewhat different account is given in "What is Terrorism, Why Is It Wrong and Could it Ever be Morally Permissible?" (Jaggar 2005, 202–17).
4. Of course, war is invariably harmful to civilians and often provides occasions for deliberate terrorism, but the rules of war forbid direct military attacks on civilians, who may be harmed only as an unintended by-product of military activity, nowadays called "collateral damage."
5. Such crimes are usually portrayed as expressions of personal prejudice, but when they are also intended to intimidate other members of the group in question, they are better understood as acts of terror. Although the FBI categorizes attacks on abortion clinics or employees as hate crimes, it is difficult to see how they are not also terrorist.
6. Thus, Hitler's bombing of London, the British and U.S. carpet bombing of Dresden, and the nuclear bombing of Hiroshima and Nagasaki, which some regard as acts of state terror, were different from the My Lai massacre perpetrated by U.S. forces in Vietnam, which was punished by the U.S. authorities. Although the distinction between state and non-state terror is conceptually clear, it is often difficult empirically to discover whether or not particular military atrocities were officially condoned.
7. Despite Savimbi's well-known record of terror, U.S. President Ronald Reagan described him as Angola's Abraham Lincoln, and he described the contras as "freedom fighters," famously asserting, "I am a contra."
8. When the World Trade Center, Pentagon, Congress, and White House are seen in this light, those who work there might be conceptualized as more than private citizens. Alternatively, their deaths could be regarded as collateral damage. Construing the objects of the 9/11 attacks as political targets supports interpreting those attacks as acts of war. However, the attacks were unlike

acts of war in that they seem not to have been part of a large-scale assault on the United States and no state has claimed responsibility for them.

9. These conventions are listed on the UN Web site at www.undcp.org/terrorism_ conventions.html.

10. In World War I, 20 percent of the casualties were civilians, but in World War II, 50 percent were civilians. Eighty percent of the casualties in the Vietnam War were civilians, and about 90 percent of the casualties of today's wars are estimated to be civilians (Pettman 1996, 89; cited in Peterson and Runyan 1999, 117).

11. For instance, an excellent article by Daniele Archibugi and Iris Young, "Envisioning a Global Rule of Law" (2002), argues very persuasively that terrorism should be addressed through law enforcement rather than military strategies.

12. In a speech given to the Southern California Americans for Democratic Action at the University of Southern California in Los Angeles on February 17, 2002, U.S. Congressional representative Dennis J. Kucinich (D-Ohio) charged that the Patriot Act violated the First, Fourth, Fifth, Sixth, and Eighth Amendments to the U.S. Constitution. These amendments guarantee the rights to free speech, peaceable assembly, probable cause, due process, a prompt and public trial; and protect from unreasonable search and seizure, indefinite incarceration without trial, and cruel and unusual punishment.

13. Kamala Kempadoo presented this perspective on the Convention against Transnational Organized Crime in a lecture on "Trafficking for the Global Market: State and Corporate Terror" at the University of Colorado on March 8, 2002.

14. This inference is mistaken; as Claudia Card points out, "Evildoers need not be evil people" (2003, 4).

15. See www.un.org/News/dh/infocus/terrorism/sg%20high-level%20panel %20report-terrorism.htm.

References

Archibugi, Daniele, and Iris Young. 2002. Envisioning a global rule of law. *Dissent* 48 (Spring): 27–32.

Card, Claudia. 2002. *The Atrocity Paradigm: A Theory of Evil.* Oxford: Oxford University Press.

———. 2003. Questions regarding a war on terrorism. *Hypatia* 18 (Winter): 164–74.

Gould, Carol, et al. 2002. Gender and Terrorism symposium at the Pacific Division meetings of the American Philosophical Association, Seattle, Washington, March 2002.

Jaggar, Alison M. 2003. Responding to the evil of terrorism. *Hypatia* 18 (Winter): 175–82.

———. 2005. What is terrorism, why is it wrong and could it ever be morally permissible? *Journal of Social Philosophy* 16 (2): 202–17.

Peterson, V. Spike, and Anne Sisson Runyan. 1999. *Global Gender Issues.* Boulder, Colo.: Westview Press.

Pettman, Jan Jindy. 1996. *Worlding Women: A Feminist International Politics.* London: Routledge.

Schott, Robin May. 2003. Introduction: Special issue on feminist philosophy and the problem of evil. *Hypatia* 18 (Winter): 1–9.

13 The Vertigo of Secularization: Narratives of Evil

María Pía Lara

Those who hurried to write something about September 11, 2001, were prone to make errors of judgment because the events of that day were so difficult to comprehend. A few years have passed, and this act of terrorism still haunts us. The legacy of terror is something that will reverberate in our global era until we are capable of properly analyzing this new type of terrorism that worships death and destruction, disguising itself behind the excuse of fundamentalist "religious views." If we are to believe the terrorist's claims of righteousness, their means and their ends were disproportionate. Clearly, their ultimate goal was to erase the notion that politics can play a role when disagreements appear in the realm of world affairs. For those who were trained by Osama bin Laden, and for those who supported him and his followers in Afghanistan and elsewhere, nothing is subject to dialogue, to negotiation, or even to public confrontation. This is what makes them a new breed of terrorists. Their goal is to erase the enemy by whatever means are necessary.

In order to learn from this disaster, it is important to study Hannah Arendt's work closely. Arendt does not suggest that any good can be derived from such evil actions (1976, viii). She distrusted the idea that we could learn something useful from pure cruelty, yet she believed that in order to recover the political realm of human affairs, we need to exercise some kind of judgment. She once called such judgments "reflective" (1992, 54), although most of the time, she referred to it as "understanding" (1994). It is not possible to speak in terms of "reasonable causes" because there can be no justifiable cause for terror and cruelty exercised against other humans. This much was clear for Arendt when she first set her agenda of understanding the features of totalitarianism.

The first thing Arendt focused on was the need to seek new categories for what she called the "unprecedented" (1976, viii). She then attempted to understand the unprecedented characteristics of deeds, what they suppress from ordinary life, and the way their goal of erasing human reactions was achieved (439–41). We could not have done this in the first few weeks after September 11, even though we learned a great deal about the perpetrators and their goals during those early days after the terrorist attacks on the World Trade Center and the Pentagon. What has come out clearly now is how carefully the terrorist's goal of total destruction was constructed. Their disregard for life, even of their own members, was evident after we saw the video of bin Laden mocking his own agents' lack of understanding of the ultimate reason they were flying those planes.[1]

Adding to our understanding of these terrible events, the *New York Times* began to publish the documents found in the places where the terrorists were trained. With such information available to us now, we can see how carefully they were trained, how sophisticated their skills and tactics became, and how wide their influence in many Muslim countries remains (Chivers and Rode 2002).

In order to learn from Arendt's approach, I will focus on some of the unprecedented features that make this kind of terrorism representative of a newly emerging world political confrontation. First, the terrorist attacks on the World Trade Center and the Pentagon must be understood as a part of the radical expression of the vertigo of secularization. I define this concept as a historical reaction that we humans repeatedly feel when pluralist conceptions of life-worlds confront others. We face these vertigos when we question the rules of social interaction and the efforts we must provide for grounding politics to authority. Plurality forces us to learn how to live with others.[2] The idea of the "vertigo" emerges when societies cannot return to previous ways of thinking about political authority and about the legitimating role that religions used to play. Arendt captured a perfect image of this "vertigo": "Nothing perhaps distinguishes modern masses as radically from those of previous centuries as the loss of faith in the Last Judgment: the worst lost their fear and the best have lost their hope. Unable as yet to live without fear and hope, these masses are attracted by every effort which seems to promise a man-made fabrication of the Paradise they had longed for and of the Hell they have feared" (1976, 446). Thus the vertigos of secularization are caused by our need to justify the autonomy of political authority.

I believe that we have not understood the problems and complexities that our societies face in grounding political orders when challenged by wider claims of justice, especially when excluded groups struggle to defend the rights of individuals and minorities. It is when societies confront injustices exercised against different groups that we face the need to separate our political orders from totalistic religious views. All religious views have ideas about justice, but they are not really universal in scope and range; they all tend to exclude different groups, and women are an important target of most religions. Historically, most of the West sought a way out of these problems when they thought that political institutions should be separated from the religious realm in order to avoid conflict. Just how the West did it, and how it still copes with its fears, would now need to be revisited in light of the historical rise of many religious communities that define themselves by their opposition to leaving religion out of the public sphere. Thus, the problem of vertigos of secularization remains an open subject.

There are no easy answers to the many questions that arise when we face our vertigos (see, for example, Euben 1999). Max Weber called these Western processes of secularization a measure—not a solution—to cope with them. He described the demise of a transcendent order of things from which to derive standards and criteria for establishing all kinds of truths. Weber linked these processes to the ways in which purposive rationality rearranged our values in terms of efficiency and orderly goals for capitalist societies. He argued that as a reaction, societies felt "disenchanted," a phenomenon that entailed the gradual disappearance of magic and of the religious forces that had previously given meanings to the world (1978, 30). Under our global conditions of communication and interaction, of immigration and of massive mobility of people from all over the world, all values have been eroded. Worldviews have multiple influences, and it is impossible to keep religious views uncontaminated or unquestioned. These are the factors that seem to have triggered new vertigos, new fears and violence. Even if there is a significant Islamic geographical expansion (North Africa, Middle East, South Asia, sub-Saharan Africa—and in the wake of immigration, now Europe and North America must be included in this list), there are other religious views that reflect the importance of the need to question the reasons for these revivals. The argument of this chapter is that this revival obeys political-fundamentalist goals.

Weber's disenchantment has become widespread in our global era, not because societies can aspire to live in idyllic harmony, but rather because the pressures of global mobility force us to confront the challenge of living inside a plurality of worldviews. Nonetheless, we will need to bring new concepts that express "the doubts and demands that were already just below the surface of consciousness" about our need to rethink the role of religions in our post-metaphysical times (Bellah 1991, 158).[3]

Thus, I agree with Roxanne Euben's conclusion that "despite crucial differences, Christian as well as Islamic fundamentalists share a preoccupation with the erosion of values, traditions, and meaning seen as constitutive of post-Enlightenment modernity" (1999, 15). Conservatives from all over the world experience the erosion of values as new vertigos of secularization. People have struggled to bring back religious views, and their insistence on closing themselves off from the rest of the world is part of their strategy to prevent the contamination of religious beliefs. I see this dynamic of renewal of the vertigo of secularization equally felt between East and West, even among highly respected Western intellectuals. Alasdair McIntyre (1984), for example, has argued about the need to recover the virtues of closed religious communities. In the well-known collective book *Habits of the Heart* (Bellah et al. 1985), Robert Bellah argued about the need to find redemption and learning from ancient biblical traditions. For his part, Daniel Bell (1976) described the loss of Western religion in social life as a fall into pure hedonism. It is not a coincidence that Bell referred to this loss as "falling into a void." The concept of the "vertigo of secularization" seems to connect with Bell's expression by giving a literal meaning to the fall caused by vertigo. He concluded that such a fall could only lead to "nihilism" (333).

Nihilists, meanwhile, seek to re-enchant the world at all costs. One extreme example of a nihilist was Hitler, who used the imaginary fate of the German people to erect its outcome as a war against non-Germans (Bellah 1991, 66).[4] Jews and outsiders were portrayed as the embodiment of "Satanic" forces (Burke 1984, 79). Another example of this vertigo was expressed by some intellectuals in Japan who saw a "spiritual breakdown" to be the result of contact with the modern West. Even a left-wing progressive intellectual from Japan, Takeuchi Yoshimi, claimed that "the modern remains an unsolved problem for Japan" (Bellah 1991, 65). Bin Laden emerges as a warrior-prophet whose aim is to re-enchant the world. He uses weapons and narratives to craft his story carefully and defines his view with a symbolic construction of good and evil. His narra-tive of re-enchantment recreates a world where all the symbols of the Muslim past are brought back to justify his view of jihad. He portrays Muslim history as a continuously linear saga of humiliations (see Bellah 1991, 149).[5] These are described, not as historical failures of the Muslim peoples, but as explanations of the way they became victims of the West and of its "satanic" forces (see Lewis 2001, and Miller 2001).

Similarly, George W. Bush has used his own narrative of political theology to justify the need for a state of emergency (a state of exception from the law). In this narrative, Muslim fundamentalists appear as pure evil, and security is the model by which the United States has managed to become an international police.

With regard to bin Ladin's narrative, we can see how it becomes useful for various purposes. The first is to capture the interest and unconditional support of disenchanted young men who have lost hope in the promise of modernity. Postcolonial experiments to build modern societies were not achieved because of inner corruption and authoritarian rule (Lewis 2002). Thus, young men no longer believe that the promise of a democracy can foster important new devel-opments to their countries. The second purpose is to ensure that the influence of the West is seen by these young men as a false promise. After all, all of their life experiences have been defined by poverty and tyranny (Lewis 2001). Third, this all-encompassing narrative renders these disaffected young men incapable of questioning, in their own political terms, the authoritarian regimes under which they live. It is much easier to blame others for their problems. Fourth, this type of narrative has always been a useful way for authoritarian regimes that foster anger toward the West to disguise their own failures.

Meanwhile, the second kind of narrative—that employed by the Bush administration—is also orchestrated to reach specific political goals. The first is to use the need for security as an excuse to extricate the government from the constraints of law. Shortly after September 11, 2001, a debate about the political and social construction of these events, as played out by the Bush administra-tion's narrative, emerged. What began as a description of tragedy became a fa-talistic rhetoric intended to shake up and frighten Americans. The goal was to build a police operation against an enemy that had already become intangible because this new kind of terrorism was not represented by a state or one single ideological group. This was a very effective excuse used by the Bush administration to justify the state of exception and the U.S. decision to go to war against Iraq.

On the other hand, politically speaking, authoritarian regimes feel the need to prevent collective discussions of their political institutions, their inner corruption, and their failure to treat their societies respectfully. Their citizens' past inexperience in building democratic institutions leads them to believe that the Western promises of modernity will not relieve their fears or fill their needs. Instead, they look to the magical power of religion. This constitutes the new re-enchantment: a belief that the promise of redemption that has been lost can be resurrected by fighting a "religious war" to bring it back. Thus, bin Laden offers them a vision of redemption and of re-enchantment. Through this vision, he becomes the new prophet of fundamentalism.[6]

Thus, bin Laden's narrative traces the origins of his people's suffering to the destruction of the Muslim empire. It goes back to its historical defeat in the seventh century, where he situates the beginning of Muslim victimhood.[7] The metaphor of victimhood is always useful because it immediately appeals to hidden emotional and psychological states of being. These appeals are then fused with the idea of revenge. Numerous examples demonstrate the way victimhood easily becomes the imperative of revenge. Think, for example, about the Serbs' quest for revenge against Croatians because of the role Ustashi (secret police) played during World War II. Serbs also blamed other ethnic groups for grievances that went far back in history (Cohen 1998).

To maximize the emotional elements of his narrative, bin Laden needed the figure of Satan. His goal was to portray the United States as the embodiment of all evils. The United States is thus seen as a civilization that unleashes the dark forces of Satan. The Koran describes Satan as "the insidious tempter who whispers in the hearts of men" (Lewis 2001, 63). As Seyla Benhabib noticed recently, these young terrorists only see the United States in relation to movies and television shows, not in relation to parliaments and institutions of democracy (2001, 36). This description should help us understand the temptations they experienced while being exposed to life in the West, and their need was to replace those "sinful" feelings with struggle, and finally with redemption. This may well be one of the factors that drive young men to seek their jihad as a way out of their fear.

Fear has also been used by the Bush administration's discourse to capture the approval of American citizens. Its policies seem to offer concrete, pragmatic ways of fighting terrorism to achieve security. What began as a tragedy was successfully manipulated to define good and evil in a theological narrative reminiscent of the clear binary descriptions of friends and foes given by Carl Schmitt (1996). Americans were portrayed as the forces of good. Christianity needed a new crusade against all infidels. To respond to an extreme fundamentalism, there must be universal ideas at state. Thus, the United States became the world police defending the sacred values of the West, and this new kind of war became the best expression of a state of exception.

Both narratives portray the enemy either in the abstract or in nonhuman terms. Civilians are represented as having no particularities—no individuality. Both enemies are portrayed as infidels, and Satan possesses their souls. These narratives prepare the groundwork for an understanding of the world as a struggle between purity and sin: the world is divided into those who possess faith and those who side with Satan. The rigorous work of trying to understand complex societies is replaced by a much simpler exercise. Instead of seeing a complex web of failures to understand each other, they see those "others" as conspiratorial forces. Instead of critically assessing the concrete successes of certain societies as interesting examples embodying certain values, those narratives portray them as manipulative and heartless. Instead of understanding how each society develops certain characteristics and not others, all are classified either as sinful or as struggling to become pure. Bin Laden's account never mentions factors such as hunger or poverty. His tale about the imperial drive of Satan to control the world has influenced many Muslim people who see the terrorist attacks as a "hard-core plot" orchestrated between Americans and Jews (Miller 2001). For those who naïvely believed in the narrative of the Bush administration, the Muslim world became the geography of fear and all true Muslim believers became a possible threat to their lives. Paradoxically, in both tales the Manichean version of the enemy as the embodiment of all evils leads to the idea of radicalizing the political goal that Carl Schmitt once imagined when thinking about war (1996, 26–35). Rather than opt first for legalizing war as Schmitt wanted (33), however, the goals of bin Laden and the Bush administration are to erase the exercise of deliberative politics from the global scene by making religion the most political of issues. Their war knows no rules.

The politicization of religion is the worst expression of the vertigo of secularization. For example, in the training camps where bin Laden orchestrated his plot, criminals became Afghanistan's aristocracy. Benhabib has called attention to the similarities between totalitarian states and nation-states in decay like Afghanistan: "The breakdown of the rule of law, the destruction of representative and democratic institutions, the pervasiveness of violence, and the universalization of the fear are features of both state-forms" (2002, 36). Thus, the similarities drawn by Benhabib allow me to understand what Arendt meant when she concluded that in places like Nazi Germany—or in this case, Afghanistan—everything can happen, everything becomes possible (1976).

The political theology used by the Bush administration is also the result of a vertigo of secularization. The political virtues of democracy have been eroded as a reaction to the terrorist attacks of September 11. A new arbitrary system of security has eroded the rights of non-citizens, who have ultimately become the subjects of persecution by a state. This state of emergency has not allowed for an open legal defense of those accused in military courts. The rule of exception also led Hitler to destroy the connection between democracy and the rule of law.

In terrorist states like Afghanistan, women, who become stateless and homeless, are the most deeply affected. Women became another key component in this new form of totalitarianism when also portrayed as the embodiment of evil. Women represent all the possible temptations that Satan whispers to Muslim men (Rashid 2002; Mardsen 1998). This has striking similarities to the way the Nazis portrayed the Jews before abducting them from their society. Thus, it is interesting to note that religion provides an excuse for making the other a political enemy to be feared even from the inside.

Recently, we have also learned about the obscured conditions of the prisoners at Guantánamo Bay and the way they have been kept hidden from public view. Indeed, Guantánamo Bay itself points to the deliberate selection of a site intended to be outside the parameters of the Constitution and resembles past historical experiences with concentration camps. What we see is the suppression of rights of individuals and the erosion of international law.[8]

Internal debates over how to cope with new expectations from women in Muslim societies and the inability to fill their needs under the most rigid interpretation of Islam law are reflected in the hardening of fundamentalist strategies against any aspirations by women. If women feel entitled to the same rights as men, there will be no possibility of a world re-enchantment or of continuing with an uncontested patriarchal rule, and no more certainty about the purity and virginity of women. Men will stop viewing women as acceptable objects of honor. By constructing a system in which women were treated as less than human, the Taliban created a new kind of apartheid. Ahmed Rashid argues that "the oppression of women became a benchmark for the Taliban's Islamic radicalism, [and] their aim to 'cleanse' society and to keep the morale of their troops high" was set accordingly (2000, 111). The Taliban's fundamentalism reacted against women with anger. The Taliban proclaimed that women's hearts had succumbed to Satan's temptations. As a result, women were banned from public view so as to be controlled and punished without public scrutiny. In sum, women were put in a contemporary form of concentration camp. Their absolute innocence was paired with a perfect state of terror (Rashid 2000, 112).

An understanding of this emerging figure of confrontational narratives of evil or of the ways in which a state becomes the police of the world should not lead us back to Samuel Huntington's (1996, 2) simplistic view of a division of us against them, a recycling of the "clash of civilizations." This reverse image of "the enemy in the mirror," to use Roxanne Euben's phrase (1999, 7), reproduces again the Manichean view that those fundamentalists held against each other. As we press forward to understand the complexities triggered by the vertigo of secularization, we should try to reconstruct the effects of those narratives through a careful, critical, political exercise of hermeneutic analysis. We must think about religion and politics by identifying the way one is used to erase the other. Religious fundamentalism is presented as an alternative to politics, not as a subject in need of public debate. We must examine the real political goals of religious views that insist on presenting themselves as redemptive narratives. The only way out of this new kind of vertigo is to understand that when religion becomes political fundamentalism, it is an artificially constructed view more connected to emotions than to reasonable arguments.

Western societies have fought for and against secularization. These different processes are still unfolding. For some fundamentalist groups of politicians from the West, religion has been brought back as an important device against their fears. Many different groups in our society are concerned now with the loss of values. Even in the most pluralistic societies such as the Netherlands, we have seen that the challenge of preserving their values is being put into question both by the Dutch people and by their immigrants' claims. They have both reacted with new fears about being contaminated. Western societies have not been free from outbursts of religious fanaticism or liberal fanaticism.[9]

Only in recent times have we tried to reconstruct how it was possible that some Western societies have dealt with grounding a legitimate political order without the sanctions from religion as their very particular creative process of understanding the meanings of religious views in secular terms. This effort was developed as a long process of creating a new realm for the political as an autonomous sphere. It did not mean that in building up this new sphere, they did not make use of religious sources for the creation of political concepts. In recent revisions of such processes we learn, for example, that "religion lies at the heart of Machiavellian politics" (Beiner 1993, 662). We have also refocused our attention in Hobbes's construction of the social contract, and we have learned that he "too, belongs to the civil religion tradition" (624). Even Rousseau, who has been the founding father of secular political thought, "left [us] with an unbridgeable tension between Christian universalism and pagan parochialism" (633).[10] The reconstruction and understanding of all these processes of creating the political reveal some of the tensions that should alert us to the importance of what I have called the vertigo of secularization.

In his very influential article "Civil Religion in America" (1991), Robert Bellah argued that in the United States the separation of state and church did not occur by denying a religious dimension in the political realm. Rather, "these have played a crucial role in the development of American institutions and still provide a religious dimension for the whole fabric of American life." Bellah recalled that this dimension of "civil religion" was found originally in Rousseau's work, and he traced the new signs of this religious understanding of symbols in the Americans who became the architects of the American Constitution. It was precisely in finding the hermeneutic traces of the interconnections between religion and politics that Bellah concluded that civil religion was still very much alive in the contemporary history of the United States. As an example, Bellah offered his analysis of Kennedy's inaugural address because "the whole address can be understood as only the most recent statement of a theme that lies deep in the American tradition, namely, the obligation, both collective and individual, to carry out God's will on earth" (1991, 171–72).

Thus, we have never fully understood the dangers and the possible liaisons that arise from a relationship between politics and religion. Our surprise at bin Laden's success in the Middle East offers us a proof of our profound ignorance. As a result of this shock, secularization is now questioned as a universal project. A recognition of the particularity of the success that the West experienced in providing an autonomous sphere for the political should not lead us to the other extreme—namely, of accepting without further examination that religion can be used for political purposes and that these goals are presented as fundamentalist claims. Thus: Are we really prepared to give up our views about the need for a separation between state and religion? Are there no interesting arguments that we can still offer for the defense of the autonomy of the political? Do we give up this way of thinking about religion and politics because Europeans were the only ones who achieved a secular state? All these questions need to be answered, and we must insist on a very open debate about these matters.

In Search of an Answer: Religion or Politics?

Our Western historical legacy owes much to those who decided that the conditions for a public political life needed the introduction of a normative criterion based on an idea of justice that included all human beings. Recent studies have shown us, however, that justice is also a term embedded with religious meaning (Escalante-Gonzalbo 2000).[11] We might even accept that the force of religious traditions in articulating moral intuitions with regard to social norms lies in the origins of political life. Certain religious representations of relevant political issues became viable candidates for acceptance into political vocabulary. How were these processes achieved? First, this is not an easy question, and things did not happen all at once. Second, before granting that Carl Schmitt was right to think that the political is merely a translation of the religious, we must understand the way a political concept captures the moral content from a religious view. Perhaps the difference between a literal translation and a disclosive creation lies in the way religious content is taken from the perspective of an emotional narrative function into the creation of a political-*semantic* space. The vocabulary of the political needed some interesting disclosive views of the way societies imagined the possibility of living a good life. We can then say that when discussing matters that concern us all, we move into a space where imagination and intuition are needed, but where we possess no definitive answers.

Religion can be a source of inspiration, as we have seen. Only if there is a focus on the moral or political quality of the story can one capture its possible normative dimension. Take, for example, the creative way Hannah Arendt used religious concepts from Christianity to produce important categories of the political. She was concerned with the question of political action. Arendt knew that action is related to its indeterminacy. She was also concerned about the plurality of views in the public sphere. She carefully tried to find the ways in which our needs to socialize with each other would not suppress our freedom and individuality. Thus, she relied upon the Christian concepts of forgiveness and promises. She claimed that "the possible redemption from the predicament of irreversibility—of being unable to undo what one has done though one did not, and could not, have known what he was doing—is the faculty of forgiving." And, she added, "The remedy for unpredictability, for the chaotic uncertainty of the future, is contained in the faculty to make and keep promises" (1958,

237). Only with both categories was she able to deliver a notion of action that copes with its problematic dimension of indeterminacy and with the notion of freedom as a determinant for human action. Thus, she took from Christianity the meaning of those experiences and transposed their semantic content to a secular narrative. In doing so, she enhanced the strength of her creative view of politics with a new concept of action. The idea of political actions both as unpredictable and as possible ways of reconfiguring freedom makes forgiveness and promises good political categories. Forgiveness and promises are human actions, not universals founded as truths, shared faith, or common identity. She detached all these *essentialist* meanings always related to religious validity and managed to secularize the concepts by disclosing the new meanings in the autonomous realm of the political.

The need to understand our present crisis through a hermeneutic perspective should focus on the historical reconstruction of the secular idea of justice. In connecting this question to a religious view, we can also say that it belongs to the definition of what makes life dignified. Locke was one of the first modern thinkers to separate church from state.[12] Church and state had to be separated because heaven and earth are separate. He argued in favor of the need to recognize these two dimensions as different realms. Locke also understood that religion was a realm of unlimited debate, while the state needed measures granting political authority to the very problems of daily life. Kant's understanding of the idea of human authority was extricated from the notion of religious authority. He thought that reason should allow us to see why rational debate would better provide us with clues to configure a way to grant the moral and political authority for our social and political norms. Kant also sought to divide justice from the realm of the good life. By visualizing justice in the territory of the public sphere, he secured the enjoyment of religious practices as parts of the private life of individuals, granting them a freedom of existential choices. Thus, Kant gave reason its authority by identifying it as an exercise of public deliberation.

This historical discussion has never been settled. In later developments Rawls occupies an important position because he was concerned with the place of religion in a liberal order. In his view, religion and questions of the good life were first excluded from the public use of reason, as Kant once claimed. Later on, however, Rawls transformed his comprehensive doctrine from *A Theory of Justice* to *Political Liberalism,* where he used his concept of overlapping consensus as the collective measures accepted by the different parties participating in debates in the political life despite their differences in the reasonable comprehensive doctrines of citizens. In the latter work, Rawls demonstrates that religious believers can be as respected as those who are nonreligious if they are able to reach political and social agreements based on reasonable attitudes.[13] With this move, Rawls was able to provide the fact of pluralism without giving up the mutual respect from parties as morally and politically reasonable equals. The challenge of transforming the members of diverse parties into rational individuals was replaced by the challenge of finding a way to encompass the greatest possible number of these diverse parties to agree on certain matters without fundamentally transforming them.

Though Rawls meant to dispel the vertigo of secularization, his position brought to light interesting nuances about the complexities of plural societies when engaging in public deliberation. One possible objection, claims Habermas (2005), would be to believe that religious citizens would accept the division of public/private when their religious modes of behavior cannot separate existential beings from the rest. This is an objection that relates to the way persons see themselves in everyday life and how their beliefs feed each and every action with pious meaning. I am sure we could also argue about other problems in Rawls's views, but what interests me is the fact that the idea of plurality remained *the most* complicated problem that the Rawlsian view was unable to solve in a satisfactory way. Rawls was not naïve about his position; he acknowledged that political reason entails the need for an autonomous sphere.

Recently, Habermas has taken a bolder and further step by arguing that we might have entered a post-secular stage. With massive migration and global mobility, we have realized that our perspective of a secular state has imposed an asymmetrical burden on the religious part of the population. This is why Europe is living under a new crisis, for as Habermas argues, "against the background of the rise of religion across the globe, the division of the West is now perceived as if Europe were isolating itself from the rest of the world. Seen in terms of world-history, Max Weber's Occidental Rationalism appears to be the actual deviation. The Occident's own image of modernity seems, as in a psychological experiment, to undergo a switchover: what has been the supposedly 'normal' model for the future of all other cultures suddenly changes into a special-case scenario" (Habermas 2005). As a result, those communities distrust liberal and secular views of societies and question their ideas as prejudices. Thus, Habermas argues, we must undertake a collective effort of hermeneutic self-reflection. We cannot envision modernity as a faith and then speak coherently of the separation of religion from the state. By criticizing secularists as falling prey to their own vertigos, Habermas stresses that we must realize the limits of secular reason and begin a wider debate between secularist and religious views with the aim of recovering important insights for a political life from both views. Habermas now defines this postmetaphysical stage as one that rejects a narrow, scientific conception of reason that is skeptical of the exclusion of religious doctrines from the genealogy of reason.

Habermas's new position has immediately generated a very interesting and clarifying debate. One of his main interlocutors has been Cristina Lafont, who responded to Habermas's Holberg Prize lecture with her own critical input. Lafont's paper not only revises Rawls's position but also clarifies why Habermas's further step does not solve Rawls's problems and might even open new ones. Indeed, Lafont argues that in trying to spare religious citizens from the burden of losing their integrity because of the need to leave behind their religious views, Habermas puts the burden now on the secular citizens, who would have to leave behind their cognitive claims about their secular and political reasons. Lafont claims that the real danger lies in the cases where conflict will not be capable of allowing the translation of religious arguments into their secular form.[14] She clarifies that because the state is a political institution, it needs secular rules. We cannot and must not confuse political justice with the legitimate claim about the need to think of how to expand our notions of equality and reciprocity, which should be granted to citizens in the informal public sphere.

Our need to defend the political institutions of a state that aims to achieve neutrality toward all citizens cannot fall prey into the other extreme side of the vertigo of secularization. Allowing the religious views to come back into the public sphere without a translation can be a dangerous step. Neutrality should help promote the secular ends of a democratic state by equally protecting all of the citizens and their rights of participating only if they accept the extra obligation of checking their arguments against other people's critical views. It is also Habermas (2001a) who has explained this stage as "the reflective thrust" of societies (2001c). It takes permanent effort to force people to be open to self-reflection. If Habermas's conditions seem hard to accomplish, it is because the reflective thrust requires that persons be willing to accept others with different faiths, to accept the epistemological difference between secular and sacred knowledge, and to recognize the priority of secular reasons in the political and social arenas because they make the transparent connection of egalitarian individualism with the universality of law and morality.

We should recall that Habermas works by means of an overarching proceduralism: Agreements are met only on the grounds of rules of communication.[15] The reason is that a reflective thrust was possible only because of the simultaneous creation of public spaces of democracy. The more the others were present, the more evidence of the impossibility of a pure, closed, idyllic society appeared. Building a political space that allows different worldviews to coexist has never been an easy goal. Globalization has only exacerbated those conditions. Why certain groups are willing to give up violence in order to survive as members of an open community is still an important question for us to answer. Perhaps the need to survive as a community has to do with learning to become an open, decentered society. This reflective thrust cannot be grounded in a Hobbesian view of the political (Hobbes 1985). It takes the efforts of others, such as Kant (1912) and Rousseau (1978), to say that fairness, not fear, should be the reason we obey political rules.

Our understanding of the basic conceptions for an open world has since been discussed as an open end in itself (Benhabib 2001). If the secular state is not a sufficient condition for guaranteeing equality of freedom for everybody, there must be proposals of what we are capable of allowing to become the new normative conditions for a real plurality of views to be represented in the public sphere. Conflicting parties should establish agreements based on a fair compromise about their exercise of positive freedoms (to act by the informed faith) and negative freedoms (to refrain from banning or allowing others to believe). The basic principles of respect and tolerance need to be developed from a new concept of what it entails to be impartial—"blind to any religion." They should allow us to see that it is fair to accept the shared respect for our mutual beliefs. Tolerance should be a device that promotes a suspension of our judgments until public debates allow us to see clearly, with reasons, what can or cannot be tolerated by all sides. Tolerance should be defined as a civic obligation of learning to take the perspective of the other.

In the end, this is what Arendt would say about our effort to build up an artificial world of human affairs. She praised the political as the most creative—albeit complex—part of the life of communities. When plurality is seen as an important and irreversible fact of a growing global world, we are confronted with the need to define new strategies to avoid the politicization of religion while still allowing debate in the public sphere. Plurality and openness can become worthy political virtues. To open oneself to others is to ensure no success of dispelling the vertigo once and for all. In accepting the political rules for modern social interaction, we reach an understanding about the irreversibility of the process of modern complex societies as being decentered. If, on the contrary, we close ourselves to the demands of plurality, violence becomes a necessary resource. No totalitarian regime has been possible without violence.

The vertigo of secularization only shows the way humans struggle to live without an idea of a final judgment. Secularization should not be seen as an ultimate goal, but rather, as a particular complex process of building up a political state. Secularization, then, is not a Western panacea, but rather one political example—a model—in which we Westerners continue to learn how to cope with our religious fears in an open society. If we are conscious that societies struggle against the growing complexity of pluralism, we need to be in permanent alert about our own vertigos. Contemporary Western democratic societies should start discussing their way into this stage of becoming or not becoming a post-secular society. Such a project implies that we face the challenge of learning to open a dialogue with many non-Western cultures in a fair way. If we are already living with clear notions of rights, we need to examine the question of how to cope with the demands that religious people make when they are confronted by a secular state. The terrorist attacks seem to have had a profoundly negative effect on perceptions of whether Western societies see those goals as truly possible. Thus, the imperative for us is to try to understand how the vertigo of secularization assumes newer shapes whenever society's basic beliefs are confronted with the beliefs of others.

In conclusion, Muslims are not the only societies that seem to be experiencing a struggle with this kind of vertigo. We are questioning whether we need to convince others of some of the advantages about what it means to live as an open society (see Stille 2002; Cahill 2002; Sengupta 2001; and Rushdie 2001).[16] The fundamentalists' appeal to violence on both sides is proof that we do not possess a consensual view in these matters. But the danger of becoming a closed society remains in both sides as well. In the face of this crisis, we should remind ourselves about the challenge of our modern societies when reacting against terrorist threats in theological terms. Western societies have fought fiercely with different forms of fanaticism. At the dangerous crossroads where we are now situated, violence has forced us to take part in this struggle, but we must do so by reinforcing the democratic institutions that can make our world possible. Our global world has forced us to enter into this stage anyway, for nothing will ever again be only "theirs" or "ours." That is because of the continuing complexity of plurality: we all live now in a small world, but on a global scale.

Notes

For their commentaries, I wish to thank Nancy Fraser, Eli Zaretsky, Maeve Cook, Andreas Kalyvas, Nadia Urbinati, and most especially, Massimo Rosati, Martin Saar, and Ina Kerner.

1. I am talking about the third video, first presented by Al Jazeera (the Arab media) and then widely viewed in the United States in December 2001. For written information about bin Laden's images on video, see Sachs 2001; Kifner 2001.

2. As it will be clear throughout the development of this chapter, I claim that most political concepts have a connection to religious meanings or derive their meaning from religious roots (see, e.g., Bellah 1991).

3. See Bellah's essay "Islamic Traditions and the Problems of Modernization" (1991, 146–66). See also Geertz 1968.

4. See Bellah 1991, especially chap. 4. See also Burke 1984.

5. Bellah argues that "the early community under the prophet and the rightly guided caliphs is a paradigm to which they [Muslims] return again and again [and] from which they draw an understanding of their own times" (1991, 149).

6. Recall Weber's definition of the prophet: "We shall understand 'prophet' to mean a purely individual bearer of charisma, who by virtue of his mission proclaims a religious doctrine or divine commandment," and "The prophet, like the magician, exerts his power simply by virtue of his personal gifts" (1993, 46–47).

7. Bernard Lewis explains that "under the medieval caliphate, and again under Persian Turkish dynasties, the empire of Islam was the richest, most powerful, most creative, most enlightened region in the world, and for most of the Middle Ages Christendom was on the defensive. In the fifteenth century, the Christian counterattack expanded. The Tartars were expelled from Russia and the Moors from Spain. But in southeastern Europe, where the Ottoman sultan confronted first the Byzantine and the Holy Roman Emperor, Muslim power prevailed, and these setbacks were seen as minor and peripheral. As late as the seventeenth century, Turkish pashas still ruled in Budapest and Belgrade, Turkish army were besieging Vienna, and Barbary corsairs were raiding lands as distant as the British Isles. . . . Then came the great change. The second Turkish siege of Vienna, in 1683, ended in total failure followed by headlong retreat. . . . This defeat, suffered by what was then the major military power of the Muslim world, gave rise to a new debate, which in a sense has been going on ever since" (Lewis 2001, 52). *New York Times* journalist Susan Sachs

claims that "the historical episodes Mr. bin Laden chose to invoke revealed much about his view of the conflicts that continue to simmer in the Arab world, placing them among Islam's greatest defeats. His reference to 80 years of 'humiliation and disgrace' was apparently a timeline that began with the end of the Ottoman Empire and the beginning of the British colonization of the Middle East after World War I" (Sachs 2001).

8. With regard to the way International Law has also been eroded by these new kinds of policies, see Günther 2005.

9. See Juergensmeyer 2000.

10. I consider Beiner's article (1993) illuminating in relation to how the Western tradition of secular politics is embedded in religious views.

11. The Mexican historian Escalante-Gonzalbo (2000) argues that we have a wider concept of justice because suffering became a moral feature of societies in the secularization of Judeo-Christian worldviews.

12. See Waldron 2002.

13. Cristina Lafont has called this the "overdetermination thesis"; see Lafont 2005.

14. Lafont argues that "if the fact that secular translations cannot be found is a good reason to allow citizens to appeal to exclusively religious reasons, why are matters so different for those citizens who happen to be politicians? [Thus], in cases of conflict, religious citizens, officials included, would remain incapable of discerning any pull from any secular reasons [and] if this is a compelling objection against Rawls' proviso, it will remain equally compelling against Habermas' proviso" (Lafont 2005).

15. Habermas argues that "this form of communication cannot even begin, unless there is prior consensus concerning important preconditions of communication. The relevant parties must renounce the violent imposition of their convictions—an imposition by military, governmental or terrorist means. They must acknowledge each other as partners with equal rights, regardless of their reciprocal evaluations of traditions and forms of life. They must also acknowledge each other as participants in a discussion in which, as a matter of principle, each side can learn from each other. In this respect, the overcoming of a fundamentalist self-understanding—of a 'fanaticism which breaks off all communication'—implies not only the reflexive tempering of dogmatic truth-claims, in other words a cognitive self-limitation, but also the transition to a different stage of moral consciousness. The boundless 'will to communication' invoked by Jaspers is driven by a moral insight which precedes everything which can be disclosed within existential communication" (2001a).

16. As Alexander Stille (2002) argues, "Despite fear, a handful of experts have been quietly investigating the origins of the Koran, offering radically new theories about the text's meaning and the rise of Islam."

References

Arendt, Hannah. 1958. *The Human Condition*. Chicago: University of Chicago Press.
———. 1976. *The Origins of Totalitarianism*. New York: Harcourt, Brace, Jovanovich.

———. 1992. *Lectures on Kant's Political Philosophy.* Edited and introduced by Ronald Beiner. Chicago: University of Chicago Press.

———. 1994. *Essays in Understanding: 1930–1954.* New York: Harcourt Brace and Co.

Beiner, Ronald. 1993. Machiavelli, Hobbes, and Rousseau on civil religion. *Review of Politics* 55 (4): 617–38.

Bell, Daniel. 1976. *The Cultural Contradictions of Capitalism.* New York: Basic Books.

Bellah, Robert N. 1991. *Beyond Belief: Essays on Religion in a Post-traditional World.* Berkeley: University of California Press.

Bellah, Robert N, et al. 1985. *Habits of the Heart: Individualism and Commitment in American Life.* Berkeley: University of California Press.

Benhabib, Seyla. 2002. Unholy wars. *Constellations* 9 (1): 34–45.

Burke, Kenneth. 1984. The rhetoric of Hitler's "battle." In *Language and Politics,* ed. Michael Shapiro. Oxford: Basil Blackwell.

Cahill, Thomas. 2002. The one true faith: Is it tolerance? *New York Times,* 3 February.

Chivers, C. J., and David Rhode. 2002. Turning out guerrillas and terrorists to wage holy war. *New York Times,* 18 March.

Cohen, Roger. 1998. *Hearts Grown Brutal: Sagas of Sarajevo.* New York: Random House.

Escalante-Gonzalbo, Fernando. 2000. *La mirada de Dios: Estudio sobre la cultura del sufrimiento.* Barcelona and Mexico City: Paidós Mexicana.

Euben, Roxanne L. 1999. *Enemy in the Mirror: Islamic Fundamentalism and the Limits of Modern Rationalism.* Princeton, N.J.: Princeton University Press.

Geertz, Clifford. 1968. *Islam Observed: Religious Development in Morocco and Indonesia.* Chicago: University of Chicago Press.

Günther, Klaus. 2005. World Citizens between Freedom and Security. *Constellations* 12 (3): 379–91.

Habermas, Jürgen. 2001a. *Glaube, Wissen-Öffnung. Zum Friedenspreis des deutschen Buchhandels.* Frankfurt am Main: Surkhamp Verlag.

———. 2001b. *The Liberating Power of Symbols: Philosophical Essays.* Trans. Peter Dews. Cambridge: MIT Press.

———. 2001c. Peace Prize for the German Publishers and Booksellers Association Lecture. 14 October.

———. 2005. Religion in the Public Sphere. Holberg Prize Lecture. 28 November.

Huntington, Samuel. 1996. *The Clash of Civilizations and the Remaking of World Order.* New York: Simon and Schuster.

Juergensmeyer, Mark. 2000. *Terror in the Mind of God: The Global Rise of Religious Violence.* Berkeley: University of California Press.

Kant, Immanuel. 1912. *Gesammelte schriften.* Berlin: Preussischen Akademie der Wissenschaften.

Kifner, John. 2001. America's Muslim allies: A time of trial. *New York Times,* 10 October.

Lafont, Cristina. 2005. Religion in the public sphere. Remarks on Habermas's conception of post-secular societies. A reply to Habermas's speech at the Holberg Prize. 28 November.

Lewis, Bernard. 2001. The revolt of Islam. *New Yorker,* 19 November, 50–63.

———. 2002. *What Went Wrong? Western Impact and Middle Eastern Response.* Oxford and New York: Oxford University Press.

MacIntyre, Alasdair. 1984. *After Virtue.* Notre Dame, Ind.: University of Notre Dame Press.

Mardsen, Peter. 1998. *The Taliban: War, Religion and the New Order in Afghanistan.* London and New York: Oxford University Press.

Miller, Judith. 2001. Bin Laden's media savvy: Expert timing of threats. *New York Times,* 8 October.

Rashid, Ahmed. 2000. *Taliban.* New Haven, Conn.: Yale University Press.

Rousseau, Jean-Jacques. 1978. *On the Social Contract.* Trans. Judith R. Masters, ed. Roger D. Masters. New York: St. Martin's Press.

Rushdie, Salman. 2001. Yes, this is about Islam. *New York Times,* 2 November.

Sachs, Susan. 2001. Bin Laden images mesmerize Muslims. *New York Times,* 9 October.

Sengupta, Somini. 2001. Turkey's secular experiment. *New York Times,* 16 December.

Schmitt, Carl. 1996. *The Concept of the Political.* Chicago: University of Chicago Press.

Stille, Alexander. 2002. Scholars are quietly offering new theories of the Koran. *New York Times,* 2 March.

Waldron, Jeremy. 2002. *God, Locke, and Equality: Christian Foundations in Lock's Political Thought.* Cambridge, U.K.: Cambridge University Press.

Weber, Max. 1978. *Economy and Society.* Ed. Guenther Roth and Claus Wittich. Berkeley: University of California Press.

——. 1993. *The Sociology of Religion.* Boston: Beacon Press.

——. 2002. *The Protestant Ethics and the "Spirit" of Capitalism and Other Writings.* Trans. and ed. Peter Baehr and Gordon C. Wells. New York: Penguin Books.

14 Willing the Freedom of Others after 9/11: A Sartrean Approach to Globalization and Children's Rights

Constance L. Mui and Julien S. Murphy

Jean-Paul Sartre has said that hell is other people, referring to the other's freedom as the greatest threat to our own freedom (1976, 45). The terrorist attacks on September 11, 2001, which turned lower Manhattan into a roaring inferno, represent a profound experience of evil. In less than ninety minutes, nineteen young al-Qaeda hijackers on a suicide mission killed more than three thousand people. In the aftermath of that fateful day, our nation struggled to comprehend the enormity of evil in their horrific acts. We quickly learned that the attacks were linked to a notorious Saudi terrorist named Osama bin Laden and the al-Qaeda training camps he ran largely in Afghanistan. With an elusive structure, a leader on the loose, and links to an international Islamist network, al-Qaeda would serve as a formidable adversary in our new "war on terror." And Afghanistan, once a foreign and even forbidding part of the world to most Americans, would become the first target of our new war.

As the American public learned about the Taliban's brutality, the disenfranchised young Arab men of al-Qaeda, the opium trade, the anti-American propaganda of the *madrases,* and the Taliban's sweeping repeal of women's rights, the Bush administration would capitalize on the latter politically to bolster public support for a war to depose the Taliban. But faring even worse than Afghan women under the Taliban were their children, who comprise the majority of the population. These children, many of whom were displaced or orphaned, are the most vulnerable victims of decades of war and drug trafficking, for starvation, disease, and violence define their everyday existence. The possibilities for these children are circumscribed by the same economic and political conditions that supported the Taliban and the terrorist training camps.

In this chapter, we adopt a Sartrean framework of freedom to explore questions concerning our moral obligations toward children in desperate regions of the world such as Afghanistan. As a superpower, what is our responsibility toward children in cultures that are different from our own, in war-torn regions that have been unaffected by globalization? When our leaders sent troops to Afghanistan and Iraq in the name of promoting freedom, this opened up the debate concerning our role and duty toward others who do not necessarily share our view of freedom or our values. To take up the question of the welfare of children in different parts of the globe, we propose an interpretation of Sartrean ethics—one that offers a broadly normative view of intersubjective freedom—to address the contemporary meta-ethical problem of pluralism. In our view, the Sartrean framework provides the foundation of an ethics that is much broader and more flexible in normative extent than traditional ethics without rejecting normative objectivity the way relativism does. All told, we find in Sartrean ethics the space to consider moral problems in a pluralistic world, especially those concerning children of different cultures, who are the worst victims of evil.

Sartre once remarked that the French were never so free as during the German occupation, suggesting that political freedom is most noticed when it is challenged. It is no surprise that after the 9/11 attacks public support for the war in Afghanistan maintained an all-time high. Unlike Vietnam or Desert Storm, it was easy to assume that in sending troops into Afghanistan the line between good and evil was perfectly clear. This was truly "our" war, named "Enduring Freedom" after our highest value. But as Sartre said, "We get the war we deserve" (1992, 708), and that war, like the war we would later wage in Iraq, was no different. This does not mean that we brought the 9/11 attacks on ourselves, as some critics contended (see discussion in Judt 2002), but rather that we were the ones who would ultimately decide what these attacks, and our subsequent military response in Afghanistan and Iraq, would mean to us. Indeed, we have chosen our meanings rather selectively. In Afghanistan, amidst all the talk about bringing bin Laden to justice and restoring peace and democracy there, very little was voiced in our press about the effects of *our* military operations on Afghan children. Occasionally, American camera crews provided us with images and stories of what has become of Afghanistan since our extensive bombing campaign. But while these images and stories heightened our awareness of the suffering of some of the world's most desperate children, we have yet to realize the extent to which our own freedom depends on the fate of these children.

In Iraq, our government used political freedom for Iraqis to justify the 2003 invasion. However, patriotic support for this military action, strategically named "Operation Iraqi Freedom," was much weaker, in part because the administration was unable either to demonstrate solid evidence of an al-Qaeda link in Iraq or to prove that Saddam Hussein had weapons of mass destruction that he intended to use against us. Indeed, the line between good and evil in this war was muddied by debates over Iraq's political sovereignty and the legitimacy of a preemptive strike, by our lengthy occupation, and by the mounting U.S. casualties there. But for all our skepticism, the plight of Iraqi children received little serious attention even as it became increasingly dire under the bombing campaign and subsequent insurgent strikes. Bush and bin Laden would mention Iraqi children in political speeches, but only to promote their own positions by pointing blame. For instance, in a triumphant speech shortly after the toppling of Saddam Hussein's statue in Baghdad, Bush claimed, "As Saddam Hussein let more than $200 million worth of medicine and medical supplies sit in warehouses, one in eight Iraqi children were dying before the age of five. And while the dictator spent billions on weapons . . . nearly a quarter of Iraqi children were born underweight" (Bush 2003). Similarly, bin Laden charged that U.S. sanctions against Iraq were "the greatest mass slaughter of children mankind has ever known," as he also condemned Bush for the "throwing of millions of pounds of bombs and explosives at millions of [Iraqi] children" (bin Laden 2004).

Certainly, children are harmed by tyranny, economic sanctions, and bombing campaigns, but appeals to these harms that do not prioritize children's rights are woefully insufficient. The harsh conditions for children's survival in many regions of the world are indisputable facts. Iraq and Afghanistan have ranked near the bottom on international development indexes. Under the sanctions, the quality-of-life ranking for Iraq, an oil-producing country, dropped to 127 out of 178 countries according to the 1994 UN Human Development Index. The situation has worsened as scores of Iraqis have been displaced since our invasion there. Likewise, Afghanistan has a long history of poor rankings due to decades of foreign invasion and civil wars, and its children have predictably borne the brunt of that history. Afghan children rank fourth in the world in early childhood mortality, with as many as one in four dying before the age of five (UNICEF 2005). The lack of food, clean water, sanitation, medicine, and vaccines has left people, children especially, severely malnourished and diseased. Moreover, children are more susceptible to being killed by land mines, and the United Nations has estimated some ten million mines remained buried throughout the country (Machel 1996). Afghan children have faced many other forms of brutality, including sexual assault, abduction, military recruitment of young boys, and torture of children by warring factions (Machel 1996). Conditions in Afghanistan remain quite dire years after Enduring Freedom, with infant and maternal mortality rates among the highest in the world and an average life expectancy of only forty-three years (UNICEF 2005).

Sadly, as with the oppression of Afghan women, much of the talk about the welfare of Afghani and Iraqi children has been part of a media relations campaign to buttress support for our military actions. For example, President Bush urged American children to become involved in a "character-building lesson" by sending dollars for food and medicine for their Afghan counterparts during Enduring Freedom (Bush 2001b). But while the president emphasized that the very survival of many Afghan children is dependent on this aid, he failed to point out that it was our air strikes after 9/11 that had disrupted relief efforts there, making it unsafe for relief workers to move food and medical supplies to areas where they were needed most. And yet Bush was not alone in exploiting the interests of children for political purposes. To garner support for al-Qaeda, bin Laden made numerous taped appeals on Al Jazeera television to the suffering of children in the Islamic world. Interestingly enough, considering his exploitation of Afghanistan for terrorist training camps, it was not the welfare of Afghani children but that of Iraqi children that concerned him.

Indeed, the media campaign after 9/11 exploited not only children's interests but their patriotism as well. When President Bush announced to the nation his decision to start the bombing campaign in Afghanistan, he closed his remarks by reading a letter written by a fourth-grader from a military family. She wrote, "As much as I don't want my Dad to fight, I'm willing to give him to you." What is remarkable is how the president used a child's intimation of self-sacrifice to herald a new view of freedom, signaled as much by the name he assigned to the military operations he ordered. As Bush remarked, "This young girl knows what America is all about. Since September 11, an entire generation of young Americans has gained new understanding of the value of freedom, and its cost in duty and in sacrifice" (Bush 2001a).

But exactly what is this new understanding of freedom, "its cost in duty and in sacrifice," that children are learning after 9/11, after Afghanistan and Iraq? For the president, it has much to do with the lesson of self-sacrifice valorized in the "Great Generation" of World War II. In fact, the Afghan Children's Relief Fund, which few remember, was a deliberate reinvention of similar war relief efforts. If anything, however, the new lesson on freedom is not simple. Not all acts of self-sacrifice, even those motivated by a noble desire for a better world, are laudable. After all, it was self-sacrifice that motivated the 9/11 hijackers and, more recently, other Islamist terrorists who planted bombs in Bali, Madrid, London, Sharm el-Sheikh, Iraq, and elsewhere. This raises many questions concerning the increasingly ambiguous meaning of freedom when a pluralistic worldview, one that is central to Western democracies, is a terrorist target. For example, what is reasonable or morally permissible to do in the name of freedom—should one nation impose democracy on another? Or should a person resort to terrorism whether to promote freedom for all or to promote religious fundamentalism? What are the existential costs of freedom, and what price should one be expected or willing to pay? What value does freedom have for young people in the Islamic world who would give up their own freedom so recklessly, and for young people in our country who would voluntarily enlist themselves to fight the "war on terror"? To be sure, the concept of freedom has been redefined both by the suicide bombers and by those who support the "war on terror."

Given the contrasting views of freedom that have become increasingly evident after the post-9/11 wars in Afghanistan and Iraq, we must exercise caution in adopting a Sartrean framework of freedom to sort out our responsibility toward the most vulnerable members of the global community. Who should speak for the world's children, especially those who are orphaned or live in countries without established governments, and what notions of freedom should we assume when it comes to the young? Can we philosophize about the rights and welfare of children in non-Western cultures without deference to political hegemony, without challenging assumptions of nationalism and sovereignty? In fact, some postmodern and leftist theorists, such as Jacques Derrida, have criticized human rights language as a discourse for the exportation of Western values (see Derrida 1994; Derrida 2002, 383; Grime 2000, 4). In view of such criticism, what position should we, as American feminists, hold?

While the conditions of children are a flash point for our analysis, we are mindful that it is the conditions of families that must culminate the analysis. As feminists, we see a direct link between the conditions of children and those of women. Shulamith Firestone (1970, 72) was among the first feminists to connect the oppression of women with that of children when she argued that it is only by liberating women that children could be free. Hence, our basic assumption in subsequent discussion is that any talk of children's rights must involve a serious examination of women's rights. At the same time, we recognize that the conditions of men and boys, who are often the economic providers for families in Afghanistan and elsewhere, are major factors in the quality of life for families.

It should also be recognized that questions of Western imperialism that challenge attempts to theorize across national boundaries are inevitably reframed in the present age of globalization, when even terrorism has been globalized. For instance, members of the al-Qaeda network act in the name of a common religion but not a common country; they are often connected by the Internet, which allows them to move nomadically around the world with the financial backing of global networks. Sartre's notion of practical freedom, which was shaped by the struggle for sovereignty against colonialism in Algeria that he witnessed, must cross borders to be a viable philosophy. The challenge before us is to do *philosophie sans frontières*. In the current context, this means understanding Islamic terrorist attacks against the West in part as a clash between pluralism and fundamentalism, exacerbated by rapid technological changes and vast discrepancies in wealth and resources within and among nations. At issue are the scope and limits of freedom, the possibilities for an open future for the young, and for that matter, for every one of us.

Recalling Sartre's famous warning against the danger of quietism in the face of evil (1975), we turn now to him for guidance in sorting out some of the ethical issues in question. Granted, Sartre does not do ethics in the traditional way, nor has he, to our knowledge, specifically addressed the plight of children in any of his writings. Nevertheless, we find his ethics of freedom helpful in providing a fresh angle from which to approach the problem of children's welfare in the global community. For Sartre, the promotion of human freedom is the only ethical value. But this is not as simplistic as it might sound, because in Sartre's view, freedom does not amount to doing whatever one pleases. Indeed, Sartre understands freedom, not as a unilateral concept, but one that must be analyzed in multiple dimensions. We would like to focus specifically on two dimensions of freedom, one taken from the later Sartre and the other from the early works. We find them to be particularly useful in assessing the rights of children, their developing capacity for moral agency in the context of globalization, as well as the corresponding moral responsibility toward them, responsibility that is shared by Westerners and non-Westerners alike.

The first aspect of freedom is developed in *Search for a Method* (1963, 91), in which Sartre speaks of the priority and urgency of meeting our material needs as the first condition of freedom. While cultures can and do disagree on what it means to be free, the fact remains that the freedom to do anything at all is invariably predicated on our ability to overcome the demands of the body. Thus, by connecting freedom with materiality, as Sartre has done in the later works, we can argue for certain basic freedoms that stem from our basic needs, such as the freedom from hunger, exposure, preventable diseases, and violence, the same freedoms that children of Afghanistan, Iraq, the Sudan, and other destitute regions of the world so desperately seek. Since such freedoms are so fundamental to survival, and the survival of children is vital to the survival of the human species, we have a moral responsibility to meet the material needs of the world's children that transcends cultural and religious differences.

It is therefore not an imposition of Western values to speak up on behalf of the world's children to ensure that their basic needs are met. One important effort is the United Nations' Convention of the Rights of Children (CRC), which defines children as all human beings under the age of eighteen. The CRC supports the right to life and health, the right to be with family and community, and the right to be nurtured and protected. It also condemns the trafficking of children and the recruitment of boy soldiers. To be sure, the treaty is framed in the context of human rights, which to some is a bourgeois concept that raises the question of whose values it represents. However, we must guard against any hasty or blanket dismissal of the treaty as imperialist, because it represents an important attempt by an international body to identify the most basic material conditions—life, health, nurturance, and shelter—that must be met if a person is to carry out any kind of project anywhere in the world. As Sartre would point out, one needs above all freedom from hunger to philosophize about freedom and hunger (1948; 1965, 94). In an interview, he stressed that "alienation and undernourishment relegated metaphysical evil, which is a luxury, to the background. Hunger is an evil, period" (1965, 94). We would add that hunger is an equal opportunity evil that knows no borders: the ghettos of America have starving children, just as the streets of Kabul, or Calcutta, or Niger have malnourished children.

Equally important to children's welfare are international support and compliance with the Land Mine Treaty. The treaty prohibits the manufacture, distribution, stockpiling, or use of land mines. Land mines are a major health threat to children in many parts of the world, and the freedom from mutilation and dismemberment is as basic as the freedom from starvation and disease. Afghanistan, one of the most heavily mined countries in the world, joined over a hundred nations to sign the treaty in 2002. The United States, China, and Russia are among those that have refused to sign the treaty. Recently, the Bush administration has defended the use of mines with timing devices (Bush 2004).

The second dimension of freedom, a more intricate one that we wish to develop in greater detail here, is taken from Sartre's early writings. In his essay, "Existentialism Is a Humanism" (1975, 350), Sartre offers an explicit account of freedom as the foundation of morality. Contending that all hopes of finding intrinsic values in an intelligible heaven disappear with the absence of God, Sartre proclaims that there are no preestablished moral imperatives for us to follow, no absolute principles that can prescribe in advance how we should act. As the being whose existence precedes essence, we choose without reference to any definitive, a priori conceptions of good and evil. Sartre would take this connection between freedom and morality further by arguing that authentic moral choices—what he calls "the actions of men of good faith"—have always, "as their ultimate significance (or value), the quest of freedom as such" (1975, 365). To see Sartre's point, we must again situate it in its intended atheistic framework. On a moral plane devoid of any divine guarantee or preestablished values, we have no written script for acting morally but are left to make our own ethical decisions freely. Whatever choices we make, however, must reflect our *will* to uphold freedom as our ultimate value. Now to uphold freedom as our ultimate value is to act in such a way as to aim resolutely at respecting and promoting, in every situation, "freedom for freedom's sake, in and through particular circumstances" (1975, 365). As far as Sartre is concerned, the person of good faith has but one ethical imperative: to will freedom as "the foundation of all values" (1975, 365). For him, to will oneself moral and to will oneself free are but one and the same project toward authenticity.

Sartre builds upon this position by maintaining, paradoxically, that to want freedom for oneself and to want freedom for others are one and the same will. It is here that Sartre directs his attention to intersubjectivity, the realm from which ethics emerges as a concrete possibility and from which freedom derives its concrete content. Sartre explains that

> in thus willing freedom, we discover that it depends entirely upon the freedom of others and that the freedom of others depends upon our own. . . . I am obliged to will the liberty of others at the same time as my own. I cannot make liberty my aim unless I make that of others equally my aim. Consequently, when I recognize, as entirely authentic, that man . . . is a free being who cannot, in any circumstances, but will his freedom, at the same time I realize that I cannot not will the freedom of others. (1975, 366)

To see Sartre's point, it is helpful first to reflect on the very principle behind the commitment to uphold freedom as our ultimate value. If we exercise our freedom at the expense of other people's freedom, what is revealed in our action is the value we place upon selfishness or domination over freedom for freedom's sake. Indeed, we have not held freedom up as our highest value unless we make it our responsibility to promote it consistently for everyone and in every situation. The true test of this commitment to freedom thus lies in our resolve to advance other people's freedom as much as our own, and as if it were our own. It is a moral commitment through which we fashion ourselves as authentic beings.

This clarification of what it means to proclaim freedom as our ultimate value gives us a better handle on Sartre's paradoxical conflation of the commitment to will our freedom with the commitment to will the freedom of others. But there is still a second way to make sense of the paradox, and that is by focusing on the interdependence between our own freedom and the freedom of others. Whereas Sartre merely invokes the interdependent nature of human freedom in his essay, it is Simone de Beauvoir who provides a lengthy analysis on the subject. In *The Ethics of Ambiguity*, Beauvoir observes that, to actualize my freedom concretely, I must surpass the given toward an open future by realizing a series of possibilities situated concretely in the world. The latter is a human world shaped by the freedom of my fellow human beings, whose projects to surpass the given have endowed the world with meanings and structured it with possibilities. Hence, it is the existence of other people as freedom, their existence as world-forming subjects, that sets the condition of my freedom. As Beauvoir puts it, "it is other men who open the future to me, it is they who, setting up the world of tomorrow, define my future" (1948, 82). In this way my freedom depends as much on other people's freedom as their freedom depends on mine. That explains Sartre's enigmatic claim that I cannot not will other people's freedom equally as I will my own.

Now to will freedom universally in this sense is to help one another to become conscious of our freedom and to work in solidarity with others to build a more open future for all. But more importantly, it is in this process that we undergo a radical transformation in our relationship with one another. We no longer experience other people as a source of conflict, but as a community of free subjects working toward a common goal, effectively surpassing our being-*for*-others toward our being-*with*-others. Notice that this understanding of the authentic moral choice echoes, in a qualified sense, the Kantian notion of being self-legislators in the universal realm of ends. To be authentic is freely to live by the only valid ethical imperative to uphold freedom as our ultimate value, a choice that ultimately puts us in the realm of the "we-subject." Thus, by connecting freedom with intersubjectivity, as the early Sartre has done, we can argue that our own freedom is in an important sense bound up with the freedom of others, in this case the most vulnerable members of the global community. To be sure, the question of how to act responsibly toward the children of the world must be addressed in a relevant way within the current context of globalization.

This understanding of Sartrean ethics, however, raises a number of questions. Why should freedom be seen as central to ethics? Moreover, given that the general precept to will freedom cannot, for the sake of freedom, have any predetermined content, but must remain more or less a "hollow" prescription, what can Sartrean ethics offer us by way of an ethical stance that crosses cultural boundaries? Finally, how do we apply concretely the precept to will freedom universally to our responsibility toward children in desperate areas of the world? We will address these issues in the discussion that follows.

Regarding the privileging of freedom that is the hallmark of Sartrean ethics, we can defend this position by pointing out that freedom is in fact a necessary precondition, if not the most essential precondition, for any ethics. Beauvoir puts the point succinctly when she says, "There can be no ethics outside of action" (1948, 22), while quickly reminding us that "action loses its meaning if we aren't free" (1948, 20). Because morality involves concrete choices between good and evil, freedom is therefore the first precondition for morality, given that only a free being can make moral choices and only a free being can assume moral responsibility for those choices. And it is because morality requires free agency and therefore entails moral responsibility that moral anxiety is a meaningful concept in philosophy and in psychiatry. The feeling of anguish is often exacerbated when we make moral choices because of the high existential costs involved in such choices. We have seen this in Sartre's famous example of the student who was torn between joining the Resistance and staying home to care for his mother (1975, 354, 356). Only a free being can exercise moral choices, free in the sense of existing as a Being-for-itself. After all, "one does not offer an ethics to a God" (1948, 10).

The first criterion for ethics is therefore our ontological existence as lack-of-being, as nothingness, as freedom from an unchanging nature, that causes there to be value by nihilating our facticity toward our possibility. Every possibility we realize results in the creation of meanings and values that are laden with moral significance. Thus, Beauvoir concludes that "ethics is the triumph of freedom over facticity" (1948, 41). Now the same is true as we move from the ontological to the ontic realm. Empirical freedom is a necessary component to moral freedom, insofar as we must work to maintain an already existing field of possibilities or open a new one in which people can express themselves in morally meaningful ways. If oppressive forces constrain the field, then we must work to open the field for all.

The moral enterprise not only requires the choices of an agent who exists as freedom, but it also involves other free moral agents by and for whom the world is endowed with a multiplicity of values and meanings. It is in this pluralistic world of intersubjectivity that we realize ourselves morally. We can create our values and express ourselves in morally meaningful ways only on a basis created and expressed by other free beings. As such, our project can be defined only in relation to, and often by its interference with, other projects. This further reveals that the moral context is made up of concrete situations where freedoms collide and conflicts emerge. Because other people are also free to assert their will and create their own values, we experience concrete and difficult problems arising in our relations with them. And ethics is born as we attempt to negotiate our way through these problems, to surpass them toward new situations and problems in a pluralistic, ethical context.

This discussion drives home the primacy and centrality of freedom in any moral context, even as it also demonstrates that no ethical theory can operate without securing to an extent both the ontological and practical implications of human freedom as its foundation. Now Sartre would make a case for freedom as our ultimate value by appealing to his ontology. Because to be human is to exist as freedom, Sartre would insist that freedom is a value, in fact the only value, that comes, not from some transcendent external source, but from our very own existence. As the uniquely human value that is rooted in the very structure of our existence as moving-beyond-toward, freedom must be respected universally if we are to respect humanity as a whole. To operate in bad faith is therefore "inhuman" or "inhumane" in the sense of working against what it means to be human.

Admittedly, this appeal to Sartre's ontology explains primarily that the universal value of freedom is directly drawn from our existential structure. At best, it only suggests that freedom would be the one value to uphold if we are to have any value at all. And yet it does not explain why any value, including even the one value that stems from our very existence, should be upheld at all. To address this point, we must keep in mind that we exist in an increasingly global community, where power and resources are not shared equally, where our freedom and other people's freedom collide and conflict even while they are bound up with one another, and where the most vulnerable members of the world community will continue to bear the brunt of such inequalities and conflicts in the absence of any intervention. To hold a thoroughly value-free position of relativism is in essence to dismiss the moral gravity of the situation. We should take seriously Sartre's warning against the danger of quietism in the face of evil.

Having established the centrality of freedom in the moral enterprise, we now turn to the second question raised above; namely, the question of what Sartre can offer us by way of an ethical position that crosses cultural boundaries. Can an ethics of freedom have any concrete normative content to be useful in addressing international conflicts? In our view, Sartrean ethics is both normative and teleological, but perhaps not in the traditional sense. We have already seen that morality involves the fundamental project to will freedom universally. On one level, it could be said that Sartrean ethics is only vaguely or nominally normative insofar as it can never be entirely content-specific. The concept of freedom, in order to be what it is, must be left open to a large extent. It cannot dictate any particular actions, nor can it organize one's field of possibilities in any particular way. But even so, the precept to will freedom universally is not left completely hollow in the Sartrean scheme. Sartre does prescribe certain content to this mandate, although not a fully concrete one in the sense of dictating particular actions to follow. First, Sartre specifies an end toward which our project of willing freedom universally must aim—that is, we must treat other people as free, conscious subjects, as For-itself, who are capable of choosing a future for themselves. In our effort to promote freedom for all, we must respect a freedom that, like ours, is absolute. Beauvoir echoed this norm when she cautions that "an action which wants to serve man ought to be careful not to forget him along the way" (1948, 153). The goal, then, is to treat other people as freedom so that their end may be freedom. And to treat other people as freedom is to help them to achieve *their* end by joining in their struggle for freedom in solidarity.

There is a second respect in which the precept to will freedom is carefully spelled out, namely, that freedom should be respected "only when it is intended for freedom" (1948, 90). To see this point, it is important to understand that, for Sartre, freedom does not amount to a brute will to power, an anarchy of personal whim, or a conflict of opposing wills locked up in their own solitude. As such, not all freely chosen actions should be condoned simply because they are an exercise of freedom; it all depends on the intended goal or end they seek to attain. This puts us in a position to fill in at least part of the normative content of the precept to will freedom: it involves not merely the positive movement to promote for everyone a more open future, but also the negative movement to condemn any action, as freely chosen as it may be, that strays, flees, or resigns itself from freedom. We can conclude from this discussion that Sartrean ethics offers a broadly normative view of intersubjective freedom. Its normative content consists of the precept to will freedom universally, which we have spelled out in part as the affirmation of all people as free subjects and the rejection of actions that turn other people into objects by exploiting their freedom. While it has defined what authenticity requires, it nevertheless remains much more flexible in normative extent than traditional ethics, in that it is not entirely content-specific in the sense of dictating any particular actions or structuring a person's field of possibilities in any particular way. Such an ethics provides enough of a moral compass while remaining open to the many possible ways of respecting freedom in a pluralistic world.

We now turn to the question of how the precept to will freedom universally can be applied to our responsibility toward children in desperate areas of the world. As mentioned above, the CRC is a step in the right direction. Since the drafting of the CRC in 1989, a number of problems have been addressed in protocols. The issues of boy soldiers, the sale of children, child prostitution, and pornography have been added in 2002 as optional protocols and ratified by roughly half of the 192 countries. These efforts affirm the status of children as free subjects and should be supported. We must take a firm position against any practice that turns children into commodities to be exploited. It is important to treat children as free subjects—to put them in the presence of their freedom, as Sartre and Beauvoir would say—so that they will in turn value freedom.

Furthermore, in multinational dialogues and negotiations affecting the conditions of children, we urge influential governments, most notably our own, to support the inclusion of women representatives as part of their protocol. Any discussion concerning children could only benefit from women's participation because, after all, who knows more about children's needs than women, the primary caretakers of children everywhere around the globe? Recognizing, as have postmodernists such as Jean-François Lyotard (1985) and Judith Butler (1997), the power of speech and self-representation, we stress the importance of women's voices in the struggle against evil perpetrated on them and on their children. As the Revolutionary Association of the Women of Afghanistan (RAWA) points out, under the Karzai government, the Taliban and other warlords are in leadership positions again, and misogynist practices such as rape, stoning for adultery, and forced marriage have continued (RAWA, 2005). Women's voices must be heard and respected in any political discourse concerning the welfare of children.

Amidst all of the anxiety about the possibility of new terrorist attacks, it is important to track claims about freedom in the war on terrorism. Both the Islamist terrorists and the democratic liberators have shown us that much can be done in the name of freedom that actually promotes bad faith, particularly in times of widespread fear. Observing the primacy of freedom in making moral decisions, we must consider how the precept to will other people's freedom can be carried out authentically even as we experience our own liberties under siege. The Sartrean framework, which supports a normative ethics without sacrificing flexibility, gives us a useful moral compass to reassess the notion of intersubjective freedom in an increasingly pluralistic world. As a major power and a wealthy nation, America has the responsibility to take the lead in respecting freedom in the global community, first by addressing the pressing material conditions for its most vulnerable members.

Note

An earlier version of this chapter, "Enduring Freedom: Globalizing Children's Rights," appeared in *Hypatia: A Journal for Feminist Philosophy* 18 (Winter 2003): 197–203.

References

Beauvoir, Simone de. 1948. *The Ethics of Ambiguity.* Secaucus, N.J.: Citadel Press.
Bush, George W. 2001a. Presidential Address to the Nation, October 7. White House Press Release. Accessed on May 28, 2005 at: www.whitehouse.gov/news/releases/2001/10/20011007-8.html.
———. 2001b. President Asks American Children to Help Afghan Children, White House Press Release, October 11. Accessed on May 29, 2005 at: www.whitehouse.gov/news/releases/2001/10/20011012-4.html.
———. 2003. Remarks by the President on Operation Iraqi Freedom, White House Press Release, April 28. http://www.whitehouse.gov/news/releases/2003/04/20030428-3.html.
———. 2004. White House: U.S. will ban some land mines, CNN Report, February 27. Accessed on May 29, 2005 at www.cnn.com/2004/US/02/27/bush.landmines.ap/.
Butler, Judith. 1997. *Excitable Speech: A Politics of the Performative.* New York: Routledge.
Derrida, Jacques. 1994. *Specters of Marx: The State of the Debt, the Work of Mourning and the New International.* Trans. Peggy Kamuf. New York: Routledge.
———. 2002. *Negotiations: Interventions and Interviews, 1971–2000.* Trans. and ed. Elizabeth Rottenberg. Stanford, Calif.: Stanford University Press.
Firestone, Shulamith. 1970. *The Dialectic of Sex.* New York: William Morrow.
Grime, Jill. 2000. Different priorities: Child rights and globalisation. *Law, Social Justice and Global Development* 1:19.

Judt, Tony. 2002. America at war. In *Striking Terror: America's New War,* ed. Robert B. Silvers and Barbara Epstein. New York: New York Review of Books.

bin Laden, Osama. 1997. CNN Interview in Afghanistan with Peter Arnett, CNN March. Accessed on May 28, 1995 at http://news.findlaw.com/hdocs/docs/binladen/binladenintvw-cnn.pdf.

———. 2001. Text of Osama bin Laden's statement, AP Press, October 10. AP text of Osama bin Laden's statement. Accessed on May 28, 2005 at: www.ict.org.il/spotlight/det.cfm?id=688.

———. 2004. Transcript of video aired on Al Jazeera satellite television November 1. Accessed May 28, 2005 at: http://english.aljazeera.net/NR/exeres/79C6AF22–98FB-4A1C-B21F-2BC36E87F61F.htm on.

Lyotard, Jean-François. 1985. *The Postmodern Condition: A Report on Knowledge.* Trans. Geoff Bennington and Brian Massumi. Minneapolis: University of Minnesota Press.

Machel, Graça. 1996. *The Impact of Armed Conflict on Children.* New York: UNICEF.

RAWA. Web site accessed August 10, 2005, at: www.rawa.org/wom-view.htm.

Sartre, Jean-Paul. 1948. Avoir faim, c'est déjà vouloir être libre. *Caliban* 20 (October): 11–14.

———. 1963. *Search for a Method.* Trans. Hazel E. Barnes. New York: Vintage Books.

———. 1965. Jean-Paul Sartre Speaks. *Vogue,* 1 January, 94–95.

———. 1975. Existentialism is a humanism. *Existentialism from Dostoevsky to Sartre,* ed. Walter Kaufmann. New York: New American Library.

———. 1976. *No Exit and Three Other Plays.* Trans. S. Gilbert. New York: Vintage Books.

———. 1992. *Being and Nothingness: A Phenomenological Essay on Ontology.* Trans. Hazel E. Barnes. New York: Washington Square Press.

UNICEF. 2002. Afghanistan back to school: Special measures for infants and children, 9 October. Accessed 21 January, www.unicef.org/noteworthy/Afghanistan/index.html.

UNICEF. 2005. Afghanistan Statistics. Accessed August 10, 2005 at: www.unicef.org/infobycountry/afghanistan_afghanistan_statistics.html.

United Nations. 1989. *Convention on the Rights of the Child.* Document A/RES/44/25.

15 Terrorism and Democracy: Between Violence and Justice

María Isabel Peña Aguado
Translated by Jana María Giles

> But while violence can destroy power, it can never become a substitute for it.
>
> Hannah Arendt, *The Human Condition*

At the same time that this essay was beginning to take form, four bombs exploded in London, sowing seeds not only of terror and panic but also of mistrust and rancor. For Britain, it was a new attack, but the wounds and cries, the desperation and faces of horror, the anxiety of waiting in hospitals, as well as the official discourse of condemnation are all too familiar. Certainly, the British government appears to have been quite prudent in measuring out images and scenes of panic and pain. One has only to note the difference between two images publicizing the attack in Madrid on March 11, 2004, and that in London on July 7, 2005. Whereas in one of the most highly disseminated photos of the Madrid attacks a young man could be seen seated on the ground, face bloody and eye swollen, with a mobile phone in his hand, in a British image we see a woman with a mask covering her injuries and her fear. This difference is not a neutral one. Nor do I believe that it comprises a difference between so-called Latin passion and British phlegm. Rather, there seems to be a clear intention in the London case to deny the attackers one of the effects most sought after by terrorists: the phenomenon of spectacle, in which fear, horror, and human pain are converted into a scene in which the actors have lost their roles and no longer know their parts. In London, at least at the government level, there has been a clear intention to continue with "business as usual," which has not always succeeded in quieting the desperation and discouragement of the population.

There is much that is aesthetic in this phenomenon,[1] not only because the images that glue us to our television screens offer us what may be an exciting vision of fear and terror. Rather, I refer to an "aesthetic" attitude or reaction toward the attacks, a mixture of vulnerability and superiority that recalls what some philosophers have identified as the "sublime."[2] In the sublime experience, insisted Kant, a moment of consciousness of the superiority of reason and morality arises that seeks to exorcise the fear and danger that present themselves as a disquieting, threatening, and uncontrollable presence (Kant 2000, §§23–29, 128–48, particularly §28, 146). At the same time—and we should not forget this—this is an exorcism that carries a violence that ultimately may appear to be compensated for not only by superior reason but also by a strong sense of freedom. Echoes of this attitude resound in our times in the insistence with which politicians and commentators claim that these acts of terror assault "our" most genuine and beloved values. In the face of the fear and sense of loss of control that these attacks awaken in us, we respond with the affirmation, also violent, of our own values, declaring them superior. The question is, which values are we speaking of, and who is included when we say "we"? Terms like *civilization, democracy,* and *liberty* immediately emerge from beneath the surface, naturally in their Western guise. Almost in the same breath we identify an implacable enemy which—to the extent that it is indeterminate—lends itself to all kinds of fantasies and speculations. These fantasies are an aesthetic phenomenon also in that they provide us with a screen on which—why not admit it?—to project and manage a threat that we concretize as a malicious and diabolical "other."

In an age when the Internet has put the world at our fingertips and when the economy, with its highs and lows, has repercussions at the global level, the political and cultural discourses nevertheless are making a detour along roads leading to a division—each day more marked—between those who consider themselves civilized and the "others," who are considered to be uncivilized. The image of Tony Blair, flanked by the leaders of the world's richest countries, condemning the London attack is significant. To the separation between wealth and poverty we now add the even more devastating difference between cultures, more devastating because its effects can be, and in fact are becoming, as dangerous as those of hunger and poverty. I do not deny that more human beings die daily of hunger than from terrorist attacks. What I refer to is a game with death and violence that not only sows terror but also, and above all, undermines confidence in a shared reality, what Hannah Arendt calls the "feeling for reality" (1998, 51). That is to say, truth is more than a shared reality; it is more a trust that has the feeling of certitude and is equally shared. It is the sensation of dependability that allows us to leave our houses and freely walk through the streets while attending to our activities, expecting and assuming a similar attitude on the part of our fellow citizens. We walk automatically when the streetlight changes, and it does not occur to us that someone will fail to respect the streetlight and take off into the intersection when we are crossing. Whoever is now placing bombs at rush hour in places such as trains and metros knows well what such loss of confidence and certitude means.

The terrible irony of the situation—as described by Pakistani novelist and essayist Tariq Ali in a newspaper article—is that it is not exactly poverty that is compelling young Muslims to strap on bombs in order to terminate their lives and take hundreds more with them at the same time. Many of those who adhere to these fanatical and violent groups believe they are reinforcing their values (and let us not forget that they also put an "our" before "values"). They justify the terror they cause as a defense of their values, a response to the way the West continues to devalue what they consider most sacred. The sad thing is that we, who do not dedicate ourselves to planting bombs, send our soldiers instead to die and kill the innocent in our place. Since we are "civilized," we speak of "collateral damage" when innocent civilians die in Iraq or Afghanistan. In contrast, what they do, in their attacks on our countries, is terrorism and savagery. We should therefore be careful of how we use language in this situation and be more honest in our use of certain concepts.

Violence

It is difficult, however, to find a language with which to express something so contrary to dialogue as violence,[3] a difficulty that increases when, as in the case of terrorism, there is a clear intent to use violence, destruction, and fear as instruments with which to accomplish a goal or impose an idea. Such an idea appears singular and irreplaceable but is nothing other than a sense of conviction in the superiority of that idea for the sake of which people are willing to kill and terrorize, an idea that legitimizes all acts of violence used to protect and feed itself, including its own destruction.

Terror, death, and their use to gain an advantage or impose an idea appear to be phenomena as linked to human history as the idea of progress or reason. Despite all their initial sympathy with the French Revolution, the Enlightenment thinkers, through whose eyes we continue to see the world, became alarmed at the dimensions that legitimate violence reached for the sake of a superior idea. Seen in this way (that is, reducing terrorism to a matter of ideas), the question becomes: When and for what reason does an idea legitimate violence in its transmission or defense? Stated another way, When does it seem just or not to fight for an idea?

In her analysis of the concept of violence, Hannah Arendt observes that one of the ideas most employed in the moment of rationalizing the use of violence is that of progress (1970, 25–31). Our faith in progress—not only social but scientific, cognitive, and technical progress—continues without slackening. Not even the pessimism that shadows our societies at the dawn of the twenty-first century is capable of dislodging the idea that in its nucleus the human collective also carries the same processes of biological and spiritual evolution that characterize each individual of the species.[4] To treat history as if it were a living thing, containing from its beginning the gene of progress, seems to be genetically programmed. It is obvious that what sustains this idea is the imperative we have to sustain hope in a future that, by virtue of its being in the future, allows us to project and sometimes postpone our most fervent desires—desires that ultimately we ourselves will not experience, but that will become the inheritance of future generations (Arendt 1970, 26–27).

Understood in this way, the present justification of the use of violence for the sake of a better future vanishes. It can only be sustained by grounding it in certain religious concepts. Ultimately, the idea of progress carries within itself the idea of a secularized divine providence, an idea that resurges in the context of the secularization of Western societies, in which a provident God is translated into a history programmed toward a necessarily better future.[5]

To repeat the question, then: Is there a good violence and a bad one, a legitimate one and an illegitimate one? It is only from this vantage point that we can understand what is happening today. The conviction that our politicians wish to sell us that ours is a "just" cause, reinforced by the discourse of progress that this idea of "justice" carries with it, is used to justify the violence and intimidation that foreign troops patrolling a city would supposedly instill. For their part, Islamic fundamentalists use terror as a tool of vengeance and a persuasive means for obliging the population to mobilize for political change in their respective Muslim countries. All these groups appeal to their own common cultural values and to an "us" that in the end represents no one, since even in Western democracies, populist movements condemning the war go unheard.[6] For our part, we not only condemn the attacks, but in criticizing the motivations of this terrorism we implicitly reject at the same time their unenlightened, fundamentalist convictions. All fundamentalism, religious or not, carries within itself the latent seed of violence. Think of Nazism, Stalinism—perhaps even Neoconservatism? As I have noted, terrorism is essentially an attitude proper to believers in a concrete ideology. The legitimization of this ideology, whether religious, political, or scientific, is marked by a fierce belief in one single fundamental truth to which we must all accordingly bow down.

A Matter of *Différend*?

Translating this scene to the philosophical terrain, we can identify our current situation, using the term Jean-François Lyotard created: the differend (*le différend*). With this concept, Lyotard precisely described the impossibility of finding a common language, a metalanguage, with which to join the different and plural ways of encountering reality.[7] It deals with a conflictive situation in which the parties fail to find a means of regulating the conflict, since such regulation is only possible by failing to do justice to one of the parties. The root of such injustice resides precisely in the failure of a universal law capable of regulating, in a plural mode, pluralism itself, which, at least in theory, presides in the heterogeneity of our democratic lives today.

Rather than understanding the state of the differend as an exception, it is necessary to see it, according to Lyotard, as the fruit of the postmodern condition on which we have disembarked since renouncing a discourse founded in the universal legitimation of one way of understanding rationalism, history, society, and progress. The pluralism of the "we" is immediately diluted by the exclusion of others who also participate as "we" (Lyotard 1988, 97–106, 147–49), a "we" that, as international terrorism exemplifies, only seeks to impose itself by means of violence and, I repeat, as rationalized in the superiority of an idea.

The problem arises not so much from the act itself as from our living in a heterogeneous world. The conflict bursts forth when all parties insist on justice without compromise. It is here, in this "agonistic" attitude, that Lyotard appears to mark one of the important characteristics of the postmodern condition (1984, 10). The question remaining is how to create a policy from these agonistic positions in which the different discourses—Lyotard speaks of language games—never appear to converge. Thus, the "war on totality" catchword with which Lyotard responded to the question of postmodernism (1984, 82), appears to be contributing, perhaps unintentionally, to maintaining these differences rather than finding means of regulating them.

In the beginning of this chapter I referred to the Kantian sublime to signal the degree to which the response of the Western world to the threat of Islamic terrorism indicates a philosophical tradition in which a concept of singular and universal reason is imposed and also in which the process of secularization and modernity begins, a philosophical tradition still prevailing to some degree today. In this context it is interesting that the reappearance of the sublime in philosophy at the end of the twentieth century would be tied precisely to the criticism to which postmodernism subjected Enlightenment rationalism, whose liberal humanism and tolerance have turned out to be a construction of "a" history that ignores others. As a model of rational and spiritual superiority, the feeling of the sublime is converted in postmodernity into a symptom indicative of the differend. Is this feeling the only possible response for those who see their vindications silenced by universalist and uniform ideas?

But if the "political philosophy" Lyotard propounds at the beginning of *The Differend* is one whose task consists in signaling the insoluble conflict that the differend expresses (1988, XIII), and this is manifested by means of a feeling of impotence and vulnerability that Lyotard reinscribes as the sublime, then what is the margin of action that is conceded us in order to put theory into practice? Or, put another way, what political praxis can arise from a ground that is ruled by silence and the insistence on absolute and total justice for each party? The options are not many, as we witness today and as was manifested in the war that shocked the former Yugoslavia at the end of the twentieth century. Absolutist assertions, although made in the name of justice, and those expressed only in the shadow of silence can only with difficulty open up space for real political action. Experience tells us that these conceptions are instead, perhaps without intending to do so, feeding resentment and the exaggerated and exalted affirmation of what are considered genuine values, which at the same time enforce boundaries of difference. I am not affirming that the political model proposed by Lyotard pretends to violence (Peña Aguado 1994, 45–52). But I do wish to indicate the dangerous game on which we are embarking while the compass of difference continues to mark the uncertain course of the imposition of the irrational superiority of each player. The violence proceeding from this idea of superiority derives, in any case, from a violence designated legitimate or illegitimate, depending upon who is using the compass.

Which Justice?

Since September 11, 2001, terrorism has ceased to be a fundamentally "provincial" phenomenon and has become a war without frontiers, displacing those national terrorisms that continue in some European countries;[8] it also has ceased to be so with regard to the equally international response that has arisen. Terrorism's indiscriminate and spectacular form of action—more ferocious and with shades of religious fundamentalism—which operates apparently with little difficulty in different zones of the planet, has been made even more clear in the attacks on Madrid and London, attacks that have likewise reinforced this transnational union in a solidarity sustained precisely by this continued appeal to common values. The German sociologist Ulrich Beck has even proposed the creation of cosmopolitan states (*kosmopolitische Staaten*), open and recognizing all types of differences, as a response to the transnationalism with which terrorism is operating. The extreme arrogance and—perhaps for that very reason—the weak point of his proposal can be discerned when he expresses what he considers a "realist utopia" in which a "cosmopolitan Europe of nations sure in themselves [*selbstbewußt*]" could arise, "acquiring [*schöpfen*] its strength from an open world-wide war against terrorism" (Beck 2002, 53). No hermeneutic feat is needed to comprehend that the "world" Beck speaks of is that marked by the patterns and cultural mores of the Western world, understanding as "Western world" the legacy of the Enlightenment tradition in which—and this should not be forgotten in the present moment—the important process of secularization has been in progress since its inception. What is most frightening in this proposal is that the foundations of such a Europe would be grounded in violence.

There has recently been a great deal of emphasis on the idea that we are confronting a "clash of civilizations." There is something in this phrase that emits an unhealthy odor of impotence and resignation. At the same time, to allow oneself to grow dizzy from the voices of those who insist on religious differences seems, in my opinion, tremendously dangerous and difficult to understand from the historical perspective that we gain—or should gain—from living in the twenty-first century. We have room for more tolerance and perspective by analyzing our much-vaunted rationalism. Undeniably, the Islamic terrorism that confronts us now, as well as the manner in which we are reacting, tends to indicate a political sphere characterized more by religious and cultural emotions, thus contaminating what could result from dialogue and joint nonviolent actions.[9] This contamination, in my opinion, clouds the fact that we are above all talking about violence and the legitimization of its use on the basis of one or another set of cultural and religious values that each side sees as legitimately responsible and defensible.

The rejection of terrorism is, or should be, consubstantial to the defense of democratic values, values based in the belief in pluralism of ideas and concepts that can, or at least should, coexist peacefully in a civil society. Nevertheless, the problem arises of how to understand this democratic coexistence, in which, at least in theory, no form of radicalism could fit, since it would essentially threaten the very idea of democracy. Disgracefully, experience tells us that we are still far from living in a true democracy, and at the same time, it makes us aware of the difficulty of maintaining the conquests of democratic values. This difficulty emanates not only from threats, real or imaginary, coming from anti-democratic sectors or ideologies. The problem arises more seriously when democracy undertakes the defense of its most genuine values by using the same methods of violence as those who it feels threatened by and whom, at the end of the day, it wishes to combat. This is when democracy begins to unravel, and the moment in which its most grave threat arises, in which it senses that the trademark of the violence—as much as that includes a "controlled" violence—is organized by the state itself. In the case of Spain, for example, the question arises: Is it legitimate that a state organizes its own terrorist group to conquer the Basque separatist group *Euskadi ta Askatasuna* (ETA)?[10] Are we not criticizing and considering terrorism as the indiscriminate use of violence to defend an idea or political choice and including, if I am pressed, a territory? If the state deploys its legitimacy in order to take advantage of those means it has at its disposal to "combat" the plague of terror, then in justifying this combat it would have to ask itself, Is there a "good" terrorism and a "bad" terrorism, a benevolent violence and a malevolent one? Apparently the answer is yes.

The question then arises as to which criteria we use to justify this benevolence or malevolence. This supposes, of course, the existence of such criteria, something problematic in itself, in its implication that violence can be accepted as a course of action, something even the early Christians absolutely rejected. Nor in the case of self-defense is the use of violence legitimized. What can be gained by the path of nonviolent resistance may be no small thing, as Gandhi showed us. Still, today only the most convinced pacifists radically defend such a position. The rest of society appears to suffer no major inconvenience in accepting the "necessity" of this "evil," which is apparently less if we employ it in defense of the honor of an Enlightenment reason but may still be represented as diabolical if it arrives with the taint of other ideologies and, even more terrible, if it originates in cultures that the West considers to be second class for not having passed through the sieve of the Enlightenment.

In this context, the present situation seems likely to result in a "clash of civilizations" in that, on the one hand, we are questioning from the perspective of postmodernity the idea of progress, and on the other, we confront theocratic concepts of "unenlightened" societies such as the Muslim world. Such a "clash," however, has many aspects to unfold before it will be induced. The same effort directed at such a clash could instead be focused on understanding that the Muslim as much as the Christian world is the descendant of Aristotle and that much of what we consider ours, including Aristotle himself, is the inheritance of the transmission of Islamic culture through Europe (Goody 2004). We also should not forget that if Islam contemplates holy war, the leading figures of our Christian tradition have similarly justified war. The concept of just war, which finds its roots in the classical thought of Aristotle and Cicero, reaches the Christian tradition via Augustine and Thomas Aquinas and certainly contradicts the radical principle of nonviolence of the early Christians, who denied even the use of violence in self-defense. The great scholastic theologians such as Suárez and Victoria and Grocio and Vattel inherited the concepts of Aquinas.

Now more than ever—and as ever—dialogue seems the single "reasonable" solution, reasonable not only from the point of view of our culture but from that of others. The cultural bridges are more numerous and stronger than we may be led to believe, since they are grounded in more shared roots than is commonly acknowledged. When all is said and done, our ignorance and mutual misunderstanding play a dirty trick on us. To recover the dialogue of cultures— which assumes, also, undoubtedly, an economic collaboration—is indispensable for our mutual peace. A true dialogue, however, is only possible if the cultures that participate are considered equally valid interlocutors. To reply that the Muslim world, for example, has not passed through the Enlightenment process— which is tantamount to saying that they have not had an emergent bourgeoisie —does not mean that they are not valid interlocutors with the West and that they are not heirs of a common millennial and absolutely respectable culture. The respect we owe their culture should not blind us to the very real economic problems they confront, on the one hand regarding development, and on the other hand as possessors of a natural resource of prime strategic importance for Western industry; it is no coincidence that Iraq as well as Chechnya are two regions with great petroleum resources.

This is the dilemma. Neither dialogue nor violence can ever resolve in favor of violence, since the justification of violence shakes the foundations of democracy to the point of its possible demise. Unfortunately, such violence has begun to emerge imperceptibly through the back door as a normal practice of democratic society. By continuing in this way, democracy will become totally delegitimized by the same appeal to violence on the part of the state that on the one hand fails to respect established democratic channels, and on the other hand nourishes and sustains the same idea of democracy. The danger comes not only from external terrorism but equally from that which is hidden in democracy's reply to this external attack. It will not serve us to slam our doors shut; the enemy is already in the house. His face is our own, his values ours. The only possibility of confronting him is to attend to ourselves and exercise our common sense. Evil, as Hannah Arendt told us, does not have a diabolical face.[11] It grows more in the swamps of ignorance and the lack of reflection.

Female Terrorists

Writing these lines I have considered many times whether the phenomenon of violence can be attributed to one sex alone. In my experience as a female intellectual and a feminist, the question acquires great relevance. If one further considers that in my own country, Spain, many women have died, and continue to die, as a result of domestic violence, the question is difficult to evade. Since they are commonly victims of violence at home, the image of female terrorists armed to the teeth and ready to put their bodies at the mercy of bombs and destruction is a shocking one. Even from the most egalitarian principles, we find ourselves surprised by the Chechnyan "black widows" who are willing to sacrifice children to their political beliefs. These images do not square with the idea of the feminine that we have learned in our patriarchal societies, yet we cannot ignore the figure of the female terrorist.[12]

From the first anarchist terrorists in Russia at the end of the nineteenth century to the Palestinian and Chechnyan suicide terrorists of today, the women who participate in these acts of violence appear to have evolved on a par with their masculine colleagues. Still, the evaluation of their actions is measured by different standards. The topic of terrorism does not appear to be the place for talking about feminism. Nevertheless, it is interesting to observe that in this matter a patriarchal vision again reigns when one tries to analyze and assess the figure of the female terrorist. When I speak of "patriarchal vision," I refer to the fact that even in this arena women continue to be evaluated by purely sexual coordinates and as rationally and morally inferior. The Palestinian terrorist Leila Khalid, who participated in the first hijacking of an airliner in 1969, was characterized as a "girl terrorist" and "deadly beauty," her actions described in terms of the idea of "beauty mixed with violence." I do not know if the beauty and attractiveness of male terrorists have ever been pondered, but it does not appear to be one of the imperative criteria for speaking of them.

The Israeli security forces, who also signal the exploitation of the image of the feminine in the unwillingness of Israeli soldiers to register Palestinian women because of the problem of physical contact, present us with an image of the female terrorist as a victim of the social and moral manipulation of the society in which she lives. These women seem to die for the Palestinian idea in order to cleanse their shame and dishonor. I am not sure if they are even promised a place in paradise. They are presented as betrayed, coerced, and victims of their own emotions and passions—and, of course, as participants in illicit relations. In the case of the Chechnyan terrorists, the above-cited "black widows," they are also presented as extensions of the masculine ideals of their fathers, brothers, or husbands fallen in battle.

The historian Walter Laqueur states that women act according to their emotions, not their reason, and that they are more fanatical and have a stronger capacity for suffering (Townshend 2002, 18). The logic of this argument is very clear and fits perfectly within the framework that has constructed the image of females, at least since the Enlightenment. Unable to use reason, and guided by their emotions and feelings, women need someone to direct their existence. On these grounds, we could argue—as Kant reminds us (1960, 81)—that if virtue in women is not authentic, neither is female evil, at least not in the sense of being justifiable beyond a mere passionate inclination. The problem is that we are always faced with the image of an extremist, whether a virtuous woman (a madonna) or an immoral one (a whore or a witch).

In their study of female terrorists, Luisella de Cataldo Neuburger and Tiziana Valentini (1996) remind us that there is a third way to interpret the phenomenon: to deny or suppress those attributes considered to be feminine. On several occasions, the terrorists interviewed by de Cataldo and Valentini point to the need to annihilate their image, transforming it into a masculine one—not only in an external way (short hair, no makeup, etc.) but also in their attitudes and the kind of language they use.[13]

De Cataldo and Valentini's study, which was first published in Italian in 1992, refers to women active in terrorist groups in Europe. Since that time, the phenomenon of terrorism has changed substantially. What we still do not know is the extent to which the traits of female terrorists have also changed, since there are few studies on this topic. Once again, there seems to be a kind of tacit but uncritical explanation of the reasons why a woman might use violence in pursuing certain aims. The figure of the woman continues to be regarded as a mere sexual object or even worse, as an asexual object, but always defined in relation to her body and seen as inferior with regard to her rational and moral capacity. Ironically, there seems to be no "clash of civilizations" in the way such a feminine image is depicted; rather, a universal criterion appears to reign.

The conclusions of de Cataldo and Valentini after interviewing several terrorist women and men are not very encouraging. The reasons that women are moved to belong to terrorist groups appear to be related to attitudes and behaviors that come from a typical feminine socialization. As Laqueur also points out, this study shows that feminine self-giving is more radical and committed when the time comes to face the consequences. The number of penitent women, for instance, is lower than the number of penitent men, contrary to what one might expect. De Cataldo and Valentini suggest that the cause of this radical self-giving, which derives from forgetting oneself, could come from the feminine model of the mother who never questions anything and lives in total self-sacrifice.[14] Both the answers of the women interviewed and the comments by the interviewers reflect the consequences for women of living without a history or an identity of one's own. From these too-often-silenced women, we see and hear that the consequences of this loss go far beyond the private realm. I will finish by quoting the words with which de Cataldo and Valentini conclude their investigation:

> No doubt the adventure of armed subversion was for women yet further tragic proof of their ephemeral social dimension. But at least they began to tell their story in the first person. They began to recoup, along with what had always been granted them by "right"—knowing how to suffer and to pay (and the resistance to penitentism is perhaps further proof of this)—even the right to tell their own story. (1996, 96).

Notes

I thank my good friend Antonio del Mazo de Unamuno for all our illuminating conversations about terrorism and violence. I would also like to thank Jana Giles for some theoretical suggestions, as well as Ruth Eppele Dickens and Mark Dickens for carefully reading through the text several times.

1.   In speaking of the aesthetic, I speak of a capacity for reflection that since the seventeenth century has been considered as the expression of excellence in humanity and culture. Beginning with Baltasar Gracián and his "man of taste" (*hombre de gusto*), passing through the Kantian capacity to judge (*Urteilskraft*), and culminating in Schiller's *On the Aesthetic Education of Man in a Series of Letters*, the aesthetic converts into a program of values and sensibilities regarding what is considered the ideal manner of human reasoning and feeling. At the same time, the aesthetic reflects the ambitions, fantasies, and fears that converge in concrete societies. This is particularly illustrated in the opposition between the concepts of the beautiful and the sublime, as seen in eighteenth-century aesthetics as well as in the recent renaissance of the sublime in the context of postmodernism. See Eagleton 1990.

2.   The feeling of the sublime is developed throughout the eighteenth century as an aesthetic feeling whose source is fear or pain. In contradistinction to the beautiful, which is peaceful and harmonious, the feeling of the sublime is caused by an experience that moves and disconcerts. The sensation of the sublime feeling therefore results in a greater feeling of relief and euphoria. The sublime reaches its highest culmination as a philosophical concept with Kant's elaboration in his *Kritik der Urteilskraft* [*Critique of Judgment*]. See Peña Aguado 1994.

3.   "Only sheer violence is mute" (Arendt 1998, 26).

4.   Arendt points out that even the "New Left" believes in this old idea of progress (1970, 23–25). Ulrich Beck also remarks that our current thinking and actions are still governed by obsolete concepts (2002, 10).

5.   It is interesting to observe how close the concepts of the sublime and progress are to each other. Since the feeling of the sublime requires a particular sensibility ("receptivity") that prepares us for culture and morality, this feeling can be understood as a sign of human and cultural superiority (Kant 2000, §29; Lyotard 1988, 170).

6.   The great irony of this situation is that the Islamic terrorist strategy of placing bombs in the most populous areas, such as metros, trains, buses, etc., reveals a faith in the democratic process even greater than that of the people in such democracies themselves, in that it shows their belief that the popular will can change, with its protests and pain, the decisions of our elected representatives.

7.   "As distinguished from a litigation, a differend (*différend*) would be a case of conflict, between (at least) two parties, that cannot be equitably resolved for lack of a rule of judgment applicable to both arguments. One side's legitimacy does not imply the other's lack of legitimacy. However, applying a single

rule of legitimacy to both in order to settle their differend as though it were merely a litigation would wrong (at least) one of them (and both of them if neither side admits this rule)" (Lyotard 1988, XI; 9).

8. As is the case with Spain, whose citizens have for the past forty years been obliged to live with the impotence and pain that terrorist acts leave in their wake.

9. "The practice of violence, like all action, changes the world, but the most probable change is to a more violent world" (Arendt 1970, 80).

10. ETA is the Basques separatist organization. The *Grupos Antiterroristas de Liberación* (GAL) is a terrorist group organized by the government that has also planted bombs, killing innocents.

11. "The trouble with Eichmann was precisely that so many were like him, and that the many were neither perverse nor sadistic, that they were and still are, terribly and terrifyingly normal" (Arendt 1963, 253).

12. Charles Townshend points out the "remarkable prominence of women in terrorist operations," looking at their presence in war. See Townshend (2002, 16).

13. "Women in armed struggle become totally interchangeable with their comrades in arms, physically and psychologically; the *mulier* becomes the *vira* of archaic Latin; women correspond in all and for all purposes to men; they are exact duplications" (de Cataldo and Valentini 1996, 94).

14. "In researching the psychological path of the terrorist, we dwelled at length and in depth on the psychodynamic mechanism that underlines the phenomenology of idealisation and on the reason that might explain the greater resistance of women to repentance. These are reasons, as we have seen, that are rooted in the specific feminine experience in the alienation of the maternal-sacrificial code by which women lived armed subversion" (de Cataldo and Valentini 1996, 92).

References

Arendt, Hannah. 1963. *Eichmann in Jerusalem. A Report of the Banality of Evil.* London: Faber and Faber.

———. *On Violence.* 1970. London: Allen Lane.

———. *The Human Condition.* 1998. Chicago: University of Chicago Press.

Beck, Ulrich. 2002. *Das Schweigen der Wörter. Über Terror und Krieg.* Frankfurt am Main: Suhrkamp Verlag.

De Cataldo Neuburger, Luisella, and Tiziana Valentini. [1992] 1996. *Women and Terrorism.* New York: St. Martin's Press.

Eagleton, Terry. 1990. *The Ideology of Aesthetics.* Oxford: Blackwell.

Goody, Jack. 2004. *Islam in Europe.* Cambridge: Polity Press.

Kant, Immanuel. 1960. *Observations on the Feeling of the Beautiful and Sublime.* Berkeley: University of California Press.

———. 2000. *The Critique of Judgement.* New York: Cambridge University Press.

Lyotard, Jean-François. 1984. *The Postmodern Condition: A Report on Knowledge.* Minneapolis: University of Minnesota Press.

———. 1984. Answering the question: What is postmodernism? In *The Postmodern*

Condition: A Report on Knowledge, 71–82. Minneapolis: University of Minnesota Press.

———. 1988. *The Differend: Phrases in Dispute*. Minneapolis: University of Minnesota Press.

Peña Aguado, María Isabel. 1994. *Ästhetik des Erhabenen. Burke, Kant, Adorno, Lyotard*. Vienna: Passagen Verlag.

———. 1994. Krieg dem Ganzen' oder Wie postmodern ist der neue Nationalismus? *Widerspruch. Münchener Zeitschrift für Philosophie* 14 (26): 45–52.

Townshend, Charles. 2002. *Terrorism: A Very Short Introduction*. New York: Oxford University Press.

16 Those Who "Witness the Evil": Peacekeeping as Trauma

Sherene H. Razack

> States like these, and their terrorist allies, constitute an axis of evil, arming to threaten the peace of the world.
>
> President George W. Bush, referring to North Korea, Iran,
> and Iraq in his State of the Union Address, 2002

> We came into contact with absolute evil.
>
> Canadian peacekeeper and witness of ethnic cleansing
> and other atrocities in the Croatian wars

It is said that a Canadian speechwriter in the Bush administration coined the phrase "axis of evil" that has been so much a part of American political vocabulary since the September 11, 2001, terrorist attacks on the World Trade Center and the Pentagon (Walker 2002). If this is true, it is fitting. For the better part of the 1990s, Canadian peacekeepers have described their activities in Somalia, Rwanda, Haiti, Bosnia, Kosovo, and Croatia as encounters with "absolute evil." The American president and the Canadian peacekeeper quoted above[1] both imagine the international as a space where civilized peoples from the North go to the South to do battle with evil. So great is the evil that (mysteriously) dwells in the South that it defies description.

Without a specific history, "absolute evil" is nonetheless understood *through* history. The biblical overtones of the phrase take us back to Indian or "savage" wars fought long ago against "heathens," and to an even more distant memory of crusades, starting in the eleventh century, when Christian knights battled Muslim armies and the future of Europe itself was believed to be at stake. Providing the "resurrected togetherness and enabling of 'religion'" (Anidjar 2002, 3), the encounter between good and evil promises a *racial* togetherness. An "axis of evil" reassures people of the North that, as in a colonial era, they belong to a family of civilized nations, a family forced to confront the savagery of the nether regions of Africa, the Middle East, and Eastern Europe. Whether in peacekeeping or in the apocalyptical encounters of George W. Bush (and his father) with Saddam Hussein, color gives the phrase "axis of evil" its currency; and it is color too, through a call to join the family of civilized nations, that gives peacekeeping its allure. Citizens of nations who join the alliance against evil come to know themselves as members of a more advanced race, whose values of democracy and peace are simply not shared by others.

An apocalyptic encounter between good and evil is hard to resist. Myths evoke "a complex system of historical association by a single image or phrase" (Slotkin 1992, 6). John F. Kennedy, for example, relied on the idea of the frontier to mark himself as a president ready and able to fight communism abroad, recalling in a single word cowboys and Indians, the undeniable civilization (and victory) of the one and the savagery of the other (Slotkin 1992, 3). The remembered past evoked by the phrase "axis of evil," a past of the internal colonization of aboriginal peoples and external colonizing ventures across the South, culminates in a contemporary encounter. As this latest installment goes, the West's historic burden to fight against evil must be taken up again with the end of the cold war and the birth of what has come to be widely described as the New World Order. We thought we could rest. We hoped that with the collapse of the Soviet Union, "a new order of free nations" would begin to take shape. Michael Ignatieff describes "our" state of mind: "With blithe lightness of mind, we assumed that the world was moving irrevocably beyond nationalism, beyond tribalism, beyond the provincial confines of identities inscribed in our passports, towards a global market culture which was to be our new home" (1993, 2). Impossibly naïve, we became victims of our own innocence. Instead of our hoped-for global fraternity, the New World Order is "the disintegration of nation states into ethnic civil war; the key architects of that order are warlords; and the key language of our age is ethnic nationalism" (1993, 2).

In these New World Order stories, warlords and ethnic nationalism, indisputable scourges of our age, are often pictured as though they have risen up from the landscape itself and not out of histories in which the West has featured as a colonizing power. No longer anchored in a history, nationalism and the violence that accompanies it seem to be properties of certain people and certain regions. Following the media story of ethnic violence, for instance, leads to three inescapable conclusions, observes Jan Pieterse: "(1) the perpetrators are mad, (2) the West and onlookers are sane, and (3) humanitarian intervention under these crazy circumstances, although messy, is the best we can do" (1998, 244). We are easily tempted into believing that no sooner had they ended than the "savage wars of peace," Rudyard Kipling's description of nineteenth-century Western colonial activities, are strangely upon us again. Myth, in this instance of an inexplicable rise in savagery, "disarms critical analysis" because it appeals to a deeply racially inflected memory: for North Americans, the golden age of cowboys and Indians, and for Europeans, African and Asian colonial adventures (Slotkin 1992, 6). It is not surprising that North American soldiers in Vietnam and peacekeepers in Somalia both described where they were as "Indian country." When racial chords are struck, it becomes difficult, as I will show, to think beyond the simple story lines of mythology.

Peacekeeping has a starring role to play in the mythologies of the New World

Order. Under the auspices of a United Nations dominated by the United States, peacekeepers are entrusted with the task of sorting out the tribalisms and the warlords, protecting the people of the South from the internal evil that threatens them. The evil, however, is powerful, and the international realm is fraught with danger. Human rights violations mark the Third World "as a region of aberrant violence" (Grewal 1998, 502). Confronted with such savagery, First World peacekeepers sometimes "lose it," descending into savagery themselves, as some are seen to have done in Somalia and upon their return home, or else they can become traumatized from too close a brush with "absolute evil." Increasingly—this is perhaps true more of middle powers like Canada than it is for the United States[2]—peacekeeping encounters are narrated as captivity narratives once were a century ago, although the hero of the peacekeeping trauma narrative is most likely to be a man, and the "capture" by the "Indians" is no more than an encounter:

> The hero of the captivity narrative is a White woman (or minister) captured by the Indians during a "savage war." The captive symbolizes the values of Christianity and civilization that are imperiled in the wilderness war. Her captivity is figuratively a descent into Hell and a spiritual darkness which is akin to "madness." By resisting the physical threats and spiritual temptations of the Indians, the captive vindicates both her own moral character and the power of the values she symbolizes. But the scenario of historical action developed by the captivity narrative is a passive one that emphasizes the weakness of colonial power and ends not with a victorious conquest but with a grateful and somewhat chastened return home. (Slotkin 1992, 15)

In documentary films and news features about traumatized white men (and only a few white women) in Africa and Eastern Europe, peacekeepers bear witness, upon their return, to an alien world, a world so savage that only a powerful alliance of civilized nations can intervene to stop the carnage. Like the narrative about an axis of evil, the story of traumatized peacekeepers depends for its coherency on the logic of rational men and women from white nations who encounter people and things in the South that are beyond rationality, things that can literally drive them mad.

To speak of the racial logic of peacekeeping trauma is to speak about the work that is done by narratives. A narrative is different from a personal story, and it is important to hold the difference in mind. Peacekeepers do experience trauma and the rotting bodies; snipers and child soldiers are real enough; but the events of trauma, Kali Tal notes, are codified in narrative form until they become a signifier for something else (1996, 6). It is the codified story, and not the individual experiences, that I refer to when I consider trauma. Deconstructing narratives, that is, looking for the way in which they are about something else, means separating the experiences of individuals from the way their stories are assembled for our consumption.

Attending to the work that narratives do, Renato Rosaldo suggests, is less about demystification than it is about dismantling. As he does with the narrative of imperialist nostalgia, where people mourn the passing of what they themselves have destroyed, Rosaldo (1989) suggests that while demystification is useful, for example, revealing the connection between nostalgia and guilt or demonstrating how little about imperialism there actually is to be mourned, it is more important to dismantle narrative by probing its productive function. Imperialist nostalgia, the yearning for the glorious days of the Raj, for instance, transforms colonial agents into innocent bystanders harmlessly sipping tea in old palaces in much the same way that witnessing the evil and becoming traumatized by it transforms peacekeepers and their nations into hapless victims of a timeless evil rather than agents implicated in the complex histories of colonialism and neo-colonialism. In probing what is produced by stories of traumatized peacekeepers, we might ask, as Kali Tal suggests for narratives of the trauma of the Holocaust and of sexual violence, "[What] is the connection between individual psychic trauma and cultural representations of the traumatic event?" (1996, 3). Focusing on cultural representations of peacekeeping in the 1990s, stories about trauma, the special qualities of middle-power nations, and the burden to be borne by the family of civilized nations in the New World Order, I explore in this chapter what it means for us in the North to cast ourselves as traumatized in both a national and an international story about the West's confrontation with absolute evil.

Those Who "Witness the Evil"

It is worth noting at the outset what is at stake in dismantling peacekeeping stories of trauma. Reflecting on the embracing of traumatized figures in national U.S. culture (in Berlant's example, the figure is the child worker traumatized by exploitation), Lauren Berlant asks about "the place of painful feeling in the making of political worlds" (2001, 128). What the frame of trauma accomplishes is the installation of "the feeling self as the true self, the self that must be protected from pain or from history" (2001, 131). Traumatized subjectivity replaces rational subjectivity "as the essential index of value for personhood and thus for society" (132). One important consequence is that we can no longer talk about injustice and how it is organized. Instead, we talk about pain and how to heal. When "feeling bad becomes evidence of a structural condition of injustice" and "feeling good becomes evidence of justice's triumph," then both the problem and the solution are removed from their material and historical contexts (133).

In the case of peacekeeping, the television documentaries and news features of traumatized soldiers that are considered here visually draw us to dead and mutilated African and Eastern European bodies, but mostly so that we might feel the horror of what it was like for Northern men and women to witness such atrocities. With their experiences at the core of what we feel, it becomes difficult to contest the story. To challenge such pain, Berlant reminds us, is to inflict violence on already damaged persons (2001, 133). How, in the face of the enormous personal pain of witnesses (we do not talk much about the actual survivors of these atrocities), do we talk about our complicity in the production of the atrocities? And how do we move toward responsibility? Keeping in mind what the trauma narrative dislodges and renders unspeakable, and in particular the way it traps us in a story about a civilized West in a primeval encounter with evil, I begin the task of dismantling.

Roméo Dallaire: The Making of an Icon

The Rwandan genocide in 1994 in which over 800,000 people were slaughtered while a skeletal UN peacekeeping force watched helplessly remains one of the century's enduring images of evil. Not surprisingly, Rwanda (and not Somalia) is the context most often referred to in Canadian trauma narratives. It is not difficult to understand why any peacekeeper who confronted the thousands of corpses, most displaying signs of brutal violence, would be traumatized by the sight. Canadian peacekeepers found themselves in the middle of the Rwandan genocide. Early in 1994, the commander of the UN peacekeeping mission, a Canadian, General Roméo Dallaire, had gathered evidence of an approaching and well-planned Hutu massacre of Tutsis. He appealed to his Canadian superior at the United Nations for help. Remembered for his now famous telex of January 11, 1994, to General Maurice Baril in which he inserted a personal plea for intervention, "Where there's a will, there's a way, let's go," Dallaire has since been described as a "voice in the wilderness of horror" (Death and duty 2000). When no help was forthcoming and the genocide ensued, Dallaire returned to Canada a traumatized man—suicidal and unable to put the horrors behind him.

Dallaire is not without his critics, but they have been remarkably few for so controversial a mission. Only one journalist has suggested that Dallaire's inexperience and infatuation with the idea of the ideal peacekeeper as someone without a gun who simply tries to talk people out of things might have cost the lives of at least the ten unarmed Belgian paratroopers whom the Hutus killed and perhaps the lives of many more (Koch 1996). Another newspaper, renowned for its conservative and anti-feminist stance, dismissed Dallaire's trauma narrative as a fabrication, just as it dismissed women who accused their fathers of childhood sexual violence (Worthington 1999). A senate committee of the Belgian government criticized Dallaire for having failed to come to the aid of the Belgian peacekeepers he assigned to guard Rwanda's interim president (Coulon 1997). For the most part, however, although opinion is divided on whether Dallaire could have done more, most concede, as does Alison Des Forges of Human Rights Watch, that he is a tragic hero, a man who faced impossible odds (*Unseen Scars* 1998).

What Dallaire actually did or did not do has long ago ceased to matter. The narrative, a nationally specific, cultural story, has taken over. By 1998, with Dallaire as its iconic figure, there were a series of documentaries made by the Canadian Broadcasting Corporation (CBC), and a succession of newspaper and magazine articles that conveyed to the public the figure of the traumatized peacekeeper. Sometimes joined in these stories by journalists and NGO workers who describe "the physical and emotional scars that will never heal," traumatized soldiers share the pain of being witness to "unspeakable evil" (Dying to tell 1999). In 1998 the Canadian Military produced *Witness the Evil*, a documentary on posttraumatic stress disorder (PTSD) suffered by peacekeepers. Intended for use within the military and also for the media, the film became the subject of a CBC documentary *The Unseen Scars*, shown several times on Canadian television in recent years. It is in *Witness the Evil* and *The Unseen Scars* that we see the full emergence of the traumatized peacekeeper and his function in national mythology.

Witness the Evil ensures that viewers also bear witness to the Rwandan genocide. Images of mutilated bodies, fields filled with corpses, and large piles of machetes dramatically convey a brutality that is frequently described as apocalypse. In an opening scene a Canadian soldier makes the sign of the cross in his tent, and we know that we are watching a story unfolding in an unholy place. The soldiers give their testimony, breaking down in tears when they describe the smell of rotting bodies, the packs of dogs fighting over corpses, and most of all, the hundreds of beheaded and mutilated children. They narrate their utter helplessness and vulnerability when confronted with the barbarism and irrationality of Rwanda Patriotic Army (RPA) soldiers. Medical units describe being watched by RPA soldiers from the bushes, others tell of dangerous roadblock encounters in which the Rwandan troops slap a Canadian soldier and try to buy a female medical officer for the price of a chicken. Soldiers describe their duties searching for mass graves and the surreal experience of accidentally stepping into a hole that turns out to be the chest cavity of a corpse, the first of several layers of corpses. We are easily convinced by these scenes that nothing is left of Rwanda but bodies piled upon bodies.

Corporal Daines reveals that his encounters with the bodies of massacred children have deeply affected his own family life. Corporal Cassavoy describes how certain smells and sights (roasted meats, newborn children, rusted-out vehicles) trigger his flashbacks. Dallaire, himself deeply sad, confirms that he too is haunted by smells and sounds, and often wishes he had lost a leg instead of his "marbles." The soldiers all report their terrible frustration that wearing the blue helmet of the United Nations meant very little. Major Lancaster found himself in the middle of a massacre, able to grab babies off their mothers' backs but to do little else. Village elders stopped the killing in this instance. The following day, Lancaster recounts, he was unable to get out of bed, overwhelmed by feelings of helplessness. The images of the genocide give way at the end of the documentary to images of Canadian soldiers bathing African children, and a voice-over lists the clinical symptoms and chemistry of PTSD, suggesting that it is a physical condition that can affect behavior both during and after active duty. "Helpless witnesses to evil" and immobilized by the overwhelming knowledge that "all the best thinking in the world went into the UN" and yet the West could not prevent a genocide, the soldiers return home. We, the television viewers, understand that even the best institution the West had to offer was no match for the evil of Africa. A voice-over reassures us that at least we made things a little better. Tearfully, the soldiers conclude that while they have enormous pride in the good they did, the price was often too high.

The trauma of peacekeepers is of a different order than that of other trauma victims, and the biggest difference is what they are traumatized by. Mapped on to the nation, peacekeeping trauma narratives produce a biblical narrative of a First World overwhelmed by the evil of the Third World. As Dallaire himself describes, his trauma was born out of an encounter with the devil, and what followed was a slow descent into hell. *"Je suis couvert de sang,"* he told journalists, describing vividly his nightmares upon return to Canada,[3] a direct connection between the hacked-up bodies and ourselves that is made clear in the only display case in Canada's national war museum devoted to 1990s peacekeeping missions. The display case shows Dallaire's bulletproof vest worn in Rwanda, his UN blue helmet and beret, and two Hutu machetes. The machetes were aimed at us, the display implies; the invisibility of the Rwandans is more or less complete.

As Liisa Malkki has suggested, the erasure of the experience of Rwandans themselves, and their "speechlessness" in the stories that are told of the genocide, should greatly concern us. It signals our investment in understanding ourselves as outside of history (Malkki 1996). We come to know of the Rwandan genocide as a horror that is unknowable and unthinkable. The "flood of terrifying images" tells us all we need to know, and in place of history and context, the very information needed to consider the future, we install "absolute evil" and the good soldiers overwhelmed by it. If time "must be given to the tasks of witnessing and testimony of Rwandans" (1996, 397), then this is a bearing witness that is fundamentally different from the peacekeepers' witnessing of the evil. Whereas the one requires us to pursue accountability (ours as well as theirs), the other invites us only to consider genocide as timeless and unchangeable, a feature of the landscape. Throughout *Witness the Evil*, the act of aggression that is the source of trauma remains amorphous, overwhelming, and African. Visually, it is hacked-up black bodies on an African landscape. These images not only "displace narrative testimony" of the Rwandans themselves, but they actively silence and dehumanize Africans by presenting them as a "mere, bare, naked, or minimal humanity" (1996, 390).

As witness, the peacekeeper is not personally implicated in what has traumatized him. He stands in the place Dana Nelson (1998) describes as the "objective and disembodied space of the universalist standpoint." From this vantage point, he is witness to a depravity that can be named but is no less mystical. His is an "occulted standpoint," the viewpoint of the observer who is not himself of the landscape, yet who is able to understand hidden things (the presence of the devil) that the Rwandans themselves presumably cannot see (Nelson 1998, 10–11). For Mary Louise Pratt (1992), "a fantasy of dominance and appropriation" is built into this "otherwise passive, open stance," a position she notes of imperial naturalists and scientific observers who thought themselves unconnected to imperial conquest but whose assumption of the right to define and name what they saw, and to encode the landscape as empty and awaiting European improvement, was a cornerstone of imperialism. "The improving eye" of Pratt's "anti-conquest man" (her term for the naturalists and scientists who saw themselves as different from conquerors) is clearly in evidence in refugee experts and relief officials, as Malkki has pointed out for Rwanda, standing "surrounded by milling crowds of black people peering into the camera, and benevolently, efficiently, giving a rundown on their numbers, their diseases, their nutritional needs, their crops, and their birth and mortality rates" (1996, 390). And it is in evidence when the camera scans the mounds of bodies and we let it tell us all we ever need to know about Rwanda.

The story of an encounter with unfathomable evil is only intelligible through race. It is perhaps no accident that so many writers of Dallaire's story compare Rwanda to Joseph Conrad's Congo in *Heart of Darkness* (1966), and Dallaire to Marlowe, the narrator of Conrad's novel. Journalist Carol Off, for instance, writing of Dallaire, begins her chapter "Into Africa" with an epigraph from Conrad. For her, Dallaire is like Marlowe, who sees the folly of colonial greed in Africa (in Dallaire's case the folly of the UN) as well as the "lusty red-eyed devils" lurking in the jungle (Off 2000, 29). For those caught between "two strains of the truly sinister" (29), there is only madness, either as trauma, or as violence. When peacekeepers are violent, as they were in Somalia, we are easily able to forgive it and even to expect it, understanding that it is the cruelties of Africa and Africans who push Western men to violence.[4] Edward Said, in discussing Conrad's understanding of imperialism in *Heart of Darkness,* points out that Conrad is largely unable to think outside of imperialism. For him there are no subjects who inhabit Africa (Said 1993, 25). Chinua Achebe put it more forcefully: Africa, for Conrad, "is a metaphysical battlefield devoid of all recognizable humanity, into which the wandering European enters at his peril" (1988, 8).

Witness the Evil and the news features on Dallaire invite us to understand ourselves racially as well as nationally, that is, as good people forced to stand helplessly by as evil unfolds and as more powerful nations refuse to help. To be invited, as these documentaries do, into the "abstracted space of universalizing authority over others" is to join a fraternity of those who are neither of the hacked bodies on an African landscape nor of the unscrupulous United States or incompetent United Nations. Before long, we begin to feel the bond that comes from sharing such high moral ground. The international domain thus constituted is an "affective space," a place where middle-power nations can experience belonging (Nelson 1998, 10–11). Dallaire himself has made explicit the affective space of the middle-power nation. Upon his return from Rwanda, Dallaire spoke passionately of Canada's noble calling. As he put it in an interview, "To be that intermediary between the superpowers—who don't give a s___ anyways—and the Third World countries who know they need the presence of our capabilities . . . *tabernacle,*[5] you've got a hard time to find a more noble concept" (Thompson 1997). Canadians have a unique destiny to fulfill as a middle power. Our nobility lies in "keeping the big boys out of it" (Howard 2001).

Canadians have turned with alacrity to the vision of ourselves as a good nation overwhelmed by the brutalities of the New World Order. Recent Canadian novels have been written, journalist Graham Fraser (2000) approvingly observed in a review, "in support of Canada's role on the world stage." In Alan Cumyn's novel *Man of Bone* (1998), a fictional Canadian diplomat, Bill Burridge, is taken hostage. Described by Fraser as a "trauma-damaged idealist," Bill Burridge is captured and tortured by guerrillas in a fictional Third World country whose history he barely knows. Burridge does not even know where Santa Irene is when he is first told of his posting there. In Cumyn's second novel, Burridge appears before a UN Human Rights Committee, and like Dallaire, who broke down when he took the stand, Burridge is humiliated by losing control of his bowels. "This is a risky time for Canada," Fraser writes sympathetically of Cumyn's hero, reading the novel as a story of the plight of a middle-power nation in the New World Order. Conservatives insist that we stay home and avoid the risks, even abandoning our historic role of peacekeeping. However, Liberals know, Fraser reassures us, that politics is not only about the local. Most "Canadians want their country to be engaged with the world" (Fraser 2000).

Our engagement with the world is everywhere depicted as the engagement of the compassionate but uninvolved observer. In November 2002, Toronto artist Gertrude Kearns held an exhibition of paintings entitled "Undone: Dallaire/Rwanda." The exhibition included large canvasses of earth-colored, military camouflage markings within which figures were discernible: Dallaire with his hands covering his face, Dallaire showing horror and helplessness, a landscape of corpses and machetes, and a UN jeep that sits uselessly atop a mound of bodies. Only the blue of Dallaire's eyes and the blue of the UN helmet relieve the unrelenting brown of the camouflage landscape. For the artist, the camouflage signals the jungle, the land itself. It also reflects Dallaire being deceived by the Hutus, by the United Nations, and by his own mind. The title "Undone" suggests the UN's responsibility, its failure to complete its mandate, and Dallaire's own state of coming apart. As the show's curator explains,

> Gertrude Kearns uses camouflage as a metaphor for psychological deception. Its pattern thinly veils the hard silhouette of what we deeply know. We hide our vulnerability, sometimes to the point of unfeeling. Better to conceal the truth and shun what we cannot change than admit our fallibility. Dallaire's voice and stories advance and recede in the fabric of Kearn's canvasses. She pulls his guilt and frustration through the camouflage screen. We are left with the prospect of our collective impotency. (Hudson 2002)

Impotent, moved, undone: this is our fate. Viewers of the exhibition congratulated Kearns in the gallery's book of comments for her depiction of what it is to be "powerless in the face of colossal evil." Both Dallaire and the artist are saluted for their courage in revealing to us "man's inhumanity," an inhumanity that leaves us stunned and overwhelmed. Trauma narratives help to organize our place in the world in just the way the novels and art exhibitions illustrate. We come to know ourselves as a compassionate people; indeed, trauma suggests that it is our very vulnerability to pain that marks us as Canadians. From our position as witness, we help to mark out the terrain of what is good and what is evil. Possessed of unique sensibilities, sensibilities that take us to the depths of grief and trauma, we can diagnose the trouble and act as the advance scout and the go-between. In this way, trauma narratives furnish middle-power nations such as Canada with a homemade, that is to say, a specifically *national* version, of the politics of rescue. What can be so wrong with this? Again, Malkki elucidates the problem:

> It is difficult to see what might be so problematic in seeing the suffering of people with the eyes of "humanitarian concern" and "human compassion." It is surely better than having no compassion or simply looking the other way. But this is not the issue. The issue is that the established practices of humanitarian representation and intervention are not timeless, unchangeable, or in any way absolute. On the contrary, these practices are embedded in long and complicated histories of their own—histories of charity and philanthropy, histories of international law, peace-keeping and diplomacy, histories of banishment and legal protection, histories of empires and colonial rule, histories of civilizational and emancipatory discourses and missionary work, histories of the World Bank and other development initiatives in Africa, and much more. (1996, 389)

When we produce narratives of "anonymous corporeality and speechlessness," when we hide our own implication and stand outside of history, preoccupied with our own pain, we stake out the color line, producing ourselves as individuals and as a nation on the civilized side of things (1996, 389). In this we have not been alone, although the position of "trauma-damaged idealist" has suited our middle-power aspirations to a tee.

Complicating the narrative lines of the peacekeeping and humanitarian experience is necessary if we are to escape the snare of the color line—the belief that peacekeeping is primarily about civilized nations sorting out, at our great peril, the tribal antagonisms and ethnic nationalism of the South. Restricted to this narrative, we do not see the historical, social, political, and economic contexts in which atrocities, as well as the tragedy of trauma for those who witness and are unable to stop them, occur. To go beyond our pain and our helplessness, to take responsibility, we must begin with our investments, investments that trauma narratives have revealed to be deeply national.

The power of the story of good and evil enacted globally, whether in peace-keeping trauma narratives or in President Bush's speeches, should give us pause. For while it is its very refusal to consider history and context that gives the story its power, its psychic appeal surely comes, paradoxically, from the mythology that informs our history. In 1973, in *Regeneration Through Violence*, Richard Slotkin advised us to remember the power of mythology and its constitutive role in the making of the American nation. The real Founding Fathers of · America, he argued, are not the politicians who drafted the Constitution, but rather:

those who (to paraphrase Faulkner's *Absalom, Absalom!* [1951]) tore violently a nation from the implacable and opulent wilderness—the rogues, adventurers, and land boomers; the Indian fighters, traders, missionaries, explorers, and hunters who killed and were killed until they had mastered the wilderness; the settlers who came after, suffering hardship and Indian warfare for the sake of a sacred mission or a simple desire for land; and the Indians themselves, both as they were and as they appeared to settlers, for whom they were the special demonic personification of the American wilderness. Their concerns, their hopes, their terrors, their violence, and their justifications of themselves as expressed in literature, are the foundation stones of the mythology that informs our history. (Slotkin 1973, 4)

Remarkably prescient, Slotkin anticipates that writers and critics who fail to reckon with these mythological figures will be unable to understand when they take over national politics. Slotkin discusses such American moments in the nineteenth century, moments when the national aspiration becomes defined as "so many bears destroyed, so much land pre-empted, so many trees hacked down, so many Indians and Mexicans dead in the dust" (1973, 5). In the twentieth and twenty-first centuries, national politics is dominated by intrepid men who confront evil itself and who, on slow days, bring order and civility to savage lands. These men are kin to Slotkin's Indian fighters, traders, missionaries, explorers, and hunters. They regenerate or reinvent themselves through violence, to borrow Slotkin's argument. If we are to think beyond these mythologies, we first have to identify how they operate and recognize their power, the project I have pursued in this chapter.

It *is* difficult to dismantle mythology and to begin to render things like genocide and ethnic cleansing "thinkable" (Mamdani 2001). Even when we are able to dismantle mythologies and to consider the historical, social, and political contexts of the countries we set out to "help," a formula for responsible intervention does not come easily to mind. Categorically refusing to intervene is as irresponsible a position as intervening because "they" will only understand force. What is at least clear, however, is that our only chance to assume a more responsible role lies in rejecting the simple and deeply raced story lines of traumatized nations, middle-power countries and their special capabilities, and showdowns with "absolute evil."

Notes

This chapter is a shortened version of the first chapter in my book *Dark Threats and White Knights* (2004, 15–50).

1. In Gerry Bellett, "Traumatized former peacekeepers will be offered counseling in B.C.," *Vancouver Sun,* 7 July 2000, B5.
2. In a search of the *New York Times* for 2001, no articles were found referring

to peacekeepers as traumatized, whereas Canada has consistently featured them.
3.   Dallaire, quoted in Monique Giguere, "Le general Dallaire ne va pas mieux," *Le Soleil,* 14 Octobre 2000, A19.
4.   Analysis of the violence of Canadian peacekeepers in Somalia is the focus of my book *Dark Threats and White Knights.*
5.   *Tabernacle,* a word used by French Canadians as a curse, technically refers to the cup that a priest drinks out of in church.

References

Achebe, Chinua. 1988. An image of Africa: Racism in Conrad's *Heart of Darkness.* In *Hopes and Impediments: Selected Essays, 1965–1987,* 1–39. London: Heinemann.

Anidjar, Gil. 2002. Introduction. In *Acts of Religion,* ed. Jacques Derrida and Gil Anidjar, 1–39. New York: Routledge.

Bellett, Gerry. 2000. Traumatized former peacekeepers will be offered counseling in B.C. *Vancouver Sun,* 7 July, B5.

Berlant, Lauren. 2001. The subject of true feeling: Pain, privacy, and politics. In *Feminist Consequences: Theory for the New Century,* ed. Elisabeth Bronfen and Misha Kavka, 126–60. New York: Columbia University Press.

Bush, George W. 2002. State of the Union Address, January 29. Ashbrook Center for Public Affairs at Ashland University. Accessed June 23, 2003, at www.ashbrook.org/articles/bush_02-01-20.html.

Coulon, Jocelyn. 1997. Massacre de Casques bleus au Rwanda. *Le Devoir,* 6 December, A5.

Death and duty: Interview with Roméo Dallaire. 2000. Interview by Brian Stewart, CBC Television, July 3. Accessed June 23, 2003, at www.cbc.ca/news/national/magazine/dallaire/index.html.

Dying to Tell the Story. 1998. Turner Original Productions, aired on *The Passionate Eye,* CBC Newsworld, January 31, 1999, April 18, 1999, and July 23, 2000.

Fraser, Graham. 2000. In support of Canada's role on the world stage. *Toronto Star,* 17 September, A11.

Grewal, Inderpal. 1998. On the new global feminism and the family of nations: Dilemmas of transnational feminist practice. In *Talking Visions: Multicultural Feminism in a Transnational Age,* ed. Ella Shohat, 501–30. Cambridge, Mass.: MIT Press.

Giguere, Monique. 2000. Le general Dallaire ne va pas mieux. *Le Soleil,* 14 Octobre, A19.

Howard, Robert. 2001. Dallaire: U.S. troops a liability. *Hamilton Spectator,* 17 March, D04.

Hudson, Anna. 2002. Handout distributed by Propeller Gallery, Toronto, September 11. www.propellerctr.com.

Ignatieff, Michael. 1993. *Blood and Belonging: Journeys into the New Nationalism.* Toronto: Penguin.

Koch, George. 1996. The Cross. *Saturday Night* (September): 64–68, 70, 72, 83, 84.

Malkki, Liisa H. 1996. Speechless emissaries: Refugees, humanitarianism, and dehisto-
ricization. *Cultural Anthropology* 11(3): 392–93.

Mamdani, Mahmood. 2001. *When Victims Become Killers: Colonialism, Nativism, and
the Genocide in Rwanda*. Princeton, N.J.: Princeton University Press.

Nelson, Dana. 1998. *National Manhood: Capitalist Citizenship and the Imagined Fraternity of White Men*. Raleigh, N.C.: Duke University Press.

Off, Carol. 2000. *The Lion, the Fox and the Eagle: A Story of Generals and Justice in
Rwanda and Yugoslavia*. Toronto: Random House.

Pieterse, Jan Nederveen. 1998. Sociology of humanitarian intervention: Bosnia,
Rwanda and Somalia compared. In *World Orders in the Making: Humani-
tarian Intervention and Beyond,* ed. Jan Nederveen Pieterse, 71–94. New York:
St. Martin's Press.

Pratt, Mary Louise. 1992. *Imperial Eyes: Travel Writing and Transculturation*. London
and New York: Routledge.

Razack, Sherene H. 2004. *Dark Threats and White Knights: The Somalia Affair,
Peacekeeping, and the New Imperialism*. Toronto: Toronto University Press.

Rosaldo, Renato. 1989. Imperialist nostalgia. *Representations* 26 (Spring): 107–22.

Said, Edward. 1993. *Culture and Imperialism*. New York: Alfred A. Knopf.

Slotkin, Richard. 1973. *Regeneration through Violence: The Mythology of the American
Frontier 1600–1860*. Middletown, Conn.: Wesleyan University Press.

———. 1992. *Gunfighter Nation: The Myth of the Frontier in Twentieth-century
America*. New York: Atheneum.

Tal, Kali. 1996. *Worlds of Hurt: Reading the Literatures of Trauma*. New York: Cambridge University Press.

The Unseen Scars: Post-traumatic Stress Disorder. 1998. CBC National, *This Magazine,*
November 25. Accessed June 23, 2003, at www.tv.cbc.ca/national/pgminfo/
ptsd/wounds.html.

Walker, William. 2002. Frum no longer one of the president's men. *Toronto Star,*
26 February, A11.

Worthington, Peter. 1999. Editorial: Turning grief into a growth industry. *Toronto
Sun,* 11 May, 17.

17 The Evils of the
September Attacks

Sara Ruddick

The attacks of September 11, 2001, caused, and could be expected to cause, pain, injury, and death; terror and grief. The victims of the attack had no distinct relation to the attackers; no grounds for predicting attack; no means of protecting themselves or others; no time for leaving, mourning, or celebrating their lives and loves. These attacks were undeniably terrible. Were they also evil?

The September attacks were called evil on the day they occurred. "Today," the President announced to the Nation, "thousands of lives were despicably ended by evil."[1] Almost immediately, America was called to a Manichean struggle of "good versus evil." The forces of evil were expansive: if you "harbored" a terrorist, you were a terrorist yourself. Soon the U.S. military forces were bombing hideouts and training camps in Afghanistan, whose regime was, in itself, an evil. The president then discovered a three-state "axis of evil." America began planning another military campaign against one of these three evil states to save both them and us from an evil leader and his dangerous weapons.

Alarmed by crusading Americans, many people inside as well as outside of the United States tried to break the connection between the attacks and the presumption of evil. If the attacks had been a response to recent policies, they would be, though no less deplorable, more rational. If U.S. governments were responsible for the policies, then U.S. citizens might assert a measure of control by changing their governments.

Several times before September 11, 2001, in pronouncements and interviews, Osama bin Laden, the founder of al-Qaeda, enumerated grievances against "America." I list some of them, in bin Laden's words, mostly from a call issued in 1998 for a jihad against Jews and Crusaders.[2] "For over seven years the United States has been occupying the Lands of Islam in the holiest places, the Arabian Peninsula . . . plundering its riches, dictating to its rulers, humiliating its people, terrorizing its neighbors." America serves "the Jews' petty state" and diverts attention from its "occupation of Jerusalem and murder of Muslims there." Once again (i.e., in 1998) America threatens to repeat the "horrific massacres" in Iraq as though they were not content "with the protracted blockade imposed after the ferocious war or the fragmentation and devastation" (bin Laden, in McDermott 2005, 168). In the years following 2001, bin Laden has repeatedly described the attacks as a retaliation for injustices suffered, even remembering the exact moment in 1982 when, watching the bombing of Lebanon, he had the idea of bombing the World Trade Towers: "I was overwhelmed by ideas that are hard to describe. . . . As I was looking at those destroyed towers in Lebanon, I was struck by the idea of punishing the oppressor in the same manner and destroying towers in the U.S., to give it a taste of what we have tasted and to deter it from killing our children and women" (bin Laden 2004, in Lawrence 2005, 235–43).

To bin Laden's arguments and others like them, many reply that whatever insults and depredations Muslims and other Arab people suffered because of U.S. policies, the attacks were neither an appropriate nor a legitimate response. I endorse this reply. No wrong done the attackers or injustices suffered by their people can justify the attacks—they are unjustifiable. But then I also believe that military force of any kind is only very rarely, and then very briefly, a moral or an effective response to assault and aggression. Bin Laden–type arguments tend to assimilate "terrorist" attacks—the poor person's military—to conventional war. I reverse that order. If a distinctive horror accrues to certain "terrorist attacks," I will locate its analogue in state-run conventional war.

Can an idea of "distinctive horror" survive the rhetoric of "good vs. evil" purveyed by the government of the United States and much of its popular culture? Do Americans, so used to bombing but so rarely bombed, inevitably exaggerate the evil done us? The September 11 attacks, if evil, are lesser evils: deaths in the thousands rather than the millions, an assault of only half a day, quick death by force and fire rather than by extended torture and humiliation. The attacks would constitute a moment in the Holocaust; they were trivial in comparison to centuries of slavery. As bombings go, driving four highly fueled passenger planes into four particular buildings seems a lesser evil than nuclear, carpet, cluster, or fire bombing, all practices in which U.S. forces have engaged.

American self-preoccupation may well have contributed to an inflated sense of the evil we suffered. But "evil," at least in its secular form, is an intrinsically aggrandizing tool of judgment. It selects from among acts and practices that are terrible, those that are truly horrible. Anyone using a language of "good and evil" will likely be drawn into comparing harms done and cruelties suffered. A comparison need not be a competition. The lesser evil is entirely terrible for those who suffer it. A sense of proportion does not require us to minimize anyone's loss. Instead, it asks us to attend to the *specificities* of evil, to trace the details of the horror in which a judgment of evil is rooted.

I take the ideal of *specificity* from letters exchanged between Hannah Arendt and her former teacher, Karl Jaspers, in 1946, shortly after the end of the Nazi era. Arendt, who had been reading Jaspers (1946, 1947) on the question of German guilt, wrote: the "Nazi crimes . . . explode the limits of the law; and that is precisely what constitutes their monstrousness" (Arendt and Jaspers 1992, 54). Jaspers replied:

A guilt that goes beyond all criminal guilt takes on a streak of "greatness"—of satanic Greatness—which is for me as inappropriate to the Nazis as all the talk about the "Demonic" element in Hitler and so forth. . . . I regard any hint of myth or legend with horror and everything unspecific is just such a hint. (1992, 62)

Arendt agreed: "We have to combat all impulses to mythologize the horrible, and to the extent I can't avoid such formulations I haven't understood what actually went on" (1992, 69).

The correspondence of these philosophers yields for me a double injunction. The first is explicit: Combat impulses to mythologize the horrible. I derive the second from the character of the correspondence. Arendt and Jaspers struggle to describe accurately the destructive cruelty they have witnessed. They speak with scrupulous care for each other as well as for the truth. They deny nothing.

In the months following the September 11 attacks, mythologizing was obvious, deliberate, and, insofar as myth helped propel a rush to war, dangerous. Less evident was a tendency to leave unspoken and under-represented the distinctive horror of these particular attacks. The United States was soon bombing Afghanistan and then, with brazen pride, Iraq. It seemed inappropriate, if not outrageous, for U.S. citizens to call attention to what we suffered as we were actively inflicting suffering on others.

But silence has its costs. An unspoken horror may fester in the imagination, fueling fantasies of homeland security and global order even in the skeptical, especially when attacks become personally and geographically close. Moreover, feelings are epistemological resources. If we cannot bear articulate witness to the horror we suffer or identify as ours, we may be less able actually to grasp the horror we inflict, however ready we are to bemoan and ridicule our government's policies. Not that we can *trust* our feelings. Rather, we can let feelings serve as "alerts," telling us to attend and follow as our minds travel to the specific aspects of a phenomenon that move us. Horror, terror, disgust, and other feelings can inform our actions, provided that they are expressed and tested in conversational exchange. Feelings call out for thought. And sometimes a thought calls out for feeling that allows words to be imagined into lives. "No warning, no preparation, no time for leaving or farewell. . . . Nothing but the keening of loss."

I will trace the horrors of the September attacks with the specificity I can manage. I consider in turn the men who produced the attacks, the victims of their production, and the good that they violated. My hope is that by attending to the wrongs suffered in the attacks of 9/11, we will be better able to grasp in their specificities the horror of the attacks justified in their name.

The September Attacks: Evil's Producers

Two classes of people produced the September 11 attacks and hence their putative evil. The leaders of al-Qaeda first planned the attacks as part of an ongoing campaign and then directed them from a distance. These "masterminds" of al-Qaeda are personified by Osama bin Laden.[3] Nineteen men carried out the attacks. Among them were four pilots whose leader, Mohamed Atta, had considerable responsibility for the logistics, military and social, of the attacks.[4]

The masterminds, as represented by bin Laden, speak in a language loosely akin to just-war theory. Bin Laden's cause (*jus ad bellum*) seems just in conventional terms: to liberate his people and lands from occupation and to redress ongoing injustices. Though he speaks out of a specific religious faith, his claims can be translated into secular language or the language of many faiths. There is no evil here. However, bin Laden's statement of just causes, like his thought and language generally, includes an anti-Semitism that exceeds opposition to Israeli policies and exceeds his explicit anti-Christian sentiments. Anti-Semitism is evil in itself and has produced great evils.

Moreover, his justification of the conduct of war (*jus in bello*) is decidedly at odds with the demands of just-war theory. Notoriously, the attacks in their very conception involved killing civilians. Mamdough Salim, an original member of bin Laden's ruling council, skipped anything resembling just-war theory and defended the killing of Americans and Muslims. He reasoned that "if an attack on an American building killed Americans that was beneficial. If Muslims working with the Americans were killed, these Muslims were punished for helping the American infidels. If innocent Muslim bystanders were killed, they would become martyrs and go to paradise and would thus be grateful to those who carried out the bombing" (in McDermott 2005, 168).

Bin Laden's own stated principles concerning "civilians" are a mix of aggressive *lex talionis*, Muslim entitlement, and civilian culpability. "We treat others like they treat us. Those who kill our women and our innocent, we kill their women and innocent, until they stop doing so" (bin Laden, "Terror for Terror," in Lawrence 2005, 119). "It would be a sin for Muslims not to try to possess the weapons [of mass destruction] that would prevent the infidels from inflicting harm on Muslims. . . . How we could use these weapons is up to us" (Hashmi 2004, 334; Lawrence 2005, 69). "As for the World Trade Center, the ones who were attacked and who died in it were part of a financial power. It wasn't a children's school!" (bin Laden 2004, in Lawrence 2005, 119).

The hijackers express in action the plans of the masterminds. These men can be seen as near ideal combatants: willing and disciplined soldiers fighting for a cause that was deeply theirs, strictly following the battle plan they had been given. Three of the four pilots controlled the passengers and their own men, then drove their planes straight into the designated buildings. Fifteen out of nineteen hijackers achieved the victory they had hoped for. The fourth pilot, in agreement with a colleague, flew the last plane into the ground as planned in advance if a mission went awry. None of them engaged in gratuitous killing or outlaw behavior. Terry McDermott (2005) claims, persuasively on my view, that all of the hijackers knew they would die. Certainly the pilots knew.

Three of these pilots were members of a "militant" Islamic group: Mohamed Atta, the leader; Marwan al-Shehhi, his close friend; and Ziad Jarrah. The fourth, Hani Hanjour, was recruited when other potential pilots failed to get visas. The pilots are described as "fairly ordinary" by several writers (McDermott, Pape, Elster, Holmes) and not the "monsters" we might wish them to be. But they are also described by other Muslims as unusually religious. These young men differed from each other. I give brief sketches of them as a gesture toward their differences and to call into question catchphrase descriptions such as "filled with hate."[5]

Mohamed Atta, the leader, was angered by social injustices and inequalities of wealth in Egypt where he grew up and where his family still lived. He was appalled by the effects of urban development on the poor, and he allegedly viewed skyscrapers as symbols of a humiliating, marginalizing Western power (see Holmes 2005, 141). When only 28, he wrote a will that is marked by gynophobia, misogyny, what sounds like sexual phobia (no one must touch his genitals; when in their proximity, people cleaning his body must wear gloves), and what sounds like wounded pride ("I don't want anyone to visit me who didn't get along with me while I was alive"). The will is governed throughout by his desire to do what is required by Islamic law, to die as a good Muslim would. Atta is usually portrayed as cold, obsessive, introverted, and generally unlikable. But he appeared to have many friends, some close. The last time he left Hamburg for the United States, he sent a cell phone text message to a friend, Said Bahaji, mentioning two friends they had in common: "Salam: this is for you, Abba and Mounir. Hasn't the time come to fear God's word? Allah. I love you all . . . Amir'" (McDermott 2005, 225).

The youngest pilot, Marwan al-Shehhi, age 23 in 2001, was a "bon vivant," a "romantic," satisfied with an arranged marriage. Well-versed in Arab literature, he reveled in telling its stories, reciting its poems. The only one from a religious family, he loved to eat but wouldn't go into a restaurant that didn't observe strict dietary laws. In the last days before the hijacking, he and Atta seem to have been almost always together.

Hani Honjour became a pilot *faute de mieux* after more suitable men failed to get visas. He studied flying relentlessly, at flight schools and on simulators, but was a slow learner. He studied English, the international language of aviators, but had trouble learning that too. After failing several times to get his flying license, he succeeded but couldn't find a job as a pilot. He went to the training centers in Afghanistan and there was recruited for the hijacking because he had a license and because as a Saudi he could get a visa. The only one who looks (from photos) and sounds (from stories) "depressed," his one real flight was his last.

Ziad Jarrah is often contrasted with Atta. He was emotionally entangled with a German-Turkish woman for "a tough five years," married her at a dismal wedding, broke up and reconciled frequently. A "normal" hedonistic and domineering heterosexual young man who tried to curb his wife's independence, he became more secretive as he became increasingly religious and then, of course, as he became involved in a secret plot. In his diary he wrote lines like these: "The morning will come. The victors will come, will come. We swear to beat you. The earth will tremble beneath your feet. . . . I came to you with men who love the death just as you love life. . . . Oh, the smell of paradise is rising" (in McDermott 2005, 88). On the morning of September 11, he wrote Aysel, his wife, a long note that includes these lines:

> My love, my life. My beloved lady, my heart. You are my life. . . . I want you to believe truly that I love you with all my heart. . . . I am guilty of giving you hope about marriage, wedding, children, and family. . . . I did not leave you alone. Allah is with you. . . . I hug you and I kiss you on the hands. And I thank you and I say sorry for the very nice, tough five years you spent with me. . . . God willing, I am your prince and I will pick you up.
>
> See you again!!
Your man always
Ziad Jarrah
9/11/2001

The most thoughtful descriptions of these pilots, on the Web or in the literature, are concerned with "*why* they do it" where "it" often means killing themselves. I am concerned with what the pilots did and how. The deed I have in mind is killing others, strangers who were doing them no harm. As I turn to what they did and how, I will refer to "the pilots" as a group, although the evidence is strongest for Mohamed Atta.

The pilots made no speeches and left little to read. To discern evil in their acts, I had first to identify the evil I was looking for. I turned to the literature, deliberately seeking evils that were undeniable and great. I started with Hannah Arendt and literature from the Holocaust, and happened on the correspondence with Jaspers. I then took up two evils that were being discussed roundly at the time: the lynching of African American men by white Americans, and the atrocities revealed by the Truth and Reconciliation Commission in South Africa. I then read Robin May Schott's manuscript "Ethics after Mass Rape." As I read terrible passage after terrible passage, I began to identify acts and practices characteristic of evil. I then asked whether and how the pilots exhibited these characteristics.

I selected four criteria from my readings to "test" these pilots: (1) Evildoers understand what they are doing; they willingly inflict the harm that victims suffer. (2) They use whatever weapons suit their military aims, no matter how cruel. (3) They treat captives, disarmed enemies, slaves, and others who cannot harm them with gratuitous cruelty. (4) They are either cheerfully indifferent to the harm they produce or triumphant in their success. How do the 9/11 pilots demonstrate these characteristics?

1. The pilots knew what they were doing and could foresee the harm they would inflict. Indeed, they planned and trained for over two years to produce the destruction that three of the four achieved. This intense and single-minded planning was accompanied by what seemed to me a macho sense of adventure as the future pilots crisscrossed the United States and flew to Europe, the Middle East, and back again, as passengers in airplanes they were learning to master, teaching themselves what they needed to know in order to kill.

2. The men in the Hamburg group believed in the necessity of armed battle and praised weapons—swords especially. Although the pilots probably left actual violence to other hijackers, they clearly favored killing or disabling anyone in their way. Some weapons, when used instrumentally to achieve some purpose, are unacceptably cruel—torture and rape are clear examples, cluster bombs and land mines are now controversial. Collectively, the pilots used knives and "box cutters to slit throats" to kill or disable, and mace and the threat of a bomb to control the passengers and on some planes to move them to the back. "Box cutters to slit throats" may have a ritualistic aspect and hints of beheadings: "Hit very hard in the neck in the knowledge that heaven awaits you" (*Der Spiegel* 2001, 2002, 297–98).[6]

3. "Gratuitously cruel" evildoers humiliate and torture, often with evident pleasure and excitement, and without any practical purposes such as control or gathering information. The dragging murder of James Byrd Jr. and the slow tortured killing of Matthew Shepard were gratuitously cruel. Memoirs and accounts of the Holocaust and slavery are riddled with instances of gratuitous cruelty.

I see no evidence of gratuitously cruel behavior among the pilots. All of the attackers believed in the righteousness of their cause, expected to kill, and may have been excited by the prospect. But they are also told to "cleanse your heart of all bad feelings that you might hold." (*Der Spiegel* 2002, 312). When on the plane and surrounded by several nonbelievers, they are told that they must "sit quietly and remember that God will make victory possible for you in the end" (310). They prayed to God to "help us to succeed in what we attempt to do, allow us to vanquish the unfaithful peoples . . . and let us conquer and bring down the unfaithful, that they lower their heads" (311).

Lowering heads and holding them high figure repeatedly in the official rhetoric, pointing to the themes of humiliation and pride evident in bin Laden's speeches, Jarrah's diary, and accounts of Atta's anger at injustice. But the desire that the once proud will be made to lower their heads, a refrain of several Christian hymns I sang as an adolescent, seems hardly akin to the brutal degradation visited on victims of the great evils.

There were only a few minutes on the planes, but that was enough time for particular cruelty, had these been cruel men. According to the 9/11 commission, on Atta's plane someone, probably Atta himself, both threatened and reassured passengers by saying, famously, "We have some planes," then telling them not to endanger themselves or the planes, that they were returning to the airport. Two flight attendants spoke almost to the moment of impact. According to one of them, the passengers in coach thought that there was a medical emergency in first class. The stewards themselves seemed to have had no idea that they were about to be crashed.

I leave out the terrible suffering inherent in the plan, the stabbing, injuring, the blood and pain, the killing, and the final terror. These happenings were undeniably terrible. But they did not include the gratuitous humiliation and cruelty laced through many great and lesser evils visited on victims with no purpose beyond humiliating and inflicting pain.

4. Were the pilots cheerfully indifferent to the suffering they caused? "Cheerfully indifferent" evildoers delight in the success of their mission or in the numbers killed but are otherwise indifferent to the suffering they cause. Exultant high-altitude bombardiers giving each other high fives on returning from a successful bombing raid provide a familiar example. Photographic records of white people enjoying themselves at a lynching provide another infamous example of cheerful indifference.

Osama bin Laden's indifferent cheerfulness was captured on a videotape discovered in Afghanistan. Bin Laden and his associates tell how they calculated in advance the number of victims and the destruction they could expect and were happy to have their expectations exceeded. "They were overjoyed when the first plane hit the building so I said to them be patient" (bin Laden 2001b, 320). "Do you know when there is soccer game and your team wins?" one associate asks. "It was the same expression of joy" (2001b, 319).

The pilots seem neither indifferent nor "cheerful"—they are, after all, about to die. But their pride and pleasure in the destruction they will achieve is chilling. The Primer reminds them of their vow and its rewards: "The sky smiles, my young son, for you are marching toward heaven." "Angels are calling your name and wearing their finest clothes for you" (*Der Spiegel* 2001, 311). As Ziad Jarrah wrote Aysel: "I did not escape from you, but I did what I was supposed to. . . . You should be very proud of me. It's an honor. And you will see the results, and everyone will be happy!!!" (in McDermott 2005, 231).

I have judged the pilots by four selective criteria. The whole-hearted intensity of their planning clearly fulfilled the least disturbing of my criteria: deliberate, knowledgeable willingness to harm. The most disturbing criterion of evil is gratuitous cruelty that serves no purpose but to inflict pain and humiliate. But I did not find gratuitous cruelty in the pilots, nor did I find the cheerful indifference exemplified by bin Laden. I did find pride in destruction, especially suggested by passages from Zarrah.

When is a weapon so terrible that the willingness to use it seems evil? The pilots' box cutters and knives are disturbingly intimate, visibly bloody weapons. They are like the bayonets that soldiers of the First World War found so appalling that they could not use them when sober. The pilots did *not* use the most terrible weapons, for example, instruments of torture and bodily rape, which violate simultaneously a victim's bodily self- and social identity.

The pilots had another weapon, their own embodied persons, whose presence and therefore whose death is necessary to the enterprise. Until a few weeks ago the fact that the hijackers were suicides hovered at the edge of my attention. I thought of these young men as killers of others. Now I see them not only as killers but as the killers' weapon. As weapons, "suicide bombers offer many advantages to the attacker: they are quick, cheap, and extremely accurate," "the high precision artillery of the militarily challenged" (Caryl 2005). I am disturbed by the ease with which I, along with Caryl and Gambetta, called these men and women "quick, cheap, weapons." There are knives, box cutters, mace, bombs, and then "us"—an ease of depersonalization that may grease the wheels of war (see Cohn 1987). I don't see suicide as a crime against humanity, or suicide bombing as doubly atrocious (Pape 2005, 216). But at the end of the day, the sufferings these missions cause to killer and victim and everyone who loved either seem overwhelming.

The September Attacks: Evil's Victims

When I think of the four pilots as I have come to know them, I can easily include them as "still within the reach of ideal humanity" (Cornell 2003, 174). When I think of their acts as I have come to know them, I find this inclusion nearly impossible. What, I ask in near rage, did these pilots think about the suffering of their *victims*?

Perhaps they believed that the passengers they sat among and the office workers they would never meet were of a *kind* to be killed, like combatants in just-war theory. But combatants can be killed, not because of who they are, but because of what they might do. A disarmed prisoner no longer capable of harm should be as protected from injury and murder as the passengers sitting next to him. Perhaps the passengers and the workers were *nothing but* a kind—Americans, Zionists, Crusaders, hateful not because of something they might or might not have done, but because of who they were. Racism and racialized nationalism inspire violence. A less conscious racist attitude that separates "their" suffering from "ours," them from us, condones violence that would otherwise be impermissible. The pilots, especially Atta, were said to be anti-Semitic (McDermott 2005, 67–68), but we hear little about that.

In the hijacker's Primer there is no mention of Americans, Jews, or Crusaders —only one mention of "the West." The Other, the enemy is "the Unfaithful," "the Unbeliever," "the Infidel." The hijackers are told that when sitting among infidels they are to sit quietly and remember that God will give them victory in the end. The plane starts moving, stops and starts again—eerily familiar. The hijackers, still sitting among the infidels—and, though this is not mentioned, among the people whose death they are engineering—pray for the final victory.

Except for causing a particular discomfort because they were, presumptively, infidels, the people who would become the victims on the planes and in the buildings are curiously absent from reports about the pilots and from their self-preoccupied reflections. It is as if victims, who were, presumptively, *nothing but* Infidels and Unbelievers, have finally been shown to be nothing—merely fungible accessories or potential obstacles to a plan that inevitably involved the death of passengers and office workers, whoever they might be. To paraphrase Simone Weil, who was speaking of workers on a factory floor, the people in those planes and in those buildings "were nothing. They simply did not count" (Weil 1977, 56).

This nothingness of victims, in its different forms, is familiar from the evils of the concentration camp, slavery, and war. Human beings "as human beings are totally superfluous" (Arendt in Arendt and Jaspers 1992, 166; Arendt 1958). They are constructed as "objects of property" (Williams 1991, chap. 12), transformed by sheer "force that turns anyone who is subjected to it into a thing" (Weil 1977, 153–54). The alleged "innocence" of the victims is also without connection to particular moral lives and character. In the midst of an attack where she counts for nothing, someone stealing from her parents' savings is no less innocent than someone taking on extra work to support them. Theirs is a metaphysical innocence "beyond goodness or virtue" (Arendt in Arendt and Jaspers 1992, 55).

Gratuitously cruel attackers need to reduce their victims to nothing: they torture, humiliate, *make* them exist, just so that they can count them as nothing before their own eyes. To repeat: there is no sign of the need to make someone "hang their head down"—to borrow language that they themselves used. For them the victims really did not count.

The September Attacks: Evil's Good

Good and evil reveal each other. In the presence of evil, we comprehend the good that evil violated. In the light of that good, we see the violation as evil.

On September 11 victims were counted *as if* they were nothing. That "as if" allows a space for reversing the valuation, creating narratives that re-count the passengers and workers as someone for themselves and each other.[7] President Bush was an early storyteller, posthumously recruiting Trade Tower victims as casualties in the War on Terror he declared. By contrast, I choose to tell the story of people who knew they were going to die and called on cell phones or left messages in emails and on answering machines. As reported, remembered, and sometimes recorded, the dominant theme of the messages was affection and love. From a Trade Tower email: "I don't think I am going to get out. You've been a really good friend." From United Flight 93: "She called to tell me that she loved me, loved me dearly, and to tell the boys that she loved us. All that she was going through . . . To call me to tell me she loved me is embedded in my head" (Clines 2001).

I hear these stories as evoking "another world" that Simone Weil recognized from *The Iliad* in the moments of love that interrupted the desolate scene of war:

> More poignant still for its pain of contrast is the sudden evocation . . . of another world, the far off world, precarious and touching of peace, of the family, that world wherein each [person] is, for those who surround him, all that counts most. (Weil 1977, 154)

I call this other world "Home"[8]—a symbolic representation of a material dwelling place, a network of attachments, and an array of relationships guided by the principle of nonviolence. "Home" offers safety first and then the privacy necessary for mementos and memories, a space for the "construction and reconstruction of oneself" (Young 1997, 163). Home dwellers create festivals, secular and religious, celebrating their people and their history. No one is of a kind that cannot enter; walls that protect need not exclude.

This is, of course, a fantasy. Homes often thrive on exclusions, some arising from race or sexuality or class arrogance, some from intimate cruel battle. Only a small minority of the world's inhabitants live in safe dwelling places. Of these, many may not want, and most do not have, the privacy in which selves are constructed. Homes that are well-ordered still exploit the affections and labor of women who live in them and of employees who work in them. Homes are often bastions of exclusion. When the doors are closed and vulnerable people have no place to go, home may become a safe place for torturers and abusers (Card 2000).

We should identify and defeat these vices of/at home. Yet a new vision of home is a fantasy we should value. Homes are not inherently the preserve of the fortunate. "We should be ashamed of a world in which safety at home is a privilege" (Young 1997, 162). Nor are risky attachments the luxury of the sensitive few. We should suspect anyone who describes the other, either friend or enemy, as someone who "doesn't put the same high price on life as does a Westerner," who doesn't love and lose as we do (General Westmoreland, in Davis 1974).

When waters and winds are quiet, and neighborhoods are mostly safe and fairly governed, the physical space that is home may become the holding place for an ideal defined by its activities. At home pain is never disregarded, nor is it ever regarded as deserved (Noddings 2002, 147). Calls for help are answered by "I am here" (Noddings 2002, 129); no one is expected to make her way alone (Kittay 1999). This is a place of illness and frailty; of tenderness, restraint, comfort, and relief. This is a place where bodies are treasured, whatever their sex; where birth is celebrated, therefore never forced; where pleasure and sensual delight are expressed as desire prompts and respect for the other allows (Cornell forthcoming). This is a place of dignity for people who hold their heads high and walk out smartly and for people whose backs are bent over and who can neither walk, nor talk, nor sing (Kittay 2004). This is a place of leaving, learning, wandering, returning—a place of waiting in fear and hope, preparing to welcome the wanderer returned.

Home is a place where attachments are protected. We are bound and learn to bind and be bound again in relationships that are bittersweet. What binds us down through generations and across them is the entirely irreplaceable complexity and visage of just this person, and then this one, and then another. The love we yearn for and then depend upon includes the desolation we fear. In a place of attachments, the art of losing may be cultivated, but it is never mastered. We must make time for reconciliation, mourning, and farewells.

On the day of the September 11 attacks, without any warning, in the absence of cruelty, maliciousness, or greed, the activities of home were halted by forces that seemed their very opposite: bodies became instruments of death; pain was disregarded; cries for help were silenced; the leaving left forever; destruction became its own deliberate aim.

And yet the stories I told, and many others like them, were also true. Messages were sent from office buildings and planes, received at home, passed along. At the end of the day we hear, "She called to tell me that she loved me, loved me dearly." The love, and with it the loss that love always risks. Then love again in the fullness of its responsibilities: "to tell the boys that she loved us." First there was the rupture: "I don't think I am going to get out . . ." Then the bond that was ruptured: "You've been a really good friend."

These last words, meant to be private, became "messages to the world." They did not offer victory, or promise to avenge the terrible injury done them. Instead, with stunning generosity, they continued to express the love they would lose, expressed both the loss and the love. It is in this *conjunction* of a good and its violation that we begin to see what evil meant, what evil did, on the day of the attacks.

Notes

I thank Robin Schott for making the *Hypatia* forums possible, for her patience with me and her courage in writing about evil.

1. The speeches of President Bush are easily accessed on the Web or in print. I cite his address to the nation on September 11 and his State of the Union Address on January 29, 2002.

2. Osama bin Laden's words are now available in *Messages to the World* (2005), edited by Bruce Lawrence.

3. Khalid Sheikh Mohammed was a key al-Qaeda commander taken captive in Pakistan shortly before the U.S. invasion of Iraq. He is now designated *the* "mastermind" of the 9/11 attacks. See, for example, Holmes 2005, 132–72.

4. Although Afghanistan was the direct target of U.S. retaliation, I consider its regime a valuable accomplice of the masterminds, providing training camps, safe houses, and other services, but not distinctive producers of their project. That the governing regime, the Taliban, was despotic, tyrannical, and brutal to women contributed to the justification of U.S. attacks on them but did not distinctly illuminate the evils of attacks on the United States. The invasion of Afghanistan may well have been the sort of American "imperial over-stretch" that the "masterminds" hoped the September 11 attacks would provoke (Holmes 2005, 156 ff.). But the evils of the invasion—the destruction of land and people—as well as whatever good came from it—remain the responsibility of the United States.

5. The "evidence" about the hijackers is often anecdotal and changing. I am aware how little I or others know about these young men. Although *Inside 9-11: What Really Happened* is now a bit breathless and dated, it has information that other books do not and has the virtue of being compiled in Hamburg by a respected German weekly, *Der Spiegel*. The book includes a document labeled by *Der Spiegel* "Primer for Terrorists on Suicide Missions" (2002, 307–13), which I refer to as "the Primer." This document was found, among other places, in Atta's suitcase that didn't make his connection. *Inside 9–11* also includes excerpts from "A Manual for Terrorists" (2002, 262–304), found

on a computer of an al-Qaeda member in Manchester, England. I refer to it as "the Manual." Terry McDermott's *Perfect Soldiers* (2005) has proved indispensable. The notes are useful for getting a sense of the "evidence," as well as the origin of stories that are many times repeated. The report of the official government commission, *The 9/11 Commission Report,* is now available. Christian Caryl published a review of literature on suicide missions, suicide bombing in particular, in the September 22 issue of the *New York Review of Books.* The attacks are one instance of suicide bombing and are discussed as such. I recommend especially the collection by Diego Gambetta, *Understanding Suicide Missions* (2005), particularly the chapter by Stephen Holmes, "Al-Qaeda, September 11, 2001" (131–72).

6.   *The 9/11 Commission* gives the clearest reports about what happened on the planes. There is a vivid description of the tactics on Atta's plane partly because someone (probably Atta) inadvertently broadcast warnings meant for the passengers to air controllers, and partly because two flight attendants, Betty Ong and Amy Sweeney, described what they saw happening until just before the plane hit the trade towers. There were cell phone calls from other planes and a fuller but not yet fully public account of Jaarah's flight, which was driven into the ground.

7.   One chooses among stories. In an early set of stories the attacks seemed like grand disasters; strangers treated strangers as someone needing help; carrying, leading, and dragging them from collapsing burning buildings. Some were official rescuers doing their duty in impossible circumstances; others were accidental passersby. Recently, the flight piloted by Jarrah and forced or driven into the ground has become the stage for a war story with heroes, villains, and moral victory. Vastly outnumbered soldiers/passengers take over a cockpit and down a plane, thus saving the White House.

8.   I have taken the idea of "Home" most directly from Nel Noddings's *Starting at Home: Caring and Social Policy* (2002) and from Iris Marion Young, "House and Home: Feminist Variations on a Theme" (1997). From Hilde Lindemann (Nelson), "What Child is This?" (2002) and "Verdi Requiem" (2002, manuscript courtesy of the author), I take the idea that "holding someone in personhood," one of the activities I would count as defining Home, can be seen as an array of practices partly created by the stories we tell. Eva Feder Kittay (1999, 2004, 2005) has influenced my thinking about dignity and dependence. In general, I am indebted to the vast and intriguing "ethics of care" that feminists are putting together. Virginia Held has regularly provided introductions to this ethics as well as producing some of its most original work, most recently in *The Ethics of Care: Personal, Political and Global* (2005). None of these very different writers approves of, or usually even knows of, my use of "home."

References

Allen, James, ed., with forewords by Hilton Als, John Lewis, and Leon F. Litwack. 2000. *Without Sanctuary: Lynching Photography in America.* Santa Fe, N.M.: Twin Palms Publisher.

Arendt, Hannah. 1958. *Origins of Totalitarianism,* 3rd ed. New York: Harcourt Brace and World.

———. 1971. Thinking and moral considerations: A lecture. In *Social Research* (fall): 417–46.

Arendt, Hannah, and Karl Jaspers. 1992. *Correspondence 1926–1989.* Ed. Lotte Kohler and Hans Saner. New York: Harcourt, Brace and Jovanovich.

Bernstein, Richard J. 2002. *Radical Evil: A Philosophical Interrogation.* Cambridge, Mass.: Polity Press.

Bin Laden, Osama. 1998a. Interview with Rahimullah Yousafai of ABC News. In *Ethics and Weapons of Mass Destruction: Religious and Secular Perspectives,* ed. Sohail Hashimi and Stephen P. Lee, 334. Cambridge: Cambridge University Press.

———. 1998b. Jihad against Jews and Crusaders. In Terry McDermott, *Perfect Soldiers.* New York: HarperCollins, 2005.

———. 2002. Letter to America. In Bruce Lawrence, *Messages to the World: The Statements of Osama bin Laden.* New York: Verso Press, 2005.

——— 2004. Towers of Lebanon. Tape delivered to Al Jazeera, allegedly recorded October 29. In Bruce Lawrence, ed., *Messages to the World: The Statements of Osama bin Laden.* New York: Verso Press, 2005.

Bush, George W. 2001. Address to the Nation, 11 September.

———. 2002. State of the Union Address. 29 January.

Card, Claudia. 2002. *The Atrocity Paradigm: A Theory of Evil.* Oxford: Oxford University Press.

Caryl, Christian. 2005. Why they do it. In *New York Review of Books* 52, 22 September.

Clendinnen, Inga. 1999. *Reading the Holocaust.* Cambridge: Cambridge University Press.

Clines, Francis X. 2001. Before and after: Voices in the wind, a new form of grieving evolves over last goodbyes. *New York Times,* Week in Review, 16 September.

Cohn, Carol. 1987. Sex and death in the rational world of defense intellectuals. *Signs* 12 (4): 687–728.

Cornell, Drucilla. Forthcoming. The shadow of heterosexuality, in *Hypatia* Special Issue: Against Heterosexualism, ed. Joan Callahan, Bonnie Mann, and Sara Ruddick.

———. 2003. Facing our humanity. *Hypatia* 18:1 (winter): 170–74.

Der Spiegel reporters, writers, and editors. 2001. *Inside 9-11: What Really Happened,* published in German in *Der Spiegel* magazine.

———. 2002. *Inside 9-11: What Really Happened.* English edition with new preface. New York: St. Martin's Press.

Dwyer, Jim, et al. 2002. "102 minutes: Last words at the trade center, fighting to live as the towers died." *New York Times,* 26 May.

Elster, Jon. 2004. Motivations and beliefs in suicide missions. In *Making Sense of Suicide Missions,* ed. Diego Gambetta, 233–58. Oxford: Oxford University Press.

Gambetta, Diego, ed. 2005. *Making Sense of Suicide Missions.* Oxford: Oxford University Press.

Hashmi, Sohail H. 2004. Islamic ethics and weapons of mass destruction: An argument for nonproliferation. In *Ethics and Weapons of Mass Destruction: Religious and Secular Perspectives,* ed. Sohail H. Hashmi and Steven P. Lee. Cambridge: Cambridge University Press.

Held, Virginia. 2005. *The Ethics of Care: Personal, Political and Global.* Oxford: Oxford University Press.

Holmes, Stephen. 2005. Al-Qaeda, September 11, 2001. In *Making Sense of Suicide Missions,* ed. Diego Gambetta, 131–72. Oxford: Oxford University Press.

Jaspers, Karl. [1947], 2000. *The Question of German Guilt (Die Schuldfrage).* New York: Dial Press; New York: Fordham University Press, 2000.

Kittay, Eva Feder. 2005. At the margins of moral personhood. *Ethics* 116 (October 2005).

———. 2004. Equality, dependency and disability. In *Perspectives on Equality: The Second Seamus Heaney Lectures,* ed. Marian Lyons and Fionnuala Waldron. Dublin: Liffey Press.

———. 1999. *Love's Labor: Essays on Equality, Women and Dependency.* New York: Routledge.

Krog, Antjie. 1999. *Country of My Skull: Guilt, Sorrow and the Limits of Forgiveness in the New South Africa.* New York: Random House, Times Books.

Lawrence, Bruce, ed. 2005. *Messages to the World: The Statements of Osama bin Laden.* New York: Verso Press.

Lindemann, Hilde. 2005. Verdi Requiem. Manuscript courtesy of the author.

McDermott, Terry. 2005. *Perfect Soldiers.* New York: Harper Collins.

Nelson, Hilde Lindemann. 2002. What child is this? *The Hastings Center Report* 32: 29–38.

Noddings, Nel. 1989. *Women and Evil.* Berkeley: University of California Press.

———. 2002. *Starting at Home: Caring and Social Policy.* Berkeley: University of California Press.

Pape, Robert A. 2005. *Dying to Win: The Strategic Logic of Suicide Terrorism.* New York: Random House.

Schott, Robin May. Ethics after mass rape. Manuscript courtesy of the author.

Weil, Simone. 1977. Factory work. In *Simone Weil Reader,* ed. George Panichas, 53–73. Mt. Kisko, N.Y.: Moyer Bell.

———. 1977. *The Iliad* or the poem of force. In *Simone Weil Reader,* 153–83. Mt. Kisko, N.Y.: Moyer Bell.

Williams, Patricia. 1991. On being the object of property. In *The Alchemy of Race and Rights,* 216–36. Cambridge, Mass.: Harvard University Press.

Young, Iris Marion. 1997. House and home: Feminist variations on a theme. In *Intersecting Voices: Dilemmas of Gender, Political Philosophy and Policy,* 134–65. Princeton, N.J.: Princeton University Press.

18 Feminist Reactions to the Contemporary Security Regime

Iris Marion Young

The American and European women's movement of the late 1970s and early 1980s contained a large segment organizing around issues of weapons, war, and peace. By the early 1990s, the humor and heroism of women's peace actions had been all but forgotten. Prompted by events in the United States and the world since September 2001, and by the rhetoric of U.S. leaders justifying some of their actions, I do think that there are urgent reasons to reopen the question of whether looking at war and security issues through a gendered lens can teach us all lessons that might further the projects of peace and democracy. A mistake in much writing about gender and war, it seems to me, is that it aims to explain bellicosity or its absence by a simpleminded essentialism in considering attributes of men and women (see, for example, Goldstein 2001). In this chapter I take a somewhat different approach by inquiring about the meaning of appeals to security, the role of the state as protector, and the support of citizens for war and potential restrictions on their freedom.

Masculinism as Protection

Much feminist theory and gender theory has focused on forms of masculinity characterized by selfishness, coarse domination, and desires to exclude. However, it is important to recall another more benign image of masculinity, one more associated with ideas of chivalry. The gallantly masculine man faces the world's difficulties and dangers in order to shield women from harm. The role of this courageous, responsible, virtuous, and "good" man is that of a protector. Good men can only appear in their goodness if we assume that lurking outside the warm familial walls are aggressors, the "bad" men, who wish to attack them.

Central to the logic of masculinist protection is the subordinate relation of those in the protected position. In return for male protection, the woman concedes critical distance and decision-making autonomy. When the household lives under threat, there cannot be divided wills and arguments about who will do what, or what is the best course of action. Because he bears this responsibility of leadership, moreover, and because he takes risks and is ready to sacrifice, those under his protection owe him deference and indulgence in small plea-sures. In this logic, the feminine woman does not submit herself, but adores her protector, and happily defers to his judgment in return for the promise of secu-rity he offers.

Hobbes is the great theorist of political power founded upon a need and de-sire for protection. He depicts a state of nature in which people live in small families where each believes some of the others envy them and desire to enlarge themselves by stealing from or conquering them. In this state of nature every-one has reason to feel insecure, not because all have these dominative motives, but because they are uncertain about who does, and they understand their own vulnerability (Hobbes [1668] 1994, chaps. xiii, xiv, xix).

In her contemporary classic, *The Sexual Contract* (1988), Carole Pateman in-terprets Hobbes along the lines of contemporary feminist accounts of men as selfish aggressors and sexual predators. In chapter 3, Pateman accounts for the patriarchal household as formed through overpowering force over women and other men. One can just as well interpret Hobbes's text through the lens of the apparently more benign masculinity of protection. On this alternative account, then, patriarchal right emerges from male specialization in security. His will rules because he faces the dangers outside and needs to organize defenses. By this account, female subordination derives from this position of being pro-tected. Both Pateman's story of male domination and the one I have recon-structed depict patriarchal gender relations as having unequal power. It is im-portant to attend to the difference. In one relation the hierarchical power is obvious, and in the other it is more masked by virtue and love. Because the latter wears a caring face, those in its orbit may fail to notice the inequality it entails.

The State as Protector and Subordinate Citizenship

What I call a *security regime* is an aspect of all states in relation to their people and people outside the state. The security regime is what a state would have to be if Hobbes were right that human relations are always on the verge of disorder and violence, if only an authoritarian government that brooks no di-vision of power or dissent could keep the peace, and if maintaining peace and security is unambiguously the highest value. Democrats agree that a major pur-pose of government is to keep peace and promote public safety, but we deny that unquestioning obedience to a unified sovereign is the only means to achieve this, and we question that values of freedom and autonomy must be traded against the value of security.

A security regime has both an *external* and an *internal* aspect. It constitutes itself in relation to an unpredictable aggressor outside. It organizes political and economic capacities around the accumulation of weapons and the mobilization of a military to respond to this outsider threat. The state's identity is militaristic, and it engages in military action, but with the point of view of the defendant rather than the aggressor. Even when the security regime makes a first strike, it justifies its move as necessary to preempt the threatening aggressor outside. Security states appeal to their role as protectors.

Internally, the security regime must root out the enemy within. There is always the danger that among us are agents who have an interest in disturbing our peace, violating our persons and property, and allowing outsiders to invade our communities and institutions. To protect the state and its citizens, officials must therefore keep a careful watch on everyone, observe and search them to make sure they do not intend evil actions and do not have the means to perform them. In a security regime, there cannot be a separation of power or critical accountability of official action to a public. Nor can a security regime allow expression of dissent. According to Hobbes's argument in *Leviathan*, it is necessary that the sovereign be one. Unity in will and purpose is absolutely essential, even if the sovereign consists in an assembly of officials rather than one ruler.

One of the things I have learned since September 11, 2001, is how easily the state actions and political culture of a democracy like that of the United States can shift in authoritarian directions. Interpreting recent events through a gender lens of masculinist protection helps reveal the logic and desires that underlie shifts toward authoritarianism. In the security regime, the state and its officials assume the role of protector toward its citizens, and the citizens become positioned as subordinates, grateful for the protection afforded them.

A marauding gang of outsiders attacked buildings in New York and Washington with living bombs, killing thousands in barely an instant, and terrifying large numbers of people in the country. Our government responded with a security alert at home and abroad. We were frightened, and the heads of state stepped up to offer us protection. They began to "hunt down those responsible" and eliminate the threat they constitute. The United States bombed Afghanistan and overthrew its government, even though that state did not attack us. The Bush administration justified the war as a necessary response to attack and as a means to protection from further attack. At home, the government began to devote more resources to homeland security, screening, searching, and making plans for hiding government officials and documents. As in past moments in American history, moments that the government has regretted, the government has rounded up those it identifies as the enemy within, whom it detains without charge.

The separation of power, due process, deliberation, and public accountability basic to a democratic state are suspended. The U.S. security regime has expanded the power of the executive and eroded the ability of legislative or judicial branches to review executive decisions or to be independent sources of decision making. In the week after the September 11 attacks, for example, Congress passed a resolution effectively waiving its constitutionally mandated power to deliberate and decide on whether the state shall go to war. Drafted quickly and passed with almost no debate, the USA-Patriot Act signed on October 26, 2001, severely reduces the power of courts to review and limit executive actions to keep individuals and organizations under surveillance, limit their activities, search and seize, or detain individuals.

How can citizens and their representatives in a democracy allow such rapid challenge to their political principles and institutions with so little discussion and protest? Surely, one part of the answer is that *citizens* believe that their rights are not threatened, that only the aliens will suffer. The sweeping powers granted to the executive, however, clearly may include surveillance on or restriction of the rights of association and assembly of anyone. Another part of the answer lies in accepting the promise of protection. Most regimes that suspend certain rights and legal procedures declare a state of emergency. They claim that special measures of unity and obedience are required in order to ensure protection from unusual danger. We have accepted a deal: you subordinate your actions to our judgment of what is necessary, and we promise to keep you safe.

Through the logic of protection the state demotes members of a democracy to dependents, a form analogous to the patriarchal household. State officials adopt the stance of the masculine protector. Their protector position puts us, the citizens and residents who depend on their strength and vigilance for our security, in the position of women and children under the charge of the male protector (cf. Berlant 1997). Because they take the risks and organize the agency of the state, it is their prerogative to determine the objectives of protective action and their means. Good citizenship in a security regime consists in cooperative obedience for the sake of the safety of all.

Patriotism has an analogous emotive function in the constitution of the security regime. Under threat from outside, all of us, authorities and citizens, imagine ourselves as a single body enclosed on and loving itself. We affirm our oneness with our fellow citizens and together affirm our single will behind the will of the leaders who have vowed to protect us. It is not merely that dissent is dangerous; worse yet, it is ungrateful. Subordinate citizenship does not merely acquiesce to limitation on freedom in exchange for a promise of security; the consent is active, as a solidarity with the others who are uniting behind the leaders and in grateful love of country.

Under these conditions of protective leadership and emergency obedience, our role as citizens gives us a single-minded purpose. We cannot sit by and do nothing, we cannot simply go on with our work, play, and private pains as though nothing has happened. The action each of us must take is clear and simple: display the flag in the window; on the banister; in red, white, and blue bunting tied around all the trees on the block; on the car antenna; on the lapel; on the backpack. There are so many ways to display the flag, and with each the citizen knows that at least she has done something—something that both expresses and helps to constitute solidarity.

The state of emergency also brings out gender-coded impulses of sacrifice. A few stand as the masculine sacrificers: the vice president who effectively risks his life every time he goes before a TV camera; police and fire fighters who rush to save the endangered and wounded and give their lives in the effort; pilots, air stewards, and marshals ready to face the terrorists' guns and knives; sailors, soldiers, and bombardiers facing enemy fire to defeat the enemy that threatens us.

The rest of us give in smaller supportive ways, by sending money to the families of those who have sacrificed to protect us, by making parcels of food or clothing, and by giving time and money to celebrations that express our love and gratitude for their protective actions.

Is It a Good Deal?

The logic of masculinist protection constitutes the "good" men who protect their women and children by relation to other "bad" men liable to attack. Feminists have much analyzed a correlate dichotomy: The "good" woman who is protected in exchange for loyalty and submission, and the "bad" woman who refuses protection by claiming the right to run her own life. The position of citizens and residents under a security state entails a similar bargain: The state pledges to protect us, but it tells us that we should submit to its rule and decisions without deliberation, publicity, criticism, or dissent. Some of the measures in place to protect us entail limitations on our freedom, especially the freedom of particular classes of people. The deal is: you must trade some liberty and autonomy for the sake of the protection we offer. Is this a fair deal?

Some years ago, Susan Rae Peterson (1977) likened the state's relation to women under a system of male domination to a protection racket. Insofar as state laws and policies assume or reinforce the view that a "good" woman should move under the guidance of a man, the state functions as a protection racket. However, the protectors withhold protection from the women who claim autonomy; moreover, they may become attackers.

Current forms of "homeland security" in the United States look like a protection racket. As long as we are quiet and obedient, we can breathe easy. If we should step out of the bounds designated for "good" citizens, however, we may find ourselves unprotected and even under attack by the protector state. If we publicly criticize the state's policies, especially the war or foreign policy, we may land on lists of unpatriotic people published to invite our neighbors or employers to sanction us. We find that we are no longer allowed to assemble in some public places, even when we wish to demonstrate about issues other than war and the security regime, and that we might be arrested if we try. So if we confine our protests to walking on public sidewalks, we may be photographed by state agents keeping watch on dissenters. We may discover that organizations we support appear on lists of "terrorist" organizations at the discretion of bureaucrats; as a result, our phones may be tapped or our email correspondence monitored.

Some citizens become defined as not "good" citizens simply because of their race or national origin. Although public opinion only recently claimed to disapprove of police and security practices that use racial or ethnic profiling, many now accept the state's claim that effective protection requires such profiling. Residents who are not citizens, especially those from places defined as sources of danger, lose most of the protection they may have had from attack by neighbors or from arbitrary and punitive treatment by state agents.

When we consent to this bargain, we endanger democratic practice. When we allow a legal distinction between the good citizen and the bad citizen that affords less legal protection to the latter, and when we allow the rhetoric of fear to consider all foreigners as enemies within, increasing numbers of us are liable to find that our attributes or activities put us on the wrong side of the line. If we allow our fear to cow us into submission, we assume the position of subordinates rather than adult democratic citizens equal to and not above our neighbors, equal to and not beneath our government.

There is little evidence that the way America has chosen to conduct its war on terrorism has in fact made the world any safer. Indeed, it may have put Americans at even greater risk. When U.S. planes began bombing Afghanistan in October 2001, officials publicly admitted that the action put Americans inside and outside the United States at greater risk from retaliating attackers.

In the spiral of violence, each bloody act creates more distrust and desire for revenge on the part of others, who then step up their own attacks. In a Hobbesian world, none of us will be safe until there is a world Leviathan. Despite its apparent aspirations, even the United States is not likely to succeed in becoming one. It is a bad deal, I submit, one that adult citizens in a democracy would not sign on to. Adult citizens wish security, and they expect their state institutions to assign some people the job of watching out for people's safety and apprehending people found attacking or endangering others. At the same time, adults recognize that a world free of risk is impossible, and they distrust any leader who seems to promise such a world. Most of all, adult citizens demand autonomy and equality *along with* a dependence on special measures of protection. They refuse to accept the patriarchal logic that gives to protective services a right to rule over those who count on their expertise at keeping watch and apprehending.

Feminist theorists of care and welfare have argued that the rights and dignity of individuals should not be diminished just because they need help and support to enable them to carry out their chosen projects (see Tronto 1994; Sevenjhuisen 1998; Kittay 1999; Young 2002). Persons who need care or other forms of social support ought not to be forced into a position of subordination and obedience in relation to those who provide care and support; not only should they retain the rights of full citizens to choose their own way of life and to hold authorities accountable, but they ought to be able to criticize the way in which support comes to them. This feminist argument rejects the assumption behind a notion of self-sufficient citizenship that a need for social support or care is more exceptional than normal. On the contrary, the well-being of all persons can be enhanced by the care and support of others, and in modern societies, much of this generalized care and support should be organized and guaranteed through state institutions. The organization of reasonable measures to protect people from harm and to make people confident that they can move and act relatively safely is another form of social support. Citizens should not have to trade their liberty of movement or right to protest and to hold leaders accountable in return for such security.

Feminism and Global Citizenship

One final aspect of recent events that I would like to bring under this gendered lens of masculinity as protection is the Bush administration's rhetoric of saving the women of Afghanistan to legitimate its war. I wonder whether some seeds for such cynical appeals to the need to save women might not have been sown by some recent American and European feminist discourse and practice that positioned itself as protector of oppressed women in Asia and Africa.

Years before the attacks of September 2001, the Feminist Majority led a campaign directed at saving the women of Afghanistan from the Taliban. Although the everyday practices of many societies impose harsh and horrible rules on billions of women that their governments are unable or unwilling to stop, the Taliban stood with only a handful of governments in imposing such rules as a matter of law and enforcing them through the state. To my ears, however, feminist focus on women under the Taliban rang with superior tones of enlightenment and righteousness, singling out this most exotic and distant of situations, and representing the women of Afghanistan as passive victims (cf. Narayan 1997).

Certainly, the Taliban should have been condemned for its policies, as should all the world's governments that perpetrate or allow systematic and discriminatory harms to and subordination of women. In this case, as well as perhaps some others, however, I fear that some feminists adopted the stance of the protector in relation to the women of Afghanistan. What is wrong with this stance, if it has existed, is that it fails to consider these women as equals, and it does not have principled ways of distancing itself from paternalist militarism.

From its torrid beginnings as a self-interested retaliation for aggressive attack, the U.S.-led war against Afghanistan has morphed into a humanitarian intervention of behalf of women's rights. Some feminists, such as Eleanor Smeal, leader of the Feminist Majority, jumped onto the war bandwagon, and the leaders of the security regime took on the trappings of feminism (see Lerner 2001). On November 17, 2001, Laura Bush became the first First Lady to give the president's Saturday morning radio address, which was devoted to condemning what she called the Taliban's war on women and to justifying the U.S. war as an effort to free Afghan women. Some members of the administration, such as Donald Rumsfeld in an interview on National Public Radio early in 2002, have suggested that liberating women would be a good reason to go to war against Iraq.

The stance of the male protector is one of loving self-sacrifice, with those in the feminine position as the objects of love and guardianship. Chivalrous forms of masculinism express and enact concern for the well-being of women, but they do so within a structure of superiority and subordination. The male protector confronts evil aggressors in the name of the right and the good, while those under his protection submit to his order and serve as handmaids to his efforts. Colonialist ideologies have often expressed a similar logic: the knights of civilization aim to bring enlightened understanding to the further regions of the world still living in cruel and irrational traditions that keep them from developing the economic and political structures that will bring them a good life. The suppression of women in these societies is a symptom of such backwardness. Troops will be needed to bring order and guard fledgling institutions, and foreign aid workers to feed, cure, and educate; but all this is only a period of tutelage that will end when the subject people demonstrate their ability to gain their own livelihood and run their own affairs.

It is difficult for feminists in Western societies not to be heard as continuous with this stance of superiority and paternalistic knowledge of what the poor women of the world need. It is disturbing that appeal to the importance of liberating women apparently works to justify war to the American people. This means that concern for the well-being of women is not a sufficient condition of feminism. Required in addition is commitment to adult democratic citizenship on a global level. Feminist global citizenship means at least that we represent and relate to needy people of the developing world as equals in a project of creating transnational democratic governance without any hegemonic power.

Note

A considerably longer version of this chapter has appeared as "The Logic of Masculinist Protection: Reflections on the Current Security State," in *Signs: A Journal of Women in Culture and Society* 29 (1) (2003): 1–25.

References

Berlant, Lauren. 1997. The theory of infantile citizenship. In *The Queen of America Goes to Washington City: Essays on Sex and Citizenship*. Durham, N.C.: Duke University Press.

Goldstein, Joshua S. 2001. *War and Gender*. Cambridge, U.K.: Cambridge University Press.

Hobbes, Thomas. [1668] 1994. *Leviathan*. Ed. Edwin Curley. Cambridge, U.K.: Hacket.

Kittay, Eva Feder. 1999. *Love's Labor*. New York: Routledge.

Lerner, Sharon. 2001. Feminists agonize over war in Afghanistan: What women want. *Village Voice*, 31 October, n.p.

Mohanty, Chandra, and Ann Russo, eds. 1991. *Third World Women and the Politics of Feminism*. Bloomington: Indiana University Press.

Narayan, Uma. 1997. *Dislocating Cultures: Identities, Traditions and Third World Feminism*. New York: Routledge.

Pateman, Carole. 1988. *The Sexual Contract*. Stanford, Calif.: Stanford University Press.

Peterson, Susan Rae. 1977. Coercion and rape: The state as a male protection racket. In *Feminism and Philosophy*, ed. Mary Vetterling Braggin. Totowa, N.J.: Rowman and Allenheld.

Sevenjhuisen, Selma. 1998. *Justice, Care and Citizenship.* New York: Routledge.

Tronto, Joan. 1994. *Moral Boundaries.* New York: Routledge.

Young, Iris Marion. 2002. Autonomy, welfare reform, and meaningful work. In *Philosophical Approaches to Dependency,* ed. Eva Feder Kittay and Ellen Feder. Lanham, Md.: Rowman and Littlefield.

Contributors

Lynne S. Arnault is Associate Professor of Philosophy at Le Moyne College, where she is a founding member of the Women's Studies Program and serves as its director. Her teaching and research are focused in ethics, moral psychology, and cultural studies. She is currently working on a manuscript for a book that explores the meaning and moral force of cruelty.

Bat-Ami Bar On is Professor of Philosophy and Women's Studies at Binghamton University (SUNY). She is author of *The Subject of Violence: Arendtean Exercises in Understanding.* She has published her work in *Philosopher's Magazine* (London), *ORD&BILD* (Stockholm), *Hypatia,* and *International Feminist Politics.*

Debra Bergoffen is Professor of Philosophy and Women's Studies at George Mason University. She is author of *The Philosophy of Simone de Beauvoir: Gendered Phenomenologies, Erotic Generosities,* and editor of several anthologies. Her essay "How Rape Became a Crime against Humanity: History of an Error" is included in *Modernity and the Problem of Evil* (Indiana University Press, 2005).

Peg Birmingham is Professor of Philosophy at DePaul University. She is author of *Hannah Arendt and Human Rights: The Predicament of Common Responsibility* (Indiana University Press, 2006), and co-editor (with Philippe van Haute) of *Dissensus Communis: Between Ethics and Politics.* Her work on Arendt, Heidegger, Foucault, and Kristeva has appeared in *Research in Phenomenology, Philosophy and Social Criticism,* and *The Graduate Journal of Philosophy.*

Claudia Card is the Emma Goldman Professor of Philosophy at the University of Wisconsin. Her most recent books are *The Atrocity Paradigm: A Theory of Evil* and *The Cambridge Companion to Simone de Beauvoir.* She is currently working on two book manuscripts, one of which responds to atrocities and the other of which is an introduction to feminist philosophy.

Margaret Denike is Assistant Professor of Human Rights at Carleton University. She has worked extensively in Canadian feminist NGOs, engaging in social policy analysis and law reform initiatives concerning institutionalized violence, sex discrimination, gender equality, and human rights.

Mary Anne Franks is a teaching fellow at Harvard University, where she is working on her J.D. She recently worked in the Investigations Division of the

International Criminal Court in The Hague. Her philosophical work engages Continental philosophy, psychoanalytic theory, law, violence, and conflict.

Jennifer L. Geddes is Research Associate Professor in Religious Studies at the University of Virginia, where she is also Co-Program Director and Permanent Fellow at the Institute for Advanced Studies in Culture. She is editor of *Evil after Postmodernism: Histories, Narratives, Ethics* and *The Hedgehog Review: Critical Reflections on Contemporary Culture.*

Alison M. Jaggar is Professor of Philosophy and Women's Studies at the University of Colorado at Boulder. She is author of *Feminist Politics and Human Nature* and *Living with Contradictions: Controversies in Feminist Ethics.* She has edited *The Blackwell Companion to Feminist Philosophy* with Iris Marion Young.

Ada S. Jaarsma is Assistant Professor of Philosophy at Sonoma State University. Her research interests include contemporary feminist and queer ethics, critical theory, and nineteenth-century philosophy.

María Pía Lara is Professor of Philosophy at Universidad Autónoma Metropolitana in Mexico. She is author of *Moral Textures: Feminist Narratives in the Public Sphere*, and editor of *Rethinking Evil.* She has worked extensively on Hannah Arendt, and her forthcoming book is titled *Narrating Evil.*

Constance L. Mui teaches philosophy and women's studies at Loyola University, New Orleans. She has published on Sartre, phenomenology, and feminist philosophy, and is co-editor (with Julien Murphy) of *Gender Struggles: Contemporary Approaches to Feminist Philosophy.*

Julien S. Murphy is Director of the Bioethics Project and Professor of Philosophy at the University of Southern Maine. She is author of *The Constructed Body: AIDS, Reproductive Technology and Ethics,* and editor of *Feminist Interpretations of Jean-Paul Sartre.*

María Isabel Peña Aguado has lectured in universities in Germany and works now at Clare Hall College, Cambridge, England. Her philosophical publications in German include work in aesthetics, postmodernism, and feminism. She has also published some fiction, which has appeared in Spanish.

Sherene H. Razack is Professor of Sociology and Equity Studies in Education at the Ontario Institute for Studies in Education of the University of Toronto. Her recent books include *Dark Threats and White Knights: The Somalia Affair; Peacekeeping, and the New Imperialism; Race, Space, and the Law: Unmapping a White Settler Society;* and *Looking White People in the Eye: Gender, Race, and Culture in Courtrooms and Classrooms.*

Sara Ruddick is professor emerita of the Eugene Lang College, New School University. She is author of *Maternal Thinking: Toward a Politics of Peace*, and co-editor of *Working It Out* and other collections of feminist essays. She is currently co-editing *Against Heterosexualism* with Joan Callahan and Bonnie Mann.

Robin May Schott is Associate Professor of Philosophy at The Danish University of Education. She is author of *Discovering Feminist Philosophy* and *Cognition and Eros: A Critique of the Kantian Paradigm*, and editor of *Feminist Interpretations of Immanuel Kant*.

Iris Marion Young was Professor of Political Science at the University of Chicago. She recently published *Inclusion and Democracy*, and a collection of her essays on ethics and international affairs, *Global Challenges: On War, Self-Determination and Global Justice*, is forthcoming.

Index

Douglas, Mary, 26, 28–31, 47
During, Lisabeth, 55
duty, 91–92
Dworkin, Andrea, 187n11

earth, sin as violence against, 63–64
Eichmann, Adolf, 5; as normal, 269n11; phobic fantasy of, 98–99; thoughtlessness of, 112–114; trial of, 88, 91–93
Eichmann in Jerusalem (Arendt), 87–88, 91–93, 112–119; subtitle, 114
Einsatzgruppen, 5, 84
Elders of Zion, 97
elites, political, 201, 203n12
Elshtain, Jean Bethke, 11, 15n16
emotion, 172, 189n25
Enduring Freedom, 246–247
enemy: law of, 132–133; perpetrator, 110, 175, 178; portrayed in abstract/nonhuman terms, 232–233; within, 301
Enlightenment discourse, 2, 129–130, 137–138, 260
entitlement, 130
equity politics, 124
eternity, immortality vs., 100
ethico-political act, 150, 156
ethics, 14, 100, 195, 200; action and, 252–253. *See also* Sartrean ethics
"Ethics after Mass Rape" (Schott), 289
Ethics of Ambiguity, The (Beauvoir), 252–253
ethnocides, 76
Euben, Roxanne, 230, 234
Euskadi ta Askatasuna (ETA), 264, 269n10
evil: abstract concept of, 110–111, 196–197, 232–233; attributed to other, 26–28; cultural analysis of, 28–29; definitions, 4, 196, 206–207, 219; as discursive construct, 25; divinity and, 56–57; as foreseeable intolerable harms, 4, 206, 219; incarnational logic and, 59–60; limitations to understanding of, 116–119; mythologization of, 111; as ontological, 196–197; particularity of, 114–115; as political concept in war against terrorism, 142; political rhetoric of, 3–4; post-metaphysical approach to, 2–5; relational aspects of, 110–111; secularized concept of, 195–196; sexualized imagery of, 26–27; as term, 4–6; terrorism, analogies with, 197–199; thoughtlessness of, 111–114. *See also* banality of evil; radical evil
evil, rhetoric of, 3–5; absolutist language, 153–154, 219; axis of evil, 4, 140–141, 195, 220, 231, 271–272; deployed by church and state, 26–28; discursive complicity, 195–196, 199;

limits of, 219–220; September 11, 2001 attacks, 26, 178–179, 195–196
Evil in Modern Thought: An Alternative History of Philosophy (Neiman), 2
evildoers, definitions of, 207, 289–291
Examen des Sorcieres (Boguet), 43
exclusionary prohibition, 99
executive branch, expanded powers of, 301–302
"Existentialism Is a Humanism" (Sartre), 250–251
existentialist approach, 14
exorcism, 105n2
extended bereaved community, 180
extradition demands, 223

familial relations, 60–61, 249
famine, 77–78
fascism, symbolic law and, 91–93, 98–99
Fattah, 198
fear: authority related to, 97–98, 102–103; gendered phenomenon of, 167; immortality and, 102–103; universalization of, 232, 233
female genital mutilation (FGM), 7, 151
feminism: global citizenship and, 305–306; Western, and indifference to Afghanistan, 145, 150–151
Feminist Majority Foundation (FMF), 151, 157n8, 305
feminist philosophy, 7–8, 25
finitude, 58, 88
Firestone, Shulamith, 249
For-itself, 254
48 Hours, 161
Fotion, Nick, 203n11
Foucault, Michel, 21–26, 48n2
fragility of human affairs, 88, 107n10
fragmentation, as sin, 59
Fraser, Graham, 279
freedom, 2–3, 93; atheistic framework, 250–251; bad faith and, 256; dimensions of, 249; intention of, 254–255; intersubjectivity and, 251–252, 255; normative content of will to, 254–255; of others, will to, 251–253; Sartrean framework, 245–246, 248–249, 253–254
Freie, John, 180, 181–182
Freud, Sigmund, 197
friendship: heteronomy of, 132–133, 135, 137; as masculine neuter, 128; political, 88, 104–105; trust and, 134–136; as virtue unique to human beings, 133–136
frontier myth, 272
fungus metaphor, 95, 106n4

167; masculinized discourse of, 177; media images of, 258–259; militarization and, 9–10, 208–212, 221–225; as noun, 196–197, 199–200; as political coercion, 200–202, 207–208; state-sponsored, 208, 212, 220–223, 225n6; targets, 201, 207, 213, 220–221, 292–293; as war without frontiers, 263; in wartime, 222. *See also* September 11, 2001 attacks; war on terrorism, rhetoric of

terrorists, female, 265–267, 269nn13,14

Tertullian, 27, 32, 34, 48n5

text: logic of, 55–56, 61, 64; regeneration of, 67–68

Theory of Justice, A (Rawls), 237

Thinking about Gender (McCracken), 48n4

Thirteenth Amendment, 213

This Sex Which Is Not One (Irigaray), 54, 64, 156

Thomas, Lawrence Mordekhai, 80–83

thoughtlessness of evil, 111–114

To Be Two (Irigaray), 53–54, 60–69

"To Perpetual Peace: A Philosophical Sketch" (Kant), 3, 14

tolerance, 239–240

torture: committed by United States, 4, 5, 7, 189n24; destruction of trust, 134; as form of cruelty, 164; in name of democracy, 5–6; rape equated with, 122; treason analogy used to justify, 43–44

totalitarianism, 5; elimination of spontaneity from the human race, 93–94; immanence and, 90, 97; phobic fantasies, 98–99; resistance to symbolic law, 91–93, 98–99; women's role in, 233–234

Townshend, Charles, 269n12

translation, 132–135

trauma: Canadian narratives of, 271–274, 275–281; narratives of, 273–274, 279–280; witnesses, 274–275

treason: heresy associated with, 22, 34–35, 38–39; witchcraft as, 22, 42–44, 48n1

trust, 2; betrayal of, 129, 134, 168; cruelty and, 164–165, 168, 189n23; friendship and, 134–136; horror and, 172–175; social location and, 164–165, 174, 187n12, 188n16

truth, 104, 176

Twin Falls Idaho, 162, 170, 184, 185n2

Ulema, 143

Unabomber, 220

undecidability, 130–131

Undoing Gender (Butler), 135

"Undone: Dallaire/Rwanda," 279

UNITA, 221

UN Human Development Index, 247

United Nations: Afghanistan and, 145–146; Darfur resolution, 6–7; ineffectiveness of, 279; terrorism treaty, 220. *See also* International Criminal Tribunal for the former Yugoslavia (ICTY)

United Nations Charter, 222

United Nations Convention of the Rights of Children (CRC), 250, 255

United Nations Convention on the Prevention and Punishment of the Crime of Genocide (1948), 6–7, 73–74, 76–77

United Nations Special Report on Afghanistan, 145, 146

United States: American narratives about Holocaust, 162, 185n3; American popular culture, redemption in, 160–163, 177–184, 186n6; American values, 11, 15n16; effect of terror on agency of population, 167–168; ethico-political leadership, 195; fundamentalist discourse of evil, 142; gender apartheid, rhetoric of, 141–142; international law and, 4, 10, 74; Northern Alliance and, 142, 146, 152–153, 157n10; patriotic self-identity, 141; political theology of, 231–233; refusal to define terrorism, 9; rule of exception, 231–233; Taliban, affinities with, 140–141, 149, 153–156; torture committed by, 4, 5, 7, 189n24; two sides of Law in, 149–150; as victim, 11–12

universal rights discourse, 128–132

universalization: of fear, 232–233; as originary sin, 62; standpoint of witnesses, 277–278

unpredictability, 93–94

Unseen Scars, The (documentary), 276

us-against-them mentality, 2, 140–141

uselessness of suffering, 112–119, 171, 188n18

Ustashi, 232

Valentini, Tiziana, 267, 269nn13,14

Van Rysselberge, Charles, 161

vertigo of secularization: disenchantment, 230–231; loss of faith and hope, 229–230, 240; political theology, narratives of, 231–233; religion and, 231–234, 239–240; religion vs. politics, 236–241

victims: anger of, 184; appropriation of suffering of, 182–183, 190n31; bystanders as, 182, 190n31; feminization of, 177, 184, 188n21, 190n29; loss of identity, 165–167; nothingness of, 292–293; random selection of, 207; September 11, 2001 attacks and, 11–12, 292–293; terrorist view of, 292–293; Western response to, 152–153. *See also* cruelty

Vietnam, 74, 77

violence: as appropriate response, 2, 9; dialogue as solution to, 263–265; *différend* and, 261–262; against earth as sin, 63–64; female terrorists, 265–267; as inimical to justice, 263–265; justification for use of, 260–261; as noun, 196–197, 199–200

virginity, 124

visible, obsession with, 154–155

vital interests, 79–80

vulnerability, 8; of body, 125–126, 135–138, 201; of other, 137–138

Walzer, Michael, 11, 207, 209

war: as collective problem, 3; definitions, 208–209; genocide as, 73; just-war concept, 11, 195, 210–212, 287; metaphorical, 209, 221–222; rhetoric of evil as tool of, 26–27; September 11, 2001 attacks and, 208–209

war crimes, 74–75, 132–133, 222

war norms, 209

war on terrorism, rhetoric of, 11, 142, 156, 195, 222

Ward, Graham, 61, 66

warlords, 272, 273

Warminski, Andrzej, 64

weapons of mass destruction (WMD), 211

Weber, Max, 229–230, 238, 241n5

Weil, Simone, 292, 293

Wellman, Carl, 207–208, 213

West: Afghanistan, indifference to, 140–141, 145–146, 150–151; feminists, indifference of, 145, 150–151; visible, obsession with, 154–155

we-subject, 252

Weyer, Johann, 39–41, 43–44, 49n8

Whicher, Pam, 184

Whitford, Margaret, 66

Wiesel, Elie, 171

Williams, Patricia, 131–132

winged words, metaphor of, 92, 98–99

witch: as both weak and powerful, 22, 24–25, 27, 37, 43; heretic-witch, 22, 25, 42; as insatiable, 27, 40–41, 43; patriarchal need for,

23–25; powers of, as illusory, 36–37, 39–40; witch-hysteric, 24; witch-melancholic, 24, 40

witchcraft: criminalization of, 23–24, 37, 41–46; as exceptional crime, 22, 42–44; heresy associated with treason, 34–35, 38–39; medicalization of, 40, 41, 44; sabbat, mythology of, 44–45; sexuality and, 22–23; skeptics of, 38–41, 43–44, 45, 49n8; as treason, 22, 42–44, 48n1

witchcraft trials: coincide with "Golden Age of Man," 22–23; jurisdictional issues, 38–39, 41–46

Witness the Evil (Canadian Military documentary), 276–278

witnesses: trauma of, 274–275; universalist standpoint of, 277–278. *See also* peacekeeping

womb, 62

women: Beijing resolutions, 129; children's welfare and, 249, 255; evil attributed to, 22–27; fantasy of, 154–155; as incapable of reason, 266–267; mother/whore binary, 147–149; noncombatants as, 126–127; as other, 8, 25, 137–138; role in totalitarianism, 233–234; scapegoating of, 22–23; sexual division of labor, 147–148; as sexually embodied persons, 122, 124; as terrorists, 265–267, 269nn13,14; used as justification for war, 305. *See also* witch; witchcraft

women's movement, 299

wonder, 89

World Court, 74

World War II, 195

Young, Iris Marion, vi, 293, 294

Yugoslavia, former. *See* International Criminal Tribunal for the former Yugoslavia (ICTY)

Ziarek, Ewa, 3

Žižek, Slavoj, 141, 145, 151–152, 156

zoe, 102

zone of mistrust, 2